The Story of Capital

The Story of Capital

What Everyone Should Know
About How Capital Works

David Harvey

V

VERSO

London • New York

First published by Verso 2026
© David Harvey 2026

The appendix was first published in *New Left Review*, March–April 2025, entitled 'On Sraffa's Trail'

The manufacturer's authorized representative in the EU for product safety (GPSR) is LOGOS EUROPE, 9 rue Nicolas Poussin, 17000, La Rochelle, France
Contact@logoseurope.eu

1 3 5 7 9 10 8 6 4 2

Verso
UK: 6 Meard Street, London W1F 0EG
US: 207 East 32nd Street, New York, NY 10016
versobooks.com

Verso is the imprint of New Left Books

ISBN-13: 978-1-83674-211-1
ISBN-13: 978-1-83674-213-5 (US EBK)
ISBN-13: 978-1-83674-212-8 (UK EBK)

British Library Cataloguing in Publication Data
A catalogue record for this book is available from the British Library

Library of Congress Cataloging-in-Publication Data
A catalog record for this book is available from the Library of Congress

Typeset in Minion Pro by MJ & N Gavan, Truro, Cornwall
Printed in the UK by CPI Group (UK) Ltd, Croydon, CR0 4YY

Contents

List of Figures

Preface

For the last three decades, I have been involved in what I retrospectively call my 'Marx Project'. I say 'retrospectively' because I never planned it. The project has just evolved, and it is only recently that I can look back and appreciate its changing shape, growth and content. The beginning point was the Clinton years, when the US political establishment was celebrating victory in the Cold War. Actually existing communism was dead, and Francis Fukuyama could even declare the end of history with the total triumph of the bourgeoisie on the world stage. I was repeatedly told during those years that the Marx texts that I had been teaching since 1970 or so were totally irrelevant as guides to action in today's world. Enrolment in my Marx class was way down. Even those who did take it did so in a far more sceptical frame of mind.

But there was something badly wrong with this 1990s vision of a troglodyte Marxism. The collapse of the Soviet Union opened up a space for a renewed exploration of Marx's texts as the basis for a better understanding of how capital works today and what an anticapitalist alternative might look like. I did not have to explain away the particularities of Soviet and world communist history. The mainstream press in the 1990s also uncovered a raft of unseemly if not vicious labour practices in the sweatshops of the world that fed the booming demand for fashionable clothing in metropolitan centres. Such accounts, I pointed out to students, could fit all too well into Marx's chapter 'The Working Day' in Volume 1 of *Capital*. President Clinton, who had dreams of extending the Great Society into health care and other socially desirable causes, was quickly advised by newly appointed Treasury Secretary Robert Rubin (from Goldman Sachs) that the Wall Street bondholders would have none of that. So Clinton staked his legacy on supporting every good neoliberal cause he could find, from the punitive refashioning of welfare 'as we know it' to NAFTA. The Volume 1 theory of *Capital*, it turned out, was most relevant in the 1990s, precisely in the years when it was almost totally ignored if not derided. Clinton's hope of reaping a 'peace dividend' from cutting back on military expenditures was likewise thwarted by the political decision to expand NATO, even though the enemy that NATO was supposed to contain had disappeared (this policy decision was to bear bitter fruit many years later in the Ukraine War).

It seemed to me that there was a strong case for going back to Marx's original texts and exploring their utility in explicating the changing paths of capital accumulation. Step by step, I found myself losing interest in the mass of different interpretations and even whole schools of thought on how to interpret Marx's political economy. I became increasingly absorbed (some would say obsessed) with a close reading of Marx's texts, many of which were coming online for the first time. It is a valid criticism of my work that I do not pay sufficient attention to the very good output of many talented commentators on Marx. I leave the mass of critical commentaries to one side as simply unmanageable.

But how to present my findings was a problem. The difficulty was fortuitously resolved by my move from Johns Hopkins to the CUNY Graduate Center in New York in 2001. In the Graduate Center, I found a cohort of politicized graduate students. My *Capital* class in some years was so large we had to commandeer the dining room to teach it. I was eventually persuaded by my graduate students, Chris Caruso in particular, to put the classes on the web – so began a long-standing collaboration between my content and Chris's media and communication skills. Together, we created a library of freely accessible materials for opening up Marx's political economy for popular consumption.

My aim in developing the *Companions* to Marx's *Capital* and the *Grundrisse* in both the video and the Verso book version was to simplify Marx's arguments as far as possible without being simplistic. This was not always easy. I preferred the idea of a companion (in which the reader could be an active participant) rather than guide, since the latter presumes that the final destination is fixed and known. I sought for an open, creative and nondogmatic reading. Over time, my own interpretations were also evolving, and they remain open to this day. In this respect, the companion to the *Grundrisse* was, for me, of major significance, because there Marx introduces the idea of capital's mode of production as a whole, as a working totality in formation in which different circulation processes

PREFACE xi

(of labour power, of capital, of credit) work together in a world where all manner of contradictions flourish. This led me to the idea to use all of the materials assembled both in the *Companions* and in the ancillary books such as *A Brief History of Neoliberalism*, *The New Imperialism*, *The Enigma of Capital* and *The Madness of Economic Reason*, along with several more practical works on urbanization and uneven geographical development. My aim was to look at Marx's political economy through the lens of a totality in the course of construction through multiple circulation processes all in contradictory motion. That is the story that this book tries to tell. It rests on thirty years of working on the Marx Project, including a couple of dry runs of the material in courses taught at the Graduate Center and the People's Forum in New York. But, as the coda on the work of Piero Sraffa illustrates, the project is ongoing, indeed never ending. The world is perpetually changing. Likewise, our understanding of it is also constantly evolving in both positive and negative ways. This book is one more step in telling the story of capital in a way that people can, I hope, understand and use both personally and politically. Collectively, we can indeed change this world, even though, as Marx points out, this is never under conditions of our own choosing. But the theoretical dissection of those conditions is a vital precursor towards changing them, and, on that basis, I offer this text in the quest to build a more humane and ecologically sensitive alternative.

Acknowledgements and thanks to Chris Caruso for editing the text and to Miguel Robles-Duran for providing the figures.

1

A Mental Map of Capital's Domain

If the mission is to construct an adequate representation of capital, including all its contradictions, then we need to devise a theory to explain how capital works and what it does on the ground. This entails a certain strategy of enquiry and presentation. In the absence of the controlled experimental methods available to the natural sciences, historians, geographers and social scientists have had to rely on the powers of abstraction and theory construction.[1] Since the very mention of theory intimidates many readers and working with abstractions is always problematic, I begin with a simplified and, I hope, easily grasp-able picture of what capital looks like as a working totality (Figure 1). The key concept here is that of capital as a mode of production within which wages, profits, exchange, consumption, realization, rents, finance, merchant profits, interest and state functions (including interstate relations) dynamically intersect with each other to constitute the totality of what contemporary capital is all about. Marx speaks of the different elements (such as production, distribution and consumption) as 'moments' in order to capture the transitoriness and contingency of everything that happens within the totality of capital's mode of production. Thus, the moment of 'production' refers to the whole range of commodity production processes going on under the direction and class power of capital, while the moment of 'consumption' refers to how all the commodities produced for sale in the market get used up in many different ways in different times and places.

---

1   Karl Marx, *Capital*, Vol. 1, trans. Ben Fowkes (London and New York: Penguin, 1976), Preface to the First Edition, p. 90; Karl Marx, *Grundrisse*, trans. Martin Nicolaus (London and New York: Penguin, 1973), pp. 275–6.

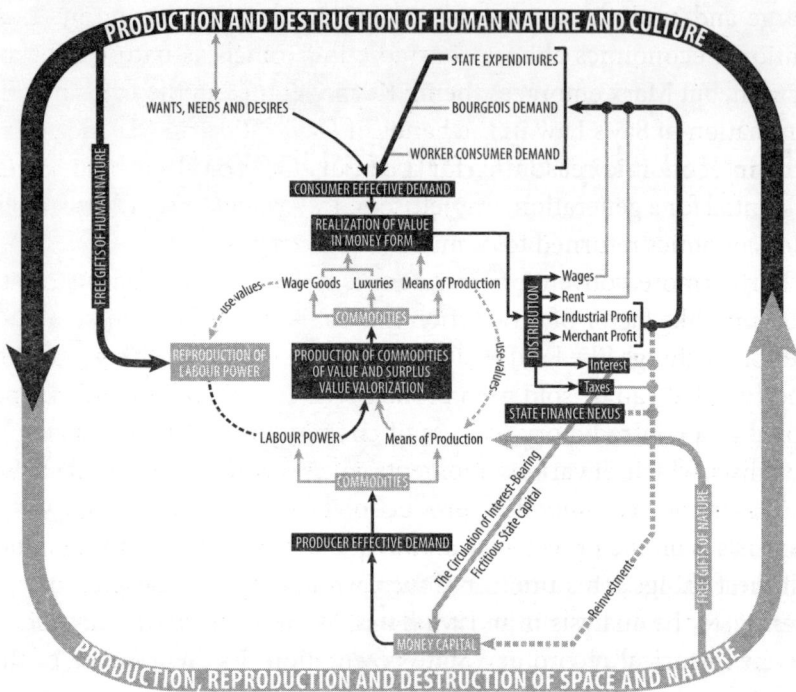

Figure 1. The Circulation of Capital

Marx develops a critique of classical political economy, and of Adam Smith in particular, for taking the rich complexity of capitalist activities (what Marx refers to as 'the concentration of many determinations, hence unity of the diverse') and hammering them into 'flat tautologies'.[2] These tautologies conveniently make everything seem harmonious with everything else. The most egregious example is Say's Law, which blithely assumes that supply creates its own demand and that therefore general crises of overproduction are impossible. When a crisis breaks out, however, as it did in the 1930s and 2007–8, these propositions are revealed as misleading if not useless. In 1960, Pierro Sraffa proved, with the aid of brilliant mathematical reasoning, that all bourgeois economics is tautological.[3] Equilibrium economics fits capital perfectly when everything is going smoothly, as when demand equals supply and all markets clear. But it is helpless when the contradictions of capital take

---

2   Marx, *Grundrisse*, pp. 86, 101.

3   Piero Sraffa, *The Production of Commodities by Means of Commodities* (Cambridge: Cambridge University Press, 1960); Geoffrey Harcourt, *Some Cambridge Controversies in the Theory of Capital* (Cambridge: Cambridge University Press, 1972). Those who adopted a positivist interpretation of Marx's political economy also became vulnerable to the charge of tautological formulations. See Ian Steedman, *Marx After Sraffa* (London: NLB, 1977).

charge and explode to generate violent crises in the economy. Conventional economics abhors contradictions much as nature abhors a vacuum, but Marx embraces them.[4] Keynes argued in the 1930s that the domination of Say's Law in the hands of David Ricardo was the crucial error in economic reasoning for a century or more. But his rebuttal, influential for a generation, was jettisoned after 1980 or so, when supply-side economics returned to dominate theorizing.

Furthermore, conventional economics typically conceptualizes capital as a thing-like factor of production that capitalists use, when combined with other things like land and labour to make another thing – a commodity – that can be sold for a profit. Marx, on the other hand, defines capital as a contradictory process of circulation of value organized by capitalists, which, at various 'moments', takes on different material forms (such as money, commodities, production processes and the like). Marx's emphasis is on the processes and the moments rather than on the static and inert things. This process–thing distinction will frequently return to animate the analysis in what follows. We live our lives as a process, but the historical record and state power registers and objectivizes us from time to time as individual, 'dot-like' things.[5] This presentation, it goes without saying, attempts a nontautological reading of the internal contradictions of capital's political economy.

In the following pages, I argue that capital's totality is an organic system in perpetual evolution. 'This organic system itself as a totality', says Marx, 'has its presuppositions, and its development to its totality consists precisely in subordinating all elements of society to itself, or of creating out of it the organs which it still lacks. This is historically how it becomes a totality. The process of it becoming this totality forms a moment of its process, of its development.'[6] The formulation may sound impossibly abstract. But consider how accurate it is.

While the idea of totality undoubtedly derives from the German philosopher Hegel, Marx reworks it and revolutionizes it (as he does with almost everything else he takes from Hegel). For Marx, the totality of capital is an ever-changing network of historically specific social practices and relations built, evolving and ultimately dissolving, only to be rebuilt again through human action. This network is constantly in the process of growth and transformation (perpetually 'becoming', as Marx puts it) even as it exhibits certain tendencies towards solidity and

---

4   Marx, *Grundrisse*, p. 351.
5   Ibid., pp. 485–6.
6   Ibid., p. 278.

permanence. Marx's concept of capital's totality is, therefore, open, evolving and self-replicating but in no sense self-sustaining, given its internal contradictions and its penchant for disharmonies and breakdowns. Capital exists as a complex ecosystem of value flows in continuous internal tension, thus forcing permanently revolutionary transformations (like artificial intelligence) and continuous historical evolution.

This economic ecosystem has a distinctive geographical structure that evolves over time. To grasp this requires the creation of a theoretical construct to represent the material qualities of myriad flows of capital occurring in space and time. Merchants take commodities manufactured in China to markets and retail outlets across the Americas. Bankers transfer investment funds from Tokyo to Brazil. Investors across the world put money into Blackstone's real estate empire with interests in industrial parks and retail complexes as well as housing from China to Barcelona, Sydney, London, Las Vegas and São Paulo. Scientists and key personnel join brain drains from Europe, China and the former Soviet Union to Silicon Valley or Seattle, while the US administration desperately seeks to protect against excessive immigration from other countries and technology transfer to China, even as it encourages such transfers between the United States, Taiwan and Japan as well as Europe. Keeping track of all of this in its myriad material forms across space and time is downright impossible, yet there are data collections on stocks and flows, on balances of payments and imports and exports between jurisdictions that indicate certain aggregate geographical and temporal laws of capital's motion within the global economy. The totality denoted as capital's distinctive mode of production is constructed through human action; its laws of motion are distinctive to itself.

Such laws of motion both reflect and produce totalities within totalities. Historically, as Marx puts it, 'the economic totality is, at bottom, contained in each individual household, which forms an independent centre of production for itself', but 'in the world of antiquity, the city with its territory is the economic totality.'[7] The totality, therefore, takes on different forms throughout history, which raises the question of how best to construe the totality of capital flow in our times. There also has to be, says Henri Lefebvre, 'a spatialized reading of the Marxian notion of totality' if we are 'to grasp the multiple relations of material co-existence between the private, urban and global levels of social life.'[8] This three-

---

7   Ibid., p. 484.
8   Lefebvre, cited in Martin Arboleda, *Planetary Mine: Territories of Extraction Under Late Capitalism* (London: Verso, 2020), pp. 177–8.

fold layering of the capitalist totality across the individual, metropolitan (regional and urban) and global scales may require modification to take into account the formation of geopolitical power blocs (Asian, European, North American) that divide up the terrain of capital flows. Political and military conflict now occurs largely at the global or regional scales. Lefebvre's reading 'challenges mechanistic determinist explanations of socioeconomic transformations' to focus on the dynamic movement of parts operating at different scales within the global totality of the capitalist mode of production.[9] The qualities of personal life and of social reproduction are embedded in economic, social and environmental conditions and processes operating at these different scales.

This theoretical perspective of scalar embeddedness was explicit in the formulation of the *Communist Manifesto*. There, the isolated labourer is construed individualistically before experiencing the collective life of labour in the factory, which expands to an understanding of broader social relations in an industrial city or region before confronting the national (state) and then global conditions of possibility for consciousness formation and political action (culminating, of course, in 'workers of the world, unite!'). The totality of capital, in this accounting, is layered according to scale. While there are obvious ways in which the internal relations between different processes operating at different scales get articulated, the 'complexification' (as Lefebvre calls it) of this process produces an ever evolving and expanding mode of production.

Marx strategically limits his enquiries to what he calls the 'inner structure' of the totality of capital.[10] This inner structure constitutes 'the mode of production', embedded, as shown in Figure 1, in a broader field of material and social relations that constitute 'the capitalist social formation'. While capital and the drive for profit may be the driving force within the inner structure of capital's mode of production – the foundational process within bourgeois society – Marx recognizes that it does not say everything that needs to be said about capitalism as a social formation. The theory of capital as a mode of production is one thing. The theory of capitalism as a social formation is quite another. This is where abstraction and concept formation step in to do the duty of what can in the natural sciences be done through experimental methods. Marx primarily focuses on capital as a mode of production (the inner structure). In so doing he holds everything going on in the social formation (like

---

9   Henri Lefebvre, *The Critique of Everyday Life*, Vol. 2 (London: Verso, 2008), p. 181.
10   Marx, *Grundrisse*, Introduction, p. 108.

the historical geography of religious beliefs and racial conflicts) constant in order to examine in sometimes excruciating detail how the 'inner structure' of capital works.

From time to time, Marx does, however, examine the critically important contextual conditions (such as the relation to nature and to divergent cultural histories and traditions) that connect what is happening in the social formation with the dynamic laws of motion operating within the inner structure of the mode of production. As a result, Milton Santos writes, 'the relations between space and social formation' are special, 'since they are formed in a particular space (a place) not in space in general like the modes of production.'[11] In the social formation, we encounter all the infinite variety of human activity in different places and times. Santos then provocatively suggests that 'modes of production write history in time; social formations write it in space.'[12] What he means by this is that the study of social formations inevitably has to confront the particularities of capital in a multitude of places, while the study of the mode of production can abstract from these and appeal to the universality of 'time's arrow', as capital's laws of motion guide capital's economic evolution according to the principle of 'accumulation for accumulation's sake'. In academia, different disciplines conceptualize the distinctive totality (or totalities) that are the focus of their enquiries. In political economy, the temporality of flows takes precedence, whereas in anthropology, history and geography, the particularities of places, spaces and divergent natural environmental and social conditions are a primary focus even as the universal engine of capital circulation and accumulation throbs incessantly and sometimes threateningly in the background. As a geographer, my eyes focus on what is going on in a few neighbourhoods in a city. As a political economist, I focus on macroeconomic conditions for housing provision, mortgage rates, employment and fixed capital formation.

This distinction between the perspectives of a capitalist mode of production and capitalism as a social formation has been the site of needlessly acrimonious debate within the Marxist theoretical tradition. E. P. Thompson, author of the classic work on the history of class formation in Britain, ridiculed Louis Althusser's structuralist abstractions concerning capital as a mode of production in much the same way that

---

11   Milton Santos, 'The Devil's Totality: How Geographic Forms Diffuse Capital and Change Social Structures', *Antipode* 12: 3 (1980): 41–6.

12   Milton Santos, *For a New Geography* (Minneapolis: University of Minnesota Press, 2021).

Ralph Miliband on historical and political grounds disputed Nicos Poulantzas's theorizing of the capitalist state. While there are legitimate grounds for exploring differences between these authors and their formulations, many of the seemingly intractable differences disappear when the complementarity of the two perspectives of social formation and mode of production is unpacked. In my own work, *The Limits to Capital* (1982) prioritized the study of the mode of production (following Marx's *Grundrisse* and *Capital*) while *Paris, Capital of Modernity* (2003) focused on the particularities of the social formation in France's Second Empire (following Marx's *Eighteenth Brumaire* and *The Civil War in France*). In my later works, such as *A Brief History of Neoliberalism* (2005) and *The Enigma of Capital* (2010), I sought to bring these two perspectives together. What then becomes apparent is that Marx derived his theory of capital's mode of production from a close study of Manchester industrialism as a social formation. His chapters 'The Working Day' and 'Machinery and Large-Scale Industry' in *Capital* clearly illustrate this. Furthermore, in Chapter 25 of *Capital*, Marx specifies the General Law of Capitalist Accumulation in the first four sections before elaborating at great length and depth on the implications for conditions of daily life and employment within the British social formation. Chapter 25 of Volume 1 of *Capital* is a good place to look if one wants an example of how Marx handles the relation between mode of production and social formation.

Tactics of this sort are not unusual even in the exact sciences. In *Marx, Capital, and the Madness of Economic Reason* (2017), I used the conception of the hydrological cycle (Figure 2) as a useful analogy for thinking about the circulation of capital within a mode of production. The cyclical movement of H_2O entails transformations of form rather like those that occur in the circulation of capital. Water in liquid form in the oceans evaporates with the heat of the sun and moves as a vapour upwards until it condenses out as the droplets that form clouds. As the particles merge and become heavier they fall to ground as precipitation (rain, fog, dew, snow, ice, hail, freezing rain). Once returned to the surface of the earth some of the H_2O passes directly back into the oceans, some of it gets stuck at high elevations or in cold regions as ice that moves extremely slowly if at all, while the rest flows downwards across the land as streams and rivers (with some water evaporating back into the atmosphere) or under the surface of the land as ground water. En route, it is used by plants and animals that transpire and perspire to return some H_2O directly to the atmosphere through evapotranspiration. Large amounts of water are stored in ice fields or in underground aquifers. Like capital,

USGS
science for a changing world

The Water Cycle

Sun

Volcanic steam

Atmosphere

Ice, snow, and glaciers

Sublimation

Condensation

Precipitation

Precipitation

Permafrost

Deposition

Evapotranspiration

Evaporation

Precipitation

Fog drip

Snowmelt runoff

Dew

Saline lakes

Surface runoff

River discharge

Wetlands

Rivers

Infiltration

Seepage

Soil moisture

Evaporation

Springs

Plants and animals

Oceans

Freshwater lakes

Plant uptake

Ocean currents

Groundwater recharge and flow

Groundwater storage

Vents

U.S. Dept. of the Interior
U.S. Geological Survey
Howard Perlman, John Evans, USGS
https://www.usgs.gov/water-science-school
This diagram shows the Earth's "Natural" water cycle, omitting the significant impacts of human influences.

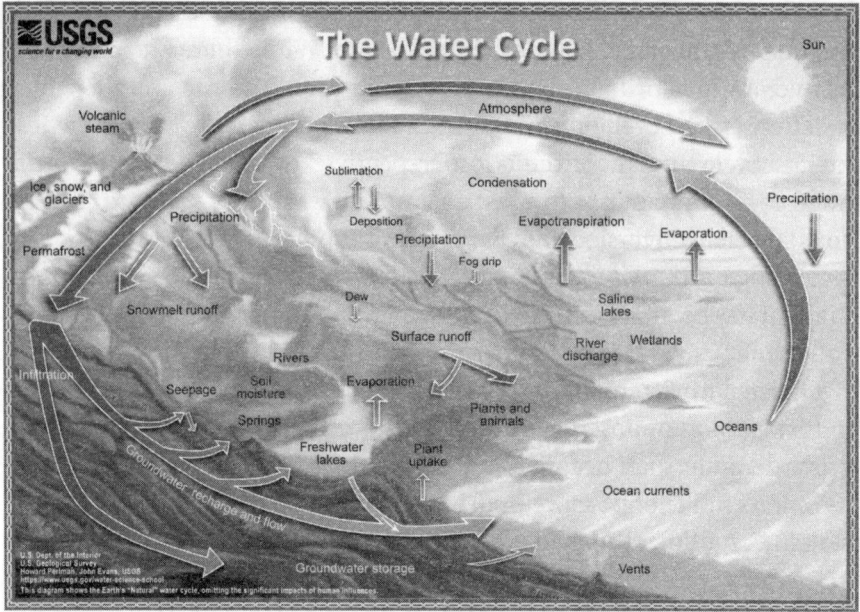

Figure 2. The Hydrological Cycle

not everything is in motion at the same pace. Glaciers move at the proverbial glacial pace, torrents rush downhill, groundwater sometimes takes many years to travel a few miles. The cycle is depicted in Figure 2 as a totality with many moving parts. This is how we will examine capital in what follows.

In this model of the hydrological cycle, water takes on different forms and passes through different states at different rates before returning to the oceans to start all over again. This is very similar to how capital moves. H_2O behaves very differently when it is in the upper atmosphere where the jet stream dwells, with all of its notorious turbulence, compared to how it behaves underground. Capital, similarly, behaves differently at global financial versus local and individual levels. Disruptive turbulence in the global financial system often passes unnoticed at the neighbourhood level, where daily life unfolds. The relationships between Wall Street and Main Street are not automatically registered in the daily lives of working people, except when mass disruptions and crises occur. Look closely at Figure 1. Capital begins as money capital. It then takes on commodity form (through the purchase of both labour power and means of production as commodities) before passing through production systems only to emerge at the end of the day as new commodities to be sold (monetized) in the market. This money is first distributed to different claimants (in the forms of wages, interest, rent, taxes, profits) before some of it returns to the role of money capital once more (with the help of the bankers and financiers) to begin the circulation process all over again.

There is, however, one very significant difference between the hydrological cycle and the circulation of capital. The driving force in the hydrological cycle is incoming energy from the sun and that is fairly constant. Its conversion into heat has in the past changed a great deal (plunging Earth into ice ages or phases of tropical heat). In recent times, the heat has been increasing significantly due to entrapment of radiation by greenhouse gasses (largely from fossil fuel use). The total volume of H_2O circulating remains fairly constant or changes slowly (measured in historical as opposed to geological time) as ice caps melt and underground aquifers are drained dry by human uses. In the case of capital, the sources of energy, as we shall see, are more varied, and the volume of capital in motion is constantly expanding at a compound rate because it has to grow or die. This growth requirement derives from the necessity for profit-making. Profit implies that there is, somehow, more output and more value at the end of the day than at the beginning. The hydrological cycle is closer to a genuine cycle, whereas the circulation of capital is, for reasons we will soon explain in more detail, a spiral in constant expansion.[13] In the theory of capital as a mode of production, the totality takes the form of a spiral of endless growth: 'accumulation for the sake of accumulation, production for the sake of production' as Marx puts it in *Capital*.[14]

But the two totalities of the water cycle and capital accumulation are, in certain respects, joined at the hip. The massive increases in the use of fossil fuels deriving from the requirement for endless growth and capital accumulation lie at the root of the increasing heat retention on Planet Earth which, if it continues at the present rate, will ultimately render Earth uninhabitable for most if not all forms of human activity. Water deprivation (in potable form) and heat exhaustion are already visible in many regions as a result of the compounding spiral of economic growth coupled with population growth (which, as we shall shortly see, is a necessary complement to economic growth). Water supplies are threatened in some major metropolitan areas (Los Angeles, São Paulo, Monterey, Cape Town, Mexico City), and many of the world's major rivers are running low (the Colorado, Mississippi, Yangtze, Ganges, Zambezi) even

---

13   Marx, *Grundrisse*, p. 266.
14   Marx, *Capital*, Vol. 1, p. 742.

as they are periodically subjected to violent flooding. The two conceptual totalities of water and capital circulation overlap.

To shift analogies, the totality of capital as a mode of production is, in some limited respects, also like a human body. In the human body blood circulates through the heart, oxygen through the lungs, energy through the digestive system, waste disposal is managed through the liver and kidneys while overall coordination is exercised through the brain. Each of these circulation processes is construed in medical science as autonomous and independent and subject to specialized knowledge in the hands of pulmonary specialists, cardiologists, neurologists, gastroenterologists, urologists and so on. Similarly, the Marxist library has specialized books on social reproduction, finance capital, labour processes, technological change and so on. All of these are subsumed, however, within the overall logic of the totality. This general description of a human body is what is called a 'concrete abstraction'. It is abstract because it does not refer to any human body in particular but is a composite representation of the main features of all human bodies. It is concrete because the knowledge incorporated in this model representation of a human body is drawn from the concrete experience of many medical practitioners (as well as people in general) probing into what the human body looks like (particularly when dissected) and how it works.

If the hydrological system and the human body can be analyzed in this way, then why not apply the same principles to the study of political economy? Political economists, Marx's example suggests, should position themselves as investigators into the structures, functions and contingencies of the capitalist mode of production viewed as an organic and expanding totality. Meanwhile, specialist investigations of, for example, social reproduction, the circulation of interest-bearing capital, and labour processes could alert us to the in-depth constitution and character of the various processes and moments within this totality.

In the *Grundrisse*, Marx offers a description of this totality as constituted by several different independent and autonomous circulation processes that are internally related to each other.[15] He first looks at the circulation of commodities and money. Not all money is capital. Capital is money circulating in a particular way. Money becomes money capital through its encounter with and purchase of the capacity to labour as a commodity. This is the seed that opens the way to everything that follows. Money capital is used to (1) purchase the capacity to labour

---

15   Marx, *Grundrisse*, pp. 673–9.

(labour power) along with commodities that furnish material means of production (raw materials, partially manufactured components, plant and equipment, machinery and so on); (2) these inputs are inserted into a labour process, the technology of which is under the control of capital, to produce a new commodity which is the property of capital; (3) the monetary value of the new commodity is realized through sale in the market that recoups the original monetary outlay but adds a money profit for capital; and (4) the money realized has to be divided and distributed to different factions depending on their claims. Some of it goes to workers in the form of wages, some is taken in the form of taxes going to the state, interest goes to the financiers, merchant profit goes to wholesalers and retailers as intermediaries and rent flows to the landlord in return for the use of the land. The industrial capitalist who organizes production gets whatever is left over. This distributed money power can be used in two ways. A part of it will go to purchase commodities to consume, so that the workers, along with the capitalist factions and the state employees, can live on the commodities produced. The other part is brought back together (often with the help of banks and other financial institutions) to reinvest as money capital, which then goes back through the circulation process all over again. It is only when the money goes back into circulation for a second time that we can say we are dealing with the circulation of capital rather than the particular circulations of money in exchange.

This gives us a picture of the inner structure, the distinctive circulation process for capital in general (Figure 1). This circulation process is not pregiven or predefined. It is not some ideal type waiting to be revealed or discovered, nor is it fixed and determinate with respect to its reach in space and time. It is something that has been and still is in the course of being historically constructed and reconstructed through continuous human social practices. Figure 1 is proposed as a 'concrete abstraction' of myriad processes occurring in billions of situations within the social formation.

There is, however, a far broader ecosystem within which this arbitrarily abstracted totality called 'capital' has its being. Hence in Figure 1 we see the metabolic relation to nature, the construction of a second nature through urbanization and the building of physical infrastructure along with the production of space and place relations. These are all contextually significant to the more narrowly defined and bounded model of capital circulation within the inner structure of the mode of production. The same can be said of capital's relation to accumulated human knowledge, social relations, culture, tradition and historical collective memory within the population. Capital depends crucially on conditions of social reproduction (for example, population growth to increase the labour supply) and to the constant shaping and reshaping of the wants, needs and desires of populations as these get expressed through the diversity of human consumption preferences. What happens in the realm of social reproduction has huge implications for how the circulation of capital proceeds. It is here that a vast pool of historically accumulated experiences, talents and knowledge, individual and collective, can be found and drawn on by capital for purposes of production and consumption.

Lastly, the state's role in capital accumulation cannot be ignored. 'The concentration of the whole in the state' forms the third level of Marx's enquiries, followed by the international relation and the world market 'in which production is posited as a totality together with all its moments, but within which, at the same time, all contradictions come into play. The world market then, again, forms the presupposition of the whole as well as its substratum. Crises are then the general intimation which points beyond the presupposition, and the urge which drives towards the adoption of a new historic form.' Globalization, the new world order and new economic possibilities are clearly on the agenda.[16]

The tentacles of the state stretch far and wide within the inner structure of capital and a case can be made that capitalist states (or at least significant elements within them) are now a foundational form of capital itself. In other words, part of state power (like social reproduction) is internal to rather than external to the inner structure of the circulation of capital. To use a formulation that applies to all the distinctive moments within the totality of capital circulation, significant elements within the contemporary capitalist state (such as a Treasury department) are 'independent and autonomous, but subsumed within' the laws of motion governing capital's mode of production. This goes against a mythical account of capital being created purely by capitalists, collectively dragging reluctant states along behind them. From Bismarck's Germany, Meiji Japan and the military dictatorship in South Korea to the state-led revivals through the MITI organization in 1960s Japan, state-centred development in de Gaulle's post-war France and the ordoliberalism of the post-war West German state, in all of these instances state-led or -guided capital accumulation has been and, in many respects, increasingly is in the vanguard. Even in the United States, Hamiltonian politics

---

16   Ibid., pp. 227–8.

and state-led initiatives on land distribution played a critical role in its economic development. In spite of all the rhetoric to the contrary, state-sponsored capital accumulation (typically managed through tax incentives rather than direct state intervention) remains a critical feature in US political economy. China's astonishing growth since 1978 rests une-quivocally on state-led accumulation even when orchestrated by private means, thus confirming the general point. It is also worth noting that state expenditures as a proportion of GDP have remained fairly constant (between 35 and 45 per cent) even over the period of neoliberal anti-state hegemony in policy-making.

Adam Smith's major treatise, you'll recall, was *The Wealth of Nations* and not *The Wealth of Capital*. The wealth of the state, he argued, could best be achieved by allowing the free functioning of capitalists operating in a price-setting market economy. Smith was giving advice to states-men, not to capitalists, on how wealth could be created and captured by and within the state for the public good. It is in this context that the otherwise mysterious title of Giovanni Arrighi's book *Adam Smith in Beijing* makes sense.[17] It gestures to what happened in China after the liberation of market forces in 1978. The significance of state-led accu-mulation has not, of course, been without its contradictions. Processes of class formation, racialization and gender discriminations within the state have often led to arrested development of capital instead of accel-erating growth. The innumerable state links to institutions and the life of civil society often produce antagonistic currents in how state powers are deployed. These deployments may check and regulate rather than facilitate the ambitions of capital. The ambitions of nationalists, socialists and monopolists compete within the corridors of state institutions with those of capitalists and their class formation.

The totality of capital's inner structure exists within this much broader totality of capitalism as a social formation. Marx's reason for conceptual-izing this distinction between mode of production and social formation is that he sees the mode of capital's production as the economic engine, the foundational powerhouse, the source of the abstract forces, to which all of us who live under the regime of capital are willy-nilly obligated. This general form of capital's inner circulation within the social forma-tion is depicted in Figure 1. This is the picture of the inner structure within the totality of the social formation. We need to keep this picture in our heads as we probe deeper and deeper into the details.

---

17   Giovanni Arrighi, *Adam Smith in Beijing: Lineages of the 21st Century* (London: Verso, 2009).

From this perspective, it makes no sense to assign a hierarchical structure of importance or causality to the interactions and interrelations between the different circulation processes at work. The failure of any one of them threatens the body's life. All the different circulation processes are co-dependent on each other. Without oxygen in the lungs, the heart, liver, stomach and so on cannot function. The same is true, as we shall see, of the economy. Without consumption, no production.[18]

I here need to interject an important political comment. The Hegelian legacy of totality as 'diversity within unity', with emphasis on the unity, has long posed a serious challenge in the history of Marxist thought. In the Hegelian idealist (albeit dialectical) tradition, the totalizing forces make it difficult to imagine any socialist escape from the prison-house of bourgeois formulations and capitalist practices. The end-point, the culmination, is teleologically given in the Hegelian system. The only revolutionary option seems to be blowing up the whole system and starting from scratch, to build something totally different. This is neither feasible nor appealing in our day and age. For this reason, some Marxist thinkers (such as Lukács) gave up on the concept of totality entirely while others quietly buried it. Marx, on occasion, flirts with the Hegelian concept of totality, substituting communism for Hegel's Absolute State as humanity's final destination. The teleological presupposition in this formulation led the Hegelian political theorist Francis Fukuyama to erroneously announce 'the end of history' when the Cold War ended in the early 1990s. But there is no such teleological presumption in the *Grundrisse*. Indeed, at one point, Marx rebukes himself for the 'too idealist' (that is, Hegelian) manner of his presentation and goes back to start the analysis all over again.[19]

Marx's open concept of totality as an ever-expanding ecosystem invites consideration of contingencies, the internal mutations, the innumerable seeds of alternative practices. There are openings at every level to doing things differently, establishing different social relations, cultivating alternative patches of human practices in Zapatista Chiapas, in Kurdish Rojava, in the recuperated factories of Argentina, in the communitarian and collective agrarian practices and solidarity economies sprouting in all sorts of places around the world. There are plenty of abandoned spaces and places and derelict zones open throughout the world to experiment with noncapitalist alternatives. While capitalist

---

18 Marx, *Grundrisse*, pp. 91–2.
19 Ibid., p. 151; see also Martin Jay, *Marxism and Totality: The Adventures of a Concept from Lukács to Habermas* (Berkeley: University of California Press, 1984).

and bourgeois practices are overwhelmingly hegemonic, particularly in the centres of political and economic power, the possibility to cultivate alternatives is everywhere apparent. The seeds of an alternative to capitalism are liberally scattered around the world, and from time to time they fall on fertile ground. This would be virtually impossible within the constraints of the Hegelian conception. We have to lay to rest at the outset, therefore, the idea that the concept of totality (with its emphasis on the unity in the diverse) is so totalizing and limiting as to make the construction of alternatives almost impossible.

Marx's *Grundrisse* is structured as an enquiry into the different circulation processes that produce and support capital as a totality.[20] Elaborating on them, we have:

1   The Circulation of Commodities through Exchange
2   The Circulation of Money as Money (commodity moneys, coinage, fiat moneys regulated by the state and so on)
3   The Circulation of Money as Capital (Figure 1)
4   The Circulation of Capacity to Labour (Figure 3)
5   The Circulation of Capital as Fixed Capital and the Consumption Fund (Figure 12)
6   The Circulation of Interest-Bearing Capital (loan capital and private debt)
7   The Circulation of Fictitious Capitals (taken up in Volume 3 of *Capital*)
8   The Circulation of State Revenues and State Debt Creation

The overall circulation process of capital can be disaggregated in other ways. In Volume 2 of *Capital*, Marx distinguishes between the circulation of capital as money, the circulation of capital as commodities, the circulation of capital through production and the circulation of all three forms taken together. Marx's point here is to show that the form capital takes opens up radically different possibilities and opportunities for the capitalist on the ground at the same time as it imposes certain constraints. When capital is in its money form, it offers all sorts of open possibilities, such as mobility across sectors and regions compared to when it is locked into the moment of production, which may require heavy investment in immobile plant and equipment. A capitalist industrialist may have a steel plant valued at $10 million, but that is very different from a capitalist armed with $10 million in cash who can use it, as did George Soros, to

---

20   Marx, *Grundrisse*, p. 678.

bet on currency exchange rates so as to quadruple his money capital in one week. If money is the butterfly form of capital and commodities are the caterpillar form, production is the chrysalis form where value and surplus value are incubated.

In *Marx's Economic Manuscript of 1864–1865* (which Engels relied on in compiling Volume 3 of *Capital*), these technical features are enriched by the emergence of class factions: merchant capitalists concentrate and specialize in the sale of commodities in the market, finance capitalists and bankers concentrate on money flows and industrialists concentrate on production, much of which is locked into place because of sunk investments.[21] While it is true that the industrialists operate at the heart of the creation and production of value and surplus value, the same cannot be said about appropriation or realization. Merchant capitalists can, in certain circumstances, dominate appropriation, exercising the power of monopsony (the power of controlling producers by monopolizing market outlets). This is what Walmart, IKEA, Home Depot and the major shoe and clothing brands do. Even electronics operates this way. Apple, for example, dominates at the front end of design of product and operates, in part, as a merchant appropriating much if not most of the surplus value at the sales end. In between are Foxconn and a whole supply chain of parts makers who employ most of the labour and produce most of the surplus value in Asia that Apple appropriates through its sales in the United States and Europe as well as in China. In automobiles, on the other hand, the producers hold the power, mobilizing a network of dealerships and financiers in their service. General Motors, for example, created a whole finance unit to extend credit for car purchases, which ultimately evolved into General Motors Acceptance Corporation becoming an independent bank.

The power relations between these factions are fluid and contingent, depending on sector and geographical situation. Plainly, since the 1970s, capital in general has witnessed a shift in which the merchant and finance factions have expanded their power at the expense of industrial capital, though unevenly, depending on place and sector. One measure of this is to look closely at the sectors and countries from which billionaires emanate today as opposed to yesteryear.

In *Capital* Volume 2 and the *Grundrisse*, Marx also examines the circulation of fixed capital (including infrastructure for production) and

---

21   Karl Marx, *Marx's Economic Manuscript 1864–1865*, trans. Ben Fowkes (Chicago: Haymarket, 2015), Section 4, pp. 376–443; Marx, *Grundrisse*, p. 851.

investment flows into the consumption fund (fixed equipment for consumption in the forms of houses, hospitals, schools and so on). These forms of circulation have become far more prominent in contemporary capitalism than was the case even in the 1970s (see Figure 12). Marx also studies different working periods and turnover times in Volume 2, followed by chapters on the circulation of variable capital (as wages) and surplus value (as profit), culminating in the modelling of circulation relations between capital and labour in a macroeconomic setting. The reproduction schemas presented at the end of Volume 2 (inspired by the work of the eighteenth-century French economist Quesnay), it is now acknowledged, were one of the first coherent attempts to build a macroeconomic model of the capitalist economy as a totality. Conventional economics only got around to doing something like this in the 1930s.

The boundedness of the totality (both structurally and geographically) is to some degree arbitrarily imposed by the investigator, even when material conditions support a particular definition of boundedness. In the case of the human body, to continue this analogy, there are strong reasons to consider it as a working totality for purposes of medical investigation. But the general social conditions in which that body operates cannot be ignored in any approach to health conditions in society. For example, a cause of death might be very specific from a medical standpoint, but the social context of substance abuse and opioid addictions, of alienation and social anomie, and all the economic and social reasons that lie behind these phenomena are of great significance to understanding recent trends in morbidity. Furthermore, the disaggregation of medical knowledge into distinctive specialisms becomes problematic when it leads to the neglect of interrelations between the different circulations. The loss of a holistic perspective in medicine sometimes turns out to be at the root of failures to understand certain critical mental and material aspects of human well-being.

We might also ask how Marx's organic ecosystemic approach is distinct from the widespread application of conventional systems theory to evolutionary processes. Biologist Richard Levins draws this distinction: 'Despite systems theory's concern with complexity, interconnection and process and despite the power of its mathematical apparatus, it does not deal at all with the richness of dialectical contingency, contradiction or historicity.'[22] Conventional systems theory thus remains, at heart,

---

22   Richard Levins, 'Dialectics and Systems Theory', in Bertell Ollman and Tony Smith (eds), *Dialectics for the New Century* (London: Palgrave Macmillan, 2008).

static and reductionist. The difference lies in Marx's turn to dialectics to embrace contradictions and mediations. The latter become critical as the mediating power not only of market exchange but also of alienated class relations (of both capital and labour). These take centre stage in Marx's theory of capital as a totality. In this theory, the economy is not powered by external forces (which do, from time to time, have a huge impact on economic life, as in the case of Covid-19) but by the inner contradictions driven by the antagonism inherent in the class relation between capital and labour.

The reason for this emphasis on contradiction is to demonstrate the inner instability and the crisis-prone character of the capitalist mode of production and to disprove the bourgeois presumption that a capitalist mode of production can ever be harmonious (in equilibrium). In the bourgeois view, major crises are solely due to external events such as harvest failures or resource scarcities. 'In the crises of the world market, the contradictions and antagonisms of bourgeois production are strikingly revealed. Instead of investigating the nature of the conflicting elements which erupt in the catastrophe, the apologists content themselves with denying the catastrophe itself and in insisting, in the face of their regular and periodic recurrence, that if production were carried on according to the textbooks, crises would never occur.'[23] The problem, says Marx, is that the apologists cling 'to the concept of unity in the face of contradiction'. Crises are inevitable expressions of the internal contradictions of capital.

The dialectical perspective also presumes that all forms of behaviour are purposive. In capital's case, the immediate purpose is the pursuit of profit or, as Marx prefers to call it, surplus value. But it turns out that this is merely a means (and a primary one at that) for the creation and appropriation of monetary wealth as a source of social, economic, political, military and above all class power. Surplus value, produced by labour, is the means for the production and reproduction of capital, the capitalist and capitalist class power. Capital is produced by labour.

This obvious purposiveness at the heart of capital led influential thinkers in the past such as Lukács to deny Engels's theses on the dialectics of nature. Since science could discern no overwhelming purposiveness in the natural world, it followed that dialectics had no application in the evolutionary sciences. Recent thinking presumes purposiveness

---

23   Karl Marx, *Theories of Surplus Value*, Vol. 2 (Amherst, NY: Prometheus Books, 2000), Chapter 17, Section 8, p. 500.

in nature even as it accepts that we do not know and perhaps can never know what that purpose might be. Our mistake is to presume that purposiveness has a moral goal. Yet we do know that, if the humble bee failed to fulfil its purpose of pollination, human life on Planet Earth would be seriously compromised. Dialectics has an increasing role in the sciences, it turns out, though not in the way that Engels had proposed. It is the dynamic dialectics of becoming of the mode of production as a totality that is central to our concerns here.

The purposiveness that lies at the heart of the theory of capital is in no way exceptional. It clashes, moreover, with the purposiveness of the labourers forced by circumstance to sublimate their desire for a decent house in a decent living environment at a decent standard of living with abundant time to pursue their pleasures at will. The alienated labourer and the equally alienated capitalist work together at cross-purposes. 'The decisive factor is not the health of the worker', Marx observes, 'but the ease with which the product must be constructed … which is on the one hand a source of growing profit for the capitalist [and] on the other hand the cause of a squandering of the worker's life and health.'[24] This clash of perspective and purpose lies at the heart of what class relations and class struggle is all about within a capitalist mode of production. The realization of one purpose, however, frequently denies the capacity to realize another. Take the history of just one commodity, sugar. The capacity to produce and to realize surplus value and to accumulate huge fortunes of wealth and power through the West Indian plantation system, based in slave labour, played a highly significant role in the rise of capital accumulation worldwide from the seventeenth century onwards. It was astonishingly profitable, but at the expense of a bitter legacy of racism and slavery. It also left a legacy of sugar-based diets with acute problems of obesity and diabetes as a worldwide problem. This has contributed markedly to the ill health and misery of human populations even as they continue to love to consume sugary things, oblivious of their horrendous history.

A simple version of systems thinking can, however, be usefully extended to illuminate the problematic role of the state within a capitalist mode of production. A sovereign state is an economy functioning within a defined territory. It was only in the 1920s that data began to be collected as if there were such a thing as nation-state economies. The

---

24 Karl Marx, *Capital*, Vol. 3, trans. David Fernbach (London and New York: Penguin, 1981), p. 185. See also Marx, *Capital*, Vol. 1, Chapter 10, 'The Working Day'.

behaviour of each sovereign state within the interstate system depends
on political and economic conditions as well on the forms of collective
action (such as tariffs and quotas) organized politically for the defence
of state interests. And those interests can be remarkably diverse as well
as broad. Sovereign states are organized as crucibles for accumulating
economic wealth and power in competition with other sovereign states.
Much of that wealth is appropriated by ruling elites and institutional
powers. The effects of interstate competition and geopolitical strategizing
on the productivity of capital in general are of great significance. But this
does not necessarily contribute to the health and well-being of working
populations within these states. Indeed, it is more often than not the
source of their misery and mental anguish. They are the ones who fight
the wars and then pay for their consequences. The flows of capital that
may augment the wealth and power of a capitalist state typically line the
pockets of its ruling class and their hangers-on.

In Marx's conception of capital's totality, the dialectical emphasis is on
the fluidity, instability and creativity of the contradictory processes (both
social and natural) that sustain and create it. The theme of contradiction
therefore plays a critical role in the unfolding of Marx's presentation.
Marx opens *Capital*, for example, with the unitary concept of the commodity, which has a use value and an exchange value. Its owner cannot
sell it and use it at the same time. The contradictory unity of use and
exchange within the commodity is brought back together by the labour
value that all commodities possess in order to be exchanged. Value as
a numeraire in the market rests on socially necessary labour time. But
labour time comes in two forms: abstract and concrete. The latter is the
particular labour input of a given producer in a given place and time,
which is very different from the average amount of time taken by multiple producers to create a comparable commodity. The concrete and the
abstract, in turn, come together at the moment of exchange, which produces a distinction between equivalent and relative forms of value. These
are unified in the universal equivalent which is a money commodity (for
example, gold and silver). This performs several contradictory functions.

It takes many successive steps of this sort to get to that opposition
between alienated labour and alienated capital in the act of production
which produces surplus value. This gives rise to the forms of absolute
and relative surplus value (to be taken up later) which produces the contradiction between rate and mass of profit and so on. I shall, in this text,
follow Marx's technique of presentation and project it forward into topics
that Marx left somewhat open. When the opposition between fixed and

circulating capital posits the circulation of interest-bearing capital as essential, it then poses the question of the contradiction within interest-bearing capital. This I propose to present as the contradiction between fictitious and real capital, which achieves a contradictory unity through the interventions of the state-finance nexus. This then opens up for exploration the contradictions within the state-finance nexus.

There is one further foundational question that has to be posed. Capital takes on multiple material forms (commodities, productive activity, money) as it circulates. But what is it that these different forms ('moments') have in common? What renders them commensurable and convertible into each other? Marx's answer is that they all, in one way or another, reflect something important about the qualities and quantities of human labour applied in their creation. Marx calls this quality 'value'. While all commodities exchanging in the market are valued in terms of their relation to human labour, not all products of human labour are commodities. If I prepare a tacos lunch for family and friends on Sunday, that entails the application of human labour. But it entails the production of a use value that is not value. If I do exactly the same thing on Monday for sale in a restaurant, then the tacos have potentially both a use value and an exchange value. Their value is realized through sale to a customer. Marx thus notes, 'Labour with the same content can therefore be both productive and unproductive.'[25]

There is, as Marx points out, plenty of room for ambivalence in this distinction. For instance, Milton, who wrote *Paradise Lost*, was an unproductive worker. On the other hand, a writer who turns out work for his publisher in a factory-style setting is a productive worker. Milton produced *Paradise Lost* as a silkworm produces silk, as the activation of *his own* nature. He later sold his product for £5 and thus became a merchant. But the literary proletarian of Leipzig who produces books, such as compendia on political economy, at the behest of his publisher is pretty nearly a productive worker since his production is taken over by capital and occurs only in order to increase it. A singer who sings like a bird is an unproductive worker. If she sells her song for money, she is to that extent a wage labourer or a merchant. But if the same singer is engaged by an entrepreneur who makes her sing to make money, then she becomes a productive worker, since she *produces* capital directly. A schoolmaster who instructs others is not a productive worker. But a

---

25   Marx, *Capital*, Vol. 1, Appendix, 'Results of the Immediate Process of Production', p. 1044.

schoolmaster who works for wages in an institution along with others, using his own labour to increase the money of the entrepreneur who owns the knowledge-mongering institution, is a productive worker.[26]

In writing this text, I am an unproductive worker and I can claim the same imperative that leads the silkworm to produce silk. It is in my nature! But, when a publisher takes this content and turns it into a book for sale in the market, I may receive a royalty for permitting the publisher to use my content to generate surplus value (profit). If I am lucky enough to write a bestseller, I can then retire and do whatever I want by living the life of a rentier.

At a certain point, however, Marx makes a qualitative shift in his ruminations on the topic of productive versus unproductive labour. He recognizes Adam Smith's concern to restrict if not abolish the parasitic activities of state, church, the law, the military and, above all, the landholders and to redirect the economy away from these rentiers and unproductive workers in order to support the contributions of entrepreneurs and their labourers. This idea also lay at the heart of the work of Saint-Simon in France. But Marx sees this as the creation of a distinctive social relation that allows for the production of surplus value rather than the purely physical production of useful things. Later on, he recognizes that the distinction between productive and unproductive can no longer be restricted to individuals. It has to extend to the whole collective enterprise of, for example, factory labour, within which there are all manner of specialized functions (such as cleaning and maintenance as well as active production).[27] It is the social rather than individual contribution that counts. It would then be theoretically possible to extend the definition to whole commodity chains, from copper and tin mines to coffee tables, for example. But at that point, the historical materialist definition of productive labour would become so diffuse that it would no longer be useful, leaving a residual pool of class hostility towards the parasitic rentiers.

Value gets created in the first instance through the application of living labour in the production of commodities for sale in the market at a profit. It gets represented and realized in circulation and consumption. Value courses through all the different moments. Its initial measure is given as socially necessary labour time, the time on average taken by labour to produce a commodity ready for market. This definition of value needs, at this point, to be taken on faith. Value is immaterial in the

---

26   Ibid.
27   Ibid., Vol. 1, p. 644.

sense that it is impossible to cut a commodity open and extract the value from it. Yet it is objective because, if I take a commodity to market and no one buys it, the labour embodied in it is socially unnecessary and hence not-value. Value is a conceptual abstraction of the sort familiar across the sciences and social sciences. We cannot measure gravity directly but we can infer its existence from its effects. We cannot measure the political power of someone like Donald Trump directly, but we can infer its existence because of its effects. Capital is not an objectified thing (as in conventional economics) but a process. It is value in motion. It passes through the different moments of money, commodity, production, consumption and distribution before once again appearing as money to be used as capital. The speed of its motion is constantly changing. In the course of its motion, capital exhibits the capacity to expand itself, to be the fount of profit, the lust for which powers the whole system ever onwards, building more and more class power.

This leaves us with the first major conundrum: Where does the increment in value – the surplus value – come from? What grounds the surplus value (or monetary profit), which is the object of capital's purpose?

2

The Circulation of Labour Capacity and the Origin of Profit

The category of labour lies at the heart of Marx's analysis. Labour in itself is, of course, a category common to all modes of production. Historically, the organization of labour (work) in general and of wage labour in particular has taken on many forms. But, as Marx writes in the *Grundrisse*, 'One of the historic presuppositions of capital is free labour' exchangeable for money and separated 'from the means of labour and the material for labour'. This presumes 'release of the worker from the soil as his natural workshop – hence dissolution of small, free landed property as well as the [dissolution of] communal landownership resting on the oriental commune'. The land, which is a foundational means of production in all modes of production, must be commodified and traded under rules of private property even though it is not in itself a commodity. In prior forms, 'the natural unity of labour with its material' is achieved and 'the individual relates to himself as proprietor, as master of the conditions of his reality.'[1] Under the rule of capital, labour is alienated in relation to itself. The labourer does not control the labour process, the product or its value (however that may be measured). It is also alienated in its relation to nature, the storehouse of use values to be used by the labourer in commodity production. Nature becomes a repository of use values to be freely extracted and appropriated by capital but rendered inaccessible to the labourer by the barrier of land ownership. Access to private property in land, and to all the resources that lie therein, depends on the extraction of ground rent by landowners.

1   Marx, *Grundrisse*, p. 471.

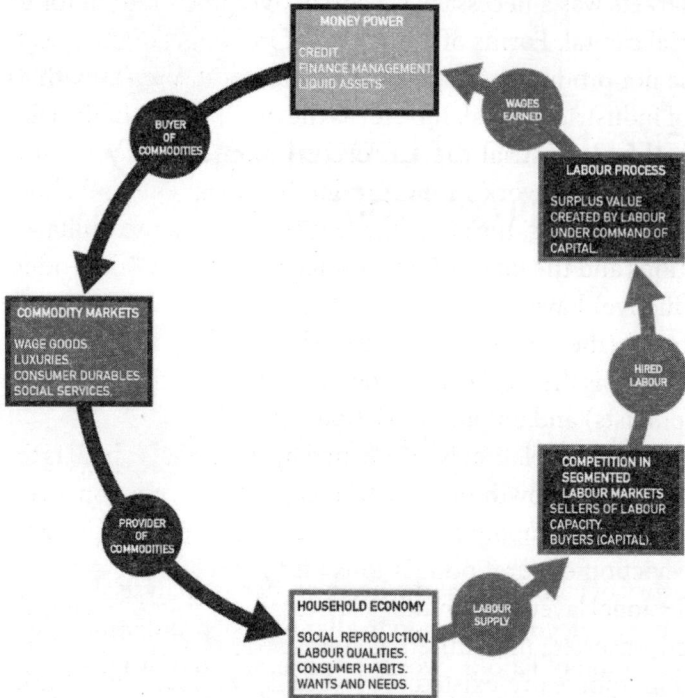

Figure 3. The Circulation of Labour Capacity

The rise of industrial capital was predicated on the dissolution or transcendence of former conditions of labour. It entailed the creation of a distinctive mode of circulation of labour capacity (Figure 3) that integrates with and supports the requirements of capital accumulation (Figure 1). These two circulation processes – of capital and of labour capacity – collide to produce value and surplus value (profit) in commodity form. The free labour that capital requires has to be free in a double sense: that unlike slave, serf or indentured labour, it is free to offer its capacity to labour to whomsoever and wherever it chooses, while being simultaneously 'freed' from any access to land as a primary means of production. Labour cannot, therefore, produce its own sustenance on its own account. For capital to exist, there had to be a labour force that had no option but to offer its capacity to labour to capitalists in order to survive.[2] In its prior existence, such a labour force – when it was not bound down by slavery, serfdom or indentured forms of labour – exchanged its capacity to labour against revenues (of the state, the church, the feudal lords or in the military). The existence of active labour and

2   Ibid., pp. 276–9.

land markets was a necessary precursor and precondition for the rise of industrial capital. Forms of employment in nonproductive sectors (that is, those not producing surplus value) did not disappear with the emergence of industrial capital. Indeed, as the productivity of the labour force employed by industrial capital rose, so more and more workers were made available to work in nonproductive forms of employment (such as personal services, the state, the law, the church, the military, cultural institutions and the like). What all wage labourers (both productive and unproductive) have in common is that their capacity to labour belongs to the buyer (the capitalist) during the hours of contract but not beyond. That contract is the legal expression of the class relation between employers (capitalists) and employees (labourers).

How this class relation is performed by industrial capital is the crucial story. The rapid growth of industrial capital depended on a continuous growth in labour supply through, for example, population growth, the forced eviction of rural populations off the land, the proletarianization of professional layers and middle classes, as well as mobilizing previously enslaved, enserfed, indentured or colonized peoples. While some sort of wage labour force pre-existed the rise of industrial capital, the dynamics of that rise required the continuous augmentation of free labour supply and important transformations in its qualities as well as in its quantities. When all other sources of surplus labour supply are exhausted, capitalists can produce their own reserve army of surplus labourers by deploying technological and organizational changes that so raise the productivity of labour as to create technologically induced unemployment.[3]

The emergence of capital out of the circulation of money is the originary moment for capital. 'Capital comes initially from circulation, and, moreover, its point of departure is money.'[4] This emergence rests, however, on the ability of the capitalist 'to find upon the market a commodity capable of creating more value than it itself has.'[5] That commodity is labour power, the capacity to labour. This is a critical point, both historically and theoretically. The only commodity that capital can find on the market that has the capacity to create more value than it has itself is labour power. No other commodity will do. This is the only commodity that can bridge the contradiction between the rule that all commodities should exchange at their value while producing the surplus value that sustains profit on a continuous basis. This first 'law of value'

---

3   Marx, *Capital*, Vol. 1, Chapter 25.
4   Marx, *Grundrisse*, p. 253.
5   Marx, *Capital*, Vol. 1, p. 270.

is not designed to explain the relative prices of commodities by way of differential labour inputs, as some economists believe (Marx explicitly rejects that idea). It simply explains the origin and continuous production of profit (surplus value) in a perfectly functioning free market society. It answers the question: Where does profit come from in a free market society?

Inspection of the spiral form reveals a contradiction that Marx only touches on rather obliquely.[6] Expansion through production of surplus value obviously implies a parallel expansion in effective demand (consumer capacity). Marx concentrates on how the surplus value is produced but does not analyze in any depth the conditions under which the surplus value is fully realized. In Volume 1, he explicitly assumes everything trades at its value in the market.[7] The problem of where the necessary increase in effective demand comes from has been the subject of intense debate. Malthus dissected the nature of the problem. The exploited workers cannot possibly be the source of sufficient effective demand. Nor can the capitalists, who are obliged to reinvest. Productive consumption through reinvestment is insufficient as a source of expanding effective demand.

To square the circle, said Malthus, there must be classes whose sole function is to consume and so provide the effective demand necessary to realize the extra value in the product. The rentiers, the monarchy, the church, the state, and the wealthy landed aristocracy therefore played an important and positive economic role as consumers. Marx even accepts that Malthus was quite right to notice the role of 'surplus idlers consuming without producing, or the necessity of waste, luxury, lavish spending, etc.',[8] something that has become an ever more conspicuous feature of our times. Without them, said Malthus, the economy would be in a state of constant overproduction (or, take your pick, underconsumption) and would lapse into permanent crisis. Ricardo rejected this proposition, preferring instead to embrace the tautologies of Say's Law, which states that overproduction is logically impossible, since every purchase is a sale and every sale is a purchase. Malthus was contemptuously dismissed as a 'general glut theorist',[9] who legitimized the economic role of the rentiers Ricardo, Saint-Simon and Marx despised. Marx and Ricardo then had to explain where the extra demand came from that could realize the

---

6   Marx, *Grundrisse*, p. 266.
7   Marx, *Capital*, Vol. 1, pp. 709–10.
8   Marx, *Grundrisse*, pp. 401–2 (footnote).
9   Ibid., pp. 417–18.

ever-expanding surplus value. To be sure, Malthus was half-right at that time, because a huge amount of residual wealth had accumulated under late feudalism and early colonialism that could be used to buy excess commodities. Injections into the money supply (for example, the California Gold Rush of 1848 or quantitative easing in our own time) could have short-term impacts. Rosa Luxemburg saw the imperialist trade with noncapitalist social formations such as China in her time as a logical answer.[10] The contemporary version of this is the vast increases in aggregate consumer demand (as well as in labour supply) from China since 1980. The automobilization of China has been a huge boon to German automobile companies like BMW. Starbucks has more coffee shops in China than in the US, and the China market has been crucial to Apple even though Apple has less than 10 per cent of it. If all this dries up, capital would then collapse unless there is another way to sustain the spiral form of endless accumulation. My own answer is that that spiral form is sustained through the credit system. If Marx recognized this, he did not want to examine it in the very opening chapters (or even the first two volumes) of *Capital*. He postponed the matter until, in Volume 3 of *Capital*, he begins to explain how an accumulation of capital increasingly and inevitably appears as an accumulation of debts.[11]

Here is a schematic version of how it works. A capitalist lacks funds to purchase a crucial input into production. He or she borrows money from the bank or from other producers to buy the commodity but then finds after production that there is not sufficient market power to buy the final commodity (including the surplus value). So the capitalist sells it on credit. Loans are, as students who take them to fund their studies clearly know, 'a claim upon future labour'.[12] Transactions in the present are thus financed by mortgaging future labour. In a trading system comprising millions of participants, the borrowing and lending can be roughly counterbalancing. Crises may occur when a large number of claims on future labour fail to be honoured and realized. As all the other ways in which effective demand can be brought to match further accumulation dry up, credit-fuelled effective demand moves centre stage to sustain the spiral, as has happened in the world economy most dramatically since 1980 or so. In a crisis, Marx notes, 'The antithesis between commodities and

10   Rosa Luxemburg, *The Accumulation of Capital*, in *The Complete Works of Rosa Luxemburg*, Volume 2, *Economic Writings 2*, eds Paul Le Blanc and Peter Hudis (London: Verso, 2016).

11   Marx, *Economic Manuscript of 1864–1865*, p. 366.

12   Marx, *Grundrisse*, p. 367; Marx, *Capital*, Vol. 3, Chapter 30, pp. 607–25.

their value form, money, is raised to the level of an absolute contradic-tion.'[13] Marx-like, we delay further consideration of the consequences of this until later (Chapter 13).

Let us return to the production of surplus value in the moment of production. Labour power, says Marx, is 'the form-giving fire' out of which capital is forged through surplus-value production.'[14] The capacity to labour is not innate. It is learned and passed on from generation to generation. Knowledge of labour processes and techniques is accumu-lated, internalized, documented and diffused across social groups and whole populations. Capital appropriates all of this as if it has the sole right to the knowledge that is embodied in the very consciousness and being of the wage labourer. Some precapitalist forms of knowledge are transformed into key use values (skills) that capital can and does appro-priate. Other customs and forms of knowledge are discarded, in some instances prematurely, as turned out to be the case of indigenous knowl-edges of medicinal uses of local plants, which have been pirated in recent times by the big pharma companies.

For example, the plantation owners in the Carolinas were much admired in the late eighteenth and early nineteenth century for their innovations in developing tidal rice production. They developed a strong commercial agriculture based, to be sure, on slave labour. But it was later shown that it was the African slaves themselves who brought the techniques and knowledge of tidal rice production from West Africa, where it had been previously well developed. The slaves continued to manage the process throughout. The only innovation attributable to the plantation owners was to substitute commercial white rice for the non-commercial West African black rice brought to the New World and used by the slave populations for their own sustenance.[15]

Labour power is not a commodity like any other. It is not a product of human labour. Its value is set by the value of the commodities that the labourer needs to consume in order to survive at a given standard of living. In the United States, the poverty level for a family of four is defined by the value of the market basket of commodities deemed nec-essary to survive at an adequate standard of living in a particular place and time. Amy Glasmeier has recently developed a 'living wage calcula-tor' for localities in the United States which 'includes the basic elements

13   Marx, *Capital*, Vol. 1, p. 236.
14   Marx, *Grundrisse*, pp. 301, 361.
15   J. Carney, *Black Rice: The African Origins of Rice Cultivation in the Americas* (Cambridge, MA: Harvard University Press, 2002).

of a cost of living: housing, food, child care, transportation costs, mis-
cellaneous – which includes clothing, as well as taxes'. It is, she says,
'designed to be a minimum living wage that someone would need to be
able to pay the basic expenses of their daily lives'.[16] In most instances
it turns out to be much higher than the existing legal minimum wage,
but it also varies significantly from locality to locality. This is the sort
of standard that Marx has in mind when thinking about the value
of labour power (the basic wage rate). This value varies a great deal
depending on environmental and cultural conditions and the definition
of necessities (for example, a mobile phone has become a necessity,
while air conditioning is considered necessary in Texas but not yet in
Maine). Class struggles over the standard of living of labour affect the
value of labour power, while, as Marx points out, a 'moral element' often
enters into its determination:[17] bourgeois reformers may seek to set up
an adequate living standard for the working citizens of a particular state
simply because living around chronic poverty is unpleasant and risky
(for example, contagious diseases do not observe class boundaries) and
because of the need to build an adequate mass market for the commodities produced. Statesmen also became aware that an exhausted,
decrepit workforce was totally inadequate for military service. Fostering consent and keeping potential unrest under control have also been
considerations.

The value of labour power in the Nordic countries is very different from that in China, Brazil or the United States. It is very different
between Alabama and Massachusetts. The definition of what constitutes
a living wage is thus highly controversial. The value of labour power
is, furthermore, sensitive to differentials in skills. Marx finesses this
problem by suggesting that the value of skilled labour is some multiple
of the value of ordinary unskilled labour. It has to include the costs and
time of training and learning appropriate skills. But, proposes Marx, for
purposes of theorization, we presume that the value of simple labour
power is fixed in a given place and time. This abstraction of the value of
labour power as a 'known datum' enables him to see more clearly where
profit comes from. It simply arises out of the fact that the value paid for a
day's work is fixed by the value of labour power, and this is less than the
value the labourer produces for capital during the hours worked. This is
what Marx calls 'surplus value'.

---

16   A. Glasmeier, New Data Posted: Living Wage Calculator, 2023, livingwage
.mit.edu.

17   Marx, *Capital*, Vol. 1, Chapter 6, particularly p. 275.

The study of the circulation of labour capacity in relation to the circulation of industrial capital is as theoretically revealing as it is politically instructive (Figure 3). The circulation process can be broken down into five distinctive moments, each with its own distinctive characteristics and conditionalities. For example, labour markets vary remarkably, both historically and geographically. The degree of regulation, the level of class conflict, the capacity for state intervention and the overall state of class struggle vary from one place to another. Marx mainly analyzes the economic roles of labour and capital as concrete abstractions and not as the qualities of actual capitalists and workers as persons in the workplace and in the market. Marx thus analyzes economic roles, not the lives of individual persons. Even so, conditions in the labour market and at the point of social reproduction of labour power are relatively fixed, though they vary substantially over space and time.

The worker begins the day by entering a labour market as a seller of labour capacity in competition with other workers. The buying and selling of labour power constitutes a labour market of some sort. That market, as we shall later see, may be segmented, segregated by race, ethnicity, religion, skills or gender and subjected to all manner of social and political regulation. Getting hired is often a difficult process. If hired, a certain segment of the working population participates in a labour process of commodity production, designed and commanded by capital to yield value and surplus value. The worker's capacity is alienated: Workers have no effective control over the labour process or the nature and value of the commodity produced, all of which belong to capital. However, as recipients of a wage, workers have discretionary freedom as to what to do with their money power. Some, if not all of it, has to be used to buy commodities in the market, both necessities in order to live and discretionary commodities that give pleasure (in Marx's case that included tobacco!). Any surplus may be saved for a rainy day, put by for old age or frittered away in reckless consumption or gambling. Finally, workers purchase the commodities they need to survive before returning to their homes with those commodities to participate in the complex processes of social reproduction, of both themselves and of others, such as children and others dependent on them. Such individuals typically live in a household (however defined) in a physical neighbourhood. The qualities of daily life within that neighbourhood world of social reproduction can vary substantially.

These are the five key moments in the circulation of labour capacity (as shown in Figure 3). When industrial capitalists encounter the labourer as the bearer of labour power, they offer a money wage in return for delivery of the capacity to labour and the ability to produce surplus value. This money wage should be sufficient for the labourer to buy all those commodities needed to live at an adequate standard of living. In return for the money wage, the capitalist has the right to employ the capacity to labour for a given period of time (subject to contract negotiation) under capital's direction, in order to produce a new commodity for sale in the market. The capitalist also needs to buy means of production (raw materials, partially finished products, plant and equipment, tools and machinery, energy and so on). Adopting a particular regime of technology and organizational form (for example, the factory and power looms), the capitalist organizes the production of the new commodity (for example, a bolt of cloth) on the presumption that someone will want to buy it for its use value (for example, in clothing manufacture). The exchange value of the new commodity rests on the past and present labour time congealed within it through production. From the standpoint of the market, this time is not the individual time of concrete labour in a particular production process that matters, but the average time taken to produce a comparable product by all producers of bolts of cloth. This is what Marx calls the socially necessary labour time (the abstract labour) embodied in the product. It often differs substantially from the concrete labour times actually expended by different producers. Marx conceptualizes the socially necessary labour time (abstract labour) congealed in the commodity as value. This value is then realized in monetary form through a sale of the commodity in the market.

The values of the inputs (the raw materials, the instruments of labour used up, the partially finished products and so on) are preserved and transferred into the new commodity (Marx designates these elements as c – constant capital). The labourers also add value to the product by congealing their labour into the new commodity. How much value is added depends on the hours worked. Capitalists know that they will have to pay a wage roughly equivalent to the value of labour power. The labourer produces the equivalent of the value of labour power (designated by v, the variable capital) in, say, six hours of work. Once that requirement is covered, the capitalist can keep the labourer working for, say, another four hours. This is the surplus value (designated by s) that underpins the money profit. The total value congealed in the product during the ten-hour day is designated as $c + v + s$.

Consider now some features of Marx's simple notation. The ratio s/v measures the rate of exploitation of labour power. The ratio c/v (variously called the organic or value composition of capital) is a measure of labour productivity, or capital intensity. The ratio $s/c+v$ is a measure of the rate of profit, while $c/s+v$ captures the relation between past and present labour in production. Marx will make much of the movement of these ratios, particularly in response to technological and organizational change, which affect the value composition. Note immediately, however, that the rate of profit is always lower (sometimes substantially so) than the rate of labour exploitation because $s/c+v$ is always less than s/v. It is also easy to infer that any increase in the value composition due to rising labour productivity will produce, everything else remaining equal, a lower rate of profit. As the ratio c/v increases the rate of profit, $s/c+v$, declines.[18]

The procurement of surplus value (profit) is the be-all and end-all of the capitalist's ambition. It is labour power that adds the value and labour power that has the capacity to produce more value than it itself has. The capitalist merely captures and appropriates the surplus value that labour produces. The encounter between capital and labour is the inception point for the systematic production of surplus value (profit). It is, above all, the point where the persona of the industrial capitalist is produced. From a materialist standpoint, it is the labourer who produces the industrial capitalist. Or, as Marx prefers to put it, 'Capital is dead labour which, vampire-like, lives only by sucking living labour, and lives the more, the more labour it sucks.'[19]

In this accounting, everything depends on the hours that labourers work beyond those required to produce the value equivalent of their own labour power. It is for this reason that struggles over the length of the working day, the working week, the working year and the working life are foundational within bourgeois society, with major implications for the capitalist social formation as well as for the theory of the capitalist mode of production. This is the moment when we see the abstract rendition of processes in the deep structure of the capitalist mode of production rising to the surface of the daily lived experience of workers. The ongoing struggles over the length of the working day, what Marx calls 'absolute surplus value', cannot be resolved by appeal to bourgeois property rights or law. As Marx puts it in *Capital*, the capitalist has the right as the owner of the capacity to labour to demand as much from that capacity as possible. Intercapitalist competition and 'the coercive laws of competition' force individual capitalists to extend the working

---

18   Marx, *Capital*, Vol. 1, Chapter 9.
19   Ibid., Vol. 1, Chapter 10, particularly p. 342.

day as long as possible no matter what individual capitalists might think appropriate. The worker, likewise, has the right to resist when the hours worked and the intensity of the labour become so onerous as to threaten the worker's health and longevity. Between these two equal rights, Marx famously observes, 'force decides'.[20]

'Force' here is political as well as physical. Class struggle ensues. The struggle over the appropriation of the labourer's time litters the history of capital accumulation. At some point, the state is obliged to intervene to regulate the length of the working day in the interests of both labour and capital. Capital's interest is not generally served, after all, by killing off workers through overwork or so exhausting and diminishing them as to lower their productivity. This is what the unlimited operation of the coercive laws of competition will likely produce. With the help of the reports of the factory inspectors, Marx presents an overview of working conditions in Britain during his time, culminating in the case of Mary Ann Walkley, '20 years old, employed in a highly respectable dress making establishment' where 'girls work on an average 16½ hours without a break, during the season often 30 hours, and the flow of their failing labour power is maintained by occasional supplies of sherry, port or coffee'.[21] Walkley quite simply died from overwork.

This plunges us into the killing fields of industrial labour. This was the fate that befell many African Americans in the wake of the emancipation from slavery in the United States. Using incarceration for the most minor of offences and legally organizing prison labour by the state, a new form of wage slavery was created in the US Southern states, in which death from overwork or from indiscipline was an acceptable practice. Death from overwork is still a formal cause of death, though not so widespread, in Japan, China and some sectors like the Thai fishing industry. Employees in Jack Ma's Alibaba in recent times worked on a schedule from 9 in the morning until 9 at night for six days a week. In response to widespread complaints and resistance to this infamous 996 system, Ma merely stated that the workers should be grateful that they have a job and feel proud to contribute to the global economic power of China through their hard work. He neglected to say that by this extraction of absolute surplus value he had become one of the richest persons in the world. The Communist Party has now stepped in and outlawed the 996 system. They have also designated the province where Alibaba is headquartered

---

20   Ibid., Vol. 1, p. 344.
21   Ibid., Vol. 1, p. 364.

as an experimental 'common prosperity' zone in which Ma and other billionaires have been invited to put much of their immense personal fortunes to the achievement of the common prosperity of all. Ma has largely disappeared from public view, and his donations are managed by Communist Party officials and not by NGOs under his control. For a while, he was living in exile in Japan. The extraction of absolute surplus value in China is in this manner currently being curbed by political intervention. In Marx's time, significant legislation to regulate the length of the working day was introduced in Britain, partly because the working class became more organized and powerful but also through an alliance, Marx tells us, with class factions 'not directly interested in the question'. In a Parliament where the landed interest and aristocracy still had a great deal of power, legislation against the interests of the loathsome upstart industrial capitalists remained feasible.[22]

But in the absence of such interventions, the constant pressure from capital to raise the rate of profit by depressing the value of labour power is matched only by pressures to lengthen the working day as much as possible. The inevitable result is 'absolute poverty [of labour] as object, on one side, and ... the general possibility of wealth as subject and as activity' on the other side, that of capital and the capitalist.[23]

The labourer's experience of capital is not confined to the workplace, and Marx takes time out to comment on the inner relations between the different moments in the circulation of labour capacity. The worker is exposed to radically different material experiences within the circulation of labour capacity: as seller of labour capacity (in a competitive and sometimes segmented labour market); as participant in a labour process (designed and commanded by capital); as recipient of a wage (which confers the discretionary freedom that goes with possessing money power); as buyer of commodities in the market (both necessities in order to live and discretionary luxuries); and, finally, as participant in and product of the multiple forms of social reproduction (including socialized provision) in the daily life of a household (however defined) in a physical neighbourhood.

Diverse experiences across the different moments of this circulation process tend to generate different political subjectivities. If the identity of working persons as workers is, as Marx puts it, 'extinguished' when they purchase commodities in the market and assume the identity of buyers,[24]

22   Ibid., Vol. 1, p. 409.
23   Marx, *Grundrisse*, p. 296.
24   Ibid., pp. 420–1.

how can class consciousness be articulated, let alone sustained, across all the moments within this circulation process? The different political subjectivities that attach to the different moments of the capitalist mode of production tend to disguise its overall class character. It is only from the perspective of capital's totality that the class character of the whole system becomes clearly visible, as opposed to the class opposition entailed in production. And it is for this reason that cultivating the perspective of capital as a totality is so important for the labour movement and why, conversely, neglecting or abandoning this perspective of capital as a totality has been so politically damaging.

In practice, workers typically relate differently to the diverse experiential worlds they encounter on their daily round through the range of moments they traverse. Some workers might succumb to the temptation of a compensatory consumerism, in which they are offered access to a cornucopia of cheap consumer goods as compensation for horrific alienation at the point of production. Others may reluctantly consent to the alienation of their labour and general exploitation in the hope that they may be able to put by sufficient money to someday open a bodega or a coffee shop. Yet others may consent to everything in this circulation process provided they have time and money enough to create for themselves a meaningful family or household life. Taking the kids to soccer games or music classes or just romping with them in the backyard may afford enough pride and pleasure to mask the alienating experiences of working for capital and going to the shopping mall. The creation of an amicable neighbourhood life has been, for many working-class populations, a compensatory though not unproblematic joy that may make class struggle against capital in production seem a remote and easily sublimated engagement.

Marx recognized the relationality within the different moments in the circulation of labour capacity.[25] If the workers are 'too industrious or demonstrate their capacity to save', capital then concludes that they are either overpaid or that they ought to be directly charged with financing their own security arrangements and not to be a burden on the capitalist state when they age or get sick. Capital is perpetually seeking ways to privatize all forms of social security. If workers cultivate abstemiousness in the hope of successfully accumulating some monetary wealth, capital typically responds by depressing wages.[26] The hypocritical and

---

25 Ibid., p. 285.
26 Ibid., pp. 287–8.

self-serving nature of bourgeois philanthropic support for piggy banks and forms of mutual support among workers, along with the general emphasis on the virtues of industriousness (for the worker but not for the capitalist), is then plain to see.[27] The ideological values of industriousness and abstemiousness are foundational precepts in bourgeois preaching to their workforces.

Like all the other circulation processes at work within the totality, we also have to recognize the contextual conditions that affect the circulation of labour capacity. Environmental pollution and degradation, much of it due to capital treating the environment as an externality for which capitalists are not responsible, have impacts on health, life expectancy and capacity to labour on an unequal basis. Living in the shadow of a plant producing noxious and carcinogenic chemicals has time and again been shown to reduce life expectancies (for example, in the so-called 'cancer alley' of Louisiana). The quality of public education is contingent on the uneven circulation of tax revenues, and consumer habits are very much driven by the creation of new wants and needs (like mobile phones) at the behest of capital. Workers' savings are likewise subject to devaluation in the course of a financial crisis, while collapses of energy networks and hurricane and tornado damage all affect, unevenly and sometimes devastatingly, this circulation process. It is in the sphere of social reproduction that older cultural relations of labouring, of patriarchy and gender dominance are both preserved and enhanced with major consequences for employment structures and economic inequality. It is here, too, that discussions of sexuality and reproduction mores are centred, again with consequences elsewhere for the circulation of labour capacity.

There are a number of deeper points to be made about the conditions that attach to each of the five 'moments' within the circulation of labour capacity. For example, competition in labour markets is often fierce and pits not only worker against worker but also frequently internalizes hostilities between different groups based on gender, ethnicity, race, religion or simply provenance. These differences often date back to pre-existing rivalries between social groups and pre-existing conditions of unfree labour (slavery in the Americas of African populations is an obvious example). To the degree that capital benefits from such competitive factionalism, it (and its dominant instruments in the media) undoubtedly does its level best to continue segmented labour markets or

---

27   Ibid., p. 289.

even to create new ones. This holds back the possibility of class solidarity among all wage workers as they attempt to negotiate an adequate wage and organize a liveable life. The greater the heterogeneity and diversity of the labour force the harder it is to organize labour along class lines to assure fair treatment in the labour market. The relative homogeneity of the labour forces in Scandinavia after 1945 played an important role in facilitating strong adherence to social democratic norms relative to the United States with its racially factionalized and immigrant labour force, divisions within which are actively crafted and exploited by capital. The resultant wage – the value of labour power – is thus dependent, unlike all other commodities, on the outcome of class formation and class struggles in which many factors, including those of clan and caste, combine.

The nature of the skills required to facilitate a labour process is sensitive to the technology deployed. A struggle ensues over the capacity for sections of the labour force to monopolize skills and thereby command a higher wage. The whole history of technological evolution carries within it the attempt by capital to combat the potential monopolization of skills by initiating technologies that disempower labour. The advent of artificial intelligence appears, in this regard, to be as threatening to service provision as automation has been for manufacturing. But the systems set up to disempower labour all too often entail the definition of new monopolizable skills. The result is a hierarchy of skills to which corresponds a hierarchy of wages, thus segmenting the workforce along technical, caste, clan and meritocratic lines as opposed to purely social and cultural lines.

It is not hard to take each moment and elaborate in this way on the diverse conditions under which that moment will be experienced by the worker. Early on in the history of British capitalism, for example, workers set up mutual aid societies and penny savings banks to attempt to collect and save money to insure against sickness, accident or the vicissitudes of old age.[28] These were precursors to modern structures of social security and insurance, while facilities for workers to save or even borrow have multiplied. Examples include the introduction of microcredit (the 'in principle' anticapitalist Grameen Bank set up by Muhammad Yunus in Bangladesh) superseded by a proliferation of Washington-based procapitalist microfinance programmes that have sought to support impoverished populations pursuing an 'entrepreneurialism of the self' in emerging

---

28   E. P. Thompson, *The Making of the English Working Class* (London: Vintage, 1966).

markets. The billions of people living on less than two dollars a day thus formed a huge market that cried out to be tapped by the financiers.[29]

Many of the active struggles we are now witnessing are over such matters as exploitation in the marketplace (protests against monopoly power and price gouging on pharmaceuticals or astronomical housing rents, for example); the perversions of the credit and mortgage debt system (consumer and credit card debt); the qualities of social provision in the state sector; and the qualities of daily life through collective consumption. Workers' struggles against capital in the workplace are just one form of struggle and by no means always the most immediately important, eye-catching or feasible. The deterioration of the qualities of neighbourhood life and stresses within families, or household reproduction units, much of which can be traced back to deindustrialization, unemployment and the political turn to neoliberalism, now lies at the root of much of the political malaise experienced by many working people in the United States. The production of a vibrant and satisfying daily life is, for many working people, just as important as holding a satisfying and well-remunerated job.[30] The ideal, of course, is to achieve both, but such a privileged, affluent worker is harder to find in these neoliberal times. Some professional positions (like my own) are, however, sufficiently well remunerated to allow for such a life. The perspective of the totality helps identify some of the daily life barriers to a revolutionary consciousness.

While the initial theory positions capital and labour as the primary locus of social, political and economic contestation, the mediating role of the capitalist state in the circulation of labour capacity must also be recognized. The complexities and chaotic conditions prevailing in the circulation of labour capacity in early industrial capitalism called forth the need for regulation and legal constraints. The concepts of private property and juridical rights were not given by nature nor mandated by God. They were arrived at as human populations increasingly sought an adequate basis on which to conduct widespread and generalized market exchange. This was how a distinctively capitalist state, adequate to the needs of capital, was formed. In the shadowy world of precapitalism, Marx notes, there existed many systems for the extraction of surpluses from dominated populations. The initial Statute of Labourers in England

---

29   Paul Collier, *The Bottom Billion: Why the Poorest Countries Are Failing and What Can Be Done about It* (Oxford: Oxford University Press, 2007).

30   C. G. Pickvance, 'On the Study of Urban Social Movements', *Sociological Review* 23: 1 (1975): 29–49.

in 1349 sought to standardize and extend the working day and penalize those 'workers in waiting' deprived of a livelihood on the land if they lapsed into vagrancy, highway robbery or other forms of undisciplined conduct. There was a long way between this and the first real attempt to regulate and limit rather than extend the working hours and conditions in Britain in the Factory Act of 1833.[31]

In contemporary advanced capitalist countries, state actions, regulations and legal interventions are omnipresent in every one of the different moments in the circulation of labour capacity. In labour markets in the United States, for example, affirmative action to compensate for past discrimination conflicts with requirements to be an 'equal opportunity' employer. But the main thrust of current judicial and legislative intervention is a bias, particularly under neoliberalism, in favour of a highly individualized labour force in a labour market with little room for collective action on the part of workers and plenty of room for capital in alliance with the state to ensure a perpetual supply of individualized low-wage labour. Within the labour process, concern over worker safety (in construction and down mines in particular) and exposure to hazardous materials underpins the work of organizations like the US Occupational Safety and Health Administration (OSHA), whose reach is severely limited by congressional refusal to appropriate adequate funds for enforcement. The state is also heavily involved in monetary matters, everything from enforcement of minimum or liveable wages to both facilitating and promoting debt encumbrance to the point of debt peonage for many in the working population (in spite of many states developing anti-usury laws). Protections against predatory credit card companies and other forms of legalized robbery are notably lacking. In the consumer market, housing, medical and educational costs reflect a lack of adequate state policies to match the needs of most consumers, while many people rely on state provision of social services as a form of collective consumption. In the field of social reproduction and social security, public policies are foundational for access to the basic qualities of a secure daily life. As Melinda Cooper so brilliantly portrays in her book on family values, current policies in the US amount to a resurrection of the punitive qualities of the British Poor Law of the 1830s.[32]

The capitalist state thus typically operates more on behalf of capital than of labour. While the chaos of disruptive and coercive conditions of

---

31   Marx, *Capital*, Vol. 1, Chapter 10.
32   Melinda Cooper, *Family Values: Between Neoliberalism and the New Social Conservatism* (Brooklyn: Zone Books, 2009).

competition may be theoretically lauded, in practice, capital works best as a rules-based and rules-enforced economic system that reflects the needs of capital in general rather than those of individual corporations or factions of capital. The pressures of organized labour can, of course, push the state to legislate in workers' favour, but as Marx's study of the history of the working day shows, this is most easily achieved when some sort of regulation is also required by capital to limit the destructive consequences of uncontrolled and potentially ruinous competition. This is, nevertheless, a situation in which organized class struggle on the part of labour and its allies can change the direction of capital's evolution in important ways.

In the *Grundrisse*, Marx on occasion appeals to a mythical figure called 'the emancipated labourer' in order to ask how labourers, armed with the kind of knowledge we are presenting here, might strategize with the aim of improving their lot and exploring alternatives. Individuals enclosed within this circulation process could seek to minimize their alienation and oppression and open spaces in which they can flourish. Collectively, they could organize to monopolize their position in labour markets and labour processes (as some immigrant groups have in the past proven skilled at doing). Or they could mobilize state powers to create a labour market as free as possible of all forms of discrimination on the grounds of race, gender, ethnicity, religion, sexual orientation and the like. State regulation of labour processes to ensure occupational health and safety, institutional supports for pension rights, health insurance, access to free education and the like, cooperative supply of food and of housing and, of course, adequate infrastructural investment are some of the social democratic programmes that could be presented politically to bring an aura of greater civility to the circulation of labour capacity from the perspective of the totality. The consequence of Marx's framing of the circulation of labour capacities as a key circulation process within the becoming of capital's totality is that it highlights what so many people have in common in their daily activities of working and living, without in any way denying the radical diversity of their skills, their individual capacities, their cultural backgrounds and all the other aspects they bring to this process but which tend to divide workforces and fragment political consciousness.

A variety of issues arise here that must be addressed even though to do so is likely to incite strong opinions and political passions. The class relation of exploitation that Marx positions at the heart of surplus value production and appropriation rests on the proposition that there is a labour force that has to engage in wage labour in order to live. This labour force is brought into being by dispossessing it of any independent access to the means of production. Hence the importance of Marx's historical account of primitive accumulation. But, as later critical commentaries have subsequently insisted, the relationships of domination on which surplus value extraction rest go far beyond those Marx envisaged. It is for this reason, for example, that Nancy Fraser insists on paralleling Marx's account of the exploitation of living labour in production with the expropriation of labour power through the persistence of neocolonial practices on capital's periphery.[33]

Conditions within the social formation affect the practices of waged workers in the mode of production. Any vector of domination by any one social group (for example, Christians) over any other (for example, Muslims) will be used to orchestrate and justify the excessive exploitation of alien labour by alien capital. Differences of race, ethnicity, culture, gender, sexuality, religion, language, history, education, expertise, social hierarchies, authority structures and the like (all of which may coexist within any social formation) can be put to use by capital to more strongly enforce labour discipline while frustrating the ability of workers to organize collective responses. Workers also find themselves in radically divergent labour markets. From the 1980s onwards, for example, much attention was paid to the distinction between formal and informal labour markets and forms of employment. In the formal sector, workers were granted legal status and their conditions of labour were often regulated, unionized and legislated to guarantee minimum rights (health care, insurance, pension provisions, guardrails against harassment and wrongful dismissal and so on), while the informal labour that dominated in most of the developing world conferred no such rights. All work was precarious at best. The most distinctive case is China, where the *hukou* system granted full citizenship rights and privileges for urban citizens while rural migrants received nothing more than the minimum wage and were expected to return to their rural homes after several years working in urban factories.

Throughout the Americas in general and in the United States in particular, a huge supplement in labour supply came from the Atlantic slave trade from the seventeenth century onwards. This imposed a racial dimension on the labour market that linked the slave labour of the cotton plantations to the wage labour of Manchester industrialism. The

---

33   Nancy Fraser, *Cannibal Capitalism* (London: Verso, 2022).

emancipation of the slaves in 1863 in the US did not eliminate the role of racism in relation to capital. Some scholars universalize this historical particularity of the social formation in the Americas and redefine capital as inherently racial.[34] In the United States, this is clearly the case. Elsewhere, however, it is not racism that dominates exploitation. In Northern Ireland or in Belgium, it is the combination of nationalism and religion (backed in Belgium's case by language) that divides, while on the Indian subcontinent it is caste (and the Dalit 'untouchables') that has played such an important role, along with the Hindu–Muslim divide, against the complicated historical background of British imperial rule up until 1948. While African labour fuelled racial capitalism through slavery in the Americas, the British organization of indentured 'coolie' labour from South Asia to work plantations around the globe from the mid nineteenth century on has left a sprinkling of Asian minorities across much of Africa and even in the Caribbean. Low-wage South Asian labour in our times has concentrated heavily on servicing the Gulf States, while Filipinos and Filipinas dominate the low-wage labour market in Singapore and domestic work (particularly care for the aged) in the United States. In Fiji, to cite another example, the clash between indigenous and South Asian imported indentured labour survives to this day, as does the African–Asian divide in Trinidad. The importance of imported labour supplies in an era of relative localized labour scarcities after 1945 in Europe cannot be ignored. The Germans took in Turks, the Swedes took in Yugoslavs, the French took in Maghrebians and so on. Marx also paid attention to the varieties of serfdom in Central and Eastern Europe including Russia. Sect-based religious divisions in the Middle East likewise provided a basis in which capital could divide and conquer. Capital makes use of every possible vector of differentiation and discrimination to naturalize and legitimize the exploitation of wage labour. But such differences may also be deployed to labour's advantage. Religious ties have often provided ready-made bonds for restricted forms of labour organization. This possibility lies at the centre of much class struggle. In the early nineteenth century, the nonconformist religious chapels in Britain laid the basis for political organizing in working-class neighbourhoods, much as the civil rights movement in the United States used the Black churches as organizing centres for political action.

Marx had, however, the long-term ambition for the abolition of wage labour altogether. While struggles against the multiple vectors

---

34   Cedric J. Robinson, *Black Marxism: The Making of the Black Radical Tradition* (Chapel Hill: University of North Carolina Press, 1983).

of domination that exist in the capitalist social formation are integral to anticapitalist struggle, no one of these vectors, such as race or gender, can substitute for the direct struggle against capital's domination over labour within the circulation of labour capacity. The collapse of the circulation of labour capacity is the ultimate aim of anticapitalist struggle. Hints of this can be seen in what was called 'the great resignation' that followed the disruption of labour markets and employment due to Covid-19. A significant segment of the US labour force did not initially come back into the labour market and refused to be reinscribed in the circulation of labour capacities. Some (mainly women) could not do so because of child-rearing or elderly care obligations, in which case the organization of household labour substitutes for the circulation of labour capacity. Others emphasized their alienation and refused to return given their history as recipients of abusive and excessive exploitation. They found, albeit temporarily, other modes of employment (for example, odd jobs) and nonpecuniary means of social provision.

Marx's dream, however, was that the associated labourers would find collective ways to organize social production cooperatively and hence abolish the power of the class relation over daily life.[35] How that might be done with the help of automation and AI has not yet been seriously considered. From the standpoint of the emancipated labourer, the superiority of good social democratic management over neoliberal malicious neglect is obvious. But that, in Marx's view, is only an intermediate step towards even more emancipatory possibilities that only become apparent in the course of class struggle. As Rosa Luxemburg put it, drawing on the lessons of the 1905 Russian Revolution: 'The proletariat requires a high degree of political education, of class consciousness and organization. All these conditions cannot be fulfilled by pamphlets and leaflets, but only by the living political school, by the fight and in the fight, in the continuous course of the revolution.' Working-class class politics, in short, is constituted in the context of class struggle.[36]

There is an important coda to this that cries out for explication. Both Ricardo and Marx accepted some version of the labour theory of value in which all value originates with the application of living labour in

35   Peter Hudis, 'Marx's Concept of Socialism', in Matt Vidal et al. (eds), *The Oxford Handbook of Karl Marx* (Oxford: Oxford Academic, 2019), pp. 757–72.

36   Rosa Luxemburg, *The Mass Strike, the Political Party and the Trade Unions*, in Axel Fair-Schulz, Peter Hudis and William A. Pelz (eds), *The Complete Works of Rosa Luxemburg, Volume 3: Political Writings 1, On Revolution 1897–1905* (London: Verso, 2019).

production. This is a difficult concept to work with, since value is postulated as a social relation, and as such is immaterial and relational though objective in its effects. Marx continued to elaborate on his version of the concept of value as his investigations progressed. The value theory he came up with was not his own. He sought to uncover the value theory inherent in capitalist circulation and accumulation practices. If, for example, capital did not put value on nature or on processes of social reproduction (for example, population growth), then Marx took his cue from those practices. Neither nature nor social reproduction are productive of value as far as capital is concerned, and Marx reflects that in his formulations. Capital treats such phenomena as free gifts of nature and of human nature. They are critically important in the theory of capital but not sources of value or surplus value.

But the labour theory of value posed a political and, for some, a serious moral problem. Why did those exclusively producing value and even more importantly the surplus value – the labourers – receive so very little of it? Many in the Ricardian school were acutely bothered by the evident injustice. They were inclined to accept some degree of socialist redistribution to better compensate the labourers. This culminated in John Stuart Mill's wholehearted and influential embrace of Ricardian redistributive socialism. Some justification for this could even be found in Adam Smith, who had earlier recognized that the inequalities inherent in a progressive market-based entrepreneurialism might require the capitalist state to redistribute some of the accumulating wealth.

The Manchester industrialists and their apologists found such ideas odious in the extreme. Marx also found these ideas wanting because Mill maintained that distribution was social and therefore amenable to human will, but that production was natural and therefore immutable. On this last point, Marx vociferously disagreed. Ricardian redistributive socialism, no matter how progressive, leaves the capitalist mode of production and all of its internal contradictions intact. The political task for Marx was the abolition of the capitalist mode of production and its distinctive labour theory of value. The acute moral and political problem posed by the labour theory of value for the Ricardians became, however, a locus of a troubling and powerful critique of capital in Britain in the 1830s and 1840s.

The marginalist revolution in economics after 1850 conveniently did away with such thorny political and moral problems. First, it abandoned what was held to be the fuzziness of the labour theory of value for an objectified and therefore presumably much more scientifically rigorous analysis of production and distribution. The marginalist economists studied the production function as a combination of the inputs of land, labour and capital as measurable and objective factors of production. Ricardo, ironically, pioneered a way to measure the contribution of each factor of production in his theory of differential ground rent. The value of land was set by the production cost on the least fertile soil that had to be brought into production in order for supply and demand for agricultural products to achieve equilibrium in the market. The marginalists took that principle and applied it to all the factors of production. The value of the inputs of land, labour and capital depended on the (money) value of the last unit of that factor of production that had to be added to achieve equilibrium of supply and demand in the market. The value of the commodity rested on the combined contribution of each supposedly independent marginal factor of production to the total cost (eliding the intractable problem of how to measure K, the capital input, when K was partially a stock of existing factories and machines). The (monetary) value of the inputs depended on their relative scarcity. This was the second great contribution of marginalist theory. If capital was scarce, then one would expect to pay more for it, whereas, if labour was abundant, then wages would be low (which, Marx insisted, they were bound to be because of capital's capacity to produce unemployment and an industrial reserve army).

The distributive shares produced by marginalism were an objective scientific, not political, determination. Each factor received its just price given the interplay of market forces. The marginalist solution internalized a persuasive notion of a just price (both wage and profit) justly arrived at. All talk of redistributive socialism could be dismissed as sentimental waffle compared to the rigorous scientific determinations wrought by market forces requiring the optimal allocation of scarce resources to production. If the result was social inequality, then it was the abstract forces of the market and relative factor scarcity, not human greed, that produced it. The source of profit was conveniently masked. Labour was condemned to gratefully accepting its scientifically determined lot of giving up its lifeblood in return for that 'mess of pottage' otherwise referred to as a 'just' wage. The problematic and moral stance of Ricardian socialism, however, has been revived in recent times: Bernie Sanders and Thomas Piketty currently represent this line of thought.

Economists have a clear choice going forward. They can either take up the positivism on offer via the marginalism of neoclassical economics around which a vast literature of materialist propositions, theoretical findings and public policies have been constructed, all of which obfuscate, objectify and fetishize the idea of a just distribution justly arrived at by way of the market exchange system. Or they can turn to the dialectical and relational basis laid out in Marx's embrace of the labour theory of value, which provides a historical materialist account of capital's economic practices in general and the origin and perpetuation of profit in particular. I will take the latter path. I note, in passing, that the 'vulgar' reasons to reject the labour theory of value as unscientific because it is immaterial and relational rather than fictitiously objective (as in neoclassical economics) fall on stony ground. By the standards set by marginalist economics, contemporary physics would also have to be rejected as unscientific because gravity is also unobservable and relational and only identifiable by its effects. Gravity is a relation between two masses. Value is likewise a relation between the host of commodities within a market system. Gravity successfully explains why apples fall to the ground. Value theory explains where profit comes from in a perfectly functioning market economy and why it, too, periodically falls to earth in long-lasting crises.

Marx offers a framework of the totality in which workers might reflect on their situation and come to terms with all of the forces that condemn them to inadequate and oppressive conditions of living and working. It is almost as if Marx plans to invite working people to join with him in dissecting the body of their discontents by reviewing the totality of their experience within the circulation of labour capacity. In the *Grundrisse*, Marx broadens his perspective on labour's travails beyond the moment of surplus value production. But here is a problem: How do workers become political subjects and class-conscious beings when their experiences within the circulation of labour capacity are so fragmented? Marx indicates where the hope might lie. 'The concrete totality is a totality of thoughts ... a product of thinking and comprehending ... of the working up of observation and conception into concepts. The totality as it appears in the head, as a totality of thoughts, is a product of a thinking head, which appropriates the world in the only way it can', even as 'the real subject' (society) 'retains its autonomous existence outside the head just as before'. Only in this way can working people see their lives as 'a rich totality of many determinations and relations' while fully recognizing the material condition that 'the concrete is concrete because it is the concentration of many determinations, hence unity of the diverse.'[37]

---

37   Marx, *Grundrisse*, pp. 100–1.

In other words, workers can theorize their world either from the per-spective of the segmented experiences across the five basic moments within the circulation of labour capacity (in which the perspective of class struggle is most firmly anchored in the labour process) or see it from the perspective of the totality in which the circulation of labour capacity as a whole is seen as a class product and a class configuration. Class politics looks very different when viewed from the standpoint of the totality. For the labourers, embedded in the circulation of labour capacity, their crisis is more or less chronic (low wages, alienation, impoverishment, unemployment, insecurity, low living standards, abysmal living condi-tions, minimal forms of social provision and so on). What is adequate for capital is inadequate for labour across all these moments. Capital thrives at the expense of labour. Not that there are not places and times when the lot of the working class has been more acceptable and stable. Nor is it the case that capital's demand for labour is constant. It is to the changing conditions and demand for labour on the part of capital that we now turn.

3

Technological Dynamism and the Productivity of Labour

In the story so far, the production and appropriation of surplus value is limited by the length of the working day and the numerical availability of a labour force in a given place and time. Fortunately, for capital, there is another way to increase surplus value. This brings us to Marx's theorization of relative, as opposed to absolute, surplus value.

More efficient producers can sell commodities at their value (the average price realized by a sale in the market) but produce at lower cost than the social average. These more efficient producers realize an extra profit. This extra profit – the first form of relative surplus value – disappears as soon as competing producers adopt the more efficient methods. Some producers will go out of business when faced with competition from more efficient producers. This form of relative surplus value is ephemeral and accrues to individual entrepreneurs only. But it generates an incentive for leapfrogging technological and organizational innovations as individual entrepreneurs struggle and fight to get ahead of each other. The result, all else remaining equal, is ever-rising labour productivity and ever-declining unit values (prices) of individual commodities. The strength of this tendency depends, however, on the intensity of competition and the availability of new technologies that increase labour productivity. When monopoly prevails, this tendency weakens unless other incentives to pursue technological change materialize (for example, the opening up of new product lines in electronics to absorb surplus capital).

This process is driven by 'the coercive laws of competition', over which, by assumption and according to both Adam Smith (the 'hidden hand of the market') and Marx, individual capitalists have no control. This assumes a world of capitalist individualism and legal structures of private property rights backed by a nightwatchman state to enforce commercial law. Marx begins his reflections in the *Grundrisse* with an account of how such a world originated. Private property did not arise as a God-given right as John Locke supposed. Nor did it originate as some noble savage sought to preserve a vestige of individual autonomy in the making of a social contract, as Rousseau supposed. Rather, according to Marx, it arose out of proliferating practices of commodity exchange in the market place, mediated by money forms that permitted an individual to '[carry] his social power ... in his pocket'.[1] The extension of private property rights over the means of production, including the commodification of land at the expense of common property and state ownership, extended the relation between the accumulation of capital and the accumulation of personal wealth. The concept of the juridical individual with exclusionary ownership rights over commodities and money underpins a whole set of legal institutions to administer and adjudicate laws of contract.

'These *objective* dependency relations' established through the market 'also appear, in antithesis to those of *personal* dependence ... in such a way that individuals are now ruled by *abstractions* whereas earlier they depended on one another. The abstraction, or idea, however, is nothing more than the theoretical expression of those material relations which are their lord and master'.[2] Market practices at their best, for example, rest on equality in exchange, freedom to trade with whomever one chooses and reciprocity, all of which turn up in the famous political slogan of the French Revolution: Liberté, Égalité, Fraternité.

This observation is followed by an interesting coda:

Relations can be expressed, of course, only in ideas, and thus philosophers have determined the reign of ideas to be the peculiarity of the new age and have identified the creation of free individuality with the ideological overthrow of this reign. This error was all the more easily committed from the ideological standpoint, as this reign ... appears within the consciousness of individuals as the reign of ideas, and because the belief in the permanence of these ideas, i.e. of these objective relations of dependency, is of course consolidated, nourished and inculcated by the ruling classes by all means available.[3]

---

1   Marx, *Grundrisse*, p. 157.
2   Ibid., p. 164 (emphasis in original).
3   Ibid., pp. 164–5.

This, of course, was exactly what Margaret Thatcher so expertly accomplished as she promoted a neoliberal orthodoxy as the ruling ideas of a ruling class for which there was no alternative (TINA). Ideas become a material force in world history and therefore a battlefield in class struggle.

But the relative surplus value that individual capitalists seek to secure by embracing competitive advantages has many forms. It is useful to distinguish, for example, between the hardware, the software and the organizational forms that increase the productivity of labour. In the early stages of capital's rise to dominance – in what Marx calls 'the manufacturing period' – the organizational forms of cooperation and divisions of labour (within the firm as well as within the market) were most prominent. But with the Industrial Revolution, it was the hardware of machine technologies and the software of the factory system that dominated. Marx considered this the moment that capital acquired a technological configuration that was uniquely adequate to its own needs. But this breakthrough did not eradicate the importance of the earlier forms. The factory system itself called for distinctive structures of cooperation and divisions of labour (including the distinction between mental and manual labour and gradations of skill).

The subsequent evolution of the means for increasing the productivity of labour has oscillated between the hardware of machine technology, the potency of innovative organizational forms (like the capitalist corporation) and facilitative software (optimal scheduling and programming) available to enhance production. The just-in-time systems that Marx hinted at and which became central in, say, the automobile industry in the 1980s, deployed an organizational form that saved immensely on the dead weight of inventories within a supply chain. Software tactics of promoting consent rather than resorting to coercion in the labour process (for example, the 'quality circles' also introduced into the automobile industry in the 1980s) have, on some occasions, come to play an important role in producing the so-called 'x factor' of higher efficiency achieved by a willing rather than recalcitrant labour force. The culture (for example, time discipline) of a potential labour force and its loyalty can on occasion be as important as its technical skills. The advantage China enjoyed in this regard after 1978 was employed by Apple, which was failing as a corporation in the United States until Tim Cook solved its production problems by targeting Chinese labour (with its distinctive discipline and skills) primarily with the help of Foxconn (a Taiwanese corporation that operated mainly in China).

The culture of management and of organizational forms varies from one corporation to another, and German, Japanese, American and Chinese corporate cultures display distinctive managerial forms that can inhibit or promote labour loyalty, adaptability and other forms of efficiency. There is a tendency, however, to emphasize the hardware of technologies in much of the literature. But it is critical to pay attention to software and organizational features as well, since these can, on occasion, be determinate in the search for advantage in the rough and tumble of competition in the marketplace.

Several important social consequences derive from systematic increases in labour productivity. First, as the cost of the commodities that determine the wage declines due to the rising productivity of labour, so the value of labour power (wage rates) can fall while sustaining the same material standard of living. If labourers need bread to live and the price of bread falls, the value of labour power declines (assuming a fixed material appetite and need for bread). This increases the surplus value (the rate of exploitation, s/v) for all capitalists, rather than only for those individual entrepreneurs who have adopted a superior technological mix. This points to a social form of relative surplus value. It is permanent, in contrast to the ephemeral form of individual relative surplus value. It then follows that, in phases of intensive technological change, it is entirely possible for the rate of exploitation s/v to continue to rise alongside a rising material standard of living of the workers. Even though the value of labour power may be falling, the volume and variety of material goods that this reduced value (wages) can command may be rising.

The material standard of living of labour in the advanced capitalist countries has risen significantly since Marx's time, but this does not mean that the rate of exploitation of that labour power has fallen. Indeed, it may have increased. This is an important observation, since bourgeois critics are fond of refuting Marx's postulate of the continuing exploitation of labour power by pointing to workers' rising material standard of living, particularly in the advanced capitalist states. Some anti-imperialists make the same error by assuming that the miserable material living standards of labour power in emerging markets such as Bangladesh or Brazil are clear and unambiguous evidence of the super-exploitation of that labour power relative to that in the advanced capitalist countries. Whether low wages translate into a high rate of labour exploitation depends, among other things, on the productivity of the labour process. A highly paid German worker living in relative luxury may be more exploited than a Bangladeshi worker forced to live on a mere pittance. Everything depends on the content of the ratio *s/v*.

A variety of other factors beyond the direct productivity of labour power may also enter into the picture. Marx noted that the abolition of tariffs on imported wheat (the so-called corn laws) in mid-nineteenth-century Britain reduced the price of bread and thereby enabled a reduction of wages. This delivered increased surplus value (profit) for industrial capital. In our own times, the creation of 'the Walmart economy' of cheap imported goods from China has permitted a rise in material living standards for working people in the US, even in the absence of any substantial increase in money wages.

Technological, organizational and software changes are internalized within a capitalist mode of production. This is, in some respects, the hallmark of the concept of capital. Innovations in techniques were by no means lacking in prior modes of production. The remarkable history of unused and abandoned technological innovation in Imperial China is a standing proof of this. But what is special about capital is the way innovation has been and still is internalized within capital's dynamic and how it has been systematically diffused as a seemingly unstoppable process. Technological and organizational progress is thus an irresistible and proliferating force within a capitalist mode of production, driven by the coercive laws of intercapitalist competition.

In *Capital*, Marx uses the case of cotton manufacturing as an example.[4] The advent of the power loom revolutionized the production of cotton cloth. This led to a massively increasing demand for raw cotton, which inspired the invention of the cotton gin for automatic processing of the raw cotton. Revolutions in chemical techniques for bleaching and dyeing also became necessary for bringing the cotton quickly to market in an adequate form (natural dyes often require weeks to take hold). This industrialization could not have worked the way it did without revolutions in transport technology (steamships and railroads) to bring the raw cotton cheaply and efficiently from the Carolinas or from Egypt and India to Manchester and take the end product to a captive market (such as that created through imperial power in India, after the Indian hand-loom industry had been destroyed by a mix of market competition and imperial administration). Innovations in one part of the industrial structure could not proceed without innovations elsewhere. The implication is that innovation and capital are synonymous. Technological progress

---

4   Marx, *Capital*, Vol. 1, Chapter 15.

is thus considered both good and inevitable, a systemic characteristic of capitalism.

The more technological, organizational and software innovation became central to capital's development, the more innovation became an independent business, creating generic technologies, such as the steam engine, electricity, automation, computers and computer management and the like (now including AI). In Marx's time, the machine tool industries anchored and drove many technological changes (for example, the proliferation of steam engine technologies), while in our own time the 'venture capitalists' of Silicon Valley have recklessly and, to some degree, successfully transformed the industry that makes and markets new technologies and new software apps and organizational forms to enhance the efficiency not only of production but of circulation and consumption. Much of this has been backed by successive cultural revolutions, for which there seems to be no fixed agenda but a plethora of marketing styles that bewilder as much as they enlighten the world in which we live.

The long history of technological, organizational and software changes goes back to well before the rise of capital's distinctive mode of production. Adam Smith considered that humanity's seemingly infinite appetite for 'trinkets and baubles' along with its innate capacity 'to truck and barter' were part of our species being.[5] The historical geography of the dispersion of technological and organizational innovations across the whole of Europe into Eurasia from the thirteenth century onwards certainly seems to support this view. The appetite for exotic spices and dyes, for jewels and trinkets was to some degree cultivated by itinerant merchants, culminating in the widespread market fairs of the late medieval world even before the rise of the Italian city-states from the fifteenth century on. Capital has reshaped our world and our mode of living in innumerable ways. It did not start from scratch but deepened and systematized elements that had been long in the making and turned them into distinctive moments within its distinctive mode of production and circulation. Already existing elements of ambition, desire and, yes, greed, were incorporated into the stream of its own development. The pursuit for something different and something new was battling against the forces of inertia and tradition, and capital thrived on that struggle.

Whole new product lines and ways of life (such as suburbanization) have burst on the scene in later times. Take, for example, the household equipment marketed as consumer durables, which today service all but

---

5   Adam Smith, *The Wealth of Nations: Books 1–3* (London: Penguin, 1982).

the poorest households in the advanced capitalist world. The modern kitchen is haven for all manner of gadgets awaiting instruction from famous TV chefs to teach everyone how best to use them. Innovations in transport and communication systems have revolutionized turnover times (through speedup) and spatial relations. Geographies of both production and consumption are in constant mutation. China's consumer market was weak in 1980, but it is now foundational for Western corporate capital (Starbucks has over 5,000 coffee shops in China, with the largest in the world in Shanghai). All such possibilities have become baked into public expectations and taken-for-granted ways of life. What is so impressive here is not so much the individual innovations but the whole evolutionary trajectory in which innovation has become big and seemingly unstoppable business.

There is, however, another aspect to the theory of relative surplus value. Whereas new organizational forms and softwares can be had for almost nothing, the hardware of machinery has to be bought in commodity form, as do all the other elements of the plant and its equipment required for production. The theory of relative surplus value consequently intersects with the rising importance of the fixed capital form of circulation. This poses both opportunities and puzzles for capital accumulation to proceed without a host of troublesome complications (which we will later take up in detail). A great deal of capital has to be sunk long-term in immovable forms, some of which, like roads, are used in common while jointly serving both production and consumption. And, finally, expanding production also requires an ever-expanding market of the sort that Marx and Engels envisaged in the *Communist Manifesto*. 'The need for a constantly expanding market for its products chases the bourgeoisie over the whole surface of the globe. It must nestle everywhere, settle everywhere, establish connections everywhere.'[6] Capital's formation of the world market, or what we now refer to as globalization, was clearly in view as early as 1848, the year the *Manifesto* was written.

Historically, up until 1970 or so, workers in the advanced capitalist countries typically shared the benefits of higher productivity. Some achieved a rising material standard of living and an increasing real wage. In the 1960s, the situation of 'the affluent worker' (the unionized worker – usually white and male – living in a suburban house with a car in the driveway, TV in the living room and dishwasher in the kitchen) was

---

6   Karl Marx and Friedrich Engels, *The Communist Manifesto* (London: Verso, 1998 [1848]), p. 39.

much commented on. Much earlier, Lenin had worried that the emergence of an aristocracy of labour would block the transition to socialism in the advanced capitalist countries while supporting capitalist imperialism.[7] In the 1960s, it looked like that was the case. Since the 1970s, most of the benefits of rising productivity have gone to capital. This is the positive impact of rising relative surplus value for capital. However, the rising productivity of labour reduces the demand for labour. Fewer workers are needed to produce the same amount of goods and services. The effect is to reduce the aggregate amount of surplus value produced because fewer labourers are employed even as the rising rate of surplus value compensates to some degree because of the declining value of labour power. The rising productivity of labour reduces the demand for labour power, which can be compensated only if the volume of demand for product increases sufficiently for the same number of labourers to be employed. If this is not the case, then a rising productivity of labour power not only increases the individual rate of exploitation (which is the positive effect for capital) but has the social effect of reducing the number of labourers employed, which all too often translates into a reduction in both wages and the corresponding standard of living of labour. The deindustrialization due to technological change that occurred from the 1970s on in many manufacturing centres had strong negative effects for large segments of the working population in the advanced capitalist countries. But the reduction in the numbers of workers employed also reduces the aggregate surplus value produced. The positive effects of technological and organizational change for capital are thus offset by this negative tendency to reduce the aggregate surplus value. This is a central contradiction which we will take up in detail later.

The theory of relative surplus value consolidates our understanding of how and why, as Marx and Engels put it in the *Communist Manifesto*:

> The bourgeoisie cannot exist without constantly revolutionizing the instruments of production and thereby, the relations of production, and with them the whole relations of society ... Constant revolutionizing of production, uninterrupted disturbance of all social conditions, everlasting uncertainty and agitation distinguish the bourgeois epoch from all earlier ones. All fixed, fast-frozen relations, with their train of ancient and venerable prejudices and opinions, are swept away, all new-formed ones become antiquated before they can ossify. All that is solid melts into

---

7   V. I. Lenin, *Imperialism, the Highest Stage of Capitalism*, in Lenin, *Selected Works*, Vol. 1, 'Preface to the French and German Editions' (Moscow: Progress Publishers, 1963).

air, all that is holy is profaned, and man at last is compelled to face with sober senses, his real conditions of life, and his relations with his kind.[8]

'Modern industry', Marx notes in *Capital*, 'never views or treats the existing form of a production process as the definitive one. Its technical basis is therefore revolutionary, whereas all earlier modes of production were essentially conservative ... Large scale industry, by its very nature, necessitates variation of labour, fluidity of functions, and mobility of the worker in all directions.'[9] The impacts of this permanent revolutionizing of production systems on the labourer are contradictory. On the one hand, 'the old system of division of labour is thrown overboard by machinery' and 'the lifelong speciality of handling the same tool now becomes the lifelong speciality of serving the same machine', thus converting workers into 'living appendages' of the machine.[10] On the other hand,

large-scale industry ... makes the recognition of variation of labour and hence of the fitness of the worker for the maximum number of different kinds of labour into a question of life and death ... That monstrosity, the disposable population held in reserve, in misery ... must be replaced by the individual man who is absolutely available for the different kinds of labour required of him; the partially developed individual, who is merely the bearer of one specialized social function, must be replaced by the totally developed individual.[11]

While the big leap came with the rise of the factory system, the proliferation of new divisions of labour and skill definitions has continued to accelerate. Whereas workers in the 1960s could look forward to employment over a lifetime, the acceleration of technological innovation now entails retraining and reskilling several times over in a working life. The history of labour demand would suggest that capital cultivates both kinds of labour, with the flexible, educated and adaptable generally achieving a more adequate standard of living than those condemned to the dull, unimaginative and badly remunerated forms of industrial labour typical of the factory system. Labour of the latter sort, with some obvious exceptions such as 'caring' functions, is particularly vulnerable to displacement by automation and AI.

---

8   Marx and Engels, *Communist Manifesto*, p. 38.
9   Marx, *Capital*, Vol. 1, p. 617.
10   Ibid., Vol. 1, pp. 547–8.
11   Ibid., Vol. 1, p. 618.

Summarizing the consequences of this argument in notational terms, we have a rising ratio of s/v (the rate of exploitation of labour power) along with a rising organic or value composition of capital, c/v, (the measure of capital intensity) but a falling rate of profit, $s/c+v$, as a result of the deployment of labour-saving innovations. We will return to consider this configuration in Chapter 5. Plainly, the dynamics of technological change lie at the centre of several foundational contradictions of the capitalist mode of production.

The emphasis on labour-saving innovations and increasing the productivity of labour suggests also that the paths of technological dynamism are deeply intertwined with the dynamics of class struggle. There is a long history, Marx notes, of the deployment of new technologies for purposes of strike-breaking and disempowering organized labour, all the while ensuring the creation of an industrial reserve army available for capital's further expansion. This puts strong downward pressure on the wage rates of those regularly employed. There is nothing new in all of this. Over the last forty years, however, the job market has been radically reconfigured through automation and robotization in manufacturing, resulting in widespread job losses (with well-paying quality jobs particularly vulnerable). The consensus view is that half and possibly two-thirds of the manufacturing job losses since 1980 in the advanced capitalist world are attributable to technological change, rather than to competition from legal and illegal immigrants and offshoring of production to places like China and Mexico, as is popularly believed. This radical reconfiguration of job opportunities now threatens to be repeated in the case of services (like health care and education). These jobs are threatened by the extraordinary strides made by AI (artificial intelligence, which is a misnomer for what should be called 'machine learning').

We cannot understand the unstoppability and depth of technological dynamism, however, without considering the role of the state. This poses, once more, a dilemma for Marx's theory: Should the state be considered as external to the inner structure of capital, though one with wide powers of intervention (particularly to rectify matters when things go wrong), or should it be considered an internal moment of the inner structure of capital? If the latter, this will require considerable modification of the general theory of the capitalist mode of production as presented in the three volumes of *Capital*. We will confront this question directly later, but some foundational elements need to be introduced here, since the state has clearly played a major role in sponsoring, fomenting and financing the technological and organizational changes that impinge so strongly on the production, circulation and realization of capital.

Let us accept for the moment Giovanni Arrighi's assertion (drawn from Braudel's work) that the motivating force behind the rise of a distinctive capitalist mode of production initially lay in the fusion of state and capital achieved in the Italian city-states (Venice, Genoa, Florence, Siena and so on) and that much of the sustaining and accumulative stimulus for capital arose out of lively competition (particularly between Genoa and Venice) within an inter-city-state system.[12] The fusion of state and capital was initially that of the merchant capitalists with state power, though, at certain points, both production and finance were radically engaged within the confines of the city-state. Siena, for example, likes to boast that it has the world's oldest bank, and Florence developed an industrial base with an industrial working class to match at an early point in its history.

Competition within some sort of interstate system has been foundational for capital ever since. Within the Italian city-states, however, there were some clear differences in the way the fusion between state and capital worked. Venice, for example, projected an image of strong centralized state power fuelled by lucrative gains from trade organized by merchants and financiers but in no way reluctant to use state-organized military force, coercion and corruption and even colonization (for example, of Crete) to achieve its goals. In Genoa, on the other hand, the dispersed power of the merchants dominated, and state power played a more muted though strongly supportive role. While competition between these two models initially favoured the Venetians, in the long run it seems the Genoese model prevailed. The Venetian trading colony-settlement was expelled from Istanbul, for example, in part through the machinations of the Genoese merchants. A parallel difference was sometimes drawn in the last decades of the twentieth century between the state-centric development of Singapore from the 1960s onwards and the more entrepreneurial-based dispersed model of Hong Kong industrialization backed by the British colonial administration prior to its re-absorption into the orbit of mainland China. In China itself, the balance between state and capital has oscillated somewhat since 1978, though at no point has the economy become seriously unmoored from the determinative power of the party-state apparatus. The big contrast on the current world

---

12   Giovanni Arrighi, *The Long Twentieth Century: Money, Power, and the Origins of Our Times* (London: Verso, 2002).

stage is between the state-centric Chinese model and the more dispersed corporate and capital-dominated model of the US, in which state power answers to capital in general and the bondholders more particularly (the Treasury secretaries over the last forty years in the US have, for the most part, come from the investment bank Goldman Sachs).

The balance of capitalist economic activity slowly shifted from the Italian city-states northwards to Western Europe in the sixteenth and seventeenth centuries. The Treaty of Westphalia of 1648 was a key moment. It brought to an end the perpetual wars of religion that had wracked the European continent for a century or more and sought to guarantee the borders of sovereign states and principalities across the European space. These states then formed the units for interstate competition over economic development (the consolidation of state wealth and power) and military advantage. This interstate system was the unique circumstance that, Arrighi hypothesizes, led to the consolidation of the capitalist mode of production in Western Europe rather than elsewhere around the world. While Napoleon's subsequent attempt to create a unified European space under French hegemony failed, it succeeded in opening up Europe to a more unified legal code and helped dissolve the monopoly power of many local ruling families, elites and clans to make way for more fluid forms of state organization, the bourgeois form of which only became fully apparent in the revolutions of 1848, followed by the unification of Germany and Italy in the latter half of the nineteenth century.

The intensity of interstate competition within Europe for economic development and relative wealth and power from the eighteenth century on, depended, as political economy was unified in proclaiming, on liberating market forces and entrepreneurial skills as much as possible, as Deng Xiaoping was to do in China a century or more later. It also depended on the productivity of its labour force for, as Marx would also show, trade between two national units with vastly different values of labour power (wage levels) and labour productivity underpinned value transfers from more labour-intensive to more capital-intensive regions (we will also take this up in detail in Chapter 6).

But it became evident, from the eighteenth century onwards, that the capitalist state had a strong interest in fostering, financing and facilitating the scientific and technological advances that would favour the higher productivity of labour along with a labour force which, in Marx's words, would be skilled, adaptable and educated enough to easily adopt new methods and standards. The state also increasingly accepted the obligation to construct the physical infrastructure (such as roads, ports and harbours) that capital would require to use in common. From the seventeenth century onwards, the national academies of science and arts began to play a significant role in basic science, while state institutions (such as Ponts et Chaussées in France and the Corps of Engineers in the US) were formed to deal with engineering the production of a built environment necessary for capital to function efficiently. These organizations were supplemented in the mid nineteenth century by the rise of research universities focused on the relation between science and technology (led by the University of Berlin). The development of science and technology became as much a mission of the state as a business mission of capital. It is here that the fusion of state and capital becomes so obvious. Contemporary US examples are research universities such as Caltech and MIT. The most celebrated example was the role of state-sponsored research and development in Japan during the 1960s by way of the Ministry of International Trade and Industry (MITI) which was solely concerned with civilian and non-military-based innovation in both products and techniques.[13] This formed the basis for the hegemony of the Japanese model of capital accumulation (along with that of West Germany) during the 1980s. All of this is intensified when it comes to the development of technologies that confer military superiority. The history of capital's innovations has been of course deeply influenced by wartime exigencies, the most epic of which was the race to build a nuclear weapon during the Second World War.

Marx had correctly postulated that the coercive laws of competition between capitals would lead to an unstoppable technological dynamism. He should have gone on to postulate that the coercive laws of competition between states for military advantage would also lead to an irresistible technological dynamism. But it would be a dynamism directed into only certain sectors of the economy. Whereas there would be minor interest in the cotton textile industry, there would be a much greater interest in the development of aerospace, naval construction engineering, the armaments and munitions industry (which is currently the most lucrative industry in the world) and, perhaps most significant of all, communications and surveillance technologies. All of this is dominated by state military interests that subcontract the making of the product to private capital, which, as in aerospace, then seeks to find and exploit civilian

---

13   Chalmers Johnson, *MITI and the Japanese Miracle: The Growth of Industrial Policy, 1925–1975* (Stanford, CA: Stanford University Press, 1982).

uses for military-based hardware. This is what Boeing, Lockheed Martin, Raytheon and Airbus do.

This highly simplified overview produces some important insights. Interstate competition on the military side has produced a cornucopia of new technologies and organizational forms in addition to those generated by intercapitalist competition. The only limits to the unstoppability of this lie either in the curbing of competition through the exercise of monopoly power or in barriers posed by the excessive cost of widespread adoption of new technological forms. This entails the devaluation of already sunk capital and of infrastructural investments. It took time, for example, for the steam engine and the railroads to give way to road haulage, the automobile and the highway.

But in the European setting, this interstate competition also produced two world wars that conferred even greater emphasis on technological and organizational innovations. It was, furthermore, interstate competition that led the leading participants into imperialist tactics and contestations in order to secure access to raw materials and markets. The British, French, Dutch and Belgian colonial possessions, along with Portuguese and Spanish special relations to the independent nations of Latin America, segmented world trade patterns, while the newly unified German and Italian states, coming rather late to the colonization feast, struggled to find a footing. Interstate and inter-imperialist rivalries played a vital role in the First World War and much of this got repeated in the Second World War as Germany sought living space (*Lebensraum*) to sustain its future. This was further complicated by the insertion of Japanese imperialist ambitions into the mix. Only the United States stood somewhat aloof until compelled to enter as an active participant. After 1945, serious efforts were made to limit the destructive role of interstate competition in Europe and to build structures of cooperation (supported if not dominated by the United States). The Common Market, NATO and the European Union resulted. But interstate competition, along with fierce investments in new military and surveillance technologies, continues to play a double-edged role, although with a different set of chief players. China, the United States, Russia and the European Union are leading the competition and now, as in the past, war cannot be ruled out as a price of perpetuating both capital accumulation and the unstoppability of technological and organizational change. The combination of AI with weapons platforms, including drone swarms, signals an ominous new phase of warmaking technology. Only a shift from competition to collaboration (as occurred internally in the European case) can work. But the signs for such a global shift are not favourable.

Technological, organizational and 'software' dynamism thus lies at the heart of any viable theory of capital's mode of production as a working totality. To the degree that this dynamism is impelled by coercive laws of intercapitalist and interstate competition, so the theory of the capitalist mode of production cannot proceed without the incorporation of some elements of capitalist state theory into the argument. This does not invite the construction of some functionalist theory of the capitalist state operating at the behest of capital. But it does suggest close attention should be paid to the intertwining of state and capital in the global competitive search for technological advantage. Research and development has become big business in its own right, and much of it rests on state-funded partnerships with private interests. In this, the major agglomerations of economic power in North America, East Asia and Europe have inherent advantages over the rest of the world. The pursuit of particular interests has global consequences. The consequent uneven geographical technological development was clearly demonstrated by the unequal capacity to produce and market vaccines in the face of the Covid-19 pandemic. It is clear also that the outcome of interstate and intercorporate competition in the production of new technologies is now dictated by the most powerful states (with the US still in the lead) and by a few megacorporations. The outcomes have little to do with increasing the well-being of the global population or dealing with critical environmental issues and everything to do with further feathering the nests of the corporate few and their shareholders (the Seven Sisters in oil and Big Pharma) and acquiring hegemony over the means of surveillance, control and violence to be applied should rival states and corporations get out of hand.

It is fashionable in research circles to seek out some single all-powerful force to account for the evolutionary path of economic and social change. But in the case of technological and organizational change, which is in itself one powerful component force in capital's evolutionary history, we find multiple threads reflecting all manner of different forces at work and that come together in ways that are, as Marx would put it, 'adequate to capital', even as the contradictions they produce can inhibit as well as promote the perpetual increase in the production of capital. It is, therefore, to how the contradictions within what might be called 'the technological and organizational moment' play out that we now turn.

4

Marx in Manchester

Marx set his theoretical investigations of capital's mode of production and its laws of motion in the context of British industrial capitalism between the 1840s and the 1860s. He initially did so in the belief that 'the country that is more developed industrially only shows, to the less developed, the image of its own future.'[1] Whether or not such a belief was justified is, of course, an open question. Towards the end of his life, after intensive anthropological investigations and detailed consideration of the Russian case in particular, Marx himself began to doubt this proposition, thus preparing the way for a subsequent critique of what many view as his Eurocentrism. But what is not open to question is the depth and range of Marx's knowledge of the state of industrial capital in mid-nineteenth century Britain.

In this, Marx was fortunate to find a huge archive of investigative materials assembled by the British state-appointed factory inspectors, public health officials and parliamentary inquiries on everything from child labour to banking practices. He fulsomely acknowledged the importance of these materials for his own interpretations and complained at the 'wretched state' of information from elsewhere:

> We should be appalled at our own circumstances if, as in England, our government and parliaments periodically appointed commissions of inquiry into economic conditions; if these commissions were armed with the same plenary powers to get at the truth; if it were possible to find for this purpose as competent, as free of partisanship and respect of persons, as are England's factory inspectors, her medical reporters

1 Marx, *Capital*, Vol. 1, p. 91.

on public health, her commissioners of inquiry into the exploitation of women and children, into conditions of housing and nourishment, and so on.[2]

The English factory inspectors and health officials like Leonard Horner, Mr Scriven and Dr Greenshaw (to name a few) were key figures.[3] Imagine how bereft and unsatisfying the first volume of *Capital* would be without the accounts provided by these state officials.

Marx also collected a vast trove of contemporary press reports, pamphlets and relevant books on all aspects of political economy (such as those of Ure and Babbage on machine technology). Finally, his friend and patron Engels not only inspired him through his early and remarkable work *The Condition of the Working Class in England in 1844* but also supplied continuous commentary on labour and life in Manchester, as recorded through Engels's first-hand experience helping to manage his family firm in the city. To top it all, Engels also got to see Manchester through the eyes of his Irish working-class companion and lover, Mary Burns. It was through her that Engels was introduced to the fetid squalor of the living quarters of the proletarian Irish immigrants of the city. The historical materialist foundation that Marx always craved in his theoretical work came from the likes of Leonard Horner, Mary Burns and Engels. It is this that gives such a powerful aura of accuracy and authenticity to Marx's writings. And it is this that then partly explains how and why Marx's theorizations from that time echo down to us so convincingly, even though we are living in such different times. Yet this also gives substance to the view that Marx's theoretical formulations may be tainted by the particularities of the Manchester case or more broadly by Anglo-centric or Eurocentric perspectives. But capital as an economic system was itself Eurocentric in origin and continued to be so throughout his lifetime. It began in its industrial form in Britain and spread worldwide but, as it did so, it had to adapt to different conditions and take on different forms. From time to time, it had to confront proto-capitalistic social formations and hybrid forms elsewhere. Marx also had to deal with regions of arrested development, regional economies where seemingly insurmountable barriers to full-fledged capitalist development prevailed (for example, the American South until very recently or the backward region of the Italian South that Gramsci confronted).[4]

---

2   Ibid., Vol. 1, p. 91.

3   Bernice Martin, 'Leonard Horner: A Portrait of an Inspector of Factories', *International Review of Social History* 14: 3 (1969): 412–43.

4   Robinson, *Black Marxism*; Michael Goldfield, *The Southern Key: Class, Race, and*

Marx universalizes the qualities and character of the capitalist mode of production by way of the particularities of mid-nineteenth century Britain in general and Manchester industrialism in particular. How to theorize its nature was the challenge that, before Marx, troubled both Adam Smith and Ricardo. How to distil a few universal concepts and relations from the myriad and voluminous record of social practices of, for example, market exchange and capitalist production everywhere and how to ensure that whatever conceptual apparatus is derived is 'adequate to' (as Marx would put it) valid interpretations of the 'laws of motion' of capital in general. To this day, it is an open question whether the laws of motion of capital that Marx laid out apply with equal force in China, Bangladesh, the European Union and the United States.

Marx's attempt to find an answer to that sort of question – a question that confronts all attempts to theorize capital – has first to deal with an intense hostility to all things Marxist, particularly in the Anglo-American tradition. As Walter Rodney wittily observes: within that tradition, 'one knows that [Marxism] is absurd without reading it and one doesn't have to read it because one knows it is absurd.' Even if Marx's presentations may have been accurate and relevant for the place and time of their origin, their validity for Lenin and Mao as well as for movements as diverse as Amilcar Cabral's revolutionary movement in Guinea-Bissau or Thomas Sankara's revolutionary government in Burkina Faso or Walter Rodney's revolutionary work in Guyana needs demonstration. Rodney has, perhaps, the most succinct answer. What matters is not so much Marx's substantive findings, which are always tainted by the circumstances of their place and time, but his method of investigation and enquiry that led him to those substantive findings. Marxism 'starts from a perspective of man's relationship to the material world; ... and when it arose historically, consciously dissociated itself from and pitted itself against all other modes of perception which started with ideas, with concepts and with words'. Marxism 'rooted itself in the material conditions, and the social relations in society'. This, says Rodney, is the starting point: 'a methodology that begins an analysis of any society, of any situation, by seeking the relations that arise in production between men.' There are a whole variety of things that flow from that: 'man's consciousness is formed in the intervention in nature, nature itself is humanized through its interaction with man's labour, and man's labour produces a constant

Radicalism in the 1930s and 1940s (Oxford: Oxford University Press, 2020); Antonio Gramsci, *The Southern Question*, trans. Pasquale Verdicchio (Toronto: Guernica Editions, 2005).

stream of technology, that in turn creates other social relations.'[5] This is the spirit of Marx's historical materialism and the *Communist Manifesto* at work. To the degree that we all now have our being within a material world dominated by capital and the geopolitics of capital's imperialism, so the method of enquiry must be directed towards understanding 'the motor within that system' in order to expose and overthrow 'the types of exploitation which are to be found within the capitalist mode of production'. The resultant theory is thereby revolutionary. As Cabral put it: there may be revolutions that have had a revolutionary theory that failed, but 'nobody has yet successfully practiced revolution without a revolutionary theory'.[6] While the material conditions of production and social relations in Guinea-Bissau may have been the starting point, the culmination, in Cabral's view, entails mobilizing the power of revolutionary theory everywhere.

In his single-minded concentration on Manchester industrialism, Marx presumes that the merchants, the bankers and the landed interest took up the subservient role of serving the needs of an all-powerful industrial capital. In the first two volumes of *Capital*, Marx largely ignores these other factions of capital. In the first volume of *Capital*, for example, he explicitly presumes that all commodities trade at their value (the market functions perfectly), that 'capital passes through its process of circulation in the normal way', and that the fragmentation of surplus value into rent, interest and profit on merchant capital in no way affects accumulation.[7] In the *Grundrisse*, Marx boldly asserts that 'the laws of capital are completely realized only within *unlimited competition* and *industrial production*'.[8] This rules out any problems that might derive from state-imposed restrictions on competition, monopolization or the excessive centralization of capital.

There is nothing wrong with abstracting in this way, but major modifications to the theory might be needed in the event of restrictions on competition and shifts in the balance of power between the different factions of capital. It is very unlikely, for example, that the laws of motion of industrial capital are the same as the laws of motion of merchant, banking or landed capital. In recent times, for example,

5   Walter Rodney, *Decolonial Marxism: Essays from the Pan-African Revolution* (London: Verso, 2022), p. 35.

6   Amilcar Cabral, 'Presuppositions and Objectives of National Liberation in Relation to Social Structure', in *Unity and Struggle: Speeches and Writings of Amilcar Cabral* (New York: *Monthly Review* Press, 1979), p. 123.

7   Marx, *Capital*, Vol. 1, p. 709.

8   Marx, *Grundrisse*, p. 559 (emphasis in original).

industrial capital has increasingly been disciplined by the monopsony power of merchant capitalists like Walmart, Ikea and the major clothing and electronics companies (like Apple). Whole sectors of the economy (such as contract farming) exist in which the direct producers dance to the tune of the merchants or other intermediaries. Likewise, the power of banking and finance, of debt and credit, and of land and property capital has, in certain times and places, been decisive in shaping capital accumulation and its crises in particular places and times. The revisions such transformations mandate in Marx's theory of capital will be examined later.

Marx's focus on Manchester industrialism entailed confronting the particularities of labour processes in the cotton mills and the nature of the labour market it defined. The power loom weavers were essentially machine minders. The transfer of skills from the labourer into the machine (a transfer that Marx makes much of in *Capital* and the *Grundrisse*) entailed a deskilling of much of the labour force. Unskilled Irish labour and women could easily substitute for what had traditionally been semi-skilled male artisans who worked handlooms, although through the 'putting out' system in which merchants provided the raw materials and gathered back the finished product. The depressing effect on wages and living conditions through the employment of Irish labourers posed a problem for Marx. Initially scathing in his criticism of the Irish for their role in redefining the value of labour power downwards, he later came to recognize that the answer lay in raising the Irish labour force up as a necessary first step in the organization of class struggle. For the millowners, division within the working class (based on gender, ethnicity, national identity and religion) was more than welcome. It helped them rule unopposed by pitting one faction of labour against another. Capital presumed the domination of labour by capital. Capital's power would be consolidated to the degree that it could mobilize other structures of domination (such as race and gender) in support of its domination over labour.

It could be argued that Marx's focus on the particularities of Manchester's industrial capitalism biased his vision and that his preoccupation with the doctrines of the free market, competition and free trade promoted by the industrialists of the so-called Manchester School of Cobden and Bright somewhat warped his vision. But the factory inspectors, the public health officials and the parliamentary reports did not confine their observations to Manchester. They went all over the country. And Marx was well aware of the distinctive influence of the Manchester industrial faction in the realm of ideology and politics as well as in their enormous (for that time) centralization of economic wealth and power. The results were, in a sense, predictable: 'One fine morning, in the year 1836, Nassau W. Senior ... a man famed for his economic science and his beautiful style, was summoned from Oxford to Manchester, to learn in the latter place the political economy he taught in the former.' What Senior learned was that the capitalist's profit was totally encompassed by the last hour of work in a twelve-hour day and that any shortening of that day to, say, ten hours would spell ruination for the capitalist system because the hours of profit making would disappear. This 'so-called "analysis"', prompted a fierce rebuttal, as much directed to Parliament as to Nassau Senior, by none other than Leonard Horner, who worked with the factory inspectors from 1833 to 1857, and 'whose services to the English working class will never be forgotten', as Marx noted.[9] And, of course, the Ten Hours Act was finally passed. The shortening of the length of the working day was, Marx opined, one small but critical step towards a socialist future. It opened a pathway to the realm of freedom – understood as free time – for the working classes.

For the Manchester industrialists of that time, a different kind of freedom – 'His Holiness Free Trade', as Marx called it – was the only kind of freedom that mattered. The economics of free trade were lauded to the skies by the Manchester school and incorporated into state policies across the country and with respect to the industries that at that time dominated in world capitalism. Free trade, it turns out, is always the mantra of the leading capitalist industries and powers. The elaboration and instantiation of the doctrine in the form of the World Trade Organization (WTO) agreements of the late 1990s at the behest of the major global corporations and the United States as the hegemonic power of the moment is the obvious case in point.

In June 1849, Marx moved to London, where he stayed for the rest of his life. While not a participant in British politics, he followed British political life closely by way of press reports and parliamentary debates. For a while, he earned some much-needed income as London correspondent of the *New-York Daily Tribune*. During the 1850s, he tried to make sense of British imperial politics for New York readers covering, among other things, the barbarity of the repression of the Indian Sepoy Rebellion of 1857–8, the equal barbarity of the Second Chinese Opium War of 1858 and the dissolution of the East India Company in favour of

---

9 Marx, *Capital*, Vol. 1, pp. 333–9.

British direct imperial rule over India. These were, incidentally, the years when Marx was intensely engaged in writing the *Grundrisse*.

The connection back to Manchester free-trade politics was obvious. As he noted in 1853:

> The ruling classes of Great Britain have had, till now, but an accidental, transitory and exceptional interest in the progress of India. The aristocracy wanted to conquer it, the moneyocracy to plunder it and the millocracy to undersell it. But now the tables are turned. The millocracy have discovered that the transformation of India into a reproductive country has become of vital importance to them.[10]

The Indian market had, for some time, been a major outlet for the huge increase in output of the Lancashire cotton industry. Imperial power had assured the destruction of a long-standing indigenous hand-loom cotton industry in favour of becoming 'inundated with English twists and cotton stuffs'.[11] 'The necessity for opening new markets or extending the old ones' was as pressing in India as it was in China and failure to do either signalled 'an approaching industrial crisis', due to 'diminished demand for the produce of Manchester and Glasgow'.[12] The millowners' answer was to rationalize the space-economy of India by building railroads. Prior to this, the Indians could not use machinery 'to work up their cotton, which is sent by ox-carts, sometimes over eight hundred miles over wet lands, to be shipped to the Ganges, thence round the Cape of Good Hope to England, to be fabricated and then returned to the natives at whatever percent above ninety such an operation costs'. The millocracy wanted, needed and eventually got a railroad system that gave access to cheap raw materials and spatially integrated markets across the Indian subcontinent. Marx records the astonishing increase in British trade in cotton goods to India from £2.5 million to £6.1 million between 1856 and 1859.[13]

It is important to recognize how global this system already was. The Manchester system rested on the slave labour of the cotton plantations

---

10   Karl Marx, 'The Future Results of British Rule in India', *New-York Daily Tribune*, 8 August 1853, reprinted in Marx, *Karl Marx on Colonialism and Modernization* (New York: Doubleday, 1968).

11   Karl Marx, 'The East India Company — Its History and Results', *New-York Daily Tribune*, 11 July 1853, reprinted in Marx, *Karl Marx on Colonialism*.

12   Karl Marx, 'Revolution in China and In Europe', *New-York Daily Tribune*, 14 July 1853, reprinted in Marx, *Karl Marx on Colonialism*.

13   Marx, *Karl Marx on Colonialism*.

in the United States and the markets for the commodities produced were to be found primarily in India, where caste distinctions prevailed. The whole system was managed by British imperial administration in which the Colonial Office in London was prepared to deploy violence and out-right repression of whole populations to keep much of the world open for trade. While the British bourgeoisie in general, and the millocracy in particular, were motivated by the vilest of interests, and promoted their endeavours with the most blatant hypocrisies, the building of the railroads would, Marx hopefully supposed, ultimately mean the building of an industrial system in India which would 'dissolve the hereditary divisions of labour, upon which rest the Indian castes, those decisive impediments to Indian progress and Indian power'.[14] The account of globalization in the *Communist Manifesto* has a contemporaneous ring:

> The bourgeoisie has through its exploitation of the world market given a cosmopolitan character to production and consumption in every country. To the great chagrin of reactionists, it has drawn from under the feet of industry the national ground on which it stood. All old-established national industries have been destroyed or are daily being destroyed. They are dislodged by new industries, whose introduction becomes a life and death question for all civilised nations, by industries that no longer work up indigenous raw material, but raw material drawn from the remotest zones; industries whose products are consumed, not only at home, but in every quarter of the globe. In place of the old wants, satisfied by the production of the country, we find new wants, requir-ing for their satisfaction the products of distant lands and climes. In place of the old local and national seclusion and self-sufficiency, we have intercourse in every direction, universal inter-dependence of nations. And as in material, so also in intellectual production. The intellectual creations of individual nations become common property. National one-sidedness and narrow-mindedness become more and more impos-sible, and from the numerous national and local literatures, there arises a world literature.[15]

The stirring up of revolutionary sentiments by these processes might, Marx hypothesized, create opportunities for socialist revolution, though this would depend on how the now ruling classes 'shall have been sup-planted by the industrial proletariat'. The relations between Manchester

---

14   Marx, 'Future Results of British Rule in India', p. 5.
15   Marx and Engels, *Communist Manifesto*, pp. 38–9.

industrialism, imperialism and class struggle were evident, though partly masked by doctrines of free trade that, in Marx's time, were supported by Manchester School economics and the works of the Ricardian socialist John Stuart Mill. The Manchester materialist anchor in Marx's thought produced a critical theory of the role of imperialism, although as experienced and understood from the centre rather than from the periphery. But this imperialism was not only about the colonization of markets. It also rested on access to raw materials from the rest of the world and, in the case of raw cotton, Marx was acutely aware that, before the US Civil War, Manchester industrialism rested on the slave economies of the Southern states in the United States. The intersection of the slave mode of production with a booming capitalist mode of production produced unfathomable brutality at the same time as 'labour in a white skin cannot emancipate itself where it is branded in a black skin'.[16] The location of Manchester in the emergent global economy of nineteenth-century capitalism, intermediating, between slave labour in the cotton fields of the southern United States and the teeming populations of South Asia as the main market, was of remarkable interest. It pioneered the global production-consumption networks that dominate global capital today.

If, however, forty years after Nassau Senior had been summoned to Manchester, he had been summoned to Birmingham, he would have encountered a rather different industrial structure in a different global situation with a different mode of labour exploitation (resting on rapidly rising labour productivity) producing for very different markets. Much of the production was relatively small scale (compared to the gargantuan cotton mills) and often highly skilled, even with some degree of primitive mechanization. The Bolton and Watt steam engine was manufactured in Smethwick, for example, a suburb of Birmingham. The whole West Midlands region was dominated by a machine tools and metal-working sector that was very different from the cotton mills of Lancashire. Above all, Birmingham was the centre of gun-making and specialized in the production of military equipment, munitions and artillery. The market for such products is very much tied to state expenditures and state contracts. But the status of the defence industries, and the role of what is conventionally referred to in the US as the military-industrial complex, is something far beyond what Marx could have envisioned. In the midst of the 'Reagan Recession' of 1982, for example, when unemployment

---

16   Marx, *Capital*, Vol. 1, p. 414.

topped 10 per cent after Paul Volcker, then chair of the Federal Reserve, raised interest rates to 14 per cent to confront an inflation rate of around 17 per cent, Reagan ruthlessly cut back on all forms of social expenditure, reduced the top tax rate from around 70 per cent to 35 per cent, confronted and broke PATCO, the air traffic controllers union. He then launched a massive increase in defence funding to challenge the Soviet Union to a gargantuan arms race, which in the long run the Soviets disastrously lost. While the rest of the US swooned in economic depression, the defence industries, scattered in a great arc from Virginia, through the Carolinas, across Texas to Los Angeles and up to Boeing in Seattle, boomed in an astonishing wave of what some called 'military Keynesianism', since it was all deficit financed, leading Republicans like Dick Cheney later to opportunistically say in the George W. Bush years that 'Reagan taught us that deficits do not matter.'

Precision engineering and making guns and steam engines require very different types of labour from minding a cotton loom. Almost a century later, the West Midlands was the industrial region in which the automobile industry took root, anchored in cities like Coventry, Aston and even Oxford, with Birmingham as its commercial centre, while totally avoiding Manchester and the cotton towns of Lancashire. In the United States, the Massachusetts industrial model of the textile towns like Lowell was likewise radically different from that of steel towns like Pittsburgh or, in later times, Detroit and the auto industry.

Marx might have ended up telling a rather different theoretical story in *Capital* had he focused on Birmingham industrialism – one where technological change had early on become, as he himself had predicted, a business in itself. Here was a form of industrial organization that drew heavily on agglomeration economies of the sort that Marx had recognized and commented on in *Capital*. In the case of Birmingham, its industrialism depended on the emergence of a labour force with distinctive machine-tool skills and modest but liveable wage levels in a cultural environment where the working class was primarily divided on the basis of mental versus manual capacities. A workman who had skills in metal forging in the making of steam engines was valuable, and employers had to prevent such workers being lured away by rival firms in Belgium, France and indeed all over the Continent. Conversely, Birmingham manufacturers were happy to employ skilled workers no matter what their background (Polish, Prussian and so on). Diversity of ethnic or religious background did not matter (as it plainly did in Manchester) as long as the skills were there.

The image of the future that this experience proposed was rather different from that suggested by the Manchester experience of the 1840s. When the International Working Men's Association was founded in London in 1864, with Marx prominent in its formation, these were the kinds of skilled and literate workers who were involved from France, Italy, Switzerland, Spain and other countries. The watchmakers of the Jura Mountain regions along the French–Swiss border in the 1860s were legendary in their political sophistication (the split between Marxist and anarchist currents had not yet occurred). These were the organizers who collected and sent money in support of strikes and other agitations occurring throughout Europe in the late 1860s, culminating in the Paris Commune of 1871, in which international participation was important and welcomed. On the other hand, these were the relatively affluent workers who constituted an 'aristocracy of labour' that Lenin later worried would not only rally to support imperialist and colonial ventures but also be all too ready to compromise with the strategies of corporate capital.

By 1860 or so, the industrialist Joseph Chamberlain (popularly known as 'Radical Joe') was exploring civic reforms in the social provision of gas and potable water, popular education and housing for the improvement of the 'respectable' and adequately skilled working classes. He eventually went some way to implementing his reformist vision as mayor of the City of Birmingham. 'Gas and water socialism' was at that time seen as a feasible answer to a whole range of ills backed by widespread local labour discontent.[17] Chamberlain took steps to realize such a possibility. With a measure of working-class support, 'Radical Joe' later became a leading advocate for colonial expansion (the South African Boer War was his most notable contribution), in part impelled by the Conservative Party's rejection of his reformism. He recognized that, if internal reform and growth of demand in the home market were blocked by bourgeois class power, the only option to expand the market was to seek out a 'spatial fix' in the form of colonial ventures and cultivation of foreign markets. The notorious partitioning of Africa by the colonial powers at the Berlin Conference of 1885 was the culmination of a phase of interstate geopolitical rivalries over access to the raw materials and incipient markets of the whole African continent.

The image of the future defined by the Manchester industrialism of the 1840s and 1850s thus plainly did not apply to Birmingham in the 1870s. If

---

17 Denis Judd, *Radical Joe: A Life of Joseph Chamberlain* (Cardiff: University of Wales Press, 1993).

Engels's father had had an industrial establishment in the jewellery, gun and machine-tool trades in Birmingham rather than a textile factory in Manchester, *Capital* might have read rather differently, as we have noted. But, against this seeming bias, Marx had the factory inspectors' reports and the writings of an increasingly militant working class that focused on capital in general rather than on cotton factories in particular.

Any casual observer might be forgiven for thinking that the Manchester image certainly still does apply to the conditions of life and labour in the Rana Plaza textile and apparel factory, twenty miles outside of Dhaka in Bangladesh, which collapsed on 24 April 2013, killing 1,129 workers, mostly women, and wounding many more.[18] Producing textiles and name-brand apparel for Western markets, the factories were under constant pressure to cut costs for the benefit of Western consumers. Wages were close to starvation levels and factory discipline fierce. The same could be said of the Foxconn production complex in Shenzhen, China, which produces most of Apple's products and employed some 250,000 (some said 400,000) workers as of 2011 in one vast factory complex. A spate of worker suicides in that year persuaded the company to festoon the cramped company-provided living quarters of the migrant workers with mile on mile of netting to capture anyone who jumped. It is all too easy to take descriptions of labour and life conditions in the euphemistically dubbed 'emerging markets' and insert them into Marx's chapter 'The Working Day' in *Capital*, without noticing much difference. To the people living under such conditions, a dollop of 'gas and water socialism' along with some internal social reformism of the 'Radical Joe' sort would seem like a gift from heaven.

Capital produces a great deal of uneven geographical development, the qualities of which are often reflected in the particular theories to which economists subscribe. Marx noted, for example, that the protectionist theories promoted in his time by the US economist Henry Carey reflected the needs of US 'infant' industries to defend themselves against the dominance of British industrialism. This was the same rationale that produced import substitution industrial policies widespread throughout Latin America in the 1960s under the theoretical aegis of the Economic Commission for Latin America (ECLA). The French economist Frédéric Bastiat, who fiercely promoted free markets and the virtues of laissez-faire in the early nineteenth century, reflected, in contrast, the struggles

---

18   Sanchita Saxena, *Labor, Global Supply Chains, and the Garment Industry in South Asia: Bangladesh After Rana Plaza* (London: Routledge, 2019).

of French industrialists to free themselves from the shackles of a costly and inconvenient patchwork of local and national state regulations, taxes and interventions. This too was later echoed in Latin America after neo-liberal refutation of ECLA and the advance of free trade policies favoured by Pinochet and the Argentinian generals from the mid-1970s on. Even in Marx's time, the image of the future that the most advanced regions projected was perpetually changing and geographically quite diverse.

The question then looms as to where and what is that contemporary form of capitalism that projects the image of our own socialist future today? Is it the Rana Plaza textile plant, Shenzhen industrialism, the Amazon warehouse workers, the Google workers in San Francisco, the Microsoft workers in Seattle or the huge labour forces at the world's major airports? But it was not only an image of everyone else's future that Marx's descriptions conveyed, but the image of what might be a socialist or communist alternative utopian reflection (of the sort that the socialist utopians of the 1840s were fond of creating and which Marx and Engels had so firmly rejected in the *Communist Manifesto*). It was instead constituted through a historical materialist negation of all that was so dreadful on the ground at that time and in that place. The immediate grounding, in Marx's case, was heavily reliant on mass production and social reproduction in the industrial region of Manchester. The cruel conditions of the workers in factories, workshops and down mines along with the equally pitiful conditions of social reproduction in the industrial urbanization that capital had created and that Engels had so pointedly described, called out for negation. The material circumstances and the socialist project to which they pointed spoke for themselves.

It follows that the socialism that must be constructed to negate what is currently alienating and threatening in today's world must be both constantly shifting and geographically diverse. These questions call for the closest attention, because, in the history of anticapitalist oppositional politics, there has been a tendency to fetishize a certain imaginary of a socialist future as an ideal, ahistorical construct. In the same way that Keynes feared that we were in perpetual danger of becoming slaves to the thought of some long-defunct economist, so the political threat of obeisance to the ideals and ideas of some long-defunct socialist or communist project also looms. The fixity of our mental conceptions acts as a drag on our ability to think, let alone freely act on the political projects now required to create a more just, more ecologically acceptable and more emancipatory socialist world. To put it in such terms is not to invite yet another bout of utopian dreaming (though a little more of that would not hurt). It is to construct an accurate, properly theorized account of what capital is currently about, much as the factory inspectors provided back in Marx's time, and, on that basis, take feasible steps towards creation of a freshly conceived socialist alternative adequate to our current situation.

What this might mean depends, however, on geographical conditions. The problems posed by capital in Latin America are quite different from those in Sweden, where the whole country went into mourning with the death of the founder of IKEA, Ingvar Kamprad, who was lionized as a national folk hero. Yet there is a distressing habit of theorizing socialism as a political project outside of any historical and geographical grounding, even if capital's basic laws of motion are invariant and universal enough within capitalism to demand and command respect everywhere.

It is significant, therefore, that, when Lenin came to power in Russia in 1917, he pursued an industrial policy based on the principles put forward by Henry Ford, as the best and fastest way to increase the productivity of labour and build an economy capable of resisting the counterrevolutionary forces seeking to undermine the fledgling communist revolution. While Lenin's strategy worked in building industrial capacity, it came at the cost of perpetuating capital's social relations. When China entered the global economy after 1978 and, in particular, when it signed on to the World Trade Organization (WTO) in 2001, it had no choice but to submit to the laws of motion of capital. It is the operation of those laws that connects the industrialism of Manchester in the 1840s to contemporary conditions in Shenzhen's Foxconn factories and those of Rana Plaza in Bangladesh. It also explains why China is now modelling itself on Silicon Valley, a very different imaginary of a capitalist future, while attempting some version of gas and water socialism along with 'common prosperity' zones through equal access to housing, health care and education (the 'three mountains' that China has to climb to quell rising discontent).

While Marx's work is open to critique and dismissal as that of some 'long-defunct (Eurocentric) economist', we still live under the rule of capital. The admittedly incomplete theory of capital circulation and accumulation that Marx laid out is plainly still relevant. His theorizing transcended the particularities of Manchester, and his 'concrete abstractions' are robust and flexible enough to encompass Manchester and Birmingham or Shenzhen and Silicon Valley, provided we allow for the particular conditions within which Marx was working. His account of relative surplus value is rooted in the British experience with strong reference to the Manchester system and the cotton industry. In Marx's time, the industrial form of capital and its distinctive laws of motion dominated only in Britain, Western Europe and the Eastern seaboard of the United States, with some mercantile outliers sprinkled across the rest of the world. But in our times, thanks to the relentless push to create an ever deepening and expanding world market, the economy is subsumed almost everywhere under the laws of motion of capital that Marx uncovered. Marx's account of those laws and how they work is thus more relevant than ever (which is not to say that our account of them cannot be improved and extended or that problems of interpretation and application should not trouble us). The charge of Eurocentrism has to be set against the fact that capital itself may be Eurocentric, in the sense that it originated in identifiable and hegemonic form in the Italian city-states before mutating under the hegemony of the Low Countries (with Amsterdam as its centre), moving to Britain (where Marx encountered it) and then in the last century to the United States. These hegemonic shifts, in Arrighi's account, entailed a change of scale as well as a deepening of institutional arrangements ordered around rising capitalist state power. But in the same way that Marx, towards the end of his life, detected a rising challenge to British hegemony by the increasing centralization of capital in the United States after the end of the Civil War, so we currently wonder to what extent a Sino-centric influence is beginning to emerge to challenge the current hegemony of the United States.

The scarcity of information about which Marx complained is no longer with us as a problem. There is no shortage of detailed information on the conditions of the world's working classes, the conditions of their social reproduction, the failures of social provision, the dire conditions close to slave labour in certain regions. There are abundant accounts of dire living and learning situations in many parts of the world and the crushing conditions of poverty in which people eke out some sort of livelihood out of almost nothing. There are research monographs galore along with voluminous reports from the international organizations such as the United Nations, the World Bank, the IMF, the Bank of International Settlements and the OECD, along with the vast trove of information collected by NGOs (for example, the OXFAM periodic reports), state authorities and commercial organizations (mainly for marketing purposes but still of relevance).[19] We suffer from a plethora

---

19 'The Challenges of Growth: Employment and Social Cohesion', Joint ILO/IMF Conference with the Office of the Prime Minister of Norway, 2010, at imf.org.

rather than a scarcity of information. Techniques of mass data mining and media manipulation have proliferated. But there is also a lot of misinformation (labelled these days as 'fake news'). The surfeit of information is in some respects a problem rather than a blessing. There is so much of it that much of the public either cannot possibly get to much of it let alone understand it. Not a few so-called 'experts' who are called on to enlighten us appear to be as confused as everyone else, even when they manage to lay aside ideological predilections long implanted by centuries of misleading bourgeois scholarship on matters to do with something called class struggle and political economy. How to analyze and interpret the information is open to controversy, and the media dress it up as much for political gain as for clear understanding. This leaves us with serious problems. It was relatively easy for Marx to see the big picture, at least from the perspective of Manchester industrialism and the factory inspectors' reports, and to envision the negations that would define a socialist project for that place and time. The challenge for us seems far more complicated and perhaps indeterminate.

The most obvious beginning point is the state of political struggle and protest in the world today, along with some sense of the dynamics, including the twists and turns from right to left and back again that bleed into and influence the present state of things. There seems to be an upsurge in labour struggles around the world – both official and union-led as well as spontaneous or merely reactive to some serious failure of public policy or excess of corporate greed. Many of these struggles, in India, Bangladesh, Indonesia and China, for example, echo the traditional struggles that arose against Manchester industrialism.[20]

But the majority of the big mass movements in recent times have been centred on the failure of the dominant economic model to deliver the necessary qualities of daily life to satisfy even the minimal needs of the mass of the population. The alienation of nature and the ever-increasing levels of social inequality as measured primarily in financial and asset wealth as well as in income terms, engenders powerful currents of resentment through relative deprivation. The austerity that is often demanded might be acceptable if we were not aware of the enormous increments of wealth and power being sucked out of the economy by the oligarchs and autocrats who wield such immense influence over public policies.

---

20   Verity Bergmann, *Globalization and Labour in the Twenty-First Century* (London: Routledge, 2016).

While the Occupy movements against the 'one per cent' failed to last, the bitter taste and alertness to increasing rather than decreasing inequalities lives on. This is the kind of situation that provides a historical materialist grounding for someone like Piketty to revive the tradition of Ricardian socialism, without appeal to the labour theory of value, and to advocate the principle of an all-encompassing global wealth tax.

So, how should we interpret this history and this situation in relation to any emergent socialist strategy? A socialist politics has to recognize the qualities, problems and contestations that arise within the totality of the circulation of labour capacity as well as at the point at which it intersects with the accumulation of capital. When alienation dominates all the different moments in the circulation of labour capacity, deep troubles lie ahead. This is something that the 'so-called analysis' of contemporary economics goes a long way to concealing rather than revealing.

5

The Falling Rate and Rising Mass of Profit

'It is a law of capital', Marx tells us in the *Grundrisse*, 'to create surplus labour' but it can do this 'only by setting necessary labour in motion ... It is its tendency, therefore, to create as much labour as possible.' But the drive to create relative surplus value by raising the productivity of labour means that 'it is equally its tendency to reduce necessary labour to a minimum'.[1] This is a contradiction with major consequences. Any increase in the productivity of labour implies that each individual labourer will be able to process more raw materials and more means of production. The ratio c/v (the organic composition of capital) will therefore tend to rise. If the rate of exploitation of labour capacity (the ratio s/v) remains constant, then the rate of profit (the ratio $s/c+v$) is bound to fall. 'The more the relative surplus value grows ... the more does the rate of profit fall.' Or, put another way, 'the smaller the portion exchanged for living labour becomes, the smaller becomes the rate of profit.'[2] But increasing relative surplus value means that the rate of exploitation of labour capacity (s/v) will tend to rise, which may counteract to some degree the tendency for the profit rate to fall. The individual capitalist's pursuit of relative surplus value means that, in aggregate, fewer labourers will be employed, assuming that the demand for the commodity remains constant.

It is important to be clear as to what is happening here. Individual capitalists seeking to maximize the surplus value they produce pursue whatever paths they can to increase the productivity of the labourers they employ. This reduces their demand for labour power (their wage

---

1 Marx, *Grundrisse*, p. 399.
2 Ibid., p. 747.

bill goes down) which, in turn, condemns more and more of the labour force to a life in 'the industrial reserve army' of the unemployed and puts further downward pressure on the wages of those that are employed. But fewer labourers employed translates into less surplus labour and therefore less surplus value and a falling rate of profit. Individual capitalists operating in their own self-interest produce a result antagonistic to the capitalist class interest. This explains why individual capitalists invest in revolutionizing the technological and organizational mix in such a way as to reduce their average rate of profit.

If labour is the source of all value and surplus value, both will decline if fewer labourers are employed at a given rate of exploitation. This accelerates the tendency for the rate of profit to fall, though by how much will depend on a variety of contingent and counteracting factors. This law (or tendency) has often been referred to as 'the most important law of political economy'.[3] This is, some Marxist economists assert, the unique law that underpins crisis formation. The influential, brilliant and indefatigable Marxist blogger Michael Roberts, for example, considers it irrefutable that the law of falling profitability is the single underlying cause of the crisis tendencies of capitalism. 'Nothing gets produced unless it yields a profit' and if the profit rate is bound to fall then there is less incentive to produce anything. All alternative explanations of crises, Roberts asserts, such as 'the inability to absorb the surplus, underconsumption, disproportion, financial fragility etc. remain unconvincing and unproven in comparison'.

Roberts's argument does not fit at all with the concept of capital as an organic (ecosystemic) totality comprising different circulatory systems. It works only with a mechanistic and positivistic scientific reading. A dialectical and relational approach to capital is one in which each of the individual moments (such as production and realization) internalizes the effects of others within the totality. The different moments co-constitute one another within the totality. It is impossible to isolate one moment as the sole or 'true' locus of crisis formation. It is impossible, for example, to conceive of production in itself without consumption, realization, exchange and distribution. The drive for consumption can just as easily shape a need for production as the other way round. The

---

3   M. Roberts, 'Monocausality and Crisis Theory: A Reply to David Harvey', in T. Subasat (ed.), *The Great Financial Meltdown: Systemic, Conjunctural or Policy Created?* (Cheltenham: Edward Elgar Publishing, 2016), pp. 55–72. See also the various blog posts that Roberts has devoted to the question of falling profits: thenextrecession.wordpress .com.

theory of a singular and unique source of crisis contrasts with a systemic interpretation in which multiple possibilities for initiating crises exist. In a circulatory system, everything at some point runs into or touches on everything else. A blockage can occur anywhere. If the market and its capacity for realization collapses, a crisis of profitability ensues. A falling rate of profit can result from underconsumption, but underconsumption can also be due to a failure to invest in response to falling profits. Falling profits can also appear to result from inability to absorb surpluses, from overaccumulation, from failure to cope with disproportionalities in the production of wage goods or means of production (for example, machinery), or because of labour or raw material shortages. All human deaths, to pursue that analogy, could technically be attributed to cardiac arrest because, in every case, the heart stops beating. But it makes no sense to consult a cardiologist when faced with lung cancer or pneumonia. The heart–lung relation is one constitutive relation within the totality of the human body. Death can occur for all manner of reasons. The fact that everything that occurs in the circulatory system of capital at some point touches on the profit rate does not justify identifying that moment as the only relevant crisis-triggering moment within the totality.

Nor is it true to say that 'nothing is produced under capitalism unless it can make a profit.' A lot of production is undertaken by the state and other institutions without regard to surplus value generation and even outside of commodification. If each moment is seen as autonomous and independent but subsumed within the totality of the circulation of capital, the problem is to figure out where, within this particular configuration of moments (for example, underconsumption, overaccumulation, scarcities in nature and so on), blockages might occur which trigger, exaggerate or ameliorate crisis tendencies. When a crisis originates in real estate markets, as it did in 2007–8, the presumption that this must be a manifestation of the tendency for the profit rate to fall is not particularly helpful. To be sure, at some point the average profit rate is bound to be affected by everything else going on within the totality (for example, a general strike of labour, demographic constraints to labour supply). But this is a secondary or collateral effect of problems that originate elsewhere (for example, in the housing market).

How the rate and mass of profit relate is a critical question. We here encounter a specific version of a general problem of how to handle relations between rates and masses. Marx notes, for example, that, while the rate of profit may be falling, the mass may be rising. This issue crops up frequently and is often a source of serious misunderstanding.[4] For example, a recent detailed study by the Bank of England of the impacts of quantitative easing on wealth distribution in Britain estimated that 'the 10 per cent of least wealthy households' saw 'a marginal increase in their measured real wealth of around £3,000 between 2006–08 and 2012–14, compared to £350,000 for the wealthiest 10 per cent'. This would seem to confirm the popular view that Central Bank quantitative easing benefited the wealthy more than it did the least well-off. But the BoE report came to the opposite conclusion. 'Quantitative Easing Reduced UK Wealth Inequality', said the *Financial Times* headline.[5] The £3,000 received by the least well off was proportionately more, given their initial average wealth, than the £350,000 received by the wealthiest 10 per cent. So quantitative easing could be considered more beneficial to the lowest 10 per cent. But £3,000 over six years is less than £10 a week, which hardly adds anything to a person's well-being, let alone political and economic power. It is a trivial gain. The wealthiest 10 per cent in Britain got more than £1,000 a week from quantitative easing. Over six years, the difference between the lowest and the highest 10 per cent was that of a few extra cups of coffee a week, on the one hand, or having enough money to buy a studio apartment in midtown Manhattan, on the other. Yet the poor were judged by the *Financial Times* to have gained proportionately more than the rich.

This same problem arose in interpreting the import of stumbling growth rates in China. After 2009 and prior to the Covid pandemic, that country contributed more than a third of global growth (more than North America, Europe and Japan combined). China, in effect, saved global capitalism from a major depression by its expansionist policies during those years (we will examine how later). Any slackening in China's rate of growth would then appear to threaten global recession. It was, of course, recognized that China's double-digit growth rates in the 1990s could not be sustained indefinitely. Yet the prospect that China's growth rate might descend to the dismal levels of Europe or Japan (or even go much below 6 per cent) sent fearful shivers through global stock markets in 2018. But the Chinese authorities appeared relatively unconcerned. Tom Mitchell, writing in the *Financial Times* in 2019, correctly explained why. It had to do with the role of the mass:

---

4   David Harvey, 'Rate and Mass: Perspectives from the *Grundrisse*', *New Left Review* 2: 130 (July/August 2021): 73–98.

5   Gavin Jackson, 'Quantitative Easing "Reduced UK Wealth Inequality", says BoE"', *Financial Times*, 1 April 2018.

A bigger but slower growing economy creates more additional demand than a smaller economy that is expanding more rapidly. Last year (2018), China's economy expanded by about $1.2tn, or twice what it did when it was growing at double-digit rates more than a decade ago. This creates enough extra urban employment (10m or more new jobs a year) to ease official concerns about their greatest fear – social instability – and any loosening of their ever tighter grip on China's body politic.[6]

If the policy objective is to create 10 million jobs, it is easier to do that with a slow rate of growth of a large mass (such as that of China's economy in 2018) than through a high rate of growth of a smaller mass (such as that of China in 2000). The rate, in itself, does not tell us very much about the distribution of benefits without knowing to what mass it is applied.

Failure to acknowledge the importance of this relationship can have serious consequences. For example, the postelection surveys concerning Trump's electoral victory in 2024 cited inflation as a critical issue that animated many voters. The inflation rate during and immediately after Covid had shot up to 8 or 9 per cent, but in 2024 it fell steadily to below 4 per cent The liberal media concluded that inflation was under control. But as the rate came down, so the price level continued to climb, and it is the price level that people confront in the supermarket, not the current rate of increase. An increase of 3 per cent on top of three years of high inflation has a big impact on the price level. Trump emphasized the price level, not the rate, and blamed Bidenomics. Add to this the fact that, after forty years of neoliberal wage repression, nearly half the US population tries to get by on $30,000 or less per year. For them, any rise in the price level poses an existential choice between putting food on the table, paying the rent or putting gas in the car. This half of the population was seriously hurt by the continuing rise in the price level, even at a lower rate of 3 per cent. Trump spoke to their anger and won the election with support from the bottom 50 per cent. Confounding the relation between rate and mass has many consequences. At the end of the day, billionaires are called that because of the mass of value they control, not because of the rate of return on their investments, even though the latter clearly contributes to the former.

The rate of profit by itself is one of the most popular metrics of how successful capitalists have been in accomplishing their mission. Articles

---

6   Tom Mitchell, 'China's Leaders Fear the Unknown amid an Economic Slowdown', *Financial Times*, 21 January 2019.

Figure 4. The Global Falling Rate of Profit

on the tendency for the rate of profit to fall abound within the Marxist tradition. Extensive empirical documentation of the tendency exists (Figure 4). The same care and precision has not been applied, however, to studying the role and significance of the rising mass. But, as the recent case of China so dramatically illustrates, again and again we are likely confronting a situation in which a serious fall in the rate of profit (say from 6 to 3 per cent) results long term in such an augmentation of the mass of output and of surplus value as to dwarf the significance of the falling rate. The question is why do so many expositions of Marx's political economy ignore this relation?

The problem initially arose with Engels's editing of the manuscripts that formed the basis for the third volume of *Capital*. Engels, it is now pretty much agreed, made it seem as if Marx was far closer to a final version of his argument on the falling rate of profit than was actually the case. The original notes form one single text entitled 'The Law of the Tendential Fall in the General Rate of Profit'. Engels divided it into three chapters: 'The Law Itself'; 'Counteracting Factors'; and 'Development of the Law's Internal Contradictions'. The titles of the last two chapters are hard to justify from the original text. They also make it seem as if the 'Law' is a primary and all-important stand-alone finding, while the counteracting factors and internal contradictions are mere modifications to the fundamental law as it operates in practice.

The original notebooks read very differently. The work appears preliminary and explorative rather than definitive. To be sure, Marx begins his manuscript with a clear, crisp and forceful explanation of how and why the profit rate might fall. The competitive search for technological advantage removes labour, the source of value and surplus value (profit), from production. Less labour input means, all other things remaining equal, less surplus value, which translates into a falling rate of profit. This argument is modified by the fact that the immense increase of productivity that occurred within the British cotton industry with the shift to power-loom weaving did not diminish the number of factory labourers employed. The Census of 1861 showed 642,000 workers in the industry. The dramatic rise in productivity reduced the price of cotton goods, which allowed the market for cheap cotton goods to expand dramatically worldwide, at the expense of domestic handloom weaving everywhere (particularly India) but also to meet a rising demand from an increasing world population. There was no effect of falling profits within the British factory sector for much of the nineteenth century. The same could be said more recently of the labour-intensive textile and clothing sectors in China and Bangladesh.

Marx was not alone in predicting a tendency for profit rates to fall. Ricardo and (more tentatively) Smith also thought profits were doomed to fall, suggesting that industrial capitalism might not be a viable mode of production in the long run. Scarcities in nature (a Malthusian explanation), rising land rents and rising wages (to cover the rising cost of food) would subject industrial capital to an increasing profit squeeze that would ultimately make the industrial form of capital impossible. Marx concluded that Ricardo and Smith were right about the outcome but wrong about the mechanism. Marx held that 'the progressive tendency for the general rate of profit to fall is ... simply the expression, peculiar to the capitalist mode of production, of the progressive development of the social productivity of labour.'[7] The competitive drive for technological advantage (relative surplus value) on the part of individual capitalists would undermine the aggregate production of surplus value, which was the basis of profit.

A few pages further on, Marx writes that 'despite the enormous decline in the general rate of profit ... the number of workers employed by capital ... hence the absolute mass of the surplus labour absorbed, appropriated by it ... hence the absolute magnitude or mass of the profit produced by it, can therefore grow, and progressively so, despite the progressive fall in the rate of profit.' He then adds: 'This not only can but must be the case.'[8] The shift from 'can' to 'must' is important. The same laws 'produce both a growing absolute mass of profit, which the

7   Marx, *Economic Manuscript of 1864–1865*, pp. 321–2.
8   Ibid., p. 327.

social capital appropriates, and a falling rate of profit'. 'How, then', Marx asks, 'should we present this double-edged law of a decline in the rate of profit coupled with a simultaneous increase in the absolute mass of profit arising from the same causes?'[9] Marx has progressed from a falling rate of profit to a double-edged law, one of falling rate and rising mass. So how, then, does he view the relation between rate and mass?

In the *Grundrisse*, Marx works through a variety of numerical examples of the rate–mass relation showing how capital can continue to grow even as the rate of profit falls. 'The gross profit' – the mass – 'will grow on the average not as does the rate of profit, but as does the size of the capital ... A capital of 100 with a profit of 10% yields a smaller sum of profit than a capital of 1,000 with a profit of 2%.' Expressed 'in general terms' this means that

> if the rate of profit declines for the larger capital, but not in relation to its size, then the gross profit rises although the rate of profit declines. If the profit rate declines relative to its size, then the gross profit ... remains stationary. If the profit rate declines more than its size increases, then the gross profit of the larger capital decreases relative to the smaller one in proportion as its rate of profit declines.

This is a typical Marx tactic of outlining different technical possibilities. It is 'this', he goes on to say, that 'is the most important law of modern political economy, and the most essential for understanding the most difficult relations. It is the most important law from the historical standpoint. It is a law which, despite its simplicity, has never before been grasped, and even less, consciously articulated.'[10]

'This' is often cited as if it refers to the theory of the falling rate of profit on its own. But the original text (and the referent of 'this' in it) indicates that it is the relation between a falling rate and a rising mass that is 'the most important law'. The context would seem to suggest that, out of the three combinatorial possibilities, it is the first – that of rising mass and falling rate – which is by far the most likely and significant. This law rests on the simple rule that 'a large capital with a lower rate of profit accumulates more quickly than a small capital with a higher rate of profit.'[11] If the mass of value in certain hands is already huge, then that mass continues to expand with potentially monstrous consequences

9   Ibid., p. 329.
10   Marx, *Grundrisse*, p. 748.
11   Marx, *Economic Manuscript of 1864–1865*, p. 335.

(environmental as well as social) even in the face of sharply falling profitability. In today's world, for example, it is relevant to ask whether the main problems we face, such as climate change and increasing inequality, are due more to the falling rate alone or to the ever-rising mass of profit resting on a declining rate? It is also relevant to ask if there are other mechanisms, such as mergers and acquisitions and accumulation by dispossession, that accelerate and augment the coming together of the mass other than by the mechanism Marx here describes? Leveraged buyouts spring to mind as convenient ways whereby particular capitalists can gain control over a huge mass of capital on the basis of very little of their own capital input. Furthermore, it is presumed in contemporary presentations of Marx's argument that the profit rate is exclusively tied to the rate of exploitation of labour power in production. But in the US pharmaceutical industry, very little of the monetary profit comes from the exploitation of labour power in production. Most of it comes from extortionate monopoly pricing in the market with the connivance of medical insurance companies and captive federal regulators.

To raise the issue of barriers to realization of value in the market is, however, to run the risk of being branded a renegade 'underconsumptionist' by those who cleave to the narrow version of crises due to falling rates of profit. However, value rests, Marx argued, on the contradictory unity of production and realization in the market. If there is no realization, the labour applied in production is socially unnecessary: there is no value. The contradictory unity between value creation in production and the realization of value in the market is foundational for Marx in the same way that the contradictory unity between rate and mass is also central to his theorizing.[12] There is an unhappy habit within the history of Marxist theorizing of choosing one side of a contradiction and erasing the other to create a one-dimensional theoretical structure – such as the stand-alone theory of the falling rate of profit proposed by Michael Roberts or the all-embracing theory of the rising mass in the work of Paul Baran and Paul Sweezy in *Monopoly Capital*.[13] The latter, for example, are very explicit that they were 'substituting the law of rising surplus for the law of falling profit' because, they argued, capital had evolved by the late 1960s from a competitive to a monopoly state. Even had this been true (which turned out not to be the case) this was no excuse for abandoning

---

12   Marx, *Grundrisse*, pp. 414–15.
13   Paul Baran and Paul Sweezy, *Monopoly Capital: An Essay on the American Economic and Social Order* (New York: *Monthly Review* Press, 1966).

Marx's law of the falling rate and rising surplus (mass), understood as a contradictory unity.

This does not mean that one or other side of a contradiction, such as realization in relation to the rising mass, cannot be abstracted for detailed analysis. Baran and Sweezy's study of the consequences of the rising mass is as helpful as Michael Roberts's studies of the consequences of a falling rate of profit. But at the end of the day, it is the interrelations between the two different circulation processes and the contradictory unity between them that matters. Marx's genius is not only to keep the contradiction in play but, as he says in his commentary on Ricardo, to elaborate at length the contradictory consequences. Both Roberts and Baran and Sweezy err in eradicating the contradiction in favour of a one-dimensional version of the theory of falling rate or rising mass.

But this still leaves us with the problem of what, exactly, is the origin of this 'double-edged' law? When Marx first introduces the figure of the capitalist in the *Grundrisse*, he observes that 'it is a law of capital' to seek profits and to 'create surplus labour'. But capital can do this only by 'entering into exchange with the worker' and 'setting necessary labour in motion'.[14] This previews Chapter 11, 'The Rate and Mass of Surplus-Value' in the first volume of *Capital*. Marx makes clear that the aim and objective of the capitalist is to command as much mass of value as possible and that in the absence of technological and organizational changes there are two ways of so doing: increase the rate of exploitation of labour power or employ more labourers. The ambition to create and employ 'as much labour as possible' rules out the possibility of the profit rate 'declining more than its size increases'.[15]

This implies, Marx goes on to argue, population growth as a continuous source of extra labour supply and of extra effective demand in the market. 'Production founded on capital' requires 'the greatest absolute mass' of necessary and surplus labour and, hence, 'maximum growth of population – of living labour capacities.'[16] This relation between capital accumulation and population growth throughout the historical geography of capitalism is rarely taken up seriously in the literature. Historically, the association has been very strong (Figure 5). The exponential growth of population has paralleled the exponential growth of capital since the middle of the eighteenth century until recently. Today, it poses a potential problem because we are witnessing accelerating population

---

14   Marx, *Grundrisse*, p. 399.
15   Marx, *Capital*, Vol. 1, Chapter 11.
16   Marx, *Grundrisse*, p. 608.

World population

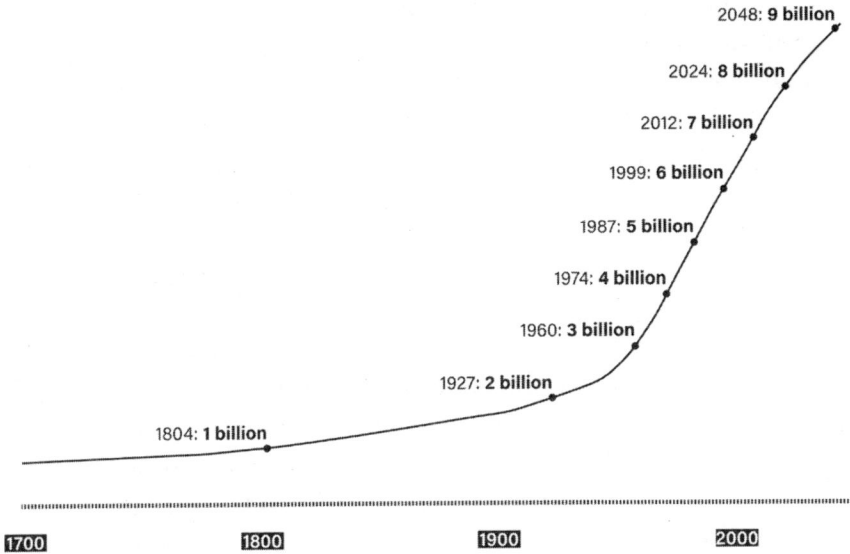

2048: **9 billion**

2024: **8 billion**

2012: **7 billion**

1999: **6 billion**

1987: **5 billion**

1974: **4 billion**

1960: **3 billion**

1927: **2 billion**

1804: **1 billion**

1700   1800   1900   2000

Figure 5. Global Population Growth Since 1700

declines in some fifty or so countries (for example, Japan, Italy and even China) and the pandemic appears to have made matters much worse. How will exponential capital accumulation continue in the absence of strong population growth to feed labour supply and expand consumer demand? It is also worth noting that countries with weak demographics, like Italy and Japan, have not performed well in the global competition to accumulate. When Angela Merkel opened the door to nearly a million Syrian refugees in 2019, she did so in the hope that the benefits from an increment in labour supply would outweigh the political costs of offending right-wing and nationalist sentiments. She was, unfortunately for her, proven wrong, at least in the short run. The right-wing critique was merciless and tainted her legacy.

But all of this does point to a long-run demographic political threat to capital accumulation in its current form. If the pursuit of individual relative surplus value through adoption of new labour-saving technology (for example, AI) prevails, at some point more and more labourers will be relegated to the industrial reserve army of the un- or underemployed. If this growing mass of surplus labour increasingly includes educated and skilled workers of the sort able to invent and apply the new technologies, the imbalance in the labour market will result in highly educated workers reduced to menial work in order to survive. Uber drivers and Amazon delivery workers with doctorates make a recipe for burgeoning anticapitalist political discontent. This was the sort of condition that produced the student movement of the 1960s in the advanced capitalist countries. A student movement in Bangladesh in 2024 ousted a long-standing government, demanding open access to adequate jobs. Signs of similar labour restiveness are evident in China. In the US there has been a dramatic shrinkage in those sectors of the job market where highly educated and seriously indebted workers were previously absorbed. The global job market is full of such troubling signs of disequilibrium disguised for the most part by low aggregate unemployment rates in many parts of the world, including China.

Since 1980, the mass of the global wage labour force has increased from around two to three billion workers. This is an immense shift in the magnitude of the working mass compared to Marx's time (Marx recorded around 2.5 million workers from the British census of 1861).[17] What both eras have in common is that many of the new workers are in the category of the labouring poor. The recent increase is attributable to three major sources above that due to population growth (which has always been important). First, the entry of China into the global economy after 1978 along with the collapse of the Soviet Empire in 1989 released into the global capitalist economy a flood of newly available wage labourers, with diversified and in some instances extraordinary skills. Second, the steadily increasing degradation of peasant, indigenous and agrarian economies (largely due to the accelerating worldwide industrialization of agriculture) augmented the long-standing flow of labour off the land and out of rural occupations into cities in, for example, China, South Asia (India and Indonesia), Latin America (Mexico and Brazil) and most recently Africa. Finally, the accelerating mobilization of women into the labour force in many parts of the world (including areas of advanced capitalism) supplemented these flows, with the result that the increasing feminization of the working class and of poverty became of huge significance. In the United States, for example, it allowed declining real wages to be offset by a stable and, in some cases, increasing household wages as women joined the workforce en masse.

These three major surges in wage labour supply cannot be repeated (with the exception of Africa, which still houses a large untapped labour reserve). The demographic conditions of compounding population growth that previously underpinned the compounding growth of capitalist production are also shifting, even going negative in some parts

17   Marx, *Capital*, Vol. 1, pp. 561–2.

of the world, as in Italy, Germany and Japan, or posing the problem of rapidly ageing populations as in China and much of Europe. Some fifty countries in the world now have negative population growth rates. Africa, the Middle East and South Asia still retain high rates of population growth.

This remarkable recent increase in the global mass of wage labour creates unprecedented problems and possibilities for accelerating the accumulation of capital by an avaricious capitalist class hell-bent on acquiring as much wealth for itself as possible. In pursuit of this goal, they have been aided, as we have seen, by the reduction of barriers to capital mobility, open capital markets and compelling and unhindered incentives to equalize the rate of profit across the world and to facilitate the increasing centralization of capital into few hands. The residual problem for capital is how to manage, secure and provision a vast increase in the labour force without simultaneously stirring it into political activism, if not into anticapitalist revolt against an ever-wealthier oligarchy that increasingly rules in its own exclusive interest.

It is not too hard, after all, for the workers themselves to identify the direct authors of their torments, which explains the lengths to which the ideological wing of the capitalist class will go to divert attention from capital as the possible root of many of our problems, by blaming immigrants, foreigners, 'lazy' marginalized populations, feminism, sexual, cultural or religious deviants, the inevitabilities of globalization, the dastardly practices of some malicious foreign power (such as China) or the dysfunctionality of the state (ruled by capital) or financial institutions (such as the central banks) for all the problems the workers experience both at work and in the home. Since the priority for labour is to survive, it also seems tactically wise for capital to make survival so difficult that the working classes have little time or energy for political matters. Raising kids with no assistance from the capitalist-imposed austerity state while working an eighty-hour week leaves little time for following politics, let alone learning and organizing.

The mass of global capital has increased since 1980, along with a huge increase in the global wage labour force, even in the face of well-documented falling profit rates. Meanwhile, the share of wages in national product has systematically declined in almost all of the world's major economies, with the United States and China in the lead.[18] This

18   McKinsey Global Institute, 'A New Look at the Declining Labor Share of Income in the United States,' Discussion Paper, May 2019, mckinsey.com.

is also consistent with Marx's argument. The precipitous decline since 2010 may have something to do with the widespread feeling that working people are being short-changed in contemporary capitalism.

It is hard to tell what proportion of the increase in the wage labour force is working for capital to produce surplus value and how much the wage labourers are exchanging their labour capacity against revenues (of the state, of the various factions of capitalist consumers or even from other workers in the case of childcare or eldercare). Evidently, much of the increase of wage labour is in informal or precarious employment. Marx, at one point, did suggest that rapid increases in the productivity of labour would allow for more and more labour to be employed unproductively (providing services to the bourgeoisie, for example). But the social (as opposed to individual) labour that is mobilized either directly or indirectly in support of surplus value production now encompasses more and more millions of workers apparently condemned to ever-lower levels of remuneration. This is hardly the description of an economy in a happy state. It may be, as Marx would put it, 'adequate' for capital and for the top 10 per cent, but it produces relative penury for everyone else. To top it all, the neoliberal turn to a politics of wage repression after 1980 leads to wage labour receiving a declining share of GDP even with a huge increase in the wage labour force. It is this that produces the situation in which the richest country in the world has half of its population trying to live on less than $30,000 a year.

But there has, at the same time, been a strong 'tendency to reduce necessary labour to a minimum' through the application of labour-saving technologies in production. This increasing productivity of labour produces 'an industrial reserve army' via technologically induced unemployment. While capital, on the one hand, perpetually seeks 'to increase the labouring population', at the same time it 'constantly seeks to reduce labour's presence in production', all the while expanding the unemployed industrial reserve army.[19] This is a major contradiction. Capital operates on a principle somewhat like that of what bourgeois economists call a backward-bending supply curve. When prices fall, the conventional theory says production should decline until supply and demand converge on an equilibrium price. But if producers have fixed costs (such as debt service) or fixed revenue objectives, a fall in prices will lead them to produce more to cover their fixed costs. This prompts further falls in price. Conversely, when prices rise producers may supply less, which

---

19   Marx, *Capital*, Vol. 1, Chapter 25.

results in further price rises. This often happens in raw commodity pro-duction (for example, indebted farmers raise output to cover their debt service irrespective of demand conditions). Oil states, to take another example, typically have a certain revenue target in mind to fund their functions, so, when oil prices decline, they pump more oil, which means lower prices (and vice versa when oil prices rise). The long-run effects can be sometimes dirt-cheap oil for consumers accompanied by wild swings in both oil prices and oil output. The oil cartel OPEC was founded in response to this problem, with the aim of stabilizing the price and assuring some stability in oil-state revenues. Conservative economists likewise worry that higher wages tempt workers to substitute leisure time for employed work and thereby increase the scarcity of labour, inducing even higher wages. Since this frustrates the achievement of the textbook condition of harmonious equilibrium in the labour market, wages must, the conservatives argue, be kept low by extra-economic means (for example, cutting unemployment benefits) to keep their 'harmonious' economic model of the labour market intact.

At the heart of the capitalist mode of production, Marx argues, there exists something like a backward-bending supply curve in the market for labour power. A falling rate of profit coexists with an increase of employ-ment of labour that stabilizes, if not increases, the mass of value and surplus value generated for capital. Meanwhile, the competitive search for technologies that increase labour productivity continues, making more and more labour power redundant. When technological innova-tion becomes a business, as Marx suggests it would, the production of generic technologies (such as the steam engine, the internal combus-tion engine, electrification, mechanization, digitalization and artificial intelligence) generalizes the forces making for a falling rate of profit. The mechanism that produces falling profits intensifies, while the thirst to maximize gross profits by employing more labour power becomes ever more compelling. The two contradictions are superimposed on each other. In the absence of any other ameliorating or interventionist force, these two tendencies would produce an infinitely expanding mass of surplus value, along with an infinitely disappearing rate of profit.

Marx, in his original draft of the theory, presses on to elaborate on some consequential modifications. He outlines some potential counter-vailing influences to counteract the falling rate of profit. These include increasing the rates of labour exploitation, hiring labour at less than its value, the falling value or devaluation of constant capital inputs, the pursuit of wasteful or unproductive investments and the like. The last of

these is of significance, as we shall later see.[20] So widespread and powerful might these influences be that Marx even envisaged phases in which
the profit rate might rise, which led Engels in his published version of
Volume 3 of *Capital* to add gratuitously the reassuring words to the text
that 'in the long run we know that the profit rate is bound to fall.' One
other key influence missing in the *1864–1865 Manuscript* appears earlier
in the *Grundrisse*. This is the opening up of new and labour-intensive
lines of production.[21] This is vitally important in two respects. First,
for many arenas of capitalist production, we witness a typical product
development cycle. A new sector, such as car production, comes online
and it is initially labour-intensive, but, as the market size and output
increase, so innovations that displace labour step by step are introduced.
Robotization and automation increasingly remove labour power from
production. But this takes several years to accomplish. Second, sectors
and lines of production are opened up which are resistant to automation. Add in the unknown consequences of artificial intelligence and the
future of labour demand looks grim. If the past is any guide, systematic
attempts to use AI to disempower and render redundant and disposable
large segments of the labour force are almost certain.

The contradictions implicit in the rate–mass question are central to
Marx's analysis. Again and again, he returns to the theme that the expansion of the capital mass can and does proceed even more rapidly in the
face of a declining rate of profit. There is, however, yet another parallel
conundrum that needs to be addressed, and to this we now turn.

---

20   For a full account, see David Harvey, *The Limits to Capital* (London: Verso,
1982), pp. 176–81.
21   Marx, *Grundrisse*, pp. 749–50.

6

The Equalization of the Profit Rate

In Volume 1 of *Capital*, Marx notes that 'the masses of value and surplus-value produced by different capitals ... vary directly as the amount of variable components of these capitals'. In other words, the more money laid out in the hiring of labour power, the larger the wage bill, and the more labourers hired, the greater the surplus value produced (assuming a constant rate of exploitation). But this poses a problem because 'everyone knows that a cotton spinner' who 'employs much constant capital' (that is, means of production) 'and little variable capital' (labour power) 'does not, on account of this, pocket less profit or surplus-value than a baker, who sets in motion relatively much variable capital [labour power] and little constant capital [means of production]. For the solution of this apparent contradiction, many intermediate terms are still needed.'[1] This conundrum was posed with the publication of the first volume of *Capital* (1867) but everyone had to wait for a much-anticipated solution until Engels had edited and published the third volume of *Capital* in 1894. The solution, when it came, posed as many questions as it answered.

The solution depended on the equalization of the rate of profit. This, Marx argued, creates a form of 'capitalist communism'. Producers contribute to aggregate value and surplus value production according to the labour they employ, while they individually appropriate value and surplus value according to the mass of the capital they advance. The model being proposed here is one in which all the surplus value produced is put into one enormous pot and then individual capitalists withdraw surplus value from that pot according to the total capital they advance,

---

1   Marx, *Capital*, Vol. 1, Chapter 11.

rather than according to the surplus value they contribute to the pot from the labour power they employ. 'The capitalist class thus ... distributes the total surplus value so that ... it [shares in it] evenly in accordance with the size of its capital, instead of in accordance with the surplus value actually created by the capitals in the various branches of business.'[2]

Labour-intensive industries thus subsidize capital-intensive industries employing few labourers. The greater the mass of capital advanced by an individual capitalist relative to the labour they employ, the greater their claim on the surplus value. Policymakers who intuit and act on this unequal distribution of rewards have achieved some spectacular results. When Singapore was cast adrift from Malaysia in the early 1960s, it decided not to pursue labour-intensive industrialization (of the sort that was developing in Hong Kong) even though it had access to plenty of low-wage labour. It constructed a capital-intensive rather than labour-intensive economy and the spectacularly favourable results in terms of wealth accumulation in Singapore are there for all to see. Conversely, Bangladesh remains an economic basket case, at least from the standpoint of the labouring population though not necessarily of its local capitalist class, because all it has to offer is labour-intensive and largely unregulated industrialization.

This explains the current Chinese ambition to transition from labour-intensive to capital-intensive lines of production by 2025 (though this may well be delayed through US obstructionism). It is not clear whether Chinese policymakers understood this theoretical point or not. They probably set out to copy the successful developmental path taken by Japan, then South Korea and Taiwan as well as Singapore (the last two Chinese-speaking). In all of these cases, the United States did not oppose and in many cases facilitated the transfer of technology in order to facilitate capital-intensive development in these countries to help contain the threat of a rising Chinese communism. This was the celebrated 'containment strategy' of China that the United States pursued during the Cold War in the Far East.

The initial thrust into market-led capitalist industrialism in China in 1978 rested on its primary comparative advantage, which was low labour costs: 'The share of labour-intensive manufactures in total exports rose from 36% in 1975 to 74% in 1990.'[3] It continued at that high level

---

2   Karl Marx and Friedrich Engels, *Selected Correspondence* (Moscow: Progress Publishers, 1975), p. 206.

3   United Nations Development Program (UNDP), 1996, Human Development Report 1996: Economic Growth and Human Development, New York, p. 94.

until 2008, when it was cut in half in response to the collapse of the US consumer market. Thereafter, labour-intensive exports, particularly to the US, have systematically declined in relative though not necessarily in absolute terms. China has now increasingly taken to offshoring labour-intensive industries to Vietnam, Laos and Cambodia (a process accelerated by Trump's tariff wars against China) or converting to automation and capital-intensive AI systems, as Foxconn, the Taiwanese firm which assembles most Apple computers in China, is proposing to do. The most recent proposals have Foxconn cutting its labour force in China by one-third. The labour-intensive production remaining will be largely oriented to satisfying the needs of the rapidly growing domestic market or exports to emerging markets. It follows that the value transfers out of China attaching to the equalization of the rate of profit may be diminishing, though by how much is hard to quantify. In China's case, however, the US has fought against technology transfers of the sort it earlier allowed to other East Asian economies, since China is construed as a hostile competitive threat rather than as a potent collaborator in the struggle to contain the spread of communism (as is the case with Japan and South Korea).

Free trade is, by definition, therefore, unfair trade when coupled with the equalization of the rate of profit. The freer and the more competitive the trade, the more unfair the outcome will likely be. This may be one of Marx's most important and striking findings.

It has largely been missed, however, because most Marxist economists believe that Marx, when he explored the equalization of the rate of profit and the resultant transformation of values into prices of production, was mainly concerned to construct a theory of price formation. If the profit rate was equalized, commodities would no longer trade at their value $(c + v + s)$ but at what Marx called their price of production $(c + v + p)$ where p is the average rate of profit everywhere. But by using the phrase 'price of production' Marx created an unfortunate confusion. Many thought he was referring to market prices, as measured in money terms, and that the transformation from values into prices of production was a market process that somehow coordinated the value theory with money price formation through actual market exchange. The exchange value system, it was thought, would incorporate this transformation.

This sparked a long and often bitter controversy in the history of Marxian political economy. The 'transformation process' seems to propose a mathematical way whereby market prices could be derived from values. But if this was the case, critics noted, then the value of the inputs (*c*) should also be measured in prices of production, not values. The effect is to render the value theory irrelevant, bourgeois critics gleefully pointed out. Paul Samuelson, the premier Keynesian economist of the 1960s, depicted the transformation process as setting up a matrix of values, erasing it and then substituting a matrix of prices of production. Economists should, he wrote, forget about the value theory and just work with market prices. Clearly, the inputs into the initial value structure ought to have been set out as prices of production rather than as values. Since Marx did not bother to do this, the prices of production he derived from the arithmetic examples he constructed in Volume 3 of *Capital* were plainly wrong. Marx acknowledged this but asserted it did not really matter. This was, I suggest, because Marx's value theory is not aimed at deriving relative prices (Marx explicitly says so in a number of places). It is primarily designed to explain the mechanisms by which a working class which produces the value receives so little of it and is thereby condemned to live and work under such appalling conditions in the midst of astonishing privatized affluence. In other words, the value theory is about the production and reproduction of class relations, not about relative price formation.

Marx, for example, uses the equalization of the rate of profit to explain 'why the capitalists are birds of a feather and why no matter how little love is lost between them in their competition with one another, they are nevertheless united by a real freemasonry vis-à-vis the workers, i.e. the working class'. It could happen, for example, that 'a capitalist who employed … not a single worker … would have just as much of an interest in the exploitation of the working class by capital and just as much derive his profit from unpaid surplus labour as would a capitalist who … laid out his entire capital on wages.'[4] This is Marx's answer to all those who ask, when first confronted with his distinctive value theory, how is it that if all value originates with productive labour that a fully automated firm that employs little or no labour can still command a profit? All capitalists, no matter how much labour they employ, have a unified interest in the repression of the working classes. It is partly the role of economic theory, through to the cruder forms of procapitalist ideology and propaganda, to sustain capital's unified front against the workers, no matter how much labour they individually employ. As Michael Roberts also admonishes us, 'The way in which there is a transfer of value from

---

4   Marx, *Economic Manuscript of 1864–1865*, pp. 305–7.

the poor capitalist economies with lower levels of technology to the rich imperialist economies has been greatly neglected.'[5]

This brings us back to the ways in which the coercive laws of competition work within the field of actual market exchange. To begin with, mature forms of market exchange are, in principle, blind to the identities and wealth of the exchangers. The market is, Marx concedes, a 'radical leveller' which 'extinguishes all distinctions'.[6] It seeks to secure the claim of neoliberal theorists such as Hayek and Friedman that the best way to protect individual liberty and freedom against the arbitrariness of state power is to build a market system based on private property and free trade. Marx does not initially dispute these propositions. In the *Grundrisse*, for example, he accepts 'that the exchange of exchange values is the productive real basis of all *equality* and *freedom*' and that these as 'pure ideas' in bourgeois society are 'merely the idealized expression of this real basis'.[7]

But while market exchange appears to be about the 'happy concordance of mutual interests' at the individual level and to embody in principle 'the exchange of equivalents', the social result is in fact unfreedom and inequality. This is so for two reasons. The first is the violence and brutality of primitive accumulation, which yields the initial commodification of much of the labour power that produces profit (surplus value). The second is competitive market exchange and profit equalization, which, for the reasons already stated, favours returns to capital and the capitalist class at the expense of returns to labour and the working class, even in the absence of overt class repression.

Conventional economic theories systematically ignore the inequalities that derive from the equalization of the profit rate. It is not even competition or trade that is the important feature here. Both may be necessary, but neither is sufficient. If the competition focuses, say, on qualities of products or on social provision, there is no problem. It is the competition and trade to produce surplus value in the context of the equalization of the rate of profit that does the damage. But this requires that capital be mobile, capable of moving rapidly from companies, sectors or regions with low rates of profit to wherever the profit rate is higher. The most mobile form of capital is the money form (as opposed to the commodity or productive forms). Internationally, the Bretton Woods

5   Guglielmo Carchedi and Michael Roberts, *Capitalism in the 21st Century: Through the Prism of Value* (London: Pluto Press, 2022).

6   Marx, *Capital*, Vol. 1, p. 229.

7   Marx, *Grundrisse*, pp. 244–5.

agreement of 1944 instituted a system of capital controls which erected a formidable barrier to the global equalization of the rate of profit. Cross-border capital mobility was circumscribed. Each country had control over its own fiscal policy, and labour could organize in each country (as could capital) without too much fear of competition from abroad. The main threat to labour came from state-sponsored importation of foreign labour (such as recruitment of Turks to work in Germany, Maghrebians to France, and Yugoslavs to Sweden, or Britain's importation of labour from its former empire, while the US opened immigration to everyone in 1965). The result has been some unfortunate (white) working class hostility to immigration, which lingers or in some places festers in the ugliest of forms to this day.

But the US abandoned capital controls (and the Bretton Woods system) in a series of world-shaking measures in the 1970s (most notably abandoning its fixed gold–dollar link on 15 August 1971). The investment bankers had long been chafing at the bit to get rid of Bretton Woods, because it restrained them far too much (in their view) from speculating and profiteering. By 1970 or so, they had a mass of surplus funds (mainly in the form of eurodollars held by branch banks in Europe) crying out for investment opportunities. In 1971, Nixon caved in to the investment bankers under pressure from speculation in the money markets against the dollar at a fixed exchange rate of $35 for an ounce of gold.

Under Bretton Woods, the auto companies in Detroit could con-struct a comfortable oligopoly position within the protected territory of the United States. When Baran and Sweezy wrote their classic study of *Monopoly Capitalism*, they focused very directly on this oligopolistic situation. The US labour market, James O'Connor observed around the same time, was partitioned between privileged, mainly white, workers in the monopoly sector and the underprivileged, marginalized work-ers – mainly women and people of colour – in the competitive sector.[8] But after 1971, both the auto companies and their workers had to defend themselves against German and Japanese imports followed by foreign direct investment (seeking out nonunionized labour in states like Alabama) to set up production in the US. Labour was no longer sheltered by capital controls from the threat of offshoring of production or the import of branch plants into nonunionized (so-called 'right to work') states in the US. Much the same thing happened in Britain as Margaret Thatcher favoured the arrival of the Japanese auto companies

---

8   James O'Connor, *The Fiscal Crisis of the State* (New York: St Martin's Press, 1973).

on greenfield sites at the expense of the British producers with their militant unionized labour forces.

Under the Bretton Woods system, it made sense to speak of the French, German, Italian, British, Swedish, US, Bolivian, Argentinian (and so on) working classes, because each state was insulated enough from global competition to form a space for worker organizing in trade unions as well as in social democratic political parties. In some states (for example, Sweden) the organization was strong enough to redistribute income and wealth to generate a much more egalitarian distribution of income. The collapse of the Bretton Woods arrangements and the turn of public policy towards neoliberalism and more open global competition disrupted this whole system from the mid-1970s onwards. The equalization of the rate of profit and its consequences moved centre stage thereafter.

The US used its power over the global mass of value circulation and production to induce or force, step by step, everyone else to liberate their capital markets. Margaret Thatcher obliged in 1982, and the 'big bang' unification of global stock markets occurred in 1986.[9] Financialization and the increased mobility of money capital ensured a far more targeted equalization of global profit rates from the 1980s onwards. The bias towards capital intensity (which particularly advantaged the US) solidified as a result. So did the degree of social class inequality everywhere in the world. The liberated investment funds, including those pulled in from the Gulf States as oil revenues spiked in the 1970s, were put to work all around the world as state loans that would subsequently reappear in the Third World in the form of the developing country debt crises of the 1980s.

Marx's finding on the equalization of the rate of profit goes against the Ricardian theory of mutual gains from trade through comparative advantage. Ricardo well understood that the doctrine of comparative advantage would not apply if capital was highly mobile. Marx instead proposes a theory of lopsided gains from trade under conditions of free movement of (money) capital, which explains why the insertion of an economy with low labour productivity (such as that of Greece) into a capital-intensive free trade zone (such as the euro zone led by Germany) facilitates the transfer of value from the weaker (Greek) to the stronger (German) metropolitan regions. Ricardo discovered, says

---

9 Eric Helleiner, *States and the Reemergence of Global Finance: From Bretton Woods to the 1990s* (Ithaca, NY: Cornell University Press, 1984).

Marx, 'that it is, in the last resort, trade which destroys the inborn beauties and harmonies of the capitalist mode of production. A step further, and he will perhaps discover that the one evil in capitalist production is capital itself.'[10]

This is a lesson that all contemporary economists desperately need to learn. Labour-intensive Greece in effect subsidizes capital-intensive Germany. This will come as a shock to the Germans, who are perpetually being told and doubtless feel they are being exploited by all those feckless southern Europeans who cannot be bothered to pay off their unpayable (according to the IMF) debts. In fact, OECD comparative data show that Greeks work much longer hours per week on average than do the Germans. Given the relative masses of the German and Greek economies, of course, the actual flow of value from Greece to Germany through the equalization of the profit rate will be relatively trivial for Germany, though highly significant for Greece. But the principle remains: free trade and profit equalization do not lead to convergence but to divergence in the accumulation of wealth. With the equalization of the rate of profit, all manner of interfirm, intersectoral, interstate and interregional value transfers occur, and the beauty of the whole system is this: that none of it is easily visible to the naked eye or even to the most sophisticated statistician.

As Gunnar Myrdal long ago theorized, from a rather different (Keynesian) vantage point, rich regions get richer by investing in and building comparative advantages while poor regions either stagnate or decline under conditions of free trade and profit equalization. Processes of what Myrdal called 'circular and cumulative causation' are always at work.[11] Capital is inevitably attracted to dynamic cities, sectors and regions, draining less dynamic cities, sectors and regions of their wealth, population, resources, talents and skills. Marx had long before noted this dynamic: 'Ease of commerce and the consequent acceleration in the turnover of capital … gives rise to an accelerated concentration of both the centre of production and its market. With this accelerated concentration of people and capital at given points, the concentration of these masses of capital in a few hands makes rapid progress.'[12] The startling contrast in recent neoliberal times between the increasing centralization of wealth and income and faster growth of the major metropolitan

---

10   Marx, Capital, Vol 1, p. 706.

11   Gunnar Myrdal, *Economic Theory and Underdeveloped Regions* (London: Duckworth Books, 1957).

12   Marx, *Capital*, Vol. 2, p. 328.

economies at the expense of everywhere else testifies to the power of this process. In the United States, the top dozen metropolitan regions produce most of the national GDP. States like California, New York and Massachusetts contribute far more in the way of per capita tax revenues than they receive back in federal spending. Those backward states dominated by a Republican politics antagonistic to federal state powers and interventions get back far more than they contribute to the federal budget.

The classical and later neoclassical economists anchored their arguments on the supposed neutrality and inherent fairness of perfectly functioning markets. But Marx shows (and Myrdal also showed) how the perfection of competition coupled with the equalization of the profit rate condemn all economic agents to suboptimal transactions and behaviours. The perfect competition that the neoclassicals laud to the skies actually confers, even as it simultaneously masks and conceals, class advantage to capital and the capitalists at the expense of everyone else. This is what Marx's value theory is designed to reveal. Meanwhile, individual capitalists operating in their own self-interest and seeking to maximize their profit undermine the sustainability of capital accumulation in general through their suboptimal but economically rational decision-making. Capital and the capitalists do very well, but the capitalist economy as a whole and working people do very badly.

Value transfers between economic entities such as corporations, regions and states occur by way of the equalization of the profit rate. This introduces spatiality and the forms of territorial political organization directly into the theory of accumulation, since the value transfer is from agents or institutional forms in one place to those in another. This contrasts with the falling rate and rising mass of profit, which is usually specified in purely temporal terms, even though the spatial effects of the increasing mass (for example, the production of space and the creation of the world market) are of the greatest significance. The conjoining of the falling rate/rising mass and the equalization of the profit rate creates a distinctive spatio-temporal frame within which the laws of motion of capital operate through the production of uneven geographical development. This is a matter to which we will later return.

Open and free access to technology for all, coupled with widespread knowledge, is a necessary precondition for a fairer trade regime. But the world is moving towards technological protectionism and centralization through the imposition of intellectual property rights, particularly when patents impede the sharing of knowledge in free markets, with

distinctive class effects. When human knowledge, which has traditionally been a part of the global commons available to all without
restriction, is encased within private property rights, it solidifies a key
distinction between manual and mental labour. This, it turns out, is a
covert basis not only for class rule but also for class formation. If the
'capitalist communism' that arises with the equalization of the rate of
profit is to prevail, it requires differential development of the global
labour force into high-tech and highly skilled labour, on the one hand,
and routine industrial and service labour, on the other. As Alfred Sohn-
Rethel puts it:

> The division between head and hand, and particularly in relation to
> science and technology, has an importance for bourgeois class rule as
> vital as that of the private ownership of the means of production. It is
> only too evident in many of the socialist countries today that one can
> abolish property rights and still not be rid of class. The class antagonism
> of capital and labour is linked intrinsically with the division of head and
> hand. But the connection is hidden to consciousness.[13]

This was, almost certainly, one of the motivations behind Mao
launching the Cultural Revolution: The educated and technologically
sophisticated elites within the Communist Party were taking control over
the manual workers and the peasantry in a way that looked dangerously
close to the reinstatement of class rule. That threat has not gone away.

The distinction between manual and mental labour as a marker of
class power is a bit too crude to capture the situation in the advanced
capitalist countries. Robert Reich, for example, thinks the key distinction in our own times is between those with symbolic and analytical
skills versus the toiling masses trained for routine and repetitive tasks
in both services and manufacturing. The whole structure of access to
learning in advanced capitalism revolves around perpetuating this class
distinction. Political elites have learned over the years that there is an
inevitable threat to their power when open access to higher education
produces a mass of educated graduating students without adequate job
opportunities. This, from Bangkok and Mexico City to Paris and Chicago
was the lesson of the '68 movement. There is an echo of this in contemporary China, where an increasingly educated labour force has difficulty

---

13   Alfred Sohn-Rethel, *Intellectual and Manual Labor: A Critique of Epistemology*
(Chicago: Haymarket Books, 2021).

of realizing its expectations in the labour market. The remedy: Ration access to higher education to the upper classes, subsume the content of that education within a corporatist, entrepreneurial and neoliberal ethic and ensure a supply of debt-encumbered and compliant supplicants for corporate jobs.

But the distinction between those with mental and manual skills is not set in stone. One of the historical strengths of capital is to be open to and foster upward mobility. This brings new cohorts of fresh recruits into the upper classes. The acquisition of symbolic and analytic skills through (debt-encumbered) education is one path to such upward mobility. The dominant structure of class-based higher education rations access to knowledge at the same time as it centralizes talent in the research universities or in corporate research labs typically located in or around capital-rich and knowledge-intensive metropolitan cities and regions. It is a vehicle for the reproduction and perpetuation for a certain structure of class rule in alignment with the capital-intensity bias that comes with the equalization of the rate of profit on the world stage. Increasingly centralized control over the media likewise limits public access to critical forms of knowledge production, even as social media and internet technologies create the illusion of decentralization of individual expression. This is one of the most beautiful examples of the rule that the best way to assure increasingly centralized power is through dispersal and decentralization. Individualistic and dispersed peer-to-peer computing activities, for example, contributed mightily to Google's current monopoly power.

The effect is to accentuate rather than counteract the increasing centralization of privilege, knowledge, expertise, wealth and power in ways that parallel the prioritizing of capital-intensive forms of economy in the privileged regions of the global economy. All manner of key institutions, be they in the state or in civil society, are subject to the gravitational attractions of the masses of capital and mental power controlled by the ruling classes in select locations (such as Silicon Valley). As public funding declines year by year for the world's major universities and cultural institutions, it is replaced by donations and grants from the ultra-rich and the major corporations, many of whom closely monitor the forms of knowledge and topics of enquiry that are permissible, remunerative and worthy of their support. While the Gates Foundation advertises its investments as dedicated to the future health and well-being of all humanity, for example, it simultaneously backs biomedical engineering breakthroughs that are protected by private intellectual property rights. The Koch brothers provide generous patronage for curative cancer research but militantly reject all forms of state environmental and occupational health protections that might control the use of the carcinogens their chemical industries introduce into the environment.

Capital-intensive bias in the history of technological innovation and diffusion thus accentuates the transfer of value from labour-intensive to capital-intensive firms, sectors and regional economies. Technological possibilities that contribute to social well-being, public health or public advancements in education and communication for the least well off tend to languish. None of this has to be part of any conscious plan. But if the benefits of technological dynamism predominantly started flowing in the other direction – towards benefiting low-paid manual labour or impoverished populations – then almost certainly capital and capitalist philanthropy would take corrective action to advantage the domain of oligarchic power where 'by natural right' it belongs. As things stand, business schools flourish while flourishing schools of labour organization are almost non-existent.

We also encounter here the associated effects of the migrations (both forced or induced) of those who are bearers of knowledge and expertise towards the main centres of research and innovation. The German rocket scientists were taken wholesale to Cape Canaveral and Huntsville, Alabama, after the end of the Second World War and became key parts of the US space programme which, during the 1960s, anchored one US path towards high-tech innovation. The flood of Russian scientists who migrated to the US after the collapse of the Soviet Union, while software engineers educated and trained in India populate US workplaces from Apple to Google to Walmart. Medical personnel educated from around the world dominate in metropolitan hospitals and health care. At the other end of the scale, we see the migration from Greece and Puerto Rico of many of those who are talented and educated because of the loss of employment opportunities on their home turf. In these matters, even marginal differences can have substantial effects. Britain offers a weak challenge to US and Chinese dominance in AI, but even those British scientists who have excelled in some area such as quantum computing end up moving to Silicon Valley rather than staying in Britain, given the inducements on offer. The difficulties of maintaining an equal geographical status in the distribution of talent and knowledge are formidable. 'Brain drains' have been a major feature in global reconfigurations of technological competitive advantage and know-how. The bias towards capital intensity in the equalization of the profit rate accentuates the powers of agglomeration and centralization of capital in ways that affect divisions of labour and the production of knowledge-based and mental skills.

7

Masses in Motion

The increasingly 'monstrous mass' (as Marx even in his day called it) of value and surplus value in circulation, along with the increasing physical mass of use values required for the reproduction of capital, ought to be in the forefront of contemporary concerns. It is this ever-increasing mass of 'everything' that threatens to exhaust possibilities for endlessly accumulating capital. Stresses and cracks in the fabric of this continuous expansionism of value and of physical material product spark periodic crises. The rising mass seriously compromises the very existence of humanity's already tenuous lifestyle, if not humanity itself, on Planet Earth. If there are global harms strongly in evidence – environmental, social and political – one of the prime engines of such harms surely lies with problems deriving from the rising mass of values and surplus values that have nowhere profitable to go. And this rising mass cannot be reversed, given the way the laws of motion of capital are structured: 'As the capitalist mode of production develops the rate of profit falls, while the mass of profit rises together with the growth of the mass of the functioning capital.'[1]

Consider the following bullet points simply to illustrate the dimensions of the problem.

- World Bank estimates of global GDP, adjusted to constant 2011 dollars, are $9.25 trillion in 1950, rising to $34.7 trillion in 1980, $63.1 trillion by 2000 and $94.9 trillion by 2011 – a more than tenfold increase since 1950 (Figure 6). How can such a compounding rate of

---

1   Marx, *Economic Manuscript of 1864–1865*, p. 357.

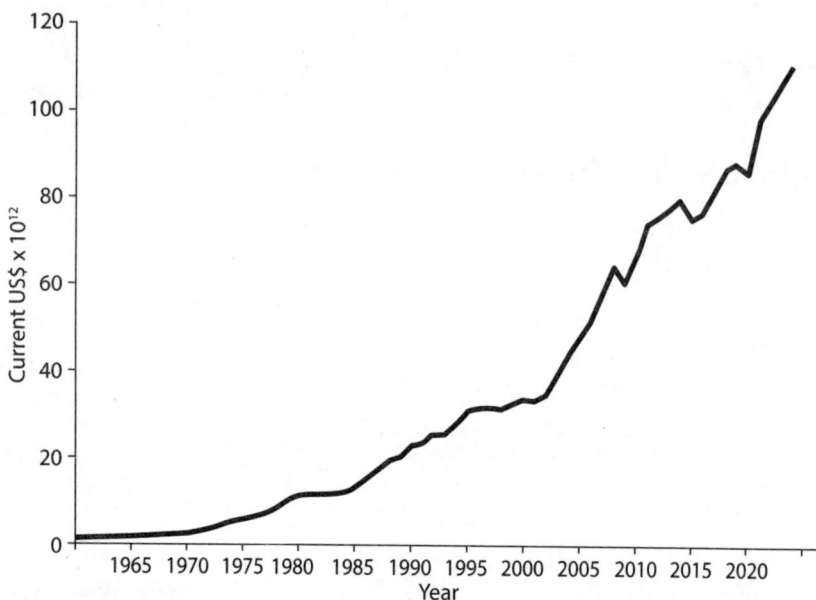

Figure 6. Global GDP Since 1960

growth be sustained into the future? Furthermore, in 1980 about 10 per cent of global GDP involved exports but that had risen (before the Covid pandemic struck) to around a quarter by 2019. Can that expansion in supply chains be resumed? And what dangers attach from a return to protectionism and autarky of the sort that proved so damaging to the world economy in the inter-war years?

- The capital value of Apple, the world's largest corporation, topped $3 trillion in 2022.[2] Elon Musk's personal wealth increased from $25 billion to $150 billion during the pandemic.[3] This is just the tip of the iceberg of astonishing centralization of wealth and power in a few hands (both private and corporate). The world's central bankers injected $9 trillion into economies to counteract Covid-19. Most of this ended up in the pockets of ultrarich oligarchs. The total wealth of billionaires worldwide rose by $5 trillion, expanding from $8 trillion to $13 trillion in twelve months. The world's wealthiest 1 per cent took 38 per cent of all additional wealth accumulated since the mid-1990s, and the global population of billionaires rose

---

2   Michael Liedtke, 'Apple Is Now the First Public Company to Be Valued at $3 Trillion', Associated Press, 20 June 2023.

3   Chuck Collins, 'U.S. Billionaires Got 62 Percent Richer During Pandemic', Institute for Policy Studies, 24 August 2021.

Global CO² atmospheric vs annual emissions

420 CO² ppm	40 CO¹ gigatons
400 CO² ppm	35 CO² gigatons
380 CO² ppm	30 CO⁴ gigatons
360 CO³ ppm	25 CO⁷ gigatons
340 CO² ppm	20 CO³ gigatons
320 CO³ ppm	15 CO³ gigatons
300 CO² ppm	10 CO² gigatons
280 CO² ppm	5 CO² gigatons
0 CO² ppm	0 CO² gigatons

1750 1780 1810 1840 1870 1900 1930 1960 1990 2020

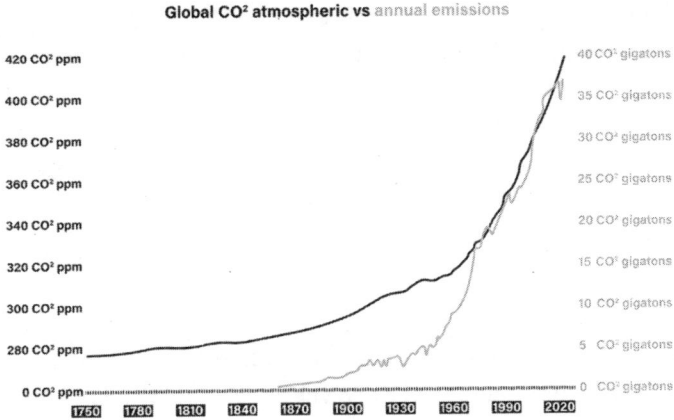

Figure 7. Global Atmospheric Carbon Dioxide Emissions Since 1880

more than fivefold (with significant numbers in China and India). Just 2 per cent of the increase in wealth after the mid-1990s went to the bottom 50 per cent.[4]

- For the last 800,000 years concentrations of carbon dioxide gas in the atmosphere had never been greater than 300 parts per million. Since 1960 CO_2 has risen continuously through expanding fossil fuel use to circa 430 parts per million in 2021 (Figure 7). The result has been a strong uptick in global warming and sea level rise, with attendant climatic and biological disruptions. While the continuing rate of emissions of greenhouse gasses is a serious problem, the mass of CO_2 already in the atmosphere is now more than enough to cause major disruptions over the next three decades without any further additions (the Antarctic and Greenland ice masses could well disappear, with catastrophic consequences for human habitats). Recent research shows that the snowpack in the Himalayas is disappearing at an alarming rate, which will turn the Indus and Ganges rivers into seasonal rivers and result in water deprivation on the whole Indian subcontinent (with more than 2 billion people affected).[5]

- The output of plastics has grown at a compound rate above 8 per cent per annum since the 1950s. Eighty per cent of the cumulative

---

4   Ruchir Sharma, 'The Billionaire Boom: How the Super-Rich Soaked Up Covid Cash', *Financial Times*, 14 May 2021.

5   Delger Erdenesanaa, 'Himalayan Glacier Loss Speeding Up, New Report Finds', *New York Times*, 19 June 2023.

output of plastics since then (some 8,000 million tons) now lies in landfills, in the oceans or in the atmosphere as microplastic polymers produced by plastic decomposition with exposure to sunlight (with unknown health effects).[6] Much of the world's potable water is now delivered in plastic containers to protect against contamination. The massive wastes produced not only in the plastics and electronics industries but also in textiles and clothing (where fast fashion prevails) is a serious environmental threat (for example, huge amounts of surplus clothing dumped in the Atacama Desert or on Ghana's beaches).[7]

- Between 2011 and 2013, China consumed 6.6 gigatons of cement – a major source of greenhouse gasses – while the US had consumed 4.5 gigatons over the last 100 years (Figure 8).[8] During those two years, China led the world in economic growth, thus saving the world from economic recession partly by spreading cement everywhere in a massive infrastructure construction boom unparalleled in human history.

- The number of international airline trips increased from 1.2 billion in 1980 to 4.6 billion in 2019 (before being briefly reduced by the pandemic). Tourism, a far cry from auto manufacture, is now a major sector for capital accumulation (Figure 9).

- The International Monetary Fund often complains at the surpluses of liquidity sloshing around in the world's money markets (Figure 14). The rising mass of money seeking opportunities for 'productive' investment is harder and harder to accommodate, prompting the suspicion that much of it is going to unproductive activity (for example, military) or rentier-type extractions.

- Finally, the upfront costs of setting up contemporary critical production systems have skyrocketed. Building a plant fabricating computer chips such as Intel in the US or TSMC in Taiwan takes an initial investment of billions of dollars. Analysts estimate that next generation of 2 nanometre chips will cost 50 per cent more to produce than current chips, with an estimated $28 billion cost for

6   Roland Geyer, Jenna R. Jambeck and Kara Lavender Law, 'Production, Use, and Fate of All Plastics Ever Made', *Science Advances* 3:7 (19 July 2017).

7   Francis Kokutse, 'Clothing Castoffs from the West Are Piling Up and Polluting Africa's Environment', *Los Angeles Times*, 27 November 2024; and 'The Fast Fashion Mountain of Shame Is Real', *Los Angeles Times*, 12 September 2024.

8   Ana Swanson, 'How Did China Use More Cement between 2011 and 2013 than the US Used in the Entire 20th Century?', *Independent*, 25 March 2015.

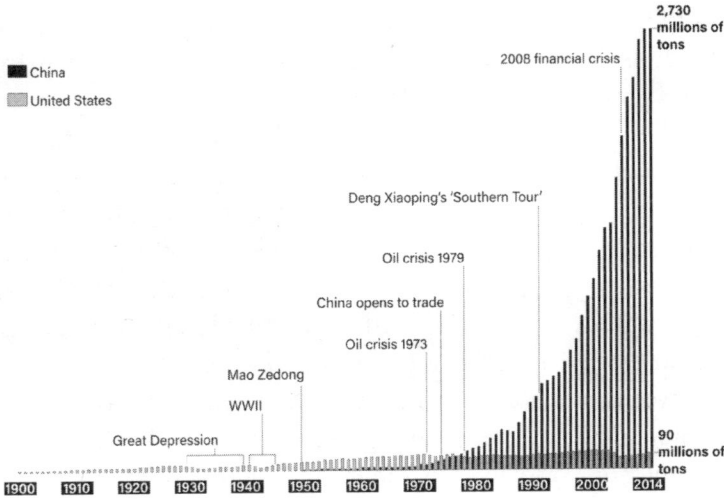

Figure 8. US versus China Cement Production Since 1900

China
United States

2008 financial crisis

2,730 millions of tons

Deng Xiaoping's 'Southern Tour'

Oil crisis 1979

China opens to trade

Oil crisis 1973

Mao Zedong

WWII

Great Depression

90 millions of tons

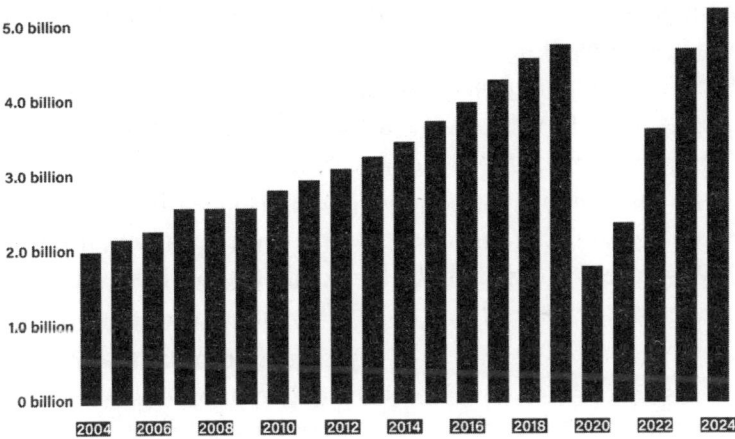

Figure 9. Number of Scheduled Airline Passengers, 2004–24

a new fabrication plant.[9] The scale that such corporations operate at has enormous implications for considering alternative forms of ownership, management and design of product under socialism.

These examples can easily be multiplied. All of them, directly or indirectly, are related to each other and all can be viewed as a product of the law of ever-increasing mass of value in circulation, no matter what the rate of profit. To seriously seek to confront or even merely regulate any

9   Anton Shilov, 'Firm Predicts It Will Cost $28 Billion to Build a 2nm Fab and $30,000 per Wafer, a 50 Percent Increase in Chipmaking Costs as Complexity Rises', *Tom's Hardware*, 22 December 2023, tomshardware.com.

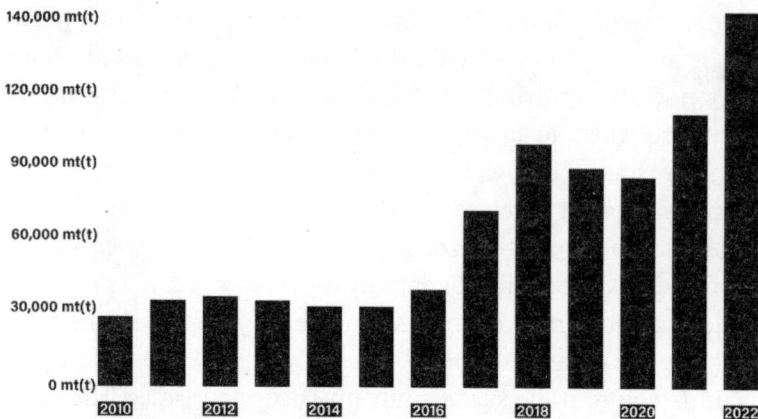

Figure 10. Global Lithium Production, 2010–22

of these masses requires taking on the process that produces them. And that underlying process is the double-edged law of the falling rate and rising mass of profit. But, in the same way that it is possible to analyze the contradictions of the falling rate of profit without too much regard for the rising mass, so it is also useful to analyze the contradictions of the rising mass of profit without much regard for what is happening to the rate. The variety of examples just listed, for example, suggests that any attempt to curb a rising mass in one sphere can easily be offset by expansions elsewhere. But it is also clear that these interrelations are the source of an overwhelming dynamism. The fact that Apple has grown so large is explained by the astonishing profitability and rapid expansion of chipmakers such as TSMC and Nvidia in relation to world demand. These, in turn, impart strong (usually debt-financed) expansionary impulses to the increasing extraction of raw materials (lithium, cobalt, rare earth metals) from the earth (Figure 10). The increasing fungibility and fluidity of unbridled money capital allows rapid reallocations of surplus capital from one sector or region of the world to another in an instant (the premier Taiwanese chipmaker, TSMC, given the potential threat of a Chinese takeover of Taiwan, is building plants in Japan, the US and possibly Germany). As a result, the world is now increasingly engulfed in an indigestible mass of physical output and of surplus value flowing down myriad interlinked channels that cross borders and pile up all over the place with consummate ease.

Masses can be mobilized and can perform as a political and economic instrument. This should not be surprising. When a mass exists in the money form, it is a claim on future labour and that means it is also a critical source and measure of economic power. Jeff Bezos founded

Amazon in 1994. He saw an opening in the emergent field of logistics, in which the aim was to rationalize distribution and create efficiencies of circulation while capturing valuable data on individual customer needs and desires sufficient to anticipate as well as shape consumer preferences. His company started in 1994 but did not make a profit until 2001. During these seven nonprofit years – coincidentally, those of the speculative 'dot-com' boom of the 1990s – Bezos kept both the hope of success and the confidence of investors alive by rapidly increasing the mass of turnover, the scale of his business enterprise and the spread of his distribution network. Faced with the choice between chasing growth of the mass or maximizing profit, he successfully pursued the former. The dot-com crash of 2001 brought down quite a few speculative ventures, which is why Amazon's declaration of a profit (however small) in 2001 was so symbolically important. To the extent that Bezos was selling change of location (productive labour in Marx's view), his enterprise created value. But his pathway to profitability lay through the increasing mass, which later anchored Amazon's rising monopoly power in the world market. Amazon turned to trafficking in information just as much as it trafficked in the exchange of things. By 2010, Amazon was big enough to have left behind the coercive laws of competition and to enjoy the privileges of oligopoly and monopoly pricing. Bezos had obeyed the first law of capital's political economy, as Marx defined it, by producing as much mass of surplus value as possible regardless of the rate of profit.

A more egregious example of how access to the mass can be used economically is George Soros's speculation that 'broke the Bank of England'. In the early 1990s, with the creation of the euro in mind, the EU states coordinated their currency movements to operate within a narrow band to facilitate cross-border trade. But the British pound was persistently trading at its lower bound within the Exchange Rate Mechanism (ERM), and the suspicion grew that it was overvalued. In stepped Soros with his Quantum Fund. He bought up as many pounds as he could and converted them into Deutschmarks. This put downward pressure on the pound. He then borrowed as many more pounds (billions) as he could to convert into marks.

Soros's unique power was almost unlimited access to a mass of borrowed funds secured by the mass of assets in his Quantum Fund. The British government had to use its foreign exchange reserves to buy pounds to keep within the ERM in the face of Soros's assault. After a few days, these reserves were exhausted, so the British government raised interest rates, hoping that the gap in interest rates between Germany and the UK would be large enough to attract investors to buy pounds. It did not work, and the pound had to be devalued. Soros converted his marks back into pounds at the new and very favourable rate, returned the funds he had borrowed to the banks, plus some interest for the few days he had borrowed pounds, and took a net profit of at least a £1 billion. Most people do not have access to the mass in this way, of course. Soros got a huge return for ten days' work, and in the process produced absolutely nothing of real value except an almighty headache for the British government.

Empirical evidence suggests that declining profits are far less likely to result in bankruptcy when there is a large mass. Many corporations strive to become too big to fail and not a few succeed. This is what kept Boeing alive after the catastrophic losses deriving from the two fatal crashes of its new line of aircraft, the 737 Max, in 2018 and 2019, followed by further problems in 2024.[10] The hegemonic position of the United States in the world after 1945 was founded on its superior economic mass (rather than its rate of growth). China's challenge lies in increasing its economic mass by a high, though now declining, rate of growth on an ever-increasing mass. It is now seen as the world's second most important and powerful economy because of its mass.

The last part of the manuscript version of Marx's chapter on the falling rate of profit takes up some of the issues created by the rising mass of value and of product. Engels called these 'Contradictions within the Law', but the proper title should have been 'Contradictions of the Rising Mass'. Issues of overproduction, underconsumption, overaccumulation and a 'plethora' of capital periodically plague capital accumulation because the rising mass gets out of control.[11] In bourgeois political economy, these questions are rendered irrelevant, given the blind faith in Say's Law, where supply automatically creates its own demand. But, for Marx, the question of the demand–supply relation is deeply problematic (as it was for Malthus, Sismondi and a smattering of other 'general glut' theorists and much later Keynes and Kalecki in the 1930s). Demand and supply, said Marx, explain nothing. They simply coordinate the laws of motion of capital, which require a completely different mode of analysis.

Capital, with its mandate to pursue surplus value at all costs, is perpetually seeking to 'go beyond'. Marx recognizes, of course, that the production of the mass is limited by the available labour force (a

10   David Gelles, 'Boeing 737 Max: What's Happened After the 2 Deadly Crashes', *New York Times*, 28 October 2019.
11   Marx, *Economic Manuscript of 1864–1865*, p. 360.

matter we have already considered). The production of surplus value is, as always, 'the immediate purpose and the determining motive of capitalist production'.[12] But, Marx now interjects, it is only 'the first act'. It remains to be completed. The 'total products must be sold … If this does not happen, or happens only partly or at prices that are less than the price of production, then although the worker is certainly exploited, his exploitation is not realized as such for the capitalist and may involve the partial or complete loss of his capital or a merely partial realization of the surplus value that has been extorted'.[13] This confirms the point Marx makes at the very beginning of *Capital*: 'Nothing can be a value without being an object of utility. If the thing is useless, so is the labour contained in it; the labour does not count as labour, and therefore creates no value'.[14] While the measure of value may, in the first instance, be socially necessary labour time, the possibility exists that much labour may be socially unnecessary and therefore valueless.

The contradictory unity between the production and realization of value moves centre stage in Marx's theorization of capital's nature. It determines his specification of capital's laws of motion and of 'becoming'. By the time we get to the end of the original manuscript on the falling rate of profit, it seems that problems of realization and of absorbing the increasing mass are just as, if not more, significant than those deriving from the falling rate of profit. Marx ends the chapter with some tentative observations on 'the plethora' of capital, overproduction of commodities and the tendency towards 'the perpetual overaccumulation of capital as a precursor to crisis formation'.[15] The presumption that the only source of crises is a falling rate of profit is here rejected in favour of overaccumulation as a potent alternative possibility.

Crises, Marx suggests, 'are never more than momentary, violent solutions for the existing contradictions, violent eruptions that re-establish the balance that has been disturbed'.[16] The balance between the production of value within the labour process and the realization of value in the market is in perpetual need of adjustment and clearly any major imbalance here will disrupt the flows within the totality of capital. Marx elsewhere has a more fulsome description:

---

12   Ibid., p. 358.
13   Ibid., p. 347.
14   Marx, *Capital*, Vol. 1, p. 131.
15   Marx, *Economic Manuscript of 1864–1865*, p. 360; and Marx, *Theories of Surplus Value*, Vol. 2, p. 468.
16   Marx, *Economic Manuscript of 1864–1865*, p. 358.

World trade crises ... as the real concentration and forcible adjustment of all the contradictions of bourgeois economy. The individual factors, which are condensed in these crises, must therefore emerge and must be described in each sphere of the bourgeois economy and, the further we advance in our examination of the latter, the more aspects of this conflict must be traced, on the one hand, and, on the other, it must be shown that its more abstract forms are recurring and are contained in the more concrete forms.[17]

The underlying balance is largely determined by the 'double-edged law' of the falling rate and rising mass, which, in turn, hinges on the contradictory relation between production and realization of surplus value (profit) within the continuous production and circulation of capital. Marx's summary statement has stunning implications. 'The market, therefore, must be extended so that its relationships and the conditions governing them assume ever more the form of a natural law independent of the producers and become ever more uncontrollable.' Supply definitely does not create its own demand, and to suppose so, Marx says, is to succumb to 'childish babble':[18]

The more productivity develops, the more it comes into contradiction with the narrow basis on which the relations of consumption rest. It is no way a contradiction, on this contradictory basis, that redundancy of capital is associated with a growing relative surplus population; for although the mass of surplus value produced would rise if these were brought together, this would equally heighten the contradiction between the conditions in which this surplus value is produced and the conditions in which it is realised.[19]

That capital so frequently produces conditions in which surpluses of capital and labour power sit side by side with seemingly no way to put them back together is thus explained:

The growing accumulation of capital involves its growing concentration. Thus, the power of capital grows, in other words the autonomy of the social conditions of production, as personified by the capitalist, is asserted more and more as against the actual producers. Capital

---

17   Marx, *Theories of Surplus Value*, Vol. 2, p. 510.
18   Ibid., p. 502.
19   Marx, *Economic Manuscript of 1864–1865*, p. 348.

shows itself more and more to be a *social power* (with the capitalist as its functionary), a power that no longer stands in any possible kind of relationship to what the work of one particular individual can create. It is instead an *alienated social power which has gained an autonomous position*, and confronts society as a thing, and as the power that the capitalist has through this thing. The contradiction between the *general social power* into which capital has developed and the *private power of the individual capitalist* over these social conditions of production develops ever more blatantly, while this development also contains the *solution to this situation*, in that it simultaneously converts the conditions of production into general, communal, social conditions.[20]

Conservative Marxists tend to dismiss any focus on realization as Keynesian which, for some reason or other, is often ruled out as illegitimate. Even to mention it is, in some Marxist circles, to depart from the scientific theory of the falling rate of profit in favour of promoting an illegitimate underconsumptionist theory of crisis formation. The rigidity of this positivist reading of Marx fails to acknowledge the importance of the rising mass (and problems of its absorption or disposal) not only in Marx's thinking but also as a compelling and ever-escalating problem in the capitalist mode of production. In the first instance, this appears as the problem of realization of value and surplus value in market exchange. While 'the production of surplus value is restricted only by the society's productive forces', the realization is restricted by the proportionality between the different branches of production and by society's power of consumption. And this is determined, as Marx shows in the *Grundrisse*, neither by the absolute power of production nor by the absolute power of consumption but rather 'by the power of consumption on the basis of antagonistic conditions of distribution, which reduce the consumption of those who form the bedrock of society' (that is, the working class) 'to a minimal level, restricted within more or less narrow limits'.[21] While individual capitalists may seek to drive wages down, they look to everyone else to raise wages and thereby promote a vibrant effective demand for their own products. The contradiction between the drive to exploit labour power up to the hilt while cultivating an adequate consumption capacity of the working class is everywhere in evidence. In extremis, 'a development of the productive forces that would reduce the absolute number of workers, thus enabling the whole nation to accomplish its

---

20   Ibid., p. 372 (emphasis in original).
21   Ibid., p. 347.

entire production in a shorter period of time, would produce a revolution, because it would deprive the majority of the population of its income', and also of its purchasing power.[22] This would be revolution by underconsumption!

Production and realization dance to the beat of different drummers. 'The conditions of realisation are affected by the division between final consumption and productive consumption (new investments).' The demand arising out of investment and reinvestment in production is stimulated by the 'constant revolutions in the methods of production themselves, from the depreciation of the existing capital which is always associated with this, from the general competitive struggle and the necessity to improve production and extend its scale, "on pain of death", merely as a means of self-preservation'. The production of new means of production is a key component in the drive to expand the mass of capital. The expansion of final consumption, on the other hand, requires that the market must 'continually be extended, so that its relationships and the conditions governing them assume ever more the form of a natural law independent of the producers and become ever more uncontrollable'.[23]

This uncontrollability is cause for concern if not for alarm. While classical political economy could aspire for capitalists to manage and control capital in motion it now transpires that the uncontrollable laws of motion control *them*.

The increasing massification of capital, quite independent of shifts in rates of exploitation or rates of growth, is a major feature of capital's history. A rising mass depends on constantly revolutionizing wants, needs and desires in human populations. It entails perpetual revolutions in the qualities of daily life and the manufacture of a culture of mass consumerism that envelops everyone in its net of engagements, desires and requirements. Early on, even in the *Communist Manifesto*, it was recognized that all of this would entail the creation of a world market and that some movement towards what is often referred to as globalization would be needed to accommodate the increasing mass of capital accumulation in commodity form. By the time Marx was writing the *Grundrisse*, he had understood the consequences of a rising mass of commodity output for the world of consumption. The production of relative surplus value 'requires the production of new consumption; requires that the consuming circle within circulation expands as did the

---

22   Ibid., pp. 371–2.
23   Ibid., pp. 347–8.

productive circle previously. Firstly quantitative expansion of existing consumption; secondly: creation of new needs by propagating existing ones in a wide circle; *thirdly*: production of *new* needs and discovery and creation of new needs and discovery and creation of new use values.'[24] The drive towards mass consumption is given within the nature of capital's drive for mass production.

This drive for mass consumption has been revolutionized over the past forty years of unbridled consumerism. In the nineteenth century, final consumers in Britain accounted for around 35 per cent of economic activity, as was also the case in China during the 1980s. In the US, final consumption now accounts for close to 70 per cent of the economy and China is rapidly catching up. Indices of consumer confidence are closely watched in the business press, since they often presage economic booms or the onset of recessions. Even Marx accepted that consumption can sometimes incentivize production, just as production creates new conditions of consumption. The typical working-class household in his time was poorly equipped with consumer durables. At the most, it would have had a kitchen range fired by wood, coal or charcoal, a few pots and pans, a table, some chairs, elementary cutlery and crockery, oil lamps and bedding. Households of this sort can still be found in much of the developing world, but in high-income countries the range of consumer durables in a working-class home is huge by comparison: stoves, refrigerators, dishwashers, washing machines, cooking equipment, coffee makers, vacuum cleaners, bedding, TV and radio, digital devices, often a car, with growing rates of home ownership. Electricity, gas, piped water and adequate sewage disposal are standard. All this constitutes an enormous and ever-growing market for surplus product.

When Marx addressed the prospects for invention becoming a business, he did not foresee the degree to which innovation would be oriented to the creation of new product lines, new needs and desires – even whole lifestyles, such as that of the suburban nuclear family or the gay ghetto. It is this that has helped make final consumer demand the chief driver of the economy in high-income countries. The governor of the San Francisco Federal Reserve Bank once commented that the US typically gets out of crises by building houses and filling them with things. Consumer durables make the consumption fund a vital core of capital's expansion, supported by a falling rate of interest on consumer loans: Since 1980, US interest rates have fallen from 15 per cent to under 2 per

---

24 Marx, *Grundrisse*, p. 408 (emphasis in the original).

cent. Only recently (post-Covid) have they risen above 4 per cent. Capitalist production also aims to support consumption rates by building in as much short-termism and planned obsolescence as possible, as with out-of-date and failing mobile phones and laptops. If capital produced only use values that lasted over a hundred years – like my grandmother's knives and forks, made in Sheffield in the 1890s, which I still use – its market would be sluggish in the extreme, making exponential growth impossible.

There has also been phenomenal growth in recent times in forms of consumerism where the commodity is not a thing, but an experience, instantaneously consumed. This, on the surface, seems to propose a mode of consumption that is far less demanding and more environmentally friendly than the making of things such as automobiles or even bicycles. Culture, sport and other events have been created or appropriated and monetized by capital, with online cultural consumption flourishing during the pandemic. Before the Covid pandemic, international tourism had expanded dramatically as a global industry – cross-border trips rose from 800 million in 2008 to 1.4 billion in 2023 (Figure 9).[25] Instantaneous consumption of this sort (the reduction of turnover time of actual consumption to almost nothing) requires, however, large-scale investment in physical infrastructure – airports, planes, cruise ships, ports, highways, hotels, stadia – as well as myriad cultural institutions: art galleries, concert halls, sports arenas, gardens and restaurants. The Netflix economy requires serious ancillary investments, both upstream in the production of a TV series and downstream in the transmission towers and the reception equipment (TV screens and household electronics), all of which gets monetized, monopolized and capitalized by the streaming organizations. Cruise liners, to cite another field of rapidly growing experiential consumerism, employ a lot of labour and entail vast investments in fixed capital, including that independent of the cruise company (for example, ports and harbours). While experiential capitalism in itself makes few direct demands on raw materials and other environmental goods, it entails the creation of massive infrastructure and a huge labour force (like the massive migrant labour force mobilized to build the stadia for the World Cup in Qatar in 2022) to cater to consumers' needs, while their destructive social and ecological consequences have provoked anti-tourism movements from Venice and Barcelona to Machu Picchu. These

25   World Tourism Organization, 'International Tourism Highlights, 2019 Edition', e-unwto.org.

negative externalities, particularly the impact on the environment, indicate potential barriers to the profitable realization of the surplus value by such means.

While Marx could not have possibly imagined the immense mass and scale of today's consumerism, nor anticipated the role of consumers in powering growth and defining lifestyles by their choices, his prescient language points to a directionality in capital's historical geography that makes such outcomes plausible and possible. 'As soon as the general conditions of production appropriate to large-scale industry have been established, this mode of production acquires an elasticity, a capacity for sudden extension by leaps and bounds, which comes up against no barriers but those presented by the availability of raw materials and the extent of sales outlets.'[26]

Mass production, most prominently represented in Marx's time by the Manchester system, generated a rapidly expanding demand for raw materials and intensified the violence of extractivism back down the supply chain, putting immense pressure on raw material producers all around the world. Mass production had also to be paralleled by mass consumption to absorb the increasing quantities of products. This meant the mobilization of the wage labour force to function as final consumers or reconfigurations of lifestyle and rising per capita incomes for significant segments of the population (such as a rising middle class). This also meant creating the world market. 'The need of a constantly expanding market for its products chases the bourgeoisie over the entire surface of the globe. It must nestle everywhere, settle everywhere, establish connections everywhere.'[27] This expansionary process refracts back on production in the main centres of capitalist development. This is spelled out in the *Communist Manifesto*:

> All old-established national industries have been destroyed or are daily being destroyed. They are dislodged by new industries, whose introduction becomes a life and death question for all civilized nations, by industries that no longer work up indigenous raw material, but raw material drawn from the remotest zones; industries whose products are consumed, not only at home, but in every quarter of the globe. In place of the old wants, satisfied by the productions of the country, we find new wants, requiring for their satisfaction the products of distant

26   Marx, *Capital*, Vol. 1, p. 579.
27   Marx and Engels, *Communist Manifesto*, p. 38.

lands and climes. In place of the old local and national seclusion and self-sufficiency, we have intercourse in every direction, universal inter-dependence of nations.[28]

What we now refer to as 'globalization' had its roots in capital's development long ago.

But we find a significant complication: 'The conditions for immediate exploitation and for the realisation of that exploitation are not identical. Not only are they separate in time and place, they are also conceptually separate.'[29] Apple computers and iPhones designed in California are assembled in Shenzhen, China, by Foxconn from parts that come from firms located all over the world. Much of the value and surplus value is realized by Apple through sales in North American and European markets. But the value is produced not only in China but all around the world. The *Financial Times* reports that Foxconn, the principle direct producer, has a profit rate of some 3 per cent while Apple, the designer and merchant capitalist, gets more than 25 per cent. But, with 1.5 million workers employed throughout China, Foxconn commands a rapidly expanding mass of capital while producing massive quantities of surplus value even though its reported rate of monetary profit is low. Foxconn produces (along with its suppliers) the value and surplus value by employing a huge mass of workers.

Apple uses a far smaller labour force to realize and appropriate much of the surplus value produced by Foxconn and others. But almost a third of Apple's market lies in China and, in recent times, that market has become unstable, in part because of competition from Chinese producers like Huawei. Apple's stock market valuation was hit badly in early 2019 when anti-US sentiment in China led to a semi-boycott of Apple products. Its capacity to appropriate surplus value in China fell and Apple's stock market valuation on Wall Street temporarily plunged. The value transfers produced through the equalization of the rate of profit are here supplemented by the divergent powers to realize and appropriate the surplus value relative to the firms, sectors and regions which organize the production of that surplus value. It is still the case that China produces far more surplus value than it appropriates, while the US appropriates far more than it produces. And this all occurs over and beyond the regional and sectoral inequalities visited on the trading world by the equalization

---

28 Ibid., pp. 38–9.
29 Marx, *Economic Manuscript of 1864–1865*, p. 347.

of the rate of profit. All of which 'heighten[s] the contradiction between the conditions in which surplus value is produced and the conditions in which it is realised'.[30]

There are further complications with respect to the organization and spreading importance of productive consumption as a distinctive field of realization of capital value. 'As the profit rate falls', Marx observes, so 'the capital minimum' for investment in search of a rising mass grows. 'This minimum is the level of concentration of the means of production in the hands of the individual capitalist' seeking to employ more labour and increase the mass in spite of the falling rate. This minimum (as shown in the case of computer chip production mentioned earlier) necessarily has to increase in pursuit of an ever-increasing mass. 'The result is increased concentration and centralization of capital', which feeds off the way 'a large capital with a lower rate of profit accumulates more quickly than a small capital with a higher rate of profit'. The credit system, which we will examine in detail later, is the main lever powering what Marx in Volume 1 of *Capital* calls 'the law of the increasing centralization of capital'.[31] In our own times, the astonishing speed of capital centralization in the high-tech sector (Facebook, Apple, Amazon, Netflix and Google – the FAANGs as they are called in the US) illustrates this tendency. The stock market valuation of Netflix, as in the earlier case of Amazon, is tied to its procurement of new subscribers (increasing the mass) rather than to its rate of profit. When its subscriptions tailed off, Netflix got into serious financial difficulties and its stock market valuation tanked. Chinese banks, it is said, are interested only in the mass of assets they control rather than profitability. Not surprisingly, the four largest banks in the world by far are Chinese, and this in spite of the fact that conventional banking was suspended in China during the Cultural Revolution. The tendency towards greater and greater centralization of the mass of value is inevitable, Marx argues, even though there are some strong counter-currents of dispersal and decentralization. State legislation curbing the powers of cartels and monopolies in the economy recognizes that there is a potential problem of excessive centralization. But weak enforcement suggests that centralizing capital still rules supreme.

The centralization of capital is often accomplished at the expense of the smaller producers, which in turn 'produces a new fall in the rate of profit' at the same time as it produces 'a plethora' of capital facing difficulty in

---

30 Ibid., p. 348.
31 Marx, *Capital*, Vol. 1, Chapter 25, Section 2, pp. 772–81.

finding productive outlets for investment. The latter condition 'arises from the same causes that stimulate the production of a relative surplus population'. This produces the signal sign of a crisis of capital: 'Unoccupied capital on the one hand and an unemployed working population at the other.'[32] This was exactly the situation in the Great Depression of the 1930s. The search for relative surplus value through technological and organizational change throws workers out of work (creating technologically induced unemployment) at the same time as it puts out of business a segment of capital (the small-scale producers in particular) that can no longer compete with the large-scale producers. The sight of unemployed capital and unemployed workers side by side in the midst of obvious chronic social needs makes no sense. It is stark testimony to the fundamental irrationality of capital.

The outcome is likely to be devaluation: the forced reduction of the mass of capital in circulation through devaluation is a periodic threat to the health and vitality of the totality. To explore this requires a major structural shift in how a capitalist mode of production is conceptualized and represented. 'One part of the old capital would lose its value completely, entirely ceasing to function as capital.'[33] Which section of capital would be subject to annihilation through devaluation would depend on the competitive struggle:

> As long as everything goes well, competition acts … as a practical fraternity of the capitalist class, so that they all share in the common booty … But as soon as it is no longer a question of the division of profit, but rather of who is to bear the loss, each seeks as far as he can to restrict his own share and saddle it on someone else. For the class as a whole, the loss is unavoidable. But how much each individual member has to bear … now becomes a struggle of enemy brothers.[34]

Now follows yet another vitally important insight into Marx's theory of the capitalist mode of production: 'The opposition between the interest of each individual capitalist and that of the capitalist class as a whole now comes into its own.'[35] Individual capitalists, acting in their own self-interest, frequently behave in such a way as to collectively jeopardize the reproduction of the capitalist class. The individual interest of the

---

32   Marx, *Economic Manuscript of 1864–1865*, p. 360.
33   Ibid., p. 362.
34   Ibid.
35   Ibid.

capitalist and the class interest do not coincide. The balance between these divergent interests can only 'be restored by the annihilation of capital to a greater or lesser extent'.[36] The penchant for increasing the mass will be punctured by crises and the bloodletting will proceed, as it did in the 1930s, until a new base for renewed capital accumulation is established. That new basis was largely established through the Second World War, which is consistent with Marx's commentary that pursuit of military and warlike activities amounts to dumping value in the ocean. The continuous expansion of the 'military-industrial complex' in preparation for the potentiality of war has played an important role in the stabilization of capital accumulation since 1945. The granting of some $40 billion in aid to Ukraine in 2022–3 to fight, from the US perspective, a proxy war against Russia was largely a huge grant to the US defence industries to supply their products freely to the Ukrainian military where much of their value and use value would be destroyed.

These are the abstractions which now rule unchallenged over both alienated labour and alienated capital.

This tension between the individual and the class perspective has enormous implications. 'No capitalist voluntarily applies a new method of production, no matter how much more productive it may be or how much it may raise the rate of surplus value, if it reduces the rate of profit. But every new method of production of this kind makes commodities cheaper'.[37] And capitalists can enjoy the individual form of relative surplus value so long as it lasts while the fall in the rate of profit and the rising mass appear 'completely independent of the capitalist's will'. Individual capitalists gain mightily from the technological advantages that collectively lead to the falling rate of profit and the rising mass of value for the capitalist class.

At first glance, this appears a rather complicated argument. But the essence of it is quite simple. Bourgeois economics has never succeeded in reconciling, let alone fusing, micro-economics (the theory of the individual firm) and macro-economic growth theory. But for Marx, this is not a problem to be solved theoretically, by contorted manipulations in the realm of ideas. It is a matter of identifying the contradictory practices through which the two perspectives intersect and relate. That is the tactic Marx is pursuing here. The ephemeral and micro form of relative surplus value which individual capitalists seek produces the macro effect

36   Ibid.
37   Ibid., p. 372.

of falling profits and rising masses, 'behind the backs' as Marx liked to put it 'of the direct producers'. Marx embraces the contradiction, whereas bourgeois political economy seeks (unsuccessfully) to ignore it or, like Ricardo 'shift them off'.

There is a dialectical principle, made much of by Engels, concerning the qualitative transformation that can arise out of incremental but cumulative quantitative changes. The classic case is when water turns to ice. We cannot walk on water, but we can on ice, if the ice is thick enough. At this point in the analysis, it is useful to apply this principle to Marx's manner of theorizing. The individual behaviours that lie behind the production of relative surplus value and the rising productivity of labour produce a world of rising mass and falling rates that coalesces into situations in which the capitalist hell can all too easily freeze over to produce paroxysms of devaluation even as it permits capital to walk on water. At what point might the incremental but ineluctable quantitative growth of the mass threaten a precipitous transformation in the modalities and dynamics of a capitalist mode of production? This is the question that arises out of the way the mass of capital in the world grew from $9 trillion in 1950 to more than $100 trillion by 2023 (Figure 6). While, as we shall later see, some of that growth has been fictitious and illusory, enough of it has been material and real as to pose substantial problems for the endless capital accumulation of use values that profit-seeking posits.

Meanwhile, we have to face up to the consequences of the social as opposed to individual form taken on by the capitalist mode of production as a comprehensive system housing all manner of contradictions and powered by abstractions. The path to any socialist alternative no longer lies in the associated labourers merely supplanting the capitalist bosses. It entails a total redesign of the whole mode of production to contain the social forces and alienations that lie behind the abstractions. It is no longer possible, for example, to distinguish between productive and unproductive labour at the individual level. Its only valid measure is across the whole social organization of production within the ever-expanding totality, from copper mine to coffee table as it were. Marx, unfortunately, evades any investigation of this problem. He leaves it as an issue to bedevil subsequent attempts of future generations to go beyond Ricardian redistributive socialism (with all its limitations) to define a revolutionary path towards building an anticapitalist alternative. This means confronting the contradictions and overthrowing the power of the reigning abstractions, one of the most potent of which is the spiral form of an endlessly accumulating and endlessly centralizing mass of value.

8

The Production of Space, Time and Place

In previous chapters, we more than once encountered the geographical, spatial and temporal aspects of capital accumulation. Capital's rootedness in the historical geography of production and consumption has been duly noted along with geographical divisions of labour, such as between town and country and a wide range of other regional specializations, often resting on specific resource endowments, both naturally occurring and humanly produced. The reproduction of distinctive kinds of labour power occurs in distinctive places, in households and in neighbourhoods usually near employment opportunities. Labour and housing markets are geographically as well as socially and culturally segmented, if not segregated, though the geographical basis of these segregations is rapidly changing as remote work spreads into certain sectors of the economy. It is now possible for some employees to work in New York City and live in Mexico City, where living costs are much lower. The geographical landscape of both capital and labour has been profoundly affected by the circulation of fixed capital, particularly that of an independent kind. Much of it is embedded in the land (like highways, rail systems, ports and industrial parks) along with those aspects of consumption fund formation (such as housing, schools, hospitals and shopping malls) that are likewise embedded in the land to form a built environment for capital accumulation and social reproduction and, on occasion, for surplus capital absorption and final consumption by people in general.

Territorial forms of organization, entities such as those pioneered by the church, the state, the interstate system, administrative districts, and private property in land all shape the 'where' of capital and commodity flows and labour migrations in and across the land. Private property in land, in particular, ensures that all competition is monopolistic spatial competition because no one can build another house where I have already built mine. This modifies how the coercive laws of competition for use of land or of space more generally operate. Metropolitan concentrations result from or impinge on the accumulation of capital and the reproduction of labour power. Agglomeration economies on the ground shape the increasing geographical centralization of capital.

This is the spatially ordered world in which transfers of value from labour-intensive to capital-intensive regions or organizations occur along with interregional, interurban and interstate competition for value production and value appropriation. In the 1980s, nonunionized Southern states in the United States offered subsidies to foreign (mainly Japanese and German) automakers to locate there. This is also the world in which imperialist practice raises its ugly head to syphon off value from one part of the world to the benefit of another. A map of surplus value production in the world looks radically different from a map of surplus value realization and appropriation, even though the two maps are tied to each other (at a distance) through the underlying contradictory unity of production and realization. Furthermore, the continuous flows of capital create geographical concentrations and centralizations of power in which particular masses become 'grand attractors' for ever greater levels of centralization (for example, London and New York), until diseconomies of scale make decentralization an attractive option. The geographical centralization–decentralization tension is an integral feature of capital accumulation, both shaping and being shaped by capital's ever-accelerating motion.

The uncertain timing of value flows and turnover times makes it imperative that the spatio-temporal dynamics of capital accumulation be carefully interrogated. Regional crisis formation and fear of cross-regional contagions of the sort that occurred in 2007–8 are closely monitored by state powers as well as the business press, but, for the most part, after the fact rather than through effective pre-emptive moves. Much depends on the performance of the international institutions whose mission is nominally to impose some semblance of order on an often wildly unstable but nevertheless rules-based motion of capital across the global stage. But more often than not, these institutions are at the beck and call of the leading economic powers (the United States in particular) and leading corporations. The evolution of the geographical landscape of capital flows and social reproduction must therefore be theorized in relation to the aggregate circulation and accumulation of capital across space and time. The theory of the capitalist mode of production is thus rendered more tangible and more concrete – but much more complicated. Locational theory rests on the 'concrete abstractions' of competitive location and placemaking in a context of the circulations and migrations of capital and labour capacity in space and time. This reflects the tangible ways in which capital gets grounded, touching down in particular places in particular ways at particular times.

The outcome is an ever-evolving geographical landscape of distinctive places networked together by communication links, migratory flows and divisions of labour broken up into distinctive neighbourhoods for social reproduction, not only of labour power of distinctive qualities but also of cultural norms, collective consumption patterns and fashionable lifestyles. The country, region or even postal code of one's birth, it turns out, is a powerful predictor of future life chances for individuals as well as for capitalist firms. How, then, are we to understand the evolving geographical landscape of capital accumulation that capital produces?

Marx writes:

> The clans of the ancient states were founded on two different principles, either on ancestry or on the locality. The ancestral clans preceded the locality clans in time and are almost everywhere pushed aside by the latter. The most extreme, strictest form is the caste order, in which one is separated from the other, without the right of inter-marriage, quite different in degree of privilege, each with an exclusive, irrevocable occupation. The locality clans originally corresponded to a partition of the countryside into districts and villages.[1]

Territorialization has played a key role in the history of human social organization and continues to do so under the sign of capital. But Marx here concedes that territorial organization rests as much on clan and caste loyalties and social practices as on the dynamics of class struggle. When the state becomes a nation-state by virtue of the clan loyalties it embraces, these geographical relations become problematized within capital's mode of production.

The 'geographical moment' within the totality requires some explanation. To begin with, its dimensions have not been constant but astonishingly dynamic: 'The more developed the capital ... the greater

---

1   Marx, *Grundrisse*, p. 478.

annihilation of space by time.'² The time it took to get from Manchester to Shanghai in 1800 bears no relation to how long it takes now. But
the barriers to movement have been just as much political and social as
physical. To this day, tariffs and regulative barriers inhibit the functioning of the global marketplace that capital perpetually seeks to establish.
Consequently, as Arrighi puts it: 'The "becoming" of the modern [terri-
torial] system of rule has been closely associated with the development
of capitalism as a system of accumulation on a world scale.' But 'the
close historical tie … is just as much one of contradiction as it is one of
unity.'³ Arrighi here cites Charles Tilly: 'Capitalism and national states
grew up together and presumably depended upon each other in some
way, yet capitalists and centers of capital accumulation often offered con-
certed resistance to the extension of state power.'⁴ The latter, conversely,
sometimes blocks the former. Capitalism and territorialism 'represent
alternative strategies of state and capital formation'. Central to this understanding 'is the definition of "capitalism" and "territorialism" as opposite
modes of rule or logics of power'.⁵ There is, in Arrighi's account, a contradiction between the brute logic of state political decision-making (such
as the decision to go to war with the aim of acquiring more territory)
and the molecular, decentralized processes of capital's motion in space
and time. These two spatial logics of power are radically different from
each other. To the degree that they coexist in the same space, they are
dialectically related more often than not in deep contradiction. Arrighi
puts it this way: 'The critical feature' of the interstate system from its
very inception has been 'the constant opposition of the capitalist and
territorialist logics of power and the recurrent resolution of their contradictions through the reorganization of world political-economic space
by the leading capitalist state of the epoch. This dialectic between capitalism and territorialism' preceded the Westphalian settlement of 1648
and continues to be a foundational feature in our own times.⁶

Space and time are, of course, foundational concepts for all forms of
scientific enquiry. As Alfred North Whitehead put it many years ago: 'It
is hardly more than a pardonable exaggeration to say that the determination of the meaning of nature reduces itself principally to the discussion

---

2   Ibid., p. 539.
3   Arrighi, *Long Twentieth Century*, p. 32.
4   Charles Tilly, *Big Structures, Large Processes, Huge Comparisons* (New York:
Russell Sage, 1984), p. 140, cited in Arrighi, *Long Twentieth Century*, p. 32.
5   Arrighi, *Long Twentieth Century*, pp. 34–5.
6   Ibid., p. 36.

of the character of time and the character of space.'[7] The historical materialism that Marx advocated is no exception. One of its most intriguing aspects is the study of how capital, through its motion, produces its own distinctive spatio-temporalities, the most obvious feature of which is acceleration and speed-up in production, circulation and realization. Yet the space-time of capital remains under-studied and under-appreciated. For critical geographers, the production, reproduction and reconfiguration of capital's space and time have always been central to understanding the political economy of capital. The problem is to integrate the theory of capital as 'value in motion' with the production and reproduction of the spatio-temporal conditions that both shape and are shaped by that motion. The competitive drive, for example, to speed up turnover times and to produce the world market, both of which have frequently been invoked in relation to the falling rate of profit and rising mass of output and value, presumes the formation of a geographical landscape that can absorb the 'plethora' of 'overaccumulating' capital in timely and, if possible, profitable ways. This theme was articulated with great clarity in the *Communist Manifesto*.

But here it is important to sound a note of warning. The classical theorizations of bourgeois political economy neglect spatio-temporality for the simple reason that their a-spatial theories of supply and demand equilibrium collapse when spatial differentiations and the qualities of place and location are introduced. This poses the question: How robust is Marx's political economy when exposed to systematic spatio-temporal interrogation? One thing is certain: That the operation of capital's basic laws of motion becomes much more intricate or, as Henri Lefebvre was fond of putting it, 'complexified'. It is perhaps for this reason that Marxist economists frequently follow the example of their bourgeois brethren and ignore historical-geographical and spatio-temporal complications. The most recent book I have on Marxian economics by David Ruccio, published in 2022, does not mention space, spatiality and territorialization even once and devotes a half-page sidebar to the topic of geography.[8] The result is an economics that presumes that all economic activities occur on the head of a pin. The key question is how to square the spatio-temporal flows of capital and labour over space and time with the conceptual image of capital's geographical evolution as a

7   Alfred North Whitehead, *The Concept of Nature* (Cambridge: Cambridge University Press, 1920), p. 33, cited in David Harvey, *Justice, Nature, and the Geography of Difference* (Oxford: Blackwell, 1996), p. 248.
8   David Ruccio, *Marx's Economics: An Introduction* (Cambridge: Polity, 2022).

totality in the process of 'becoming'. Such a reading, as Lefebvre points out, 'challenges mechanistic determinist explanations of socioeconomic transformations' to focus on the dynamic movement of parts operating at different scales.[9]

This forces recognition of the spatially differentiated qualities of personal life and of social reproduction as experienced in the daily life of the labourer. These are all embedded in divergent economic, social and environmental conditions and processes operating at different scales. To be raised in the Bronx is to encounter radically different life chances than to be raised in the Upper East Side of Manhattan. While criminality can be found in both locations, the typical white-collar criminality of the Bernie Madoff sort found on the Upper East Side of New York is radically different from a Bronx-style robbery. This theoretical perspective of scalar embeddedness was rendered explicit in the formulation of the *Communist Manifesto*. There, the isolated labourer is construed individualistically before experiencing the collective life of labour in the factory, which expands to an understanding of broader social relations in an industrial city or region before confronting the national (state) and global conditions of possibilities for consciousness formation and political action ('workers of the world, unite!'). The totality is layered according to scale. While there are obvious ways in which the internal relations between different processes operating at different scales get articulated, the 'complexification' this layering produces within the totality of an ever-evolving capitalist mode of production is fascinating, even if it is hard to follow.

The answer to the question 'What is the most relevant spatio-temporal scale?' is not given by theory but by historical materialist enquiry into dominant practices. In the period from 1945 to the mid-1970s, for example, the spatio-temporal rhythms of global capitalist development mainly derived from a specific relation between different scales of capitalist activity. The primary scale of action was that of sovereign nation-states defined as autonomous entities within the United Nations and Bretton Woods frameworks, which expanded over time to accommodate new states with decolonization. Within nation-states, industrial regions and factory-level politics rested on the base of solid working-class neighbourhoods linked to large national corporations (as in the automobile industry). This configuration constituted the typical geography of what was called 'Fordism'. But this system also rested on the basis of

---

9   Lefebvre, *Critique of Everyday Life*, Vol. 2, p. 181.

imperialist and neocolonial extractions of value from the weaker peripheral economies, unable, for example, to resist the transfers implicit in
the equalization of rates of profit. But the sovereignty of the state, armed
with capital controls, protected both national capital and the respective
working classes from too much international competition. This was the
world of Baran and Sweezy's *Monopoly Capital*, Samir Amin's *Accumulation on a World Scale*, Ernest Mandel's improperly titled *Late Capitalism*
and Giovanni Arrighi's *Long Twentieth Century*.[10]

This structure was, step by step, dissolved with the neoliberal turn
from the mid-1970s on. This new geography gradually asserted the
dominance of global multinational capital, the big banks and financial
institutions resting on the work of entrepreneurial individuals. 'There is
no such thing as society', Margaret Thatcher famously proclaimed, 'only
individuals and', she later added, 'their families.' Some influential commentators in the 1990s even pronounced the end of the Bretton Woods
nation-state as a relevant institution. As previously noted, the Hegelian
Francis Fukuyama went so far as to announce the end of history in 1992
with the end of the Cold War.[11] Traditional forms of labour organization
declined, the political institutions of social democracy were decimated
and the relevance of citizenship rights at the level of the state was called
into question.[12] This stymied the political activism within the capitalist
states as realized under the Bretton Woods arrangements. The ruling
ideas were now unquestionably those of the ruling class on the world
stage, and the state increasingly behaved as the ruling committee of
the local bourgeoisie, as Marx had long before anticipated. Much now
depends on the actual mechanics of heightened spatial competition to
transfer value by way of the increasing equalization of profit rates on
the world stage. What appeared to be a fairer and more equal system
based on individual rights was in fact a superb hidden mechanism
for the transfer of value to the most technically sophisticated states
and the most powerful corporations backed by an extremely wealthy
billionaire class.

---

10   Baran and Sweezy, *Monopoly Capital*; Samir Amin, *Accumulation on a World
Scale: A Critique of the Theory of Underdevelopment* (New York: *Monthly Review* Press,
1974); Ernest Mandel, *Late Capitalism* (London: Humanities Press, 1975); Giovanni
Arrighi, *The Long Twentieth Century: Money, Power, and the Origins of Our Times*
(London: Verso, 1994).

11   Francis Fukuyama, *The End of History and the Last Man* (New York: Free Press,
1992).

12   Kenichi Ohmae, *The End of the Nation State: The Rise of Regional Economies*
(New York: Free Press, 1996).

Trade between Manchester and China once entailed trips of a year or more, whereas now it takes twelve hours by air. By the 1980s, knock-offs of the new Paris fashion designs were being produced in Hong Kong almost immediately to be available in the chain stores of London, Paris and New York a day or two later. Most recently, China has initiated a 'Belt and Road' initiative, among other things connecting Chongqing in China with Duisburg in Germany by rail, cutting by weeks the time of the journey by sea. This is what Marx called 'the annihilation of space through time.'[13] It is a basic evolutionary law dictating capital's geography. The cutting of the Suez and Panama Canals, the introduction of the steamboat and the coming of the railroads revolutionized global space relations in the nineteenth century. Containerization and air freight transportation since their introduction in the 1960s have done much the same for the latter half of the twentieth century. The fresh-cut flowers that adorn the corner stores in Manhattan each morning were cut a day or so before in the Andean regions of Colombia and Ecuador and distributed across the United States via a staging point in Miami.

The great ports for conducting trades in commodities were once places like London, Liverpool and Bristol, Antwerp, Hamburg and Rotterdam, New York, Boston and Charleston, Odesa and Buenos Aires, but these ports were abandoned after the 1960s as too small and shallow to support containerization and the rising mass of commodity flows. Their docklands almost everywhere became empty sites for real estate ventures (spectacularly so in London). We now look on the great automated container ports of Singapore, Shenzhen and Shanghai, San Diego and Elizabeth, New Jersey, Rotterdam and Hamburg (built on entirely new sites) to accommodate the vast increase in the mass of foreign trade, while organized labour on the docks has been reduced to a pale version of its former self by automation and containerization.

Innovations increasing the efficiency of spatial movement and accelerating turnover times have been hugely prominent in the history of capital for good reason. The geographical world organized around the horse and buggy morphed into a world of railroads, of the internal combustion engine, the airplane, the containership and the internet, with electronic exchange markets functioning at unthinkable speeds enabled by quantum computing. In an era when transport costs were prohibitively high, producers were protected against the coercive laws

---

13   Marx, *Grundrisse*, p. 524; Edward Chamberlain, *The Theory of Monopolistic Competition* (Cambridge, MA: Harvard University Press, 1962).

of competition. Even the local village baker and brewer were monopolists, making monopolistic competition the name of the game. With
declining transport costs, these monopolistic protections gradually
disappeared. When I was growing up in Britain in the 1950s, almost all
beer was locally brewed. You knew what town you were in by the beer
you drank. The same was true in the United States in the 1960s. If you
were drinking National Bohemian, you were in Baltimore, if Iron City
then you were in Pittsburgh and Coors meant you were in Denver. But
by the late 1960s, beer production became regionalized and, by the
1980s, imported beers suddenly appeared on the scene, so by 2000 you
could get beers from all over the world. My local bar in New York now
has over 100 microbrews from all around the world. But many of these
local breweries are being absorbed into a single financially centralized
holding company. Most of the tequilas and many of the mezcals in
Mexico are owned by PepsiCo, though you would not know it from
the diversity of their local branding, names and labels. The power and
promise of local authenticity (commanding a monopoly price as in the
wine trade with its chateaux, terroir and appellation contrôlée desig-
nations) is merged into highly centralized financialized organizations
for value appropriation.[14] This sort of geographical history has been
powerfully affected by lower transport costs (through containerization)
but also by the new techniques of packaging, preservation and mass
distribution of the product, for example, the transportability of keg
beers. But the operative tendency here is for maximum geographical
dispersal of production in the midst of maximum centralization of
financial appropriation.

The acceleration of turnover times (the shorter 'working period' for
production) and the market (accelerating 'circulation times' of the sort
that Amazon now produces) is likewise a permanent feature of capital's dynamic. Pigs are now bred to have two or even three litters a year
rather than just one. The Japanese introduction of just-in-time production systems revolutionized the auto industry worldwide after 1980. This
pioneered the way for the production of the global car, assembled out of
parts manufactured all over the world and linked through intricate commodity supply chains in which the sites for the production of value are
separated geographically from the sites for the realization and appropriation of that value. Speed-up becomes a crucial objective. Devaluation,

14   David Harvey, 'The Art of Rent: Globalization, Monopoly and the Commodification of Culture', *Socialist Register* 38: 93–110 (2002).

Marx observed, does not occur because commodities cannot be sold in the market but because they cannot be sold in time. Hence the saying 'time is money.'[15]

There are three conceptual fields we need to negotiate regarding the nature of space and time within the totality.[16] The first is that of absolute space and time. This is the space and time as understood in Newtonian physics. It is represented by Euclid's geometry in a Cartesian space. It grounds the cadastral map of private properties in land and depicts administrative territorial boundaries on the map of the world. This is as well the absolute time of the atomic clock. Space and time are considered immutable and unchanging frameworks within which entities, locations and addresses have their being and within which their history unfolds and endless capital accumulation proceeds. Each property on the map has a unique location, assuring monopoly power for the owners and monopolistic forms of competition. Physical and social action occurs within these fixed frames of space and time. Property rights in land are exclusionary, and you trespass on them at your legal peril. In upstate New York, a woman was shot dead in her car for pulling into someone's driveway by mistake.

Absolute space is the privileged form of space for setting up territorial administrative structures of government or fashioning collective modes of action. It is here that the territorialization of capital in space and time intersects most directly with social reproduction in general as well as the social reproduction of labour power. Social reproduction by way of spatial segregation is a prominent feature in every capitalist city. Indeed, all the other moments in the theory of co-evolution laid out in Chapter 9 come together here to define the qualities and forms of a particular place, spatially defined. The partitioning of education, for example, into distinctive school districts with differential resources depending on local taxation flows plays an important role in shaping social class and racial or ethnic (clan) distinctions within the reproduction of labour power not only in the United States but nearly everywhere that capital rules. Absolute spaces can be organized to exclude, protect and assert a distinctive identity as much based on the distinctive qualities of place as on some other mark of otherness and difference. The map of social reproduction qualities and quantities in the world's major cities typically depicts social distinctions in absolute space and time.

15   Marx, *Grundrisse*, p. 543.
16   David Harvey, *Social Justice and the City* (Baltimore: Johns Hopkins University Press, 1973).

Territorial rights are usually specified in absolute space and time. The cadastral map depicts both individual and collective property rights to the land and all that lies therein. For capital, that means access and rights to the foundational means of both production and consumption. Those foundational features are not static. The French term *aménagement du territoire* (the management of territory) here appears most apt. Human activity in any mode of production, including capital, seeks to construct a landscape of adequate use values to function as the constant and usually common capital of production, while providing the infrastructure for collective and individual consumption. The scale at which education is organized is different from the scale at which electricity is generated, which is different again from the scale at which housing provision, garbage disposal or sustainable ecological practices are formulated. The management of territory entails dividing up the common territory into different more or less appropriate scales of management while assembling economic and political power at those different scales depending on prevailing circumstances. The building of distinctive places for social reproduction and the creation of local and regional loyalties to the states or other territorial collectivities adds a political dimension of governance and state's rights to capital's infrastructure. In China, for example, what seems to be a highly centralized system is, in fact, decomposed into a nested hierarchy of competitive regional and local jurisdictions. How all this plays out with respect to state formation will be taken up later.

The second field is that of relative space-time. This is the space of Einstein's relativity theory and of Riemannian geometries. While distances in absolute spaces are fixed and recorded in kilometres and time is registered and measured by the swing of the pendulum, distances in relative space-time vary according to the cost and time incurred in traversing them. The fastest or cheapest way to get from A to B is not necessarily the way the legendary crow flies. Space and time are not separable as they are in the absolute conceptual field. The uniqueness of addresses (79th and Broadway) gives way before the fact that there are innumerable properties equidistant from Times Square. The continuity of the spatial field gives way to networks of accessibility (think of airline systems in which it costs as much to go from New York to Ithaca as from New York to London). Relative space-times are perpetually shifting because of technological changes in the ability to traverse space in less and less time. While it took several weeks for the news of George Washington's death in Mount Vernon in Virginia to get to Ohio, such an event would be known within minutes via cable news today. Technological dynamism in the fields of transport and communication has, therefore, been foundational for understanding how capital as a mode of production evolves with respect to its internal structures as well as in terms of the external spatio-temporal relations it may have across social formations. In the nineteenth century, trade with noncapitalist China was, as Rosa Luxemburg for one emphasized, vital to the development of capital as a mode of production in Britain.[17] The spatio-temporal dynamics of capital shifted dramatically as the internal combustion engine displaced the steam locomotive as the dominant technology governing the annihilation of space through time. Air transport and the internet have continued the periodic reshaping of relative space-times as propelled through the coercive laws of competition. Faster and more spatially nimble production systems drive out less efficient systems of value in motion. The laws of what I call time-space compression prevail. In the theory of relative space-time, the focus shifts from the study of things, events and processes in space and time to the study of the production of space-time by processes.

The third, and by far the most problematic of the spatio-temporal frames is that of relational space-time, whose primary advocate was Gottfried Leibniz in his famous correspondence with someone called Clark (a stand-in for Isaac Newton). Newton's absolute theory of space and time made it seem as if space and time preceded the existence of God, Leibniz claimed, when our actual space and time is God's choice out of an infinite set of possible space-time worlds. The secular version of this argument concerns whether capital accumulation occurs within the fixed framework of absolute space and time, or whether capital creates its own relational spatio-temporal world out of an infinite set of possible worlds. The answer, annoyingly, is that it is both. In the same way that Marx fixes the value of labour power as stable and known for purposes of theoretical enquiry, when it is in fact fluid, diverse, geographically differentiated and perpetually changing, so he works with the absolute theory of space relations in a world where multiple spatio-temporalities prevail. Biological organisms (including we humans) create their own distinctive clocks and spatio-temporal worlds. We regulate our behaviours according to socially specified clock times. As the sociologist Georg Simmel pointed out long ago, if all the clocks in Berlin were out by only one hour, the city would come to a chaotic standstill.[18]

---

17   Rosa Luxemburg, *The Accumulation of Capital*, in *The Complete Works of Rosa Luxemburg*, Volume 2, *Economic Writings 2*, eds Paul Le Blanc and Peter Hudis (London: Verso, 2016).

18   Georg Simmel, 'The Metropolis and Mental Life', in Donald N. Levine, *Georg*

Cultural representations of space and time are incredibly diverse. This is the field of quantum mechanics, whose mysteries Einstein could never fully accept since it involved what he called 'spooky action at a distance'.[19] Particles moved in coordinated fashion at seemingly infinite distances from each other without any sign of a physical communication mechanism between them. But the mathematical equations derived from this strange quantum world have always proven correct, even though the physics appears impossible. Quantum computing is now a primary tool for the sophisticated big Wall Street traders to engage with the mysteries of movements in contemporary stock markets. It seems to work well, but nobody can explain why. Value in Marx's theory is immaterial even as it has objective material consequences. Yet some sort of relationality seems to connect, for example, the value of a plot of land in Hong Kong with one in Sydney, Buenos Aires, Jakarta, Durban or New York without any market mechanism or realtor coordinating relations. There is, as it were, a rental surface of land values cast across the whole world. Everyone is affected and everyone contributes without knowing it. Like value, these social processes appear immaterial but objective in their consequences. Social and political movements, like those in 1848 and 1968, erupt in some kind of unison to echo around the world. There seems to be an underlying political zeitgeist of the moment. A concordance of senti- ments in markets worldwide can likewise occur without any tangible material process to explicate them. The turn to more authoritarian forms of governance all around the world over the last decade is not easily explained, any more than the crash of the stock market on Black Monday in 1987 has been fully explained. Is the rise of political authoritarianism we are witnessing a response to the financial crash of 2007–8? Nobody knows, but suspicions lurk. Interestingly, even bourgeois economics has, in recent times, seen fit to emphasize the importance of 'intangibles' in economic theory: reputations, expectations and anticipations along with 'market sentiments' are increasingly evoked to explain shifts in monetary valuations that otherwise seem inexplicable.

When identifying these three conceptual fields of spatio-temporality in *Social Justice and the City* back in 1973, I insisted that they not be seen as exclusionary alternatives but as three different but complementary

Simmel on Individuality and Social Forms (Chicago: Chicago University Press, 1971 [1903]).

19   Albert Einstein and Max Born, *The Born–Einstein Letters 1916–1955: Friend- ship, Politics and Physics in Uncertain Times* (London: Palgrave Macmillan, 2004). See Einstein's letter to Born dated 3 March 1947.

perspectives on the same spatio-temporal reality: 'Space is neither absolute, relative or relational in itself, but it can become one or all simultaneously depending upon the circumstances. The problem of the proper conceptualization of space is resolved through human practice with respect to it.'[20] The absolute conception of space maps most easily onto the world of use values and private property rights. Exchange relations of commodities, capital and labour primarily posit a world of relative space-times, while the immateriality of value accords most strongly with the conceptual field of relational space-time. In the same way that capital and the commodity can be understood only in terms of the unity of the three conceptions of use value, exchange value and value, so capital's spatio-temporality rests on the concordances of absolute, relative and relational space-times. The commodity, Marx's foundational concept in *Capital*, exists in absolute space and time as a use value, in relative space-time as an exchange value and in relational space-time as value.

While all of this may seem super abstract and somewhat bewildering, the practical applications are easier to understand. The contemporary form of globalization is, for example, nothing more than another round in the capitalist production and reconstruction of space and time, as initially construed in the *Communist Manifesto*. It entails a further diminution of the friction of distances, what Marx refers to as the tendency for 'the annihilation of space through time' as a fundamental law of capitalist development. This rests on yet another round of technological and organizational innovations reducing costs and times of movement to produce the law of 'time-space compression'. This entails a geographical restructuring of capital circulation and accumulation (proliferating commodity chains, deindustrialization here while opening up of new production complexes somewhere else). The production of uneven geographical development is based on capital's pursuit of some mix of accessibility and proximity to raw materials, labour supplies and market opportunities, to say nothing of the creation of physical infrastructure in the form of built environments favourable to production, circulation and consumption. This is, in turn, associated with the increasing centralization of global economic and political power, with far greater emphasis on the Pacific (and especially China) and newly industrializing regions.

There has also been a shift in the geographical scale at which capital is organized (symbolized by the growth of supra-state organizational forms

---

20   Harvey, *Social Justice and the City*, p. 13.

such as the European Union and NAFTA and more prominent roles for international institutions such as the International Monetary Fund, the World Bank, the Bank of International Settlements, the WTO and the more directly political formations such as the G7, the G20 and various military alliances and economic pacts that currently prevail). The contemporary globalization of capital has been, it can be argued, a product of these specifically geographically grounded processes. The question is not, therefore, how the globalization of capital has affected geography, but what these distinctive geographical processes of the reconstruction and reconfiguration of spatio-temporal relations have contributed to contemporary capital accumulation. Uneven geographical development driven by competitive capital continues to powerfully shape uneven development of capital circulation and accumulation.

While transport and communications technologies have played and continue to play a leading role in producing time-space compression in spatio-temporal relations, individual capitalists play an important role by way of their locational strategies. Impelled by the coercive laws of competition, firms will locate to minimize their costs of acquisition of material inputs (including land) and costs of access to markets. For some industries, such costs seem not to matter too much – for example, the cotton industry located in Marx's time in Lancashire drew its primary raw materials from far away in North America and from the Middle and Far East, while marketing its products all around the world (particularly to India). Other industries were drawn to locate either close to raw materials and suppliers of intermediate products or to markets. The industrial city was a complex form of organization of production and marketing activities in places in which processes of increasing centralization of money capital in space play an important role alongside locational forces that work to create a particular landscape of and for capital accumulation. Agglomeration economies play a significant role in shaping urbanization and the geography of production. Cities grow, as we have seen, by virtue of the momentum of their own growth. The rich regions grow richer until some limits of congestion and overaccumulation hold them back. But then new systems of delivery and consumption suddenly arise to give a new way to overcome space by time, such as that now deployed by Amazon at a huge scale and Grubhub for restaurant takeout foods. Employment in transport and communications is, in Marx's view, value producing and applies to that vast army of delivery people who service the consumption needs of the city. The ability to annihilate space through time continues to be of great significance.

The rising mass of product generates a need to absorb the 'plethora' of overaccumulating capital. When capital is in its value or money form, then the problem is to find profitable (but not necessarily productive) avenues for expansionary reinvestment. When it exists in commodity form, the problem is to find buyers in the market who have the want, need and desire for particular use values backed by ability to pay, in particular locations. This is, in short, a problem of realization.

I address one aspect of this problem by way of a theory of 'the spatial fix'.[21] This term (and the theoretical insights it anchors) needs clarification, since it has multiple meanings. One meaning of 'fix', as in the phrase 'the pole was fixed in the hole', refers to something secured in a particular location in such a way that it's difficult to move. 'Fix a problem', on the other hand, means to resolve a difficulty, for example, to 'fix the car's brakes' so it's safe to drive. To say 'the fix is in' suggests that a particular outcome is foreclosed and predetermined. This second cluster of meanings has a metaphorical derivative, as in 'the drug addict desperately needs a fix.' Once the fix is found, the need is satisfied. But the implication is that this is a temporary rather than permanent solution, since the addict's craving soon returns. Successive technological fixes have so far counteracted the Malthusian dilemma positing that population growth will always outstrip gains in productivity to produce mass impoverishment.

It is in this last sense that I use the term 'spatial fix' to describe capital's insatiable drive to resolve its inner crisis tendencies in particular regions by geographical expansion and geographical restructuring. The parallel with the idea of a technological fix is deliberate. Capital is addicted to geographical expansion, colonialism and neocolonialism, endless technological change and never-ending growth as a solution to its internal contradictions. There is therefore a long history of spatial fixes. Globalization is a systemic outcome of spatial fixes, and it has been going on since 1492 if not before. The contradictory meanings of 'fix' reveal something important about the spatial dynamics and the crisis tendencies that attach to it. The problem of fixity (in the first sense of being immovable) contradicts the competitive drive to maintain and, if possible, accelerate the motion and spatial mobility of capital. Capital, it seems, has to fix a part of itself in space (in immoveable structures of transport and communications and urban infrastructure, for example)

21   David Harvey, 'Globalization and the "Spatial Fix"', *Geographische Revue* 2 (2001): 223–30.

in order to more easily overcome spatial barriers and ensure the much-prized continuity of capital accumulation in space and time. But, after a while, infrastructure becomes outmoded and has to be superseded. Capital builds a geographical landscape adequate to its own needs at a certain point in its history, only to have to destroy that landscape (and devalue much of the capital locked up in it) at a later point in its history, in order to make way for a new, more expansionary spatial order. The spiral form is thus imprinted in the landscape of continuous accumulation. The rising mass has a technological as well as purely economic basis. The containerization in international trade that began in the 1960s was miniscule in those early years compared to the massive container vessels that now ply the oceans.

The idea of 'the spatial fix' initially came out of attempts to reconstruct Marx's theory of the geography of capital accumulation. In an essay on this topic, published in *Antipode* in 1975, I showed that Marx's fragmentary writings could be consolidated into a reasonably consistent account to theorize the spatial as well as the temporal dynamics of accumulation. Consideration of these temporal dynamics adds an extra level of complexity to the theorization of capital.[22] Debt, for example, is a claim on future labour which immediately raises the question of the time horizon of current debt contracts. The displacing and absorption of overaccumulating capital is temporal as well as spatial – it is called 'kicking the can down the road' in political circles. When debt claims might be due and the possibility of continuing to roll them over on the never-never has a huge impact on potential crisis formation. Mainstream Marxists, for the most part, preferred to ignore this problem. I later sought to deepen the argument through an examination of the relation between Hegel's views on imperialism, von Thünen's argument concerning the frontier wage (a precursor to key formulations on marginal cost pricing in neoclassical economics) and Marx's presentations on colonialism (most particularly the peculiarity of closing the first volume of *Capital* with a chapter on British colonial land policies and the theorizations of Wakefield on colonial settlement).[23]

These studies showed that (a) capital could not survive without being geographically expansionary, while perpetually seeking out

---

22   David Harvey, 'The Geography of Capitalist Accumulation: A Reconstruction of the Marxian Theory', *Antipode* 7: 3 (1975): 9–21.

23   David Harvey, 'The Spatial Fix: Hegel, Von Thünen, and Marx', *Antipode* 13: 1 (1981): 1–12, republished in David Harvey, *Spaces of Capital: Towards a Critical Geography* (London: Routledge, 2001).

spatio-temporal fixes to its internal contradictions; (b) that major innovations in transport and communication technologies were necessary
conditions for that expansion to occur (hence capital's need to annihilate space through time, supplemented by the drive to overcome spatial
barriers to the mobility of commodities, money, people, information and
ideas over space and time); and (c) its modes of geographical expansion depended crucially on what capital most lacked for its completion
and the most significant barrier to be overcome in its search to maximize the production of surplus value. It could entail the search for new
markets, for fresh labour power, for cheaper and more accessible natural
resources, for agglomeration economies or fresh cultural configurations
that could be absorbed, monetized and appropriated by capital in place.
It could also lead, as we shall later see, to the accumulation of capital to
present itself as an accumulation of debts.

Much depends on how the rising mass and the overaccumulation of
capital is manifest and the (class) forces that determine which form of
spatial fix capital will pursue. Overaccumulation, in its most virulent
form (as occurred in the 1930s, for example), is registered as surpluses
of capital and labour occurring at the same time, with seemingly no
way to put them together in productive (though not necessarily socially
useful) ways. The temptation to put them together in unproductive ways
by 'useless' investments in the built environment will be taken up later.
Failing that, the result is potentially massive devaluation of both capital
and labour (bankruptcies, idle factories and machines, unsold commodities, unemployed workers, all often concentrated in particular regions to
produce regional crises). Devaluation is usually associated with forced
monetary depreciation (asset devaluation) and even physical destruction. But there are ways to mitigate such outcomes. Herein lies the logic
of the spatial fix and its relation to the periodic devaluations of capital.
If, for example, a crisis of localized overaccumulation within a particular
region occurs, the export of its surpluses of capital and labour to some
new territory (for example, across the Atlantic) to start up new production there becomes a tempting possibility.

Marx was well aware of these tactics and the dangers involved. When,
in the nineteenth century, the British home market for steel and railway
building was satiated, Britain lent money to Argentina to build railways
with British steel and rolling stock, with British companies sometimes
doing the work. Since 2000, the Chinese market has shown signs of sat-
uration, given the country's incredible increases in output. China has,
in the last few years, extended large credits to foreign governments to

build elements of its Belt and Road Initiative across much of East Africa (chiefly railroads, ports and dams) often using Chinese construction companies employing Chinese labour and surplus Chinese product to do the work. In the late 1960s, Japanese surpluses of both money and credit began to be used more massively abroad. South Korea followed suit towards the end of the 1970s and Taiwan did so after 1982. In these latter cases, South Korean and Taiwanese companies set up production companies abroad (many in China but also in Central America, Southeast Asia and Africa) producing consumer goods (particularly clothing and textiles) for North American and European markets.

The circulation of capital within the interstate system triggers strong currents of cooperation and competition. When things are going well, states, like capitalist firms, function as a virtual freemason society with everyone falling over each other to offer support, cooperation and loans to all and sundry. To the degree that the coercive laws of competition can freely operate, unhindered by physical, political and economic barriers (such as high transport costs or steep tariff barriers) value transfers from labour-intensive to capital-intensive sectors and regions of the global economy freely operate such that rich regions grow richer and poor regions languish. But antagonisms erupt when things go badly and the threat of widespread devaluations looms. The result is an often-violent attempt to impose the burden of the crisis onto others.

The production of space and place by both capital and labour as well as by those other classes that also require space in which to dwell has 'momentum, meaning and political economic implications for how our world will be' as well as how the capitalist mode of production works. But the introduction of the concepts of dwelling and inhabiting points to something more expansive in the field of spatio-temporal thinking which, interestingly, Henri Lefebvre took from the neofascist Heidegger in order to connect his theorization of the production of space with an understanding of the dynamics of everyday life within the capitalist mode of production.[24] At some point, 'becoming' may morph into 'belonging'. The identity politics (nationalism and localism) that flow from place-based loyalties and meanings then enter on the scene, sometimes with ugly rather than happy consequences.

But there seems to be a missing 'moment' in this analysis, which can only be addressed by inserting the 'geo' into politics and incorporating

---

24   Henri Lefebvre, *The Urban Revolution* (Minneapolis: University of Minnesota Press, 2003); and Martin Heidegger, *The Question Concerning Technology* (New York: Garland, 1977).

nation-building into the theory of capital. Capital's 'becoming' to its present state took place during a century of two world wars, multiple territorial skirmishes and interstate conflicts galore. While it would be far too presumptuous to attribute much of this to the guiding influence of capital, it would be equally presumptuous to believe that capital had nothing to do with geopolitical conflicts, either in terms of their origins or their consequences. The economic causes and consequences of territorial conflicts are there for all to see, and some way must be found to integrate them into the task of theorizing capital (see Chapter 17). The basis for this is to be found in the territorialization of capital and its contradictions when a spatial fix becomes essential to absorb the inevitable overaccumulation of capital.

Marx admired Aristotle. He approvingly noted Aristotle's opinion that humans are inherently political (and therefore social) beings, rather than isolated entities constituted as dots in the world of market exchange. In the first volume of *Capital* he admired the way Aristotle derived the principle of equality from the practices of market exchange. He pointed out that Aristotle could not, however, derive a labour theory of value because the dominant form of labour he encountered was slave labour, thus reaffirming Marx's view that the labour theory of value derives solely from the widespread use of wage labour. But Aristotle also advanced the principle that 'place is the first of all things'.[25] This is not a principle that Marx endorses, even though Aristotle plainly accords it great significance. But what social practices give rise to such a principle, and what consequences flow from the production of space and place with respect to the theorization of capital?[26]

The initial obvious 'place' to start is to focus on the role of the 'places' of social reproduction and everyday life (which is, I suspect, one of the reasons Lefebvre put so much emphasis on studying the latter). Consider the place where one is born and raised. A child born and raised in Gaza in 2010, versus a child born and raised in the Upper East Side in New York, in Kensington or Tower Hamlets in London, in rural South Dakota on an Indian reservation, in Rio's favelas, in the slums of Mumbai, in the quiet of Sweden's Norrland or the raucous streets of Johannesburg. We come to terms with the world and its ways through our experiences in particular places at particular times. Most people do not stay forever where they were born, but they carry within themselves a sense of who

25   Aristotle, *Physics* (Oxford: Oxford University Press, 2008), Book IV.
26   Edward S. Casey, *The Fate of Place: A Philosophical History* (Berkeley: University of California Press, 1997).

they are and what might be possible taken from those first places where they came to know their world and also – and this is very significant – their place in it. It is for this reason, I suspect, that Aristotle claimed that 'place is the first of all things'. It parallels Aristotle's preoccupation with the progressive search for 'the good life' as the high point of human existence and potentiality. The production of convivial, life-affirming places is a key feature of any socialist project.

While Aristotle insists that humans are, by nature, political beings, Marx insists that they are not only political beings but also, by nature, 'sentient beings'. In *The Economic and Philosophic Manuscripts of 1844*, Marx even goes so far as to propose a prospective theory of 'species being'.[27] This is a utopian vision of a future perfected 'human nature' which is broadly consistent with Aristotle's evocation of virtue at the centre of the good life and the potential for human flourishing. Marx later dropped this line of thinking as too idealist (Hegelian), as too essentialist and utopian, but he never let go of the quest for perpetual revolutionizing of the social order so that sentient beings might better realize their potentialities. The creation and production of places in which such ambitions might be realized – the sentient qualities of places, both humanly constructed and naturally occurring – links capital's production and use of places to the metabolic relation to nature and the production and use of changing spatio-temporalities. The long history of the commune as a socialist objectification for anticapitalist projects exemplifies the positive mobilization of place as opposed to the narrow, reactionary and mystical formulations of nationalism. The endless 'becoming' of capital entails perpetual transformations in these geographical moments.

Our sense of space-time as well as our conception of our metabolic relation to nature is radically different today than it was a generation ago. The same also has to be said about our understanding of the concept of place and the role of place production in capital accumulation. This has been the focus of an extensive bourgeois literature in recent years. It covers consideration of all types of places (cities, villages, hamlets, factories and so on). Multiple cognate terms exist, such as territory, region, home and hearth, and metaphorical uses abound. We can feel out of place, put in our place, in the wrong place at the wrong time. The concept of place, like that of space-time and nature, covers a multitude of specificities. Furthermore, it cannot be appreciated adequately outside its

---

27 Karl Marx, *The Economic and Philosophic Manuscripts of 1844*, trans. Martin Milligan (New York: International Publishers, 1964).

metabolic relation to the environment (natural and humanly modified) and spatio-temporal positioning.

Capital uses the qualities of places as a selling point in the course of production and circulation of real estate capital. At the same time, places and place-building lie at the core of territorialization. But the theory of place is much more about affect, identity, feelings, loyalties and internal relations. As a liberal reading of Lefebvre suggests, geography is not learned but lived, and how it is lived becomes the issue. In the same way that capital produces an alienated relation to nature and imposes an alien spatio-temporality, so it can produce a dehumanized and alienated 'placelessness' (for example, soulless suburbs) or places of incarceration (for example, prisons) that contrast with sacred places, places of collective memory and places of meaning, as opposed to the soulless placelessness that currently forms a key locus of human discontent. The physical contrast between the urban environments of, say, Sienna and Dallas, says a great deal.

There is, therefore, a form of unalienated national identity, patriotism and pride of place that appears meaningful and thoroughly consistent with the socialist project. The struggles over what kind of place we inhabit and what kind of people we want to be is a form of general political and social struggle that is central to what socialist consciousness must embrace. It is oppositional to the alienated and exclusionary nationalism that frequently attaches to the toxic form of developmentalism that too often corrupts anticapitalist politics. It was, I suspect, this tension that led Lenin to reply to the question as to whether nationalism was or was not compatible with socialism with the obvious but unsatisfying answer: 'It depends' (an answer with which Luxemburg wholeheartedly disagreed). The nationalist politics that led the British into Brexit could have expressed a desire to decouple a British socialist project from an increasingly bureaucratized and corporatized European Union, but the Brexit project was dominated by right-wing anti-immigrant, racist and xenophobic politics coupled with mindless deregulation and privatization in the name of a Thatcherite market-based fictitious human liberty. This contrasted with the Scottish referendum on independence, which envisaged the construction of a progressive social order funded by North Sea oil, the benefits of which were currently flowing south to London. The latter extracted far more value from the Scottish economy than it gave back. The Catalan case for autonomy is a mixed bag. An autonomous socialist element dominates in the city, while a right-wing nationalist strain dominates in the rural region. Much can be gained by the fusion of nationalist sentiments with a socialist project, while much can be lost by its fusion with right-wing and fascist forces.

The cultural, anthropological and historical dynamics of place-building that accompanied and, in some instances, determined the evolution of capital's geographical dynamics need to be incorporated into the story of capital. This requires a critical engagement with the theory of place in bourgeois literature. The problem is that this also has right-wing and fascist leanings, and so many socialists do not want to touch it. Here, for example, is the fascist sympathizer Martin Heidegger:

> The object character of technological dominion spreads over the earth ever more quickly, ruthlessly and completely. Not only does it establish all things as producible in the process of production; it also delivers the products of production by means of the market. In self-assertive production, the humanness of man and the thingness of things dissolve into the calculated market value of a market which not only spans the whole earth as a world market, but also as the will to will, trades in the nature of Being and thus subjects all beings to the trade of a calculation that dominates most tenaciously in those areas where there is no need of numbers.[28]

This solid critique of capitalist modernity travels on the same ground as some of Marx's views in *The Economic and Philosophic Manuscripts of 1844*. It also harks back to that side of the contradiction underpinning Marx's double consciousness — the toxic consequences of left developmentalism. Heidegger's account of the sources of contemporary alienations is trenchant.

> All distances in time and space are shrinking ... Yet the frantic abolition of all distances brings no nearness; for nearness does not consist in shortness of distance. What is least remote from us in shortness of distance, by virtue of its picture on film or its sound on radio, can remain far from us. What is incalculably far from us in point of distance can be near to us ... Everything gets lumped together in uniform distancelessness. What is it that unsettles and thus terrifies? It shows itself and hides itself in the way that everything presences, namely, in the fact that despite all conquest of distances, the nearness of things remains absent.[29]

---

28   Martin Heidegger, *Poetry, Language, Thought* (New York: Harper & Row, 1971), p. 112.

29   Ibid., p. 164.

The consequences of the increasing production of 'placelessness' in contemporary life are, as Ted Relph, drawing on Heidegger, notes, everywhere in evidence.[30] The future effects (even without the necessary violence) will be almost as devastating to humanity in the long run as the ruins of Gaza, Aleppo, Eritrea, Sudan, Haiti, Myanmar and Ukraine. We contemplate the increasing visibility of fire- and flood-devastated land-scapes, the incipient loss of water supplies and of key mineral resources capable of fuelling the new electronic systems of communication and production. This is all supposed to help sustain human life, when all the indicators point to a world of place-based creative destruction in which the increasing pace of destruction steadily outstrips our ability to create a viable alternative. A new round of moonshots is a delusional alternative that is presented as a new step for humanity when it is nothing more than the product of interstate competition between the United States and China for military control over outer space. The institutional arrangements for adequate governance in the contemporary world are totally unable to deal with problems that will, in fact, take some form of authority, perhaps even dictatorship, to address. If this is so, then the only interesting question is whether the coming dictatorship might be benevolent or malevolent. If that is the case, then Heidegger may have been right in his diagnosis. Human societies are incapable of addressing their existential problems in their present structure in which the totality of mental conceptions, technologies, social relations, institutional norms, the conduct of daily life and metabolic relations to nature infuse capital's mode of production with its distinctive dynamics. But the theory of place cannot be ignored. Loyalties to place, territory and nation produce geopolitical tensions at every turn. The full story of capital cannot be properly told without incorporating geographical perspectives on capital and labour in space, place and environment. As Lefebvre proposed when he first encountered Heidegger's work in the inter-war years, to reject the critical perspective on place-building is to throw out the baby with the bath water but to accept the mystical and un-moving roots of place-bound perspectives, as did Heidegger and Aristotle, is to risk drowning in an ocean of mystical beliefs. Lefebvre's answer was simple but effective. He replaced the deep mysticism of Heidegger's concept of 'dwelling' with the more prosaic 'inhabiting' as foundational for the everyday life taking place in the material, conceptual and lived spaces of class struggles and endless capital accumulation.

---

30   Edward Relph, *Place and Placelessness* (London: Pion, 1977).

9

Social Reproduction and the Circulation of Labour Power

'The maintenance and reproduction of the working class remains a necessary condition for the reproduction of capital.'[1] Increase of population is a necessary condition for sustaining the accumulation of capital in its spiral form. 'Production founded on capital' therefore requires 'the greatest absolute mass' of necessary and surplus labour and, hence, 'maximum growth of population – of living labour capacities'.[2] But, says Marx, in a somewhat surprising twist, the expanding mass of labour expended on producing, sustaining and augmenting the labour force in itself creates no value. 'All the social powers developing with the growth of population and with the historic development of society cost [capital] nothing.'[3] To say that no value is added by the reproduction of labour power is not to say that the activities going into social reproduction in general and the reproduction of labour power in particular are irrelevant. To begin with, as Federici notes, 'The reproduction of human beings [is dependent on] the immense amount of paid and unpaid domestic work done by women in the home.'[4] Furthermore, it is not only the quantities but the specific qualities of the labour power supplied that matter for capital.[5]

---

1   Marx, *Capital*, Vol. 1, p. 718.
2   Marx, *Grundrisse*, p. 608.
3   Ibid., p. 765.
4   Silvia Federici, *Revolution at Point Zero: Housework, Reproduction, and Feminist Struggle* (Binghamton, NY: PM Press, 2020), p. 2.
5   My main sources on this topic are Tithi Bhattacharya, *Social Reproduction Theory: Remapping Class, Recentering Oppression* (London: Pluto Press, 2017); Lise Vogel, *Marxism and the Oppression of Women: Towards a Unitary Theory* (Chicago: Haymarket Books, 1983); Susan Ferguson, *Women and Work: Feminism, Labour, and*

In the same way that some Ricardian economists, armed with their labour theory of value, were logically drawn to redistributive socialism by the obvious anomaly that those whose labour power produced value received so little of it, so not a few Marxists have been drawn in recent years to social reproduction feminism by the anomaly that, while labour power is a commodity, there is still far too little accounting as to who produces it, how, where and at what cost. Our understanding of capital is incomplete, notes Susan Ferguson, 'if we treat it as simply an economic system involving workers and owners, and fail to examine the ways in which wider social reproduction of the system – that is the daily and generational reproductive labour that occurs in households, schools, hospitals, prisons, and so on – sustains the drive for accumulation'.[6] Social reproduction theory seeks to make visible 'the relation between labour dispensed to produce commodities and labour dispensed to produce people as part of the systemic totality of capitalism'.[7]

Theoretically, according to Marx's schema, social reproduction, including that of labour power, has one foot firmly planted in the theory of capital's mode of production while the other foot stands on conditions within the capitalist social formation. This positioning 'complexifies' (as Lefebvre puts it) matters considerably and requires some explication. A medical analogy is helpful. A doctor may diagnose a patient with liver failure and treat the ailment accordingly. But doctors are acutely aware that the social conditions of opioid use and alcoholism (in, say, Ohio) or amphetamine use (in, say, Shenzhen) have much to do with the ailments they are treating. The invidious practices of drug promotion by Big Pharma against a background of work stresses and workers' alienation have much to do with the bodily deterioration of patients. These problems lie in the social formation. But all manner of political and social struggles against multiple forms of oppression and domination of one group by another coexist within the social formation, whereas it is the class relation between alienated capital and alienated labour that

Social Reproduction (London: Pluto Press, 2019); Nancy Fraser, *Cannibal Capitalism: How Our System Is Devouring Democracy, Care, and the Planet and What We Can Do About It* (London: Verso, 2022); Silvia Federici, *Revolution at Point Zero: Housework, Reproduction, and Feminist Struggle* (Binghamton, NY: PM Press, 2020); Melinda Cooper, *Family Values: Between Neoliberalism and the New Social Conservatism* (Brooklyn: Zone Books, 2017).

6   Susan Ferguson, 'Capitalist Childhood, Anti-Capitalist Children: The Social Reproduction of Childhood', unpublished paper, 2015, cited in Bhattacharya, *Social Reproduction Theory*.

7   Bhattacharya, *Social Reproduction Theory*, p. 2.

dominates within the more circumscribed theory of capital as a mode of production.

The relation between mode of production and social formation is construed dialectically. Marx is not averse, however, to treating such relations one-sidedly (as in Volume 1 of *Capital*, where he assumes all commodities exchange at their value and that effective demand in the market is always sufficient for the realization of all values). He sometimes assumes that production takes the lead in defining consumption (as today in the case of opioids), but at other times he assumes that customer-led changes in cultural and social organization and preferences (for example, the generalization of the nuclear family at the expense of the extended family) take the lead in market formation, leaving capital to adjust its production accordingly. Capital has proven very adept at so doing. The social formation is, however, perpetually 'becoming', sometimes in ways antagonistic to the current organization of capital's mode of production. The first months of the Covid-19 pandemic, for example, severely interrupted global supply chains. This dialectic does not always advantage capital. The accumulation of capital may promote forms of consumerism that affect everyday life for good or for ill. It may lead, as in the case of opioids, to deterioration in the quantities and qualities of labour supply flowing from the social formation to feed the mode of production.

The dialectical relation between mode of production and social formation is intricate and deep. But some of the main bridges between them are questions of social reproduction, precisely because they include the reproduction of labour power, which is one of the key moments in the circulation of labour capacity. Marx clearly recognizes this. In his time and place (Manchester in the 1860s), 'The capitalist may safely leave [the reproduction of the workers] to the worker's drives for self-preservation and propagation. All the capitalist cares for is to reduce the worker's individual consumption to the necessary minimum.'[8] Marx was only half-right in this. The more the workers struggle to fashion a reasonable life for themselves, the more capital concludes that this is because capital has been too generous and that a general reduction of wages is in order. When economic conditions are good for capital, however, wage cuts become less urgent.

But what has so far largely been assumed away must now be brought back into the main theoretical frame. The embeddedness of the reproduction of labour capacity in daily life poses problems of an entirely different

---

8   Marx, *Capital*, Vol. 1, p. 718.

nature to those hitherto encountered. In the same way that a urologist is not trained or enabled to deal with an opioid epidemic that in the US has killed almost as many people over the years as died from Covid-19, so collective (state) action and entirely other economic, political and social skills are required to deal with the role of social reproduction in relation to the circulation of labour capacity and capital accumulation.

A historical perspective is helpful here as a beginning point. Capital arose to dominance in a world characterized by uneven geographical development within and between a variety of social formations, traces of which persist and, in some instances, have been augmented by capital over time. In the Americas, for example, the legacy of the slave trade and racism continues daily to affect everyday lives, labour markets, labour processes and social relations. Social reproduction in many parts of the world has been tainted by this history to the point that the mode of pro-duction incorporates and feeds on racial discriminations and differences in both everyday life and in the circulation of labour capacity. From this perspective, many would now regard capital as inherently racial. A variant of this history came with the British import of indentured labour from South Asia into Africa, the Caribbean and even small Pacific Islands such as Fiji. This produced a divided legacy of ethnic conflicts that saturate social formations in ways that capital continues to prey upon. In South Asia, the history of caste has proven hard to displace, and in India the Hindu–Muslim divide against the background of the legacy of British imperial rule, indigenous Adivasi elements and mul-tiple linguistic divisions characterizes a complicated social formation that capital has to adjust to and use as best it can. In the Middle East, religious-based factionalisms, such as those that have rendered Lebanon ungovernable and Syria pulverized by a vicious civil war, provide oppor-tunities for certain forms of merchant capitalism to flourish on the basis of illegalities and violence. Across Africa, kinship structures and tribal (clan) loyalties institutionalized under indirect colonial rule continue to play a major role. A clan-based form of capital in, for example, Nigeria, struggles to cope with a globalizing capital administered by capital's international institutions, such as the IMF. In China, the traditions of Confucian caste-like hierarchies and imperial bureaucratic adminis-tration have not been erased (in spite of Mao's attempt to do so in the Cultural Revolution). It is significant, also, that almost all of the 'foreign' capital that entered China after the opening of the economy in 1978 came through or was mediated by the ethnic Chinese diaspora located pri-marily in Hong Kong and Taiwan. They were familiar with the social

and cultural codes embedded within a distinctive Chinese social formation (*guangxi*). The result has been a form of capital accumulation
that Western capitalists find hard to understand let alone negotiate. But
in Slavic regions of Central and Eastern Europe (including Russia), the
problem primarily lay with the history of serfdom and hierarchical social
relations of a traditional peasantry under landlordism and Tsarist rule.
The social formation in Northern Ireland, just to take a more small-
scale example, is, for its part, beset by 'the Troubles' which arose out of
religious and nationalist divisions of the sort that rile political conflicts
all over the world. Loyalties to place backed by a culture of belonging
assume significance almost everywhere.

It is vital to understand the role of such uneven geographical development within social formations and capital's role in adapting to, fostering
and promoting distinctive forms of that development. Massive migrations are also under way as populations search for greater security and
an elusive economic livelihood in a context where new labour-saving
technologies (such as automation, digitalization and AI) and capital
mobility are leaving the globe with vast pools of disposable surplus
labour. Labour's share of national income (Figure 15) has been steadily declining since 1980 almost everywhere (including China).[9] A rising
industrial reserve army and a slumping labour market go hand in hand,
giving rise to acute political and social problems. In the face of this
it is tempting to dissolve the theory of capital into a list of 'adjectival
capitalisms' such as Chinese, Nordic, European, North American, supplemented by further disaggregations to incorporate varieties of welfare,
racial, digital or cognitive capitalism.

This is not the path that Marx takes. He is interested in theorizing
the general nature of capital no matter what the prevailing conditions
within distinctive social formations. This is his stated intention and his
continuing quest, as we saw in his mission statement in the *Grundrisse*.
But we need to probe much more deeply into the processes at work in
the social reproduction of labour power. Without doing this, as socialist
feminists insist, the theory of the capitalist mode of production is seriously compromised.

At the micro level, the social reproduction of labour power has special
qualities. To begin with, it is pre-eminently a place-bound process. We
remember the places where we grew up, where and by whom we were

---

9   Mai Chi Dao, Mitali Das, Zsoka Koczan and Weichang Lian, 'Drivers of Declining
Labor Share of Income', IMF Blog, 12 April 2017, imf.org.

socialized into the qualities of an everyday life and the prevailing dominant (usually hierarchical) social relations in that place. Our life chances
depend heavily on the postal code of our birth. We remember the informal and formal education that supposedly prepared us to participate in
the labour market. Daily life is fuelled by the consumption of the commodities produced by capital, accompanied by a whole range of products
and processes (such as cooking and cleaning) done individually or collectively by and for ourselves, outside the reach of the market. While
the anchor of social reproduction may be the pursuit of the well-being
of individual workers and their families and dependents in a domestic
household economy, the spaces and places of social reproduction are also
key sites of collective consumption and collective action.

Populations are organized territorially. Administrative structures of
governance (for example, local and municipal governments) are created
to ensure the levels of social provision in a territory worthy of the aspi-
rations and needs of both capital and the population in general in that
place. While class struggle may traditionally focus on the point of production, the collective struggles for social provision in terms of education,
health care and housing have played a major role in dictating the shape
and form of the capitalist mode of production. Social movements in the
cities or on the land (for example, the landless peasant movement and its
urban offshoot in Brazil) wage forms of class struggle, increasingly direct
as sectors such as housing and social care become an attractive terrain
for capital accumulation. Landlords and housing mortgage financiers in
effect take back part of the social wage through the extraction of profit
through real estate operations and the renting of accommodation.

But Marx's focus was on Manchester industrialism, and that led him
to ignore the rise of bourgeois-led urban reformism of the Joseph Chamberlain variety in Birmingham after 1860 or so. This presaged the 'sewer
socialist' movements in Milwaukee and other cities in the United States
in the 1910s. Struggles over the conditions of local collective consumption
are indeed just as important as those over the wage rate. Rising housing
costs (which have increased sixfold in much of the world since 1980 or
so) negate rising wages. Rent strikes (for example, in Glasgow early in
the last century or the mortgage strikes that broke out recently in China)
have become centres of struggle. The organization of affordable social
housing through collective action, either through municipal socialist
governments (as in Britain before Thatcher) or directly through trade
union action (for example, in New York in the 1930s or more recently in
Montevideo) are cases in point. Struggles over social housing, from Red

Vienna in the 1930s to the barrios and *bidonvilles* of innumerable South American and African cities, are an essential aspect of the totality of what the theory of the capitalist mode of production must incorporate.

Forms of collective consumption depend on the existence of spatial and territorial forms of social and political organization of the population (as workers, community-based groups, and others). Much of this activity connects with the requirements of social reproduction. It takes the form of place-based and spatially segmented and segregated expressions of that social reproduction, even as it simultaneously has to accommodate the spatial dynamics of capital accumulation. The urban process under capitalism in all its aspects integrates with the circulation and accumulation of capital, as demonstrated by the operation of finance-backed real estate capital and the rise of huge multinational real estate companies, such as Blackstone, whose asset values now vie with others for the title of the largest in the world. The qualities of everyday life achieved in cities, townships and neighbourhoods are the result of decades of social struggle embedded in but not confined to the capitalist mode of production. But this is also the realm in which the reproduction of differences, of culture, religion, ethnicity and the like becomes a major feature, in some instances fuelling civil strife (as in Northern Ireland).

The fact that capital's value theory, as Marx presents it, excludes the costs of social reproduction does not diminish its relevance to understanding the material basis for capital accumulation. It also helps explain why Marx held that the path towards socialism entailed the transcendence if not abolition of capital's law of value. Social reproduction needs to be liberated from the web of restraints that capital imposes on it. The ways in which work and the production of goods (use values) are currently organized in the domestic sector outside of market forces provide some clues to how such an alternative socialist economy might work.

The consensus among social reproduction theorists is to treat social reproduction as external to capital accumulation but indispensable to the economy. I have positioned it here as straddling the relation between the mode of production and its social formation. This relation is dialectical and relational, rather than empiricist or positivist. Capital, for example, economizes as ruthlessly as possible on expenditures for social reproduction. Reducing the value of labour power expands the surplus value for capital. Capital and the capitalist state jointly furnish the material and monetary basis for much social reproduction, particularly of the collective sort (for example, schooling). In the first instance, they do so by fixing the value of labour power. How much necessary labour is required to reproduce the value of labour power depends on how much labour is freely available in the domestic sphere. This relation is fluid, not fixed. Marx, however, neglected to study this interdependency and generally ignored what is done with the income stream that flows to the support of social reproduction. This is the gap that social reproduction theory has to fill.

There are five areas in which the social reproduction 'moment' directly intersects with the circulation and accumulation of capital. First, it intersects directly with the circulation of labour capacity. The health, fitness and well-being of the labourers has to be preserved over time. The labourer has to return to the workplace refreshed on a daily basis and in a fit state to produce more surplus value for capital. The reproduction of capital depends on this, and the onus is placed on the household economy to provide, among many other things, food and shelter to workers using the commodities bought with the money wage established in the market, supplemented by all those products and services created within the household. The balance between commodities bought in the market and produce created domestically has shifted over time in many places. As more women have entered the labour force, reliance on market provision of household functions (for example, fast-food takeout, laundry and cleaning services) has increased. Capital wants to keep the value of labour power as low as possible by reducing the material standard of living of the labourer to a bare minimum. Individual capitalists drive down the wages of their own employees, but at the same time they look to their rivals to raise wages to increase consumption capacity in the market. Individual capitalists may likewise pay little concern to the health and well-being of their own employees while looking to rivals or to the state to keep the labour force fit enough and savvy enough to guarantee future quantities and qualities of labour supply. The uneasy relation between the need to accommodate and enhance the social reproduction costs of the worker as a stimulus for the market and the drive to reduce those costs as close to zero as possible, in order to maximize the extraction of surplus value, creates an inevitable contradiction.

Second, capital needs to cultivate and sustain an unemployed labour reserve ready for work. Workers' households may have enough resources to meet this task in the short run, but long term the onus falls on the state or some other set of social institutions (the workhouses of old) to support the industrial reserve army of the unemployed. During crises, unemployment can become widespread. Leaving workers and their families to starve (as happened in the 1930s) is hardly an optimal solution even for capital. State intervention, such as unemployment insurance and social welfare, is required. But capitalist class interests strictly monitor the generosity of these payments, for it is held that both the wage level and the willingness to take up wage labour depend on the level of state support offered to the unemployed. These are the kinds of constraints that put downward pressure on the material basis of social reproduction for waged workers. The bourgeoisie widely applies the doctrine of austerity to justify reducing the funding of critical social services (for example, education and health care).

The third moment overlaps with the first. It concerns the need to educate workers and to train them with the requisite skills and temperaments to match capital's ever-changing workplace demands. Adaptation and mastery of new technologies (some of which emanate from labour itself) do not come easily. The constant retraining of more and more flexible labour forces takes resources and persistent effort. Education takes its place within the field of social reproduction. It is here that the state has a significant role to play. But a lot of the basic training for the labour process (for example, time discipline) takes place in the household from a very early stage. Traditional skills inherited from long ago are also frequently called upon for free. Major shifts in capital accumulation, such as the shift from gas-powered to electric cars, entail major shifts in the labour skills required for production. If the requisite labour force is not locally available, capital may then seek to import it. For example, Seattle turns to South Asian labour (for example, Bangalore), where software skills are abundant. Apple, conversely, in the 1990s took production to China, where line engineers were in abundant supply in contrast to the US, where they were scarce.

Fourth, a new and vital moment that Marx would not have encountered, is the general rise in life expectancies, mainly but not exclusively in the upper-income countries (from the mid-thirties in Marx's time to the mid-seventies in ours). This forms the cutting edge in a remarkable expansion of employment in what is known as 'the care industry'. The organization of this industry is a source of low-paid employment or unpaid caring for the old and the sick. The 'caring industry' is now a major source of employment, some of which is nonmarket, though it is becoming more monetized and increasingly regulated. While it may legally be organized in part as a nonprofit sector, it pays out interest on loans and increasingly is a field for the investment of capital in funding retirement homes.

The fifth moment recognizes the important role of the household in promoting 'consumption capacity', aggregate effective demand in the market. Obviously, the capacity of the workforce is limited in this regard by the value of labour power and the numbers employed, and to the degree that wages have systematically declined as a share of national income. Consumption capacity thus increasingly rests on the demand from what Malthus referred to as 'consumption classes' (for example, state employees). While Marx has doubts about this formulation, he does, from time to time, accept that market demand reflects the wants, needs and desires of the population at large and that sustained working-class demand is important to the continuous accumulation of capital. There is a dynamic relation between capital's penchant for creating new products and goods for the market and the reshaping of cultural and consumer preferences within households and neighbourhoods. The invention of new fashions and lifestyles occurs on the terrain of social reproduction. In Volume 2 of *Capital*, Marx recognizes the role of 'rational consumption' (rational from the standpoint of capital) in equilibrating demand and supply in the market. Bourgeois philanthropy (today orchestrated by the NGOs) here plays a manipulative and rationalizing role. But there is another, longer-term set of considerations in the sphere of consumption that will need to be accounted for. In the same way that fixed capital of an independent kind, much of which is immovably embedded in the land (as built environment) is required to support production, so analogous investments in, for example, roads, housing, schools and hospitals require the circulation of capital in the form of a consumption fund to support consumption. We will later take up the problems of fixed capital circulation and consumption fund formation. For now, however, Marx-like, we will put these considerations to one side.

Social reproduction does not necessarily occur in the same places as production. The United States has a horrible record of economizing on its support for advanced education and skills while importing them to meet its needs from elsewhere (the 'brain drains' from Britain and Europe in the 1960s, the reliance on South Asian–trained software engineers and Russian space scientists while relying on eleven million or so illegal immigrants for its manual labour force). In the agricultural sector, migrant labour forces play a key role. On the East Coast of the United States, migrant work crews recruited from the Caribbean follow the harvest from the Southern States to New England in the season, leaving the costs of social reproduction or of care (for example, from workers' exposure to toxic pesticides) to their country of origin.

The economic conditions regulating social reproduction depend on the trajectory of both public and private policies adopted at the level of the capitalist state. In the United States, consumers account for two-thirds of economic activity but, until recently, in China, the proportion was around one-third. In recent times, policies seem to have shifted in China towards a more consumer-based model (particularly focused through housing on the consumption fund). But to date, this shift has been limited in its effects. This trend will have significant impacts on social reproduction in China. The point here is that the conditions of social reproduction in a country relate to the macroeconomic and political choices made within the framework of state power. And that depends on the social forces milling around in the social formation in general (including racial and ethnic strife and struggles over gender roles). The politics of state austerity are very different from those of economic stimulus. The latter can take the form of either expanding social expenditures for the mass of the population or tax cuts for the top 1 per cent, depending on who controls state power. Policies in the fields of education, health care and housing are highly significant at the state level and affect the social wage in ways that set the stage for other forms of collective social provision. None of this is outside the capitalist mode of production. It is necessarily embedded within it.

Finally, the capitalist process of reproduction 'produces not only commodities, not only surplus-value, but it also produces and reproduces the capital-relation itself; on the one hand capitalist, on the other, the wage labourer'.[10] It is 'the capitalist [that] produces the worker as a wage-labourer'.[11] By converting part of his capital into labour power, the capitalist 'kills two birds with one stone. He profits not only by what he receives from the worker, but also by what he gives him. [Part of the capital] is converted into means of subsistence which have to be consumed to reproduce the muscles, nerves, bones and brains of existing workers and to bring new workers into existence'.[12] Social reproduction is critical to the reproduction of the class relation on which the accumulation of capital is founded. In all of these respects, social reproduction plays an integral part in the capitalist mode of production. Eliminate or exclude it and the whole theoretical edifice collapses.

Labour is not, however, a commodity like any other. It is at this point that social reproduction incorporates elements that play a contingent

---

10   Marx, *Capital*, Vol. 1, p. 724.
11   Ibid., Vol. 1, p. 716.
12   Ibid., Vol. 1, p. 717.

rather than foundational role in the mode of production. In normal commodity production, the inputs of constant capital, c, are noted and their value is transferred by labour into the value of the final product $(c + v + s)$. In the case of labour power, no constant capital is recorded. To depict this as theoretically contingent to the concept and theory of capital does not in any way imply that it is secondary within the social formation. It merely asserts that the field of social relations is open to all manner of local determinations in relation to the motion of capital. It is no accident, of course, that opening the door to admitting the importance of wide-ranging social questions of gender, sexual preference and personal identity affects how social reproduction is configured, with clear implications for the mode of production.

Gender discrimination plainly exists in the labour market, on the job and in the distribution and use of money power. It is observable in consumer markets and of course is a major feature in the organization of labour in the household or in developing and supporting neighbourhood communal functions. The feminist 'wages for housework' movement of the 1970s was a brilliant slogan for drawing attention to the gendered aspect of almost everything going on in the circulation of labour capacity. At around the same time, welfare rights movement leaders, emerging from the feminist and Black freedom movements of the 1960s, summed up their demands (which took into account the gendered and racialized biases of labour relations as well as the oppression of wage labour itself) in a call for a 'guaranteed annual income'. As Angela Davis pointed out, this radical demand was the 'immediate alternative they have most frequently proposed to the dehumanizing welfare system. What they want in the long run, however, is jobs and affordable public childcare. The guaranteed annual income functions, therefore, as unemployment insurance pending the creation of more jobs with adequate wages along with a subsidized system of childcare.'[13]

The socialist feminist movement drew attention to the divide-and-rule tactics of capital collaborating with the long-standing role of patriarchy in regulating gender relations both in the market and in domestic lives. Major discriminations also exist in consumer markets. It was only after the Equal Credit Opportunity Act of 1974 that women in the United States could freely have and use their own chequebooks and apply for mortgage finance without a male co-signer. While changes in the laws on access to credit and mortgages responded to the pressures of second-wave

---

13   Angela Davis, *Women, Race and Class* (New York: Vintage Books, 1983), p. 237.

feminism, bankers also supported them because they unleashed a huge and profitable expansion in the mortgage market that culminated in the financial crash of 2008. The law was thus not entirely successful. Women invariably find themselves paying higher interest rates and obliged to lay down larger deposits than their male counterparts when buying a property. The equal pay for equal work movement also failed to accomplish its ambitions almost everywhere (apart from some progress in the Nordic countries).

Access to mortgage finance has been and still is an initial indicator of multiple structures of domination and of oppression within the United States, beginning with the infamous redlining of mortgages according to race that legally underpinned the production of racial segregation in US cities until 1964 and thereafter has continued to do so by informal means to this very day. Exclusions and oppressions based on ethnicity, religion, national identity, sexual preference and identity, as well as clan, class, caste and gender and even, in our times, on political ideology, are omnipresent in the social formation. But, to the degree that the configuration of these distinctions varies so radically from the United States to Northern Ireland, China, Sudan, Sweden, Catalonia, Lebanon, India and Bolivia, so Marx's tendency to hold them to one side in order to unpack the laws of motion of capital in pure form is understandable. He nevertheless recognizes that the whole history and geography of actual capital accumulation is suffused with the effects of the multiple forms of domination and oppression (beginning with slavery and later pertaining to the plight of Irish immigrants that interestingly parallels the historical treatment of Puerto Ricans in the US). All of this is internalized within the social formation and is highly concentrated in its effects within the broad field of social reproduction. The latter is strongly inflected by the reproduction of other structures of domination and oppression. Capital's mode of production takes place within contexts such as these.

Marx constructs a theory that, for the most part, abstracts from such matters. This becomes a problem when it is assumed that what is abstracted from is unimportant or irrelevant. It is often the case that questions of race and gender are the cutting edge of struggles against the structures of domination and oppression that social reproduction internalizes in a particular place and time. It is important to remain alert to when such contingent features play a leading role. The financial crisis of 2007–8 arose, for example, out of extending sub-prime mortgages in the United States indiscriminately to women (single heads of households in particular), African Americans and immigrants (Latinx in particular). When the foreclosure wave struck, it left those who had lost homes suffering massive losses in the assets they had previously controlled. African Americans lost close to 80 per cent of their assets, the value of which passed to the banks before being bought out at fire-sale prices by companies like Blackstone.

The household economy is very different from that of capital and is constructed on the basis of quite different social relations. To begin with, most activities (from washing the dishes and making the beds or cooking dinner and doing the laundry) are neither commodified nor monetized. The conditions that govern the rule of value theory are absent. Insofar as production occurs for others, it is production of goods or products that are not commodities. It is important to distinguish, however, between individuals in their households and collective forms of social reproduction involving the capitalist state along with communal and social forms of collective action. In the same way that the role of the individual labourer in production changes when production takes on a social form (within a factory or a corporation), so social reproduction looks very different from the collective communal perspective compared to how it looks from the standpoint of individuals and their immediate families.

The monetizing of social and exchange relations within the household economy takes on peculiar forms, if it occurs at all. As Tithi Bhattacharya puts it: 'On the one hand, capitalism depends heavily on the household to replenish labor power and reproduce gender hierarchies. On the other hand, as a site of mutual aid, income pooling, and the accumulation of vital reserves, the household, though always changing, has proven vital to the survival of the working class.'[14]

While the nature of the capital–labour class relation is clear enough in production, how it works in the case of social reproduction is more complicated. Clues can be gleaned from Marx's chapter in *Capital* on the working day. Why is it, he asks, that 'capital's drive towards a limitless draining away of labour power' was curbed by 'forcibly limiting the working day on the authority of the state, but a state ruled by capitalist and landlord'?[15] The depletion of the capacities of the workers by over-work was not in the long-term capitalist class interest. To avoid the 'premature exhaustion and death' of labour power led capital to agree to 'a normal working day'.[16] But also 'capital's power of resistance gradually weakened, while at the same time the working class's power of attack

14   Bhattacharya, *Social Reproduction Theory*, p. 39.
15   Marx, *Capital*, Vol.1, p. 348.
16   Ibid., Vol.1, pp. 376–7.

grew with the number of its allies in those social layers not directly interested in the question.'[17] So who were these allies? The widespread revulsion within the bourgeoisie against the conditions of factory labour, as revealed in the factory inspectors' reports, and horror at the filth and dirt of industrial capitalism pushed, for example, the romantic poets, like Wordsworth, and later on Ruskin, to retire to the bucolic lands of the Lake District to denounce capitalist industrialism. In addition, the landed aristocracy, which remained powerful until mid-century, detested the crass and heartless policies of the upstart industrial capitalist class. They broadly supported workers' rights. How capital ended up concurring with legislation to regulate the length of the working day pioneered the way for capital to accept that a capitalist state under its control would actively engage to support the social reproduction of labour power.

The apparatuses in the leading capitalist states typically support some access to social security, education, health care, housing, environmental protection and other popular and essential needs. So why would states dominated by finance and merchant corporate interests bother with topics like education and health care for the masses? Why would Treasury secretaries like Robert Rubin, Hank Paulson and Steve Mnuchin, all from Goldman Sachs, care? The short answer, of course, is that they probably do not. Mnuchin's new wife responded to critical commentary on the luxuriousness of her wedding by asserting her superior value to society because she paid more taxes than her humble critics.[18] By that measure, at least half the US population would be judged worthless. She subsequently apologized for voicing the thought (though not necessarily for having it). Since 1980, political power has sought the neoliberal holy grail of lower taxes for the rich while limiting its liabilities to provide for the population at large. President Clinton's reform of 'welfare as we know it', which put restrictive and punitive requirements on social welfare recipients, is a prime example. The longer answer needs to address the concatenation of social and political forces within the capitalist mode of production as well as in the social formation at large which would force even Treasury secretaries drawn from Goldman Sachs to pay some degree of attention to funding adequate conditions of social reproduction.

Social reproduction is sensitive to employment conditions. Deindustrialization of the sort that saw the city of Sheffield in Britain lose some 64,000 good-paying unionized jobs in the steel industry in two years in

17   Ibid., Vol.1, p. 409.
18   Maggie Haberman and Mikayla Bouchard, 'Mnuchin's Wife Mocks Oregon Woman over Lifestyle and Wealth', *New York Times*, 22 August 2017.

the mid-1980s (Pittsburgh went through the same experience) radically changed the conditions not only of production but of social reproduction in neighbourhoods and in households that had hitherto served those industries through the supply of labour power. It impacted gender roles as working women displaced men as the primary wage earner in many households. The deindustrialization of much of the so-called 'rust belt' in the United States similarly left behind a ghastly wreckage of working-class communities and lifestyles, with wrecked families riddled with opioid addiction. Capital's ruthless exploitation of the pain and misery of unemployment and dispossession in the living space through sale of opioids and fentanyl has far exceeded the misery and violence it typically imposes at the point of production. Protected to some degree against premature death at the point of production, redundant workers suffered premature death from the inability to protect against the monopoly powers of Big Pharma. Dangerous painkillers were ruthlessly foisted on vulnerable populations that were already hurting, both physically and mentally, from the violence of job losses. The conversion of an individual relation of painkiller and user into a metabolic relation between addict and painkiller to the benefit of Big Pharma and wealthy owner families like the Sacklers is one of the great social tragedies of our times. But who cares when masses of disposable and redundant workers are thrown onto the trash heap of history? Certainly not then Secretary of the Treasury Steve Mnuchin (who became a billionaire speculating on the housing foreclosures of 2008).

To fight against that fate entails class struggle at a different point in the circulation of labour capacity. In his early years, Gramsci openly wondered if neighbourhood organization, with its perspective of the working people as a whole (including the street cleaners, day-care providers and horse cab drivers along with women at home) might be as important to organizing and defining 'the will of the people' as the factory councils, where the perspective was defined by a given industrial plant, usually from a male perspective.[19] Gramsci here echoed Marx and Engels, who urged that workers must 'make each community the central point and nucleus of workers associations in which the attitudes and interests of the workings of the proletariat will be discussed independent of bourgeois interests'.[20] Strong militant organization by women on

---

19   Antonio Gramsci, *Selections from the Prison Notebooks* (New York: International Publishers, 1971), pp. 129–33.

20   Karl Marx and Friedrich Engels, 'Address of the Central Authority to the League', in *Marx and Engels Collected Works*, Vol. 10 (New York: International Publishers, 1986), pp. 282–3.

a neighbourhood basis has long been a powerful support for all forms of class struggle. In Gramsci's time, the *case del popolo*, 'houses of the people', in Italy and elsewhere in Europe (community centres organized mainly by women but expressive of class solidarities) were just as important to political action as the factory councils. They even built affordable social housing for workers. An underlying unity was thus constructed between social reproduction and class struggle at the point of production. This was very much in evidence during the great auto strikes in Flint, Michigan, in the 1930s, when neighbourhood organization played a critical role in support of the strikes.[21] While Marx, Engels and Gramsci were all alert to the advantages of working across this broader canvas, they regrettably failed to treat this as a cutting edge of the path to a socialist alternative.

State provision, when it does materialize, ought to be universal. But this often triggers opposition. In the United States, for example, this cuts against the particularities of place-based struggles. African Americans, immigrants and women are by far the most vulnerable groups, but their special treatment sparks the political resentments of white men. Universal programmes like welfare are depicted (erroneously) as privileging 'Black welfare queens' (to quote Ronald Reagan's favourite and most egregious fiction). Racial bias is thus one of the not-so-hidden barriers to the achievement of universal health care and equal educational opportunity in the United States.

The household economy constitutes a world where different concepts of work and value arise to those which capital defines. It proposes a real alternative from which 'a new state of society' might be constructed. As recipients of a wage, workers identify and act as buyers and consumers rather than as wage labourers. From this, workers can potentially construct a comfortable daily life for themselves. Their struggles in this realm are indirect class struggles. Broad movements of opposition arise against accumulation by dispossession by merchants, bankers, landlords, service providers, greedy corporations and even the state itself. Social movements form to pressure state regulation, more adequate provision of collective services (like education, affordable housing and health care) or subsidy of, for example, pharmaceuticals or protection against exorbitant credit card fees and extortionate forms of credit. The politics that Marx describes in his chapter on the working day can be generalized to the living space.

---

21   See *With Babies and Banners: Story of the Women's Emergency Brigade*, directed by Lorraine Gray (Women's Film Project, 1979).

But capital seeks to make it impossible for the worker 'to strive for wealth in general form' or to participate 'in the higher, even cultural satisfactions, the agitation for his own interests, newspaper subscriptions, attending lectures, educating his children, developing his taste'.[22] But herein lies a serious contradiction. Wage repression limits effective demand for wage goods and degrades conditions of social reproduction in the household. On the other hand, the hierarchy of wages that frequently accompanies divisions in the labour force associated with skills, talents and managerial positions builds strong blocks of consumer power in the market while stratifying the working class through housing segregation and job discrimination.

But children need to learn how to labour as well as how to socialize with others, and how and what to consume. The family and the household constitute the space that is supposed to socialize children and produce the labouring human being ready and able to participate in capital's labour processes. But it is not a space whose qualities are determined by capital alone. It is a space riven with complex and multiple social relations. While, for example, gender is omnipresent as a form of distinction and difference within the whole network of capital circulation and accumulation, it is very prominent, if not basic, to the social relations within the household (often designated as a family) which, to this day, is one of the primary institutional sites for the reproduction of labour power in most parts of the world. To begin with, systematic repression under capital of the individual wage in order to bolster the profit rate has put more and more pressure on families to double their presence in the labour market by more and more women joining the paid labour force. This revolutionizes the dynamics of the household economy. While individual wages fall, household incomes may increase.

The social wage of labour depends heavily on the state organization of forms of social provision such as education, health care, housing, water and sanitation and the like. The qualities of social reproduction are contingent on the social wage (the market wage plus the wage received in kind through state expenditures). The neoliberal state has, in recent years, typically reduced the social wage through a politics of enforced austerity and sought to substitute the politically less salient privatization of social welfare through NGOs.[23] This, when coupled with

---

22   Marx, *Grundrisse*, p. 287.
23   Tina Wallace, 'NGO Dilemmas: Trojan Horses for Global Neoliberalism?', in *Socialist Register 2003* (London: Merlin Press, 2003) pp. 202–19. For a general survey

wage repression, has markedly reduced the relative standard of living of labour over recent years in the advanced capitalist countries, though with two compensating trends. Cheaper wage goods (as exemplified by the 'Walmart economy' based in recent times on the China trade) means that the real wage (measured by what money can buy) does not sink so low as the nominal wage. While individual wages may decline, household incomes may also remain steady or even rise as (white) women enter the paid labour force en masse. Given the subsequent travails of systematic deindustrialization and the concentrated political attack on the Fordist 'affluent worker', whose income was sufficient to support the whole family, women have often become the main wage earners in the household. This in turn incentivizes the increasing market commodification of household labour. In many of the major metropolitan areas of the world, a goodly proportion of family meals are now either provided by fast-food enterprises or by takeout. The introduction of new labour-saving household technologies (washing machines, dishwashers, robotic vacuum cleaners and the like) puts pressure on the disposability of incomes at the same time as they do not necessarily save the time advertised.

At this point it is important to note, however, that Black women and other women of colour have been compelled to work outside the home throughout the history of the United States, not just in the past fifty-plus years. Angela Davis makes this point when she writes that Black women 'have thus carried the double burden of wage labour and housework – a double burden which always demands that working women possess the persevering powers of Sisyphus'.[24] Such Sisyphean tasks continue to disproportionately impact women of colour under neoliberalism.

The neoliberal orthodoxy that leans towards radical state austerity when it comes to social service provision has pushed these burdens onto the family or into whatever other social form the household might take, leading some, such as Melinda Cooper, to suggest that, in the case of the United States at least, the Fordist conception of the family and of social reproduction has been superseded by the forging of a neoliberal family form as the current basis for social reproduction.[25] Uneven gender burdens within households may be in the course of some amelioration, but the progress is slow, not only because of deeply embedded

---

of the role of NGOs, see Michael Edwards and David Hulme (eds), *Non-Governmental Organisations: Performance and Accountability* (London: Earthscan, 1995).

24   Davis, *Women, Race and Class*, p. 231.

25   Cooper, *Family Values*.

presumptions about proper gender roles but also because both the state and civil society set up institutional norms that reinforce rather than ameliorate gender distinctions. Only recently, for example, have parental leave options mandated by the state been made more gender neutral in the United States and Britain (as opposed to Scandinavia, where they were instituted several years ago).

State mandates on everything from population growth and family values to education, quality-of-life issues and mental well-being are now pretty universal within any capitalist social formation. 'But', Federici notes, 'the expansion of the service sector by no means eliminated home-based, unpaid reproductive work, nor has it abolished the sexual division of labor in which it is embedded, which still divides production and reproduction.'[26] It still is generally the case that most of this work falls to the lot of women and that this work is undertaken under traditional structures of patriarchy involving the oppression and domination of women by men, sometimes backed up by violence against women. Federici's point is that this situation is structural and embedded culturally and historically within both the capitalist social formation and mode of production. It cannot be dealt with solely by individuals changing their practices and social relations, no matter how important that may be. If women can be hired at a lower wage for comparable work, their employment becomes a weapon in class struggle. It was for this reason that the progressive anarchists in Second Empire Paris so virulently opposed the employment of women in the workshops. The definition of skill was at that time given as work which women could not do. The employment of women in the workshop, no matter how skilled, therefore amounted to deskilling.

Two generations of active struggles by women and their allies have successfully extended many civil rights to women in the advanced capitalist countries. But the fact that the gender gap in pay and access to job opportunities has not been anywhere closed, while responsibilities for household labour have not been equalized in even the most progressive countries and that domestic violence against women (which now extends in the US to state denial of women's right to abortion) is such a recalcitrant feature, has led some to conclude that capital is inherently rather than contingently patriarchal as a mode of production. This signifies that the emancipation of women, along with that of people of colour, is a key aspect of anticapitalist struggle. By the same token, the feminist

---

26   Federici, *Revolution at Point Zero*, p. 100.

struggle and antiracism must also be anticapitalist if they are to succeed. As Federici puts it: 'If our kitchens are outside of capital, our struggle to destroy them will never succeed in causing capital to fall.'[27]

The nature of household work has changed dramatically over the years. Back in the 1950s, almost all meals were prepared at home (even if in workers' lunch boxes) and, in my youth in Britain, all washing and ironing was done by hand with Mondays taken up solely by that labour. On those days, the neighbourhood was festooned with drying sheets and shirts flapping in the wind. Food preparation is now market driven and washers and dryers have become ubiquitous (even if in the local launderette). More women have been liberated from household labour in order to participate in the labour force, but, alas, child-rearing is as time-consuming as it ever was and much of that is left to women. Angela Davis pointed out as early as 1981, 'The demand for universal and subsidized child care is a direct consequence of the rising number of working mothers.'[28]

Melinda Cooper's study of the transformation in the role of the Fordist family and of family relations during forty years of neoliberal policies, particularly in the United States, is a brilliant example of the kind of study required, even if it dwells mostly on the toxic legacy at the expense of the positive possibilities that lured so many people, including thoughtful and committed feminists, to support some version of the neoliberal agenda, at least for a while.[29] A labour force that is flexible, literate, intelligent and adaptable to the shifting requirements of changing divisions of labour while learning generic skills such as those currently appropriate to a digital economy is plainly desirable as one faction within the working class. From the mid-nineteenth century onwards, it was recognized in almost all capitalist societies that mass public education was essential for maintaining a flow of adequately trained labour to supply capital's ever-expanding needs. The danger was that workers might use their critical powers to dissect the inequities of exploitation and seek to remedy their own alienation. They might wonder how the promise of equality and freedom gets diabolically and dialectically inverted into the inequalities and unfreedom they see all around them. The promise of a liberalism founded on rights and free and open individualistic competition ends up producing mass misery and wage slavery. From the very beginning, as Charles Dickens had Mr Dombey opine in the novel of that

27   Ibid., p. 29.
28   Davis, *Women, Race and Class*, p. 243.
29   Cooper, *Family Values*.

name, he was all in favour of public education provided 'that the inferior classes should continue to be taught to know their position'.[30]

This raises the question of the content of the education that grounds contemporary social reproduction. The dominant political-economic institutions and hegemonic ruling ideas are inevitably biased towards if not dictated by those of the ruling classes. Most of the world's finance ministers and central bankers are trained in US economics departments – the most infamous being the Chicago Boys, who took over the Chilean economy in 1975; they were Chileans trained by Milton Friedman's group at the University of Chicago. Ukraine's finance minister teaches at Cambridge and proposes a full conversion to neoliberal orthodoxy in labour laws and fiscal policies while opening the country's rich agricultural lands to foreign corporate ownership (hitherto banned) in return for continued support in the war against Russia. The aim is to at least pretend to confront the pressing material questions of poverty, social inequality, environmental degradation, social exclusion and identity formation around the world, all the while shaping an adequate but rationed education and training of populations to facilitate their capacity to manage, use and adapt to the rapidly evolving technologies and policies of contemporary capitalism. Contemporary education has to do all of this without ever challenging capital itself.

Education is partially oriented to meet the evolving needs of production, but it is also a vehicle for class formation, reproduction and indoctrination. Access to elite schooling from prekindergarten to postdoctoral studies assures access to well-paying jobs and managerial positions in the privileged fields of mental as opposed to manual labour. The figures of financiers, merchant capitalists, industrialists, large land and property owners, high state and military figures, legal and financial experts, media monopolists, political leaders and the leaders of major cultural institutions along with those who, for some reason or other, are independently wealthy, are all deployed in their respective niches within the capitalist class. The education and reproduction of this class is a largely closed affair, though from time to time a meritocratic element creeps in to make a plausible story about 'rags to riches'. The dynamism of capital – its technological form in particular – along with its compounding growth and increasing mass, does create new opportunities for the induction of new, ambitious and vigorous individuals into a process of class transformation and renewal. At the same time, it also renders

---

30   Charles Dickens, *Dombey and Son* (London: Penguin, 2002 [1846–8]).

redundant past skills, mentalities and cultural forms that once sold well in the labour markets of the world. The capitalist class of the 2020s in the United States is very different from the capitalist class of the 1970s which set in motion that class project we now refer to as 'neoliberalism' as a means to secure and restore its collective class power even as it became somewhat more open to multiculturalism and the rights of women.

In the course of its inevitable expansion over time to create the world market, capital has encountered an incredible diversity of social systems, of cultural habits, of social relations, of juridical presuppositions and proto-state forms as well as institutions and practices of being in the world, some of which are inherited from long ago and some of which are newly created in the turmoil that inevitably results from the penetration of the practices of capital circulation and accumulation into hitherto untouched territories and among different peoples. Capital does not, as some suppose, necessarily homogenize these differences. But it has proven adept at adapting to them and using them to its own advantage wherever possible. It nurtures, for example, niche markets around ethnic and national differences. It seeks out populations endowed with certain skills and attitudes appropriate for certain forms of productive activity.

The bearer of the commodity 'capacity to labour' lives within a dense and dynamic matrix of socio-cultural relations which defy easy characterization or description. While there is no need to abandon the concept of capital as an ecosystemic totality and as an organizing principle for enquiries, it is important to recognize that other conceptual totalities intersect and sometimes disrupt those aspects of social formations geared to social reproduction. While social configurations based on the remnants of slavery, indentured labour and apartheid to this day still provide possibilities for the mobilization of particularly oppressive forms of labour supply, they also pose a barrier to the flexible circulation of labour capacity required by innovative shifts in the capacity to accumulate capital. Ossification within the social formation often produces what Cedric Robinson calls 'arrested development' in particular places and times.

It is hard to explore the terrain of social reproduction without encountering questions of intersectionality, defined as 'the multiple oppressions that constitute the social experience of many people' particularly but not exclusively women of colour.[31] These discriminatory and oppressive

---

31   David McNally, 'Intersections and Dialectics: Critical Reconstructions in Social Reproduction Theory', in Bhattacharya, *Social Reproduction Theory*.

experiences sometimes take on a caste-like character 'that sets the presumed supremacy of one group against the presumed inferiority of all other groups'. The basis for this is the supposedly immutable traits within human populations giving a long-lasting hierarchical structure to social relations even as they often overdetermine the class relation. Such divisions and segregations reverberate in the labour market, in the labour process, in commodity markets, on the streets, in commercial establishments, in access to housing and mortgage finance, in contacts with state or private institutions such as hospitals, schools and the like. Discriminations are everywhere, and it is indeed the case that many of them look more caste-like or clan-based rather than emanations of class. But the difficulty with intersectionality, as David McNally points out in Bhattacharya's edited collection on social reproduction theory, is that it treats every vector of oppression as independent, analyzable in itself and therefore only amenable to specific forms of amelioration. This essentialist reading disintegrates into a mechanical social atomism in which an attempted amelioration in one place or at one point is unaffected by the vector of oppression at another. McNally proposes, instead, a more organicist interpretation in which the multiple moments of discrimination and oppression are integrated within the human experience construed as a totality. The political problem is not defined by all the multiple differences that exist within the global order (which can be seen as a vital resource), but when such differences become the basis for discriminations and oppressions. This allows for a more systematic approach in which, for example, reforms targeted at class configurations have implications for gender and racial oppressions and vice versa. If, for example, all labour processes became oriented to the open and constructive instead of the soul destroying and crippling sort, the need for a large workforce of, say, Black immigrant women to do the rote, repetitive and soul-destroying work of care would disappear. The political challenge is then to seek out those ameliorations of specific labour practices that have maximal effects on other connected forms of oppression. At the same time, the mass of global wage labour has been rapidly increasing, and this generates incredible pressures to expand resources (including labour power) for social reproduction.

10
Extractivism and the Metabolic Relation to Nature

Labour is, first of all, a process between man and nature, a process by which man, through his own actions, mediates, regulates and controls the metabolism between himself and nature. He confronts the materials of nature as a force of nature. He sets in motion the natural forces which belong to his own body … in order to appropriate the materials of nature in a form adapted to his own needs. Through this movement he acts upon external nature and changes it, and in this way he simultaneously changes his own nature.[1]

The universality of this dialectical metabolic relation comprises the historical geography of humanity on Planet Earth. Much has been written about that metabolic relation, which forms the material basis of capital's mode of production viewed as a totality. It also constitutes a dynamic force in capital's social formation. The natural world is constituted through evolutionary processes that are, in principle, autonomous and independent but subsumed within capital's mode of production. How to conceptualize its role within the unfolding of capital's mode of production is a controversial problem. There are many different schools of thought as to how best to conceptualize, guide, regulate and act on that metabolic relation.[2] We begin with a concrete historical materialist example.

---

1 Marx, *Capital*, Vol. 1, p. 283.
2 Over the last forty years, an immense literature on capital and the metabolic relation to nature has been published. It is almost impossible to fuse the very different

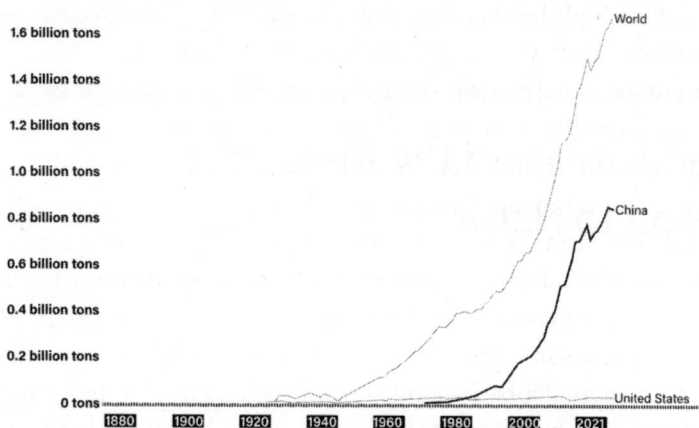

Figure 11. Annual CO$_2$ Carbon Emissions from Cement Production

In 2007–8 global capital ran into a major crisis. The epicentre was the collapse of the financial institutions supporting a speculative boom in the US housing market. The subsequent contraction in the US consumer market hit China's export industries hard. Unemployment and plant closures soared in China. The Chinese authorities responded by a massive switch to investment in domestic productive consumption. It concentrated on building the physical infrastructure required for massive urban and regional development. It built, for example, more than 20,000 miles of high-speed rail network within ten years, thus fundamentally contributing to the annihilation of space by time across the space-time of the Chinese economy. China built a significant number of wholly new cities, termed 'ghost cities' because no one was living in them at that time. It is widely accepted that, by these measures, the Chinese single-handedly held off the threat of a slide into a deep and long-lasting global depression. The demand for raw materials from China spread back down supply chains to countries like Australia and Chile, whose economies escaped the worst of the economic destruction felt elsewhere.

One of the of the consequences, however, was that China consumed, in two years, 45 per cent more cement than the US had consumed in the preceding century (see Figure 8). Unfortunately, the production of

contributions either politically or scientifically. Major recent works are John Bellamy Foster and Brett Clark, *The Robbery of Nature: Capitalism and the Economic Rift* (New York: *Monthly Review* Press, 2020); Jason W. Moore, *Capitalism in the Web of Life: Ecology and the Accumulation of Capital* (London: Verso 2015); and Kohei Saito, *Karl Marx's Ecosocialism: Capital, Nature, and the Unfinished Critique of Political Economy* (New York: *Monthly Review* Press, 2017). My own, now somewhat dated, contribution was *Justice, Nature and the Geography of Difference* (Oxford: Blackwell, 1996).

cement entails high levels of greenhouse gas emissions. Recovery from the economic crisis was largely bought at the expense of a dramatic global increase in extraction of raw materials accompanied by accelerating greenhouse gas emissions (Figure 11).[3] If, as Marx maintains, crises do not necessarily signal that the end is near for the capitalist mode of production but open up a phase of radical restructuring of how that mode of production works, the changing metabolic relation to nature was very much at stake in the resolution of this crisis. And the resolution was in any case temporary. By 2021, many of the main property development companies in China, such as Evergrande and Country Garden, defaulted on their debts, leaving the authorities in Beijing a financial mess to clean up. This was not the first time, nor will it likely be the last, when the laws of motion of capital dictate unwanted and, at some point, dangerous ecological consequences.

The increasingly 'monstrous mass' of value and surplus value (as Marx even in his day called it) in circulation across the globe, along with the increasing physical mass of use values required for the reproduction of capital, ought to be in the forefront of contemporary concerns. If there are global harms strongly in evidence – environmental, social, economic and political – one of the prime engines behind the production of these harms is the need to accommodate the rising and spiralling mass of value and use values in a limited world. In 1950, recall, global GDP stood at $9.25 trillion, rising to $100 trillion by 2023 – a more than tenfold increase in constant dollars. The resulting exponential pressure to open up new markets, to pursue new means of production, to extract more raw materials from the earth and to elicit additional labour power has been immense. Again we see that the consequent pressure on carbon emissions, climate change and habitat depletion arises out of the forces that dictate a rising mass rather than falling profit rates.

The relation to nature is a universal feature for all human societies. Its predominant qualities play a critical role in defining the characters of different modes of production. But the relation to nature implied by the laws of motion of capital is very different from the ecological impacts of indigenous bands, a feudal peasantry, a theocratic state or an imperial regime. This is not to deny the huge ecological impacts worldwide of even small indigenous bands who discovered the uses of fire. When the colonists arrived in New England, they found themselves in what they thought was a bountiful natural landscape, not understanding that the

---

3   Muriel Boselli, 'IEA sees record CO2 emissions in 2010', Reuters, 30 May 2011.

fecundity they saw was due to centuries of management of the forest edge by indigenous peoples using fire. On the other hand, the introduction of goats into Central America during the Spanish conquest, like the earlier introduction of sheep into the ecology of the Scottish Highlands, completely changed the vegetation, the soil structures and the water balances on the land.[4] The spread of non-native species with a little help from human activities has likewise had enormous and cumulative ecological impacts. The proliferation of viral diseases (of which Covid-19 is only one) is embedded in the metabolic mix of processes that combine natural processes with economic dynamics.

Contemporary capitalist corporations and capitalist states, armed with scientific understanding and all manner of powerful technologies, have the capacity to transform habitats overnight and to change, by accident or design, the course of planetary evolution. They do so through, for example, plant and animal breeding practices, genetic engineering (GMOs), the introduction of new chemical and biological agents, widespread habitat destruction (such as the deforestation of Amazonia, desertification or the ravages of open-cast mining) along with the radical transformation of contextual conditions (such as surging urbanization of populations and investments, waste disposal mountains, the rising salinity of oceans and increasing concentration of greenhouse gases). None of this would be so pressing were it not for the fact that capital necessarily proceeds in the spiral form of endless exponential growth because of its perpetual commitment to the production of surplus value and the search for profit. Burgeoning human populations (rising from 1.2 billion in 1850 to 8.2 billion today – see Figure 5) are also playing their part as significant agents of ecological and evolutionary as well as economic change. Population increase is, as I noted earlier, a vital concomitant of the exponential growth of capital.

The case of climate change is, for example, today in the forefront of debates as prolonged droughts, more frequent floods, life-threatening heat waves, hard-to-control fires and wave after wave of insect invasions and infections (viral or bacterial) plague the planet. The recent extraordinary flooding in Pakistan in 2022 (which inundated around one-third of the country's area) and the chronically diminished flows of the Yangtze and Colorado rivers through drought are examples of the changing scale of current environmental problems. To add to the mix, a military

---

4   William Cronon, *Changes in the Land: Indians, Colonists, and the Ecology of New England* (New York: Farrar, Straus and Giroux, 1983); William L. Thomas (ed.), *Man's Role in Changing the Face of the Earth* (Chicago: University of Chicago Press, 1956).

exchange of even tactical nuclear weapons is not (alas) impossible. This could threaten the habitability of much of the planet for all of humanity and most other living things. How capital and the capitalist state handle (or more often fail to handle) this range of potentialities is one of the most important political questions of our time.

Human beings, considered both individually and collectively, are of nature rather than within it. 'All production', says Marx, 'is appropriation of nature on the part of an individual within and through a specific form of society.'[5] This is Marx's first step towards a holistic, dialectical interpretation of the relation to nature. The relation to nature is deemed 'metabolic'. This refers to a relation between two or more elements, or 'moments', that are so intertwined that one element cannot exist independently of its other(s). Bees cannot exist without pollination and pollination depends heavily on bees. This constitutes a metabolic relation. Likewise, the heart cannot continue to beat without oxygen that comes from the lungs. The two elements or moments are qualitatively different but co-dependent. A hurricane, on the other hand, may knock a house down, but the hurricane does not need the house to exist anymore than the house needs the hurricane to exist. The relation between house and hurricane in this case is independent, autonomous and contingent. Important though such an event may be (particularly to the house's owner), this is not a metabolic relation. Human labour, in the sense we are considering it here, is defined by its metabolic role in transforming elements in nature into useful products to support human life. The labour theory of value rests on this metabolic relation. Marx construes the relation between production and realization as a social metabolic relation. Unfortunately, industrial capital disturbs 'the metabolic interaction between man and the earth, i.e. it prevents the return to the soil of its constituent elements consumed by man in the form of food and clothing; hence it hinders the operation of the eternal natural condition for the lasting fertility of the soil'.[6] The destructive consequences are everywhere apparent. In *Capital*, Marx puts it this way:

> Capitalist agriculture is a progress in the art, not only robbing the worker, but of robbing the soil; all progress in increasing the fertility of the soil for a given time is a progress towards ruining the more long-lasting sources of that fertility. The more a country proceeds from large-scale industry

---

5   Marx, *Grundrisse*, p. 87.
6   Marx, *Capital*, Vol. 1, p. 637.

as the background of its development, as in the case of the United States, the more rapid is the process of destruction. Capitalist production, therefore, only develops the techniques and the degree of combination of the social process of production by simultaneously undermining the original sources of all wealth – the soil and the worker.[7]

The labour of transforming elements in the natural world into commodities useful to consumers, however, presupposes a form that is distinctly and exclusively human. Thus the famous formulation in *Capital*: 'What distinguishes the worst architect from the best of bees is that the architect builds the cell in his mind before he constructs it in wax … Man not only effects a change of form in the materials of nature; he also realizes his own purpose.'[8] Note here the purposiveness of the action. Bees, it could be said, have a purpose – pollination. But 'human purpose' is changeable, perpetually shifting and open to human imagination. It differs from individual to individual and takes various social and political forms. 'Purpose' has, however, to be stripped of any teleological presumption of 'becoming', such as Hegel's transition to an Absolute State or the vision of an ultimate degrowth communism promoted in some Marxist narratives, such as the romanticized utopianism proposed by Kohei Saito.

The starting point is, then, the recognition that human labour is wholly natural even as it is social. The transformation of nature it produces is simultaneously a transformation of human nature. We cannot change the world around us without changing ourselves, and we cannot change ourselves without changing the world around us. We build vast cities, but then we have to live in them and adapt our personas accordingly. The question of what kind of city we (and capital) build is not independent of the question of what kind of people we want to become. 'Man makes himself', says Marx, by way of the metabolic relation to nature. But in 'making itself' humanity also remakes aspects of the planet and the land.[9] Capital produces and reproduces a special kind of nature modified through human action, struggling to be adequate to capital's nature at a particular moment in its historical geography, powered onwards by the pursuit of often disparate human goals and purposes, all overlain by the requirement of surplus value production. The historical geography of human nature under capital is thus a product of the

---

7   Ibid., Vol. 1, p. 638.
8   Ibid., Vol. 1, p. 284.
9   V. Gordon Childe, *Man Makes Himself* (Nottingham: Spokesman Books, 2003).

transformation of nature wrought purposively through human action. When Gramsci wrote his inspired essay 'Americanism and Fordism' in the 1930s, he fully recognized that the Fordist production system was shaping a new persona and political subjectivity through the specific qualities of the work experience on the assembly line.[10]

Human nature is perpetually changing its nature through shifts in the metabolic relation to nature. But there is many a slip between cup and lip. Engels puts it this way:

> Let us not ... flatter ourselves overmuch on account of our human victories over nature. For each such victory nature takes its revenge on us. Each victory, it is true, in the first place brings about the results we expected, but in the second and third places it has quite different, unforeseen effects which only too often cancel the first ... Thus at every step we are reminded that we by no means rule over nature like a conqueror over a foreign people ... but that we, with flesh, blood, and brain, belong to nature, and exist in its midst, and that all our mastery of it consists in the fact that we have the advantage over all other creatures of being able to learn its laws and apply them correctly.[11]

In using the term 'metabolic' to characterize this foundational labour relation, Marx is emphasizing interpenetration and co-evolution rather than separation and autonomy. He rejects the Cartesian dualism of nature versus culture in favour of more dialectical understandings, such as those laid out in Richard Levins and Richard Lewontin's *The Dialectical Biologist*.[12] The human and the natural are interwoven. They are integral to each other within capitalism as a social formation as well as within the capitalist mode of production. There is, I therefore argued in *Justice, Nature and the Geography of Difference*, 'nothing unnatural about New York City', any more than there is anything unnatural about beavers building dams and ants and birds building nests.[13] The theory of the capitalist mode of production thus has to be grounded in an understanding of the metabolic relation to nature. Capital, as a social formation, engages

---

10   Antonio Gramsci, 'Americanism and Fordism', in *Selections from the Prison Notebooks* (New York: International Publishers, 1971), pp. 279–318.

11   Friedrich Engels, *Dialectics of Nature*, in Marx and Engels, *Collected Works*, Vol. 25 (New York: International Publishers), pp. 460–1, cited in Harvey, *Justice, Nature and the Geography of Difference*, p. 184.

12   Richard Levins and Richard Lewontin, *The Dialectical Biologist* (Cambridge, MA: Harvard University Press, 1987).

13   Harvey, *Justice, Nature and the Geography of Difference*, p. 186.

with and perpetually transforms the nature it inhabits at the same time as it transforms itself. Capital – value in motion – may be the dynamic force in the social formation, but value arises out of labour's metabolic relation with nature.

This requires a very distinctive set of concepts and practices to help us theorize the co-evolution of capital's nature, even in the face of a vast array of holistic and idealist concepts and practices, such as those of deep ecology, responsibility to nature, the land ethic (Aldo Leopold), ecofeminism (Carolyn Merchant and Maria Mies) and ecosocialism (Saito), circulating within the capitalist social formation. The coming into being of capital's hegemony entailed, argues Merchant in *The Death of Nature*, a transformation of the concept of nature as sentient and alive both within and around us into a set of objectified external processes and things to be appropriated and scientifically exploited under the utilitarian calculus of use values supposedly adequate for the functioning of endless capital accumulation.[14] This is the world as defined by the empiricist and positivist 'natural' sciences that capital has historically cultivated.

The capitalist mode of production cannot be properly understood without some understanding of the far broader socio-economic, political and metabolic conditions prevailing within the totality of a capitalist social formation. In the late 1860s, according to Saito, Marx recognized that he needed to better integrate ecological perspectives into his political economy, particularly after the prominent soil scientist of the time, Justus von Liebig, switched from the optimistic view that Malthusian constraints on increasing soil fertility could be overcome by judicious resort to mineral fertilizers to recognizing that most agricultural practices rested for economic reasons on soil mining and the robbery of fertility even when mineral fertilizers were available. It was around this time as well that George Perkins Marsh published his stunning book *Man and Nature: or, Physical Geography as Modified by Human Action.*[15] In this book, deforestation, soil erosion and soil exhaustion featured large in explaining the collapse of earlier civilizations. The bourgeoisie has, therefore, known of the dangers of ecological collapse all along.

The fragmented attempts around the world to replace the overwhelming power of capital with some alternative have drawn sustenance from the loose bonding of a huge array of potentially unalienated human

---

14   Carolyn Merchant, *The Death of Nature: Women, Ecology, and the Scientific Revolution* (San Francisco: HarperOne, 1990).

15   George Perkins Marsh, *Man and Nature: or, Physical Geography as Modified by Human Action* (Mineola, NY: Dover, 2021).

practices with respect to alternative forms of the metabolic relation to nature. The need to care for some aspect of that metabolic relation to avoid, say, species extinction or soil exhaustion, depletion of fish stocks, loss of honeybees through insecticide application and so on, is imperative. Under the rule of capital, of course, it is alienated labour under the rule of alienated capital that mediates the metabolic relation to nature under capital. By extension, this implies that the labour process designed and imposed by capital necessarily entails an alienated relation of both capital and labour to nature as well as to each other. The capitalist puts labour capacity to work on the transformation of nature as if the latter is an object that can be reshaped into use values for sale as things in the market. Any quest to retrieve for labour an unalienated relation to nature or to the land at some point requires an anticapitalist politics that breaks the relation that ties labour so tightly to nature construed as a dead object.

Inherent in the concept of a metabolic relationship is the principle that all socio-economic projects, particularly those forged through the circulation of capital, are simultaneously environmental/ecological projects. Conversely, all ecological projects to achieve, for example, 'sustainability' (whatever that means) or 'harmony with nature' (as the Chinese proclaim), are necessarily socio-economic projects. Bourgeois policymakers today partially recognize the importance of this principle by requiring environmental impact statements to accompany socio-economic proposals. Scrutinizing ecological projects for their direct and indirect costs, usually calculated in the money terms of cost-benefit analysis, has become a common practice in the calculus of capital. But, as many critics point out, the monetary valuations are not only fictitious but in themselves anti-ecological in the deeper sense required for the maintenance of planetary health and for the restoration of an unalienated relation to nature. The latter ambition is expressed in bourgeois terms as the elusive but endless search for 'the re-enchantment of nature' in the face of an all-too-often soulless and alienating industrialism.

It is sometimes said that Marx lays bare the structure of his thinking in the *Grundrisse* but buries it so deep in the text of *Capital* as to make it difficult to discern. But there are occasions in *Capital*, often in footnotes, where Marx reveals a great deal about the principles that guide his scientific approach to historical materialism. This is so with the fourth footnote to the chapter on machinery: 'Technology reveals the active relation of man to nature, the direct process of the production of his life, and thereby it also lays bare the process of the production of the social relations of his life, and of the mental conceptions that flow from those relations.'[16] In this accounting, it seems that the totality is constructed out of five different but autonomous and independent moments, all in dynamic (dialectical, metabolic and often contradictory) interrelation with each other. Marx then goes on to criticize the 'abstract materialism of the natural sciences' (dominated by empiricism and positivism). He proposes, instead, a scientific historical materialism capable of developing 'from the actual, given relations of life, the forms in which these have been apotheosized'. This, he concludes, 'is the only scientific method'.[17]

The language here is important. Notice that technology 'reveals', 'discloses' or 'lays bare' but does not determine the relation to nature. Marx is not, as many believe, a technological determinist (that is the dominant positivist interpretation), even though he assigns a critical role to revolutions in the 'productive forces' in his account of capital's history. It is from this historical materialist perspective that Marx proposes to investigate the internal relations within the evolutionary totality of capital as a social formation. In the footnote in *Capital*, there are five 'moments' in dynamical and dialectical interrelation, held together to constitute the totality of the social formation. In *The Enigma of Capital*, I expanded this to seven moments through consideration of the contextual conditions implicit in Marx's texts.[18] While each moment is independent, autonomous and contingent, no moment can be fully understood outside of its relation to all the others – hence the metabolic character of their interrelations. The seven moments, in no particular order of significance, are:

1 The labour processes of surplus value production
2 Technologies and organizational forms
3 Social relations (caste, clan, class and gender)
4 Institutional and administrative arrangements (including the state, the law and the interstate system)
5 The metabolic relation to nature
6 The daily life of consumption and social reproduction
7 Mental conceptions, including scientific and cultural understandings of and beliefs about the metabolic relation to nature across the globe

---

16   Marx, *Capital*, Vol. 1, p. 493.
17   Ibid., Vol. 1, pp. 493–4.
18   David Harvey, *The Enigma of Capital: and the Crises of Capitalism* (Oxford: Oxford University Press, 2010).

The evolutionary dynamic of the capitalist social formation is shaped by transformations and inter-relations across all of these moments working together. Watch the history unfolding when one moment undergoes shattering changes (in, for example, technology or social relations) and the often-shattering effects on many if not all the other moments which reverberate throughout the totality. This conception is in line with Lefebvre's reading of totality, which 'challenges mechanistic-determinist explanations of socioeconomic transformations and ... shows how the dynamic movement of parts also exerts a constitutive effect on the unfolding of the whole'.[19] Under this reading, circumstances can arise in which one or two moments might take a leading role in promoting a particularly prominent path for the 'becoming' of capital. Uneven development among the moments may produce tensions (sometimes productive) between them. Mental conceptions and cultural beliefs, for example, may have trouble keeping pace with technological and organizational changes, and intended and unintended consequences may follow.

When people started to see the world through microscopes and telescopes, for example, their mental conceptions of the world in general and of nature in particular changed significantly, as did many social, economic and scientific practices. A world of microbes and bacteria became visible, for example, and a germ theory of disease along with adequate treatments and appropriate social behaviours also became possible. When new viruses emerged after HIV/AIDS, culminating most recently in Covid-19, autonomous transformations within a nature, though modified by human action, called forth major adjustments in mental conceptions (for example, the role of DNA), in social relations, in the daily life of social reproduction, as well as in institutional and administrative arrangements. Reflect, therefore, how the world adapted and adjusted in many ways across the seven moments in response to HIV/AIDS or Covid-19 and with what effects, both positive and negative.

This way of thinking about co-evolutionary processes generates significant insights about all of moments involved. The metabolic relation to nature is just one, though key, moment within the matrix of all the other metabolic relations that constitute a social formation. When the question is asked, 'Where do we start to organize an anticapitalist movement within the existing "becoming" of capital?', the answer has to be that we can start anywhere across the seven moments, including the metabolic relation to nature. But we also have to move relationally

19   Arboleda, *Planetary Mine*, p. 193.

and dialectically across the whole matrix of interrelations among the moments to secure substantive qualitative changes within the social formation. Struggles for environmental justice, for example, can morph into anticapitalist struggles in general and provoke quests for new technologies and organizational forms which, in turn, presuppose entirely new social relations. These can, in their own turn, raise questions of administrative structures and of law at the same time that they treat the quality of daily life for people as their testing ground. The impact has to be gauged by the accumulating effects within and across all the other moments within the social formation. Activists in the ecology movement invariably find they cannot realize their often narrowly defined ambitions for a more 'harmonious' relation to nature without pursuing substantial changes across the six other moments (social relations, in particular). Instead of giving up on such a project as too vast and too complicated, the need arises for a collective social strategy to change what in our times appears to be the suicidal path in the evolution of the metabolic relation to nature. The answer has to be through the development of a co-evolutionary dynamic opposed to that which capital itself is currently defining.

Paying attention to the dynamic interrelations between these seven moments and studying their co-evolution also invites an immanent critique of past attempts to construct anticapitalist, socialist, anarchist, feminist or communist alternatives. There is a tendency within social theory, as well as in utopian conceptions of anticapitalist alternatives, to prioritize and privilege one of these moments as the 'silver bullet' for forging all meaningful societal change. There are environmental determinists (like Jared Diamond and Jeffrey Sachs), who attribute the macro shifts in human history to environmental forces to which human societies must perforce adapt; institutionalists (economists like Daron Acemoglu), who argue that differences in the wealth of nations are explicable primarily through the forms of the state, its institutions and laws; technological determinists (many Marxists, such as G. A. Cohen), who see transformations in the productive forces as the moving force of history along with their bourgeois counterparts, like Thomas Friedman, who, in *The World Is Flat*, freely acknowledge the consummate power of technologies to reshape the world); then there are the anti-state anarchists and some feminists, who exclusively focus on the question of social relations (nonhierarchical and nonpatriarchal).[20] Other thinkers,

---

20   Jared Diamond, *Guns, Germs, and Steel: The Fates of Human Societies* (New York: W. W. Norton, 2005); Jeffrey D. Sachs, *The End of Poverty: Economic Possibilities*

like Paul Hawkins, anchor their explanations and future hopes in autonomously evolving practices of daily life; finally, there are the idealists, who see human evolution as reflecting the outcomes of vast ideological struggles in the field of mental conceptions and cultural beliefs.[21] The perspective of historical materialism sees all these moments at work in interaction with one another within the totality.

If we seek, for example, to reconstruct the hegemonic rise of neoliberalism from the mid-1970s onwards, we need to study the shifts across all of the moments in interaction. Mental conceptions underwent spectacular transformations, such that the ruling interpretation of neoliberalism these days is that it was a transformation wrought first in the world of ideas (Thatcherism, Reaganism and the turn to anti-Keynesian supply-side economics). In *A Brief History of Neoliberalism*, I interpreted it as a class project that emerged out of the crisis of accumulation in the 1970s, which entrained a huge tail of ideological baggage to disguise its class origins and character.[22] The transformation of mental conceptions was a critical feature along with social relations and institutional arrangements. Others attribute it to the coming together of new technologies and organizational forms that enabled decentralization, flexible specialization, small-batch production, just-in-time production systems and elaborate supply chains, all pinned together by new and far cheaper systems of transport and communications across the globe. This, in turn, relates to a radical transformation of labour and social relations with the turn to precarity, flexibility and deskilling of the labouring force engineered with the help of a technically skilled managerial labour force while undermining of trade union power and democratic socialist parties. Still others believe that the whole shift was primarily orchestrated by the rise of finance and merchant capital at the expense of industrial capital, all enclosed within the rise of new state forms in the wake of the collapse of the Bretton Woods arrangements. In truth, all of these moments were involved, and accounts of all are necessary in the kind of historical-geographical narrative we need if we are to truly represent what happened.

for Our Time (New York: Penguin, 2005); Daron Acemoglu and James A. Robinson, *Why Nations Fail: The Origins of Power, Prosperity, and Poverty* (London: Crown Currency, 2012); G. A. Cohen, *Karl Marx's Theory of History* (Princeton, NJ: Princeton University Press, 2000); Thomas Friedman, *The World Is Flat: A Brief History of the Twenty-First Century* (New York: Farrar, Straus and Giroux, 2005).

21   Paul Hawken, *Blessed Unrest: How the Largest Social Movement in History Is Restoring Grace, Justice, and Beauty to the World* (New York: Viking, 2007).

22   David Harvey, *A Brief History of Neoliberalism* (Oxford: Oxford University Press, 2005).

Revolutionary social change, including that set in motion by the bourgeoisie, depends on the subtle bringing together of all these different moments if it is to have even a chance to succeed. This is precisely what previous attempts to build a socialist alternative failed to do or even recognize as necessary, even though partial attempts were made and in some instances are continuing (as in China and Cuba). One major error of Stalinism was to believe that transformation of the productive forces was sufficient, without exploring more thoroughly questions of social relations, the material qualities of labour processes and, perhaps most important of all, mental and cultural conceptions that could not be easily reshaped by educational indoctrination. The ecological disasters in the Soviet Union reflected the neglect of Marx's views on the metabolic qualities of the relations to nature. But capital, too, neglects the evolving form of these relations at its peril.

Plainly, any shaping of revolutionary consciousness in the quest for alternatives cannot afford to neglect the alienation of nature as one of its critical tasks. This is what Saito desires with his portrait of Marx as an indigenous thinker. As Arboleda also puts it, 'Marx began to see in non-Western forms of landownership and social reproduction, some of the embryonic and unrealized forms of the universalized political community of the future. Furthermore, he began to identify the revolutionary potential of peasant and non-Western communities.'[23] But what thwarted such a future, Marx recognized, was not the proliferation of agro-industrial technologies and gargantuan modern technologies of extractivism in the mining sector, but the seeming inability to scale up precapitalist institutions to the global level. How can we scale up the landless peasant movement in Brazil (MST), for example, in a way that is compatible with China's industrialism in a world shaped by coercive laws of competition between both capital and states?

Saito, for example, in his book *Marx in the Anthropocene*, based on a study of Marx's later unpublished notebooks, indicates that the late (post-1868) Marx exhibited a far greater concern for the science behind the metabolic relation to nature and a far deeper appreciation of the qualities of that metabolic relation in precapitalist societies (a theme briefly touched on in Marx's *Grundrisse*).[24] He concludes, on this basis, that Marx was increasingly positioning himself as a 'de-growth communist'. Saito as a result abandons historical materialism and totally

23   Arboleda, *Planetary Mine*, p. 212.
24   Kohei Saito, *Marx in the Anthropocene: Towards the Idea of Degrowth Communism* (Cambridge: Cambridge University Press, 2023).

rewrites Volume 1 of *Capital*, as evidenced by the revisions Marx inserted into the French edition, revisions which Engels unfortunately ignored in his preparation of the definitive German (and English) versions. Saito could be correct in this interpretation, but he offers little textual evidence from the unpublished notebooks. He instead relies almost entirely on relatively minor revisions in the French edition of *Capital* in 1872 and some letters from Marx that indicate from his interest in precapitalist social formations that he might have had further revisions in mind. Abandoning the precepts of historical materialism amounts to abandoning what Walter Rodney considers the essence of Marx's contribution. It reduces the concept of degrowth communism to an empty signifier, an abstract utopian romanticism which can be transcended only by re-inserting it into the matrix of social relations, production capacities, technologies, mental conceptions, everyday life, institutional arrangements and, of course, the everchanging nature of the metabolic relation to nature.

Consider, for example, the problem of climate change, which has become dramatically more important over the last decade or so. As an idea, it originated within the ranks of a middle-class professional scientific elite back in the 1960s that sought to change the world by promoting radically different mental conceptions, regulatory practices and public policies that did not impinge on their own job prospects, lifestyles and qualities of daily life. Interestingly, there was a serious contribution by Soviet scholars that for political reasons was largely unnoticed. But none of this got anywhere, particularly in the face of intense opposition by the fossil fuel lobby with their hired guns and powerful influence over the media. It was only when the consequences of climate change began to be felt on the ground, when daily life, particularly for the impoverished and the marginalized, became increasingly insufferable, that popular mental conceptions began to shift. But its progress remains blocked by an institutional framework (the coercive laws of competition within the interstate system in particular) that remains totally inadequate to the task of collectively dealing with what is increasingly recognized as a dire situation. Nor is the present state of social relations (inequality in particular) conducive to the kind of action required to bring our metabolic relation to nature into a happier configuration. When an oligarchy rules in its own narrow interest (building, as in the case of Peter Thiel, the equivalent of survival arks in New Zealand) and promotes its own ruling ideas through media control to the exclusion of all else, it is difficult to articulate constructive responses.

Meanwhile, if we conclude that our metabolic relation to nature is headed in a such a suicidal direction as to warrant major intervention, we need to ask in what ways we could change all the other moments in the co-evolutionary process that shape the way the metabolic relation to nature is unfolding. This leads to some very simple questions that unfortunately require astonishingly complicated and difficult answers. What shifts will be required in mental conceptions and cultural beliefs? What social relations might facilitate any proposed change of direction? What production and consumption systems (and energy and raw material requirements) could help revolutionize the metabolic relation to nature? What technologies and organizational forms in production, exchange, transport and communications would be required? What qualities of daily life might need to be sacrificed, substituted or created? What administrative and legal adjustments (for example, reforms of the capitalist state and the interstate system) would we need to implement? These are all valid questions to which adequate answers have to be found, even in the face of an omnipresent problem of unintended consequences.

Capital's management practices with respect to the metabolic relation to nature call for critical dissection. The ideas of extractivism, for example, grew to prominence in the colonial period and have carried over, much reinforced, into our own time. The original use values for capitalist production are scattered over the surface or deep within the Earth. They require the deployment of human labour to discover and extract them. The monetized value of these so-called natural resources should by rights belong to the peoples living in their proximity. But colonial practice saw otherwise. While the raw materials were extracted from a particular place, they were typically processed elsewhere under the supervision of capitalist corporations and powers. The processors appropriated most of the wealth. To this day, Ecuador exports crude oil and imports refined oil at great cost.

The erroneous separation of nature from culture in thought and concept, initiated most explicitly by Descartes, was a persuasive historic product, internalized within the logic and practices of capital itself. The duality of use value and exchange value internalized a contradiction between material qualities and social relations. This distinction is still with us. Under the rule of capital, 'Nature becomes purely an object for humankind, purely a matter of utility; ceases to be recognized as a power for itself; and the theoretical discovery of its autonomous laws appears merely as a ruse so as to subjugate it under human needs, whether as an object of consumption or as a means of production.'[25] This is not, it is important to stress, Marx's own normative view (nor is it mine) of how we should properly view the metabolic relation to nature. It is Marx's representation of capital's way of seeing nature, as implied in capital's metabolic practices in market exchange and the material qualities of the built environments in which we have to live. This is what arises out of 'the actual, given relations of life, the forms in which these have been apotheosized.'[26] These are the ideas about the metabolic relation to nature 'adequate to' a purely capitalist mode of production but destructive to the qualities of the nature we inhabit.

Much also depends here on how the concept of totality is deployed. When Marx writes that capital is destined to create the world market, he is casting his thinking about capital as a totality at a global level. This market is very different from a local farmers' market. The world rules-based trade order (as defined by the World Trade Organization), largely designed and, until recently, mainly policed by the United States, is a feature cast at a global scale but seemingly irrelevant to understanding the farmers' market. Tomato growers in New Jersey are acutely aware, for example, that they are in competition in the supermarkets (but not in the farmers' market) with Dutch greenhouse produce. Plainly, scale matters. In the same way as it makes sense to conceptualize the human body as a totality operating within the totality of activity in a local region, so local economies are increasingly dependent on and integrated with other local economies. In turn, they are often part of a regional economy as a working totality – a 'structured coherence' – defined at another scale (such as the Midwest in the US, the Pearl River Delta in China, Bavaria in Germany, the pampas in Argentina). It is in these regional and local economies that natural variation, emphasized and highlighted by variations in labour productivity, produces a 'second nature' in capital's own troublesome and often faulty image.

The qualities of the current metabolic relation to nature exhibit a vast diversity across Planet Earth and regional and local divisions of labour and specializations of function depend on them. These qualities are in constant transformation through absorption, consumption, exhaustion and depletion, through soil mining and extractivism. This takes place at the same time as capital's active production of space, place and environment through fixed capital and consumption fund formation, in and on

---

25   Marx, *Grundrisse*, p. 410.
26   Marx, *Capital*, Vol. 1, pp. 493–4.

the land, permit capital to build its own geography, beginning with the distinction between the city and the country and progressing through all manner of regional specializations. This opens up the Malthusian question of natural limits. It also opens up the tradition of Prometheanism in the attempt to produce a new nature more adequate for capital (which is very different from producing a new nature for the benefit of humanity).[27]

It is vital to recognize that there is, however, nothing purely 'natural' about so-called 'natural resources' or 'naturally arising scarcities', since they are elements in the natural world subject to technological, social, cultural and economic appraisals. To attribute economic crises to scarcities in nature, as did Malthus, is to confess to an inability to adapt technologies, cultures and social and economic forms to metabolic relations more adequate to capital's (or our) requirements. The concept of scarcity is not natural but a product of capital's marketing practices. Without scarcity, market prices could not form. If relative scarcity does not exist, it must therefore be created, if only to ensure that market forces and allocations can function. To attribute scarcities to nature is to render all attempts to eradicate them moot.

The rich and diverse use values derived from nature are not initially products of human labour. By capital's (and Marx's) definition, such use values have no inherent market value until they are used, extracted, refined and otherwise manipulated through the application of human labour. So-called 'natural' use values have to be conceptualized, says Marx, as 'free gifts of nature'. Marx's position here is controversial but helpful. Yet his reasoning is widely misunderstood. Marx is simply saying that capital treats environmental goods untouched by human hands as free gifts having zero value. Capital helps itself to the fecund diversity of use values in nature without conceding the need to pay anything, no matter how important the use values extracted from nature are in fuelling the production of value and surplus value. This is capital's value theory (and not Marx's, nor, for that matter, mine) in action. Marx is merely reporting on what capital values and what it does not, as registered in its metabolic practices.

There are, however, two points of modification necessary to this position. In the first, some natural use values can be commodified, owned and therefore traded by whoever owns them at a price, even in the absence

---

27   John Dryzek, *The Politics of the Earth: Environmental Discourses* (Oxford: Oxford University Press, 1997).

of any application of labour. Marx clearly accepts the idea, at the outset of *Capital*, that commodities can exist which have a price but no value and cites the case of uncultivated land as an example. This is also the case with mineral deposits, waterfalls and other potential use values in nature. This defines the role of a landed capital class, charging rent (an unearned income) in return for granting access to the free gifts of nature. The rent is, in effect, a tax or access fee levied by landed property owners (including the state) on access to natural resources. The yield on that rent can be capitalized into a market price for ownership of the use value (for example, land or mineral deposits) in question. Such rights of access can be traded as property rights. Hence the importance of land, property and resource markets in regulating access to the free gifts of nature. This first modification derives from the ambiguous position of land and all the use values therein as a universal and basic means of production that had, to some degree, to be commodified and monetized prior to the domination of capitalist industrial production. All of this hints at the power of rentiers to exploit common property resources (such as the oceans). It also forms the basis for the operations of a class of landed capitalists. What initially appears as a feudal residual turns out to become the primary form of rentiership as capital acquires its most mature form. In this way, landed capital can secure its role in Marx's theoretical elaboration as one of the three great classes in the capitalist social formation. So-called natural scarcities are the social product of this class power.

In the second modification, the state and capital in general find that capital, impelled by competition, super-exploits in a destructive way key use values in the natural world that need to be preserved and protected for future use. Capital, left to itself, unrestrained but operating under the pressures of the coercive laws of competition, will inevitably destroy the two primary sources of its own wealth, labour and the soil. The same kind of regulatory move to defend the lives of labourers through regulating the length of the working day has to be applied to protect the fertility of the soil along with the resources contained therein from excessive exploitation and unlimited extractivism. A parallel concern is, incidentally, expressed in bourgeois economics in the theory of market failure due to what are called externalities – use values that enter into production at zero price but which get extracted and used in such a way as to restrict or destroy their future availability.

Finally, we need to confront the role of a contradiction that runs throughout much of Marx's theorizing about capital's nature. This concerns the way in which individual capitalists seeking to maximize their own self-interest and, forced by the coercive laws of competition, act in a way that undermines the conditions required for the healthy reproduction of capital as a social metabolic relation. This is the contradiction that leads capitalists to produce a falling rate of profit by way of the individual pursuit of relative surplus value. Something analogous occurs in the way the metabolic relation to nature unfolds.

Garrett Hardin's famous essay 'The Tragedy of the Commons' outlines one of the most egregious ways in which capital's dominant economic logic leads to the abuse if not destruction of ecological aggregates and common property resources (including the air we breathe).[28] Hardin imagines a common pasture used by many cattle herders. The cattle herders seek each to augment their wealth and power by adding another head of cattle to their herd. This increases the wealth of each herder by a whole unit while the cost to the herder of land degradation through overgrazing is spread across all users of the commons. It is economically rational for all herders to add cattle to the point where the land is totally degraded. Conventional economists have turned this into a parable favouring enclosure of the commons and individual property rights, because then the costs as well as the benefits would, they argue, be internalized within the individual production unit (presuming no externality effects). But that was not Hardin's point. He was concerned with population growth. A family would benefit from an extra child, but the environmental costs would be spread everywhere, eventually diminishing the Earth's fecundity. The same logic drives car ownership. I benefit from owning a car but the extra costs of air pollution and carbon emissions when I use it to drive to the local supermarket are spread over the globe. Individualized property rights are not the answer. Draconian regulation by a world authority, Hardin held, is required (China's one child policy imposed in 1980 was a step in this direction). How this works out depends very much on the scale of the phenomena in question.

Take the case of air pollution. In Marx's day, air quality was an extremely important issue within the household. Cooking over open fires in fetid slums, smoke inhalation, mouldy interiors, lack of running water and adequate sewage disposal all posed serious health problems at individual and local levels for impoverished working populations. Water-borne diseases (for example, cholera) posed serious hazards. The supposedly simple bucolic life often nostalgically conjured up around

---

28   Garrett Hardin, 'The Tragedy of the Commons', *Science* 162: 3859 (December 1968): 1243–8.

the lives of Scottish crofters in the eighteenth century as close to a pris-
tine nature was in fact based on the dangerous smoke of peat fires in the
cotters' huts. The pollution of clean water in Amazonia with the mercury
and cyanide used by rogue gold miners or the lackadaisical protections
supposedly practiced by oil companies are an overwhelming complaint
of indigenous peoples, for whom water quality means everything. This is
paralleled in the United States by siting toxic waste dumps on indigenous
lands. Particulate pollution from industrial plant and households and,
later on, from car and truck emissions, contributes to poor air quality
for many urban residents, even in upscale neighbourhoods. The affluent
Upper East Side in New York City has some of the worst concentrations of particulate matter in the city, thanks to the often-clogged FDR
Expressway that runs along its edge. The application of public health
principles to living conditions has had to confront such problems, but
to this day is only partially successful in imposing the land use management, the building design and user codes required.

The Great Smog (based on a temperature inversion) that occurred
in London beginning 5 December 1952 concentrated sulphur in the air
from the burning of coal in domestic hearths and turned the fog a dirty
yellow across the whole metropolis. Somewhere between 4,000 and
10,000 people died. The answer was to ban coal fires, switching to electricity produced in power plants with super-tall smokestacks that blew
the particulates into the atmosphere high above the temperature inversion (the most iconic was the Battersea Power Station in London). After
a few years, the Scandinavians were complaining about the acidification
of their lakes and forests and lodged complaints with Britain for in effect
dealing with externalities by blowing them somewhere else. Pollution
problems rarely get solved, but instead just get moved around. Margaret
Thatcher (a chemist by training) finally conceded the Scandinavian case
after Britain had bought time and retrofitted many of its power stations
to either capture the sulphur output or convert to cleaner natural gas.
The power stations of Ohio had similar regional effects on New England
and parts of Canada. In recent times, major air-quality events have hit
several metropolitan areas, from Delhi to Paris and across multiple
Chinese cities. Not to be outdone, New York City and the whole Eastern
Seaboard of the US had several days of major air-quality alerts from
Canadian wildfires.

And then there are the global problems: climate change, deforestation and desertification, habitat destructions and numerous species
extinctions. Systemic pollution of oceans and water supplies. Excessive

use of fertilizers and pesticides particularly in industrialized agriculture, all of which gets into rivers and oceans with pernicious effects. Some problems are very specific. For example, the use of chlorofluorocarbons (CFCs) in the massive use of refrigeration from the 1920s on, ensured, among other things, a much safer urban food supply to burgeoning metropolises, but the CFCs subsequently produced an ever-widening hole in the ozone layer that protects Earth from radiation, especially in Antarctic and peri-Antarctic regions (southern Argentina and Chile, Australia and New Zealand). It took difficult international negotiations to produce the Montreal Protocol, which phased out the use of CFCs. This was one of the first examples (though the earlier banning of DDT, thanks to the efforts of Rachel Carson, came close) of the sort of international agreement and coordination needed to deal with a whole raft of other environmental problems, including the mutations of deadly contagious viruses that may in part be the result of increasing environmental stresses attributable to the rising mass of output and of value. By far the most existential problem in these times is the question of climate change, which is running out of control with the consequent proliferation of extreme events (floods, hurricanes, droughts, intolerable heat waves, fires and so on). In this case attempts at international agreement have produced a lot of promises but not much movement on the ground. Carbon dioxide emissions are still increasing and other greenhouse gasses, such as methane, remain largely uncontrolled. The danger is that global warming may, for example, melt the global tundra, thus releasing massive quantities of methane to produce further runaway global warming.

The evolution of this issue may well be rendered doubly problematic because of the path dependencies and potential feedback effects involved. The interstate system of competition is an entirely inadequate institutional structure for confronting global ecological problems. The mechanics behind the tragedy of the commons here applies with force. The benefit of using fossil fuels lies largely within the state, but the costs of global warming are visited unevenly on the whole world. The emergent interstate system may have been adequate for capital in its early years, but it is now proving wholly inadequate to confront the internal contradictions of the capitalist social formation, let alone for properly managing the global commons in ways to protect the ecological health of Planet Earth. The biggest barrier to cogent change is administrative and state structures that are sclerotic and almost impossible to supersede or change. The effect is to block transitions across all the other moments within the social formation (from mental conceptions to social relations), while emphasizing local interests at the expense of planetary requirements.

The theory of the mode of production emphasizes the key role of the spiral form, the ever-rising mass of value and of product, which perpetually poses the problem of how to absorb that mass in ways not too damaging to environmental conditions. It is hard not to be overwhelmed by the enormous increase in scale of global output and of value and the immense increase in ecological stresses that result.

The fact that natural use values have no economic value in Marx's representation of how capital works helps us understand why Marx argued that the abolition of the capitalist law of value had a fundamental role to play in the transition to socialism. Throughout civil society, there are a variety of alternative value systems to which we might adhere. Intrinsic theories of nature's value abound (with the deep ecologists in the vanguard). Aldo Leopold's appeal to the land ethic has been influential, as have various proposals to anchor environmental practices in some version of the proper management of the global commons or the cultivation of an ethic of responsibility for nature.[29] The loss of a sentient relation to nature features prominently in internal bourgeois critiques of capital's conceptualization and materialization of the metabolic relation to nature. This objectification of nature, its commodification and monetization, signalled what the Frankfurt School referred to as the 'revolt of nature' inseparable from the parallel 'revolt of human nature'. A critique of the alienation of and from nature was outlined in Marx's *Economic and Philosophic Manuscripts of 1844*, only to be abandoned in later works in the Marxist tradition (with the exception of the Frankfurt School and, most recently, *Monthly Review*). This left the field of ecological critique to a diverse group of environmentalists, ecologists, feminists, anarchists, deep ecologists and the like who have not always been clear about any connection with anticapitalism, even as they embrace the idea of the 're-enchantment of nature' as one of their key objectives.

Environmentalism is certainly not antithetical, even if it is sometimes antagonistic, to Marxist perspectives. Nor is it possible for Marxist theory to ignore the political economy of nature. But much more work remains to be done to more clearly articulate how the metabolic relation to nature merges with all the other moments within the totality of capital

---

29   Aldo Leopold, *A Sand County Almanac* (Oxford: Oxford University Press, 2020 [1949]).

as a mode of production. From within the field of the metabolic relation to nature under the rule of capital, two tendencies brook large: a brutal and uncompromising extractivism on an increasing scale and an under-stated but profoundly pervasive Prometheanism. This is, moreover, an issue that will not easily be remedied and which is rapidly intensifying alongside the exponential growth of capital accumulation on a world scale. The lineaments for an anticapitalist environmentalism lie to hand. Accounts of environmental collapses multiply by the day. The barriers to a better articulation of an anticapitalist environmentalism are concentrated in the coercive laws of intercorporate and interstate competition, refracted through international institutions such as the IMF and the United Nations. The focus of the competition is mainly squabbling over the distribution of monetary wealth in the drive to consolidate financial hegemony come what may. But competing for pole position while the planet burns puts Nero's accomplishment in the non-existent shade.

11

Fixed Capital and the Consumption Fund

Classical political economy treated the distinction between fixed and circulating capital as a primary problem. Marx found the distinction between constant capital (the means of production) and variable capital (the capacity for labour) far more useful. It revealed the true nature of capital by highlighting the class relation that underpinned the concept and theory of surplus value production. Conceptualizing capital accumulation in terms of fixed and circulating capital conveniently concealed the class relation and thereby obscured the origin of profit. Nevertheless, Marx paid considerable attention to fixed capital. In the *Grundrisse*, he depicted its distinctive form of circulation as one of three major circulatory processes operating within the totality of capital.[1]

To avoid confusion it is important at the outset to set up some distinctions. Fixed capital within the enterprise comprises plant, machinery and equipment, all of which have to be purchased in the marketplace as commodities. The primary use value of this fixed capital is to increase the productivity of labour, and it is this, of course, which results in the tendency for the profit rate to fall. There are, however, two features of the employment of fixed capital that make its circulatory process somewhat 'peculiar'.[2] First, as a means of production, it does not contribute any material substantive input into whatever is produced. It has this quality in common with some other forms of constant capital, such as energy inputs. The commodity produced does not physically incorporate pieces of the machine or units of energy. The transfer of the value of such forms

---

1   Marx, *Grundrisse*, pp. 678–743.
2   Marx, *Capital*, Vol. 2, p. 238.

of constant capital into the final product is, therefore, a matter of social calculation rather than physical material measurement, even though the physical properties of the fixed capital, its durability and lifetime, for example, have an important role to play in its circulation.

The second feature – and this distinguishes machinery from the energy that drives it – is that fixed capital is deployed over many cycles of production and often for many years. The distinction between circulating and fixed capital rests, therefore, on some conception of a 'normal turnover time' which, if it is greatly exceeded, differentiates fixed from circulating capital. This 'normal turnover time' of circulating capital is also a social rather than purely physical determination. Marx put it on a yearly basis, which made some sense given the general turnover time for the production of agricultural commodities in the temperate regions where capital, at that time, was most active. Marx recognized, of course, that some production processes might entail several turnover times in a year and that the coercive laws of competition would incentivize the shortening of both production time and circulation time within the average turnover time of capital. So, while Marx based his analysis on the assumption of a standardized and normalized turnover time, actual turnover times are likely to be variable. Something like cotton spinning presumes, for example, production on a continuous basis, which can only be measured as volume of use and output per hour.

The history of capital suggests, however, a tendency towards the systematic reduction of turnover times (or, from another perspective, speed-up of all turnover times). Speed-up in the realm of circulating capital, stimulated by the coercive laws of competition, sometimes appears just as important as the tendency towards the falling rate and rising mass of profit in the historical dynamics of capital accumulation.[3]

Marx approaches the study of fixed capital step by step. He begins by observing that, if capital is, for some reason (either technical or social), stuck or 'fixated' in the form of commodities yet to be sold or money yet to be invested, a certain loss of value – devaluation – occurs. Hence the hustle and bustle involved in keeping as much capital as possible in motion along with speeding up that motion as much as possible.

The problem of fixation and devaluation becomes more pressing in the context of the differential turnover times required for different capitals. A cotton yarn factory requires a certain amount of raw cotton on a daily basis, while the cotton crop comes in once a year and the factory

---

3   Ibid., Vol. 2, Chapter 14.

itself lasts many years. Someone has to store the cotton (and guard its potential value) after the harvest so it can be released to the factories when it is needed. Some degree of physical fixation and lack of motion (and, hence, loss of value) is unavoidable, and strenuous efforts are made to reduce the 'downtime' of capital's motion and to minimize any loss of value due to fixation. Interestingly, Marx identified the kinds of steps that would ultimately lead to the Japanese 'just-in-time' production system of the 1980s in which inventories are reduced to a minimum by the optimal scheduling of inputs from suppliers.[4] If this continuity cannot be achieved physically, financial means can be found via the credit system to ensure a smooth flow of money between the cotton growers, the merchants and the cotton spinners to enable them to meet their daily costs. The credit system and the circulation of interest-bearing capital enter on the scene not as parasites (as is sometimes supposed) but as creative and necessary helpmates to assure the continuity of money flows in the face of radical differences in physical turnover times.

Marx abstracts from all such complications to recognize fixed capital as that part of constant capital that remains in productive use over many turnover times and over many years. It takes time, however, for the circulation of fixed capital to 'harden' (as Marx puts it) into a distinctive form of circulation, governed by its own laws of motion.

The immediate problem posed is this: How does the value embodied in the machine return into the general circulation of capital through its use in production? The easiest answer is to assume straight-line depreciation. A machine that is purchased for $10,000 and which has a physical lifetime of ten years should return the equivalent of $1,000 of its value per year by way of the commodities it helps to produce. The value returned can then be used at the end of ten years to buy another machine for $10,000. This is the simplest and least problematic form of fixed capital circulation. But matters are in practice much more complicated. To begin with, the physical lifetime of the machine is not easily determined. Variable lifetimes of particular machines can be condensed down to average lifetimes of, for example, all power looms everywhere. Some capitalists would then be advantaged because their machines last longer than the social average, while others would lose out because their machines stopped working after five years. In any case, the capitalist has to save up (accumulate) the annual return of $1,000 as an increasing amount of savings (dormant capital) to be able to buy the new machine

---

4   Ibid., Vol. 1, p. 608.

after ten years. This means the fixation of a lot of money capital over the lifetime of the machine. In practice, the industrialist may lend the increasing amount of idle money capital out to other capitalists (with the help of bankers and financiers) until the time comes to buy a new machine.

But what happens when new, more and/or cheaper machines come on the market before the straight-line depreciation schedule is complete? Competition would then ensure that the old machines are devalued before their physical lifetime is over. A gap thus arises between the physical and the economic lifetimes of the machine. Anxiety on this point leads capital to seek to recuperate the value of its fixed capital as quickly as possible.[5] Hence the incentive to twenty-four-hour use and the imposition of shift work on the labour force. This was the sort of thing that happened in the case of Manchester industrialism. The difference between recovering the value of a machine in five years instead of ten is economically significant.

The more technology becomes a business and the faster the progress of technological change, the more the problem of what Marx rather quaintly calls 'moral depreciation' affects matters. Instead of straight-line depreciation, the value of machinery is here calculated in terms of immediate replacement cost, which tends to fall over time, sometimes precipitously.[6] The general effect is periodic devaluation of existing fixed capital with the advent of cheaper and more efficient machines. One answer to this problem is to lease the machinery and equipment (where possible) on a periodic (for example, annual) basis, which allows for the periodic renegotiation of the lease to reflect the availability of new and more efficient machines. Airlines, for example, lease rather than own most of their aircraft, and industrialists lease forklift trucks to move things around in their factories.

There is a third option in which machines are valued by way of their contribution to the commodity values they help to produce and realize in the market. In other words, the value of the input is determined retrospectively by the value of the output. This method poses a huge problem for bourgeois economic theory, which likes to presume, for purposes of its perfected economic models, that the value of the capital stock (the machines) is fixed and independent of the prices of commodities produced and realized in the market with the aid of this stock. When

5   Ibid., Vol. 1, p. 528.
6   Ibid., Vol. 2, Chapter 8.

capital takes the form of money, there is no problem in valuing capital inputs. When it takes the form of a physical stock (for example, working machines), putting a money value on them is problematic because that value is typically not independent of the commodity values they help produce. In 2007–8, when the housing market collapsed, the banks had a huge inventory of foreclosed properties on their books which in the absence of a viable market had no market value. For accounting purposes, they had to be assigned some arbitrary value which reduced valuations to guesswork. Bourgeois economics here collapses into tautologies (of the sort Marx describes so critically in his introduction to the *Grundrisse*).

In the 1960s, this led to the so-called 'capital controversy' (an intense technical argument between economists like Paul Samuelson in Cambridge, Massachusetts, and Joan Robinson in Cambridge, England) about how to value fixed physical capital stock without reference to what it is used to produce. This problem has not been satisfactorily resolved in conventional economics.[7] But, as Marx noted, when bourgeois economics confronts a seemingly irresolvable contradiction, its only answer is to pretend that contradiction does not exist. So, no one mentions the capital controversy anymore. Its potentially troubling implication, that all bourgeois models of the economy are founded on tautologies, is studiously ignored. The tautologies in bourgeois economics appear as contradictions in Marx's theory, and Marx, as we earlier observed, embraces such contradictions. The bourgeois policymakers' answer to the problems of 2007–8 was to flood the world with excess liquidity so as to rescue the banks, in the hope that this money would trickle down and revive the housing market as well as the economy in general. Most of that flood of liquidity ended up (predictably in Marxian theory) in the pockets of a ruling kleptocratic oligarchy. What actually happened in housing markets and fixed capital investments will be examined later.

Marx sees the circulation of fixed capital as a special case of the contradictory unity between production and realization.[8] To begin with, fixed capital is defined by its use rather than by its material physical qualities. There are a lot of sewing machines in the world, but they only constitute fixed capital when assembled by a capitalist entrepreneur in a sweatshop employing wage labour. The sewing machine that in Britain used to be in every working-class grandmother's parlour is not fixed capital – but it *is* part of what Marx calls 'the consumption fund'.

7   See Harcourt, *Some Cambridge Controversies in the Theory of Capital*.
8   Marx, *Grundrisse*, pp. 406–15.

This distinction is important.[9] It implies that fixed capital can be augmented or diminished by changing the uses of existing things. It is frequently held that the transition to full-fledged capitalist economic development rests on a prior surge of investment in fixed capital formation. The historical data tend to support this, except for the first 'take off' into self-sustaining capitalist development in Britain after 1700 or so.[10] In that case, there is no evidence for any surge of fixed capital formation prior to the Industrial Revolution. It seems that, from the seventeenth century on, merchant capitalist robbery of much of the world of gold and materials led to its use in Britain to support consumption and state functions, creating assets that could later become fixed capital through change of use. The flexibility of definition of fixed capital is essential to Marx, but anathema to bourgeois economics because it cannot put a stable value on K, the capital input, in all its modelling equations and national accounts.

At this point, it is necessary to broaden the concept of fixed capital beyond the machines employed in production. Marx takes up the case of fixed capital of an independent kind and differentiates between that part embedded in the land and that part that is moveable.[11] Marx mainly gestures towards the importance of these distinctions without exploring them in the detail they deserve. While the use value of such investments may be to somehow contribute, though indirectly, to the productivity of labour, their contribution is not always clear or measurable as it is in the case of machines. While the Interstate Highway System in the United States clearly contributed to the overall productivity of the economy, there are plenty of 'bridges to nowhere' whose contribution is dubious.

To better understand how such investments work, consider the transport industry, which, in Marx's view, produces value and surplus value by producing change of location for both people and commodities. Fixed capital of an independent kind embedded in the land consists of highways and railways, ports, harbours and stations, cranes and loading equipment, warehouses and retail establishments and so on. The fixed capital not embedded in the land comprises engines and rolling stock, trucks, cars, scooters and bicycles, container ships, barges, ferries and boats, and aircraft and so on. All of this, taken together, constitutes the fixed capital of the transport system – a far-from-trivial mass of capital.

---

9   Harvey, *Limits to Capital*, Chapter 8.
10   Walt W. Rostow, *The Stages of Economic Growth: A Non-Communist Manifesto* (Cambridge: Cambridge University Press, 1960).
11   For a full exposition, see Harvey, *Limits to Capital*, Chapter 8.

But much of this physical stock is also used for purposes of consumption. Many, if not most, of these physical items partially belong to the 'consumption fund', defined as long-term assets created to support daily consumption. The biggest owned items in the consumption fund are housing and cars, but consumer durables also constitute a major market. Provision of health care and education, along with many other physical and social infrastructure, also characterizes the full range of items that constitute the consumption fund. Changes of use take material items from one economic category to another. When an abandoned cotton mill is converted into a residential condominium or recreation centre, this amounts to a transfer from fixed capital to the consumption fund. When the granting of microcredit to a peasant family leads into production for profit, the peasant hut moves from being part of the consumption fund to being a form of fixed capital.

There is also a problem of joint uses. A road, Marx notes, 'can be used to transport commodities or for taking walks'.[12] Cars and houses can be used for production work or for pleasure. So who builds the road, and how may its value be recuperated through use? While its uses may be individualized, it is the collective consumption that, in many instances, matters. Roads and bridges are used by millions of drivers, and their economic viability depends on monetizing individual uses for collective benefit. While it may be possible to impose user charges (toll roads and bridges, airport taxes, user licenses, congestion charges and the like), it is often impossible to assign costs and revenues to such investments in an economically equitable or rational way. Responsibility for building much of this infrastructure therefore lies as much in the public domain as it does in the domain of capital itself. Marx does suggest, however, in his lengthy discussion in the *Grundrisse* on who is going to build the road, that one measure of the maturity of capital is the degree to which such activities as road building migrate from the state sector into that of private capital. Urban infrastructure, however, is an even more complex commodity comprising many elements juxtaposed in such a way as to be as usable as possible, though for whom and for what is not always clear. It is here, too, that the collective forms of both production and consumption play a significant role. All of this exists at another level of complexity. But that level, as we shall see later, rests on a solid understanding of the simple version of how capital circulates through fixed capital and consumption fund formation (Figure 12).

---

12   Marx, *Grundrisse*, pp. 525–33, 687.

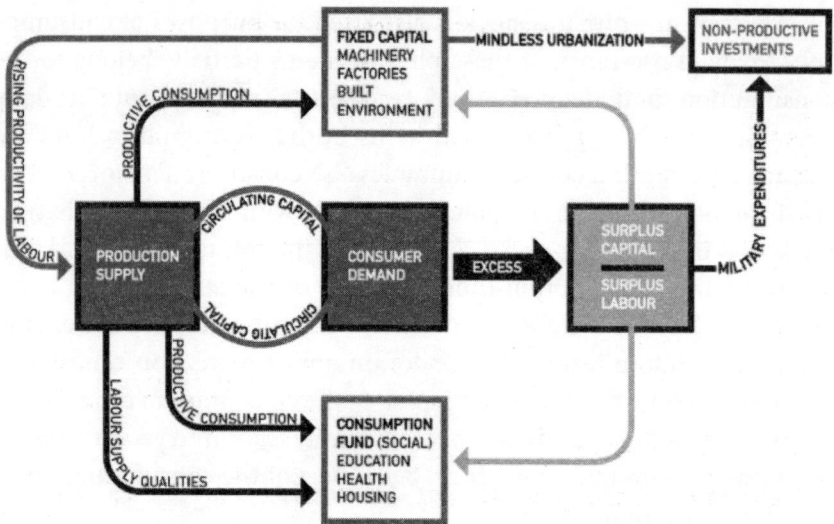

Figure 12. The Circulation of Fixed Capital and Consumption Fund Formation

Long-term investments in fixed capital and the consumption fund seemingly go against the main tendency of capital, which is to accelerate turnover times. Fixed capital and consumption fund formation entail a slowing down of circulation, while circulating capital is typically about speeding circulation up. A part of capital circulation slows down to facilitate speeding up the circulation of the rest. Investments in fixed capital and the consumption fund will therefore occur only in situations in which society is prepared to defer benefits now to reap the benefits of rising productivity later. This presumes that society can afford to wait and that the benefits of long-term investments are sufficiently well known and acceptable.

At this point, however, we encounter a strange concordance of effects and interests. The law of falling rate and rising mass tends to produce, as we earlier saw, crises of idle surpluses of capital and surpluses of labour power side by side. Investment in machinery (fixed capital) requires surpluses of both capital and labour to be held back from current consumption in order to increase future output. In the early stages of capitalism, such deferred gratification imposed considerable stress on populations living on very little. Society had to tighten its belt and be prepared to wait in order to mobilize the necessary surpluses of capital and labour power required to invest in fixed capital and reap the benefits of rising labour productivity. Once this fixed capital comes online, however, the mass of commodities on the market increases while labour is released from production.

10-Month exponential moving average

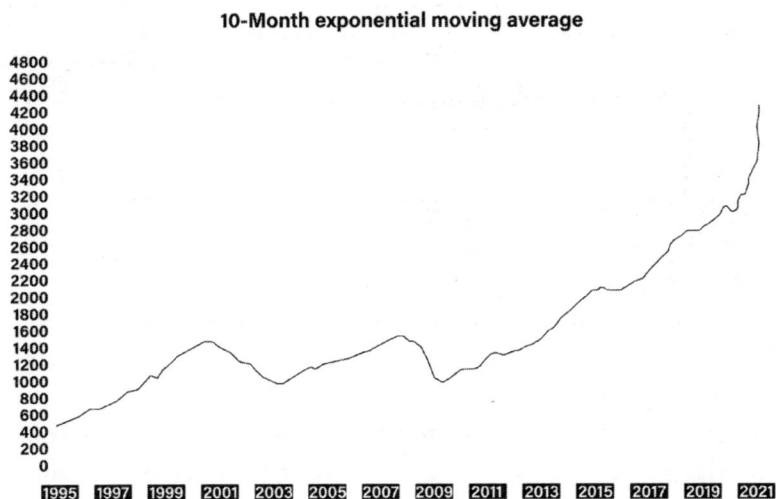

Figure 13. S&P 500 Stock Market Monthly Close Valuations Since 1995

This is the point at which the circulation of fixed capital 'hardens' into a separate circulatory process. Machine technology, moreover, transforms the category of labour input from the individual to the sociality of the labouring mass (for example, within the factory). So-called 'productive labour' (productive of surplus value) can no longer be assessed based on what an individual does, because it is the organization of collective labour in the factory (and the detailed division of labour within the firm) that now matters. Fixed capital comes into its own under conditions of mass production and mass consumption. The rising mass of ever-cheaper final product necessitates an expanding market for use values (for example, through the formation of the world market), while rising productivity creates ever-greater surpluses of use values of both commodities and labour. Fixed capital, in short, produces the surpluses of circulating capital and labour power that are required to facilitate even more fixed capital investment. This seemingly closed loop propels, in the absence of any countervailing force, a steep downward spiral in the profit rate.

But there are 'moments in the developed movement of capital which delay this movement other than by crises; such as, for example, the constant devaluation of a part of the existing capital: the transformation of a great part of capital into fixed capital that does not serve as agency of direct production; unproductive waste of a great portion of capital.'[13] This

---

13   Ibid., p. 750.

is an explosive idea. Marx does not elaborate on it, but we can. To begin with, a constant current of devaluation has a permanent presence in the basement, as it were, of capital accumulation. Crises arise when that current, for some reason, becomes a flood in which the physical destruction, the monetized depreciation and the devaluation of the assets, the skills, as well as the commodities along with their labour forces all collide to produce stasis within the capitalist economy. When value loses its motion, capital is dissolved.

The second possibility is the diversion of fixed capital investment into non-surplus-value-producing projects and surplus capital flows into consumption fund formation for which there is no market demand (a new opera house that is never used, for example). The use value of fixed capital shifts from promoting the increasing productivity of labour in production to absorbing the mass of surplus product and surplus labour through investments in fixed capital of an independent kind along with the formation of a continuously rising consumption fund that may or may not have any users. The seemingly bizarre idea of using this form of fixed capital and consumption fund formation to absorb the ever-increasing mass of surplus value and surplus labour produced by the falling rate of profit is largely ignored in the literature. It is therefore helpful to expand on it here.

Fixed capital formation, particularly that of an independent kind, becomes a sink for absorbing surplus capital and labour rather than a means for increasing the productivity of labour. Like planned obsolescence, it constitutes a means to manage the crisis tendencies of capital by way of pre-emptive but organized devaluations of portions of the rising mass. The only parallel to this possibility in Marx's writings is his view that spending money on military equipment and warlike ventures amounts to dumping value in the ocean.[14] But notice that it is the 'great part' and 'the great portion' of capital that is involved in this nonproductive but capital-absorbing activity. If this argument is correct, we might anticipate that the management of the crisis tendencies of capital since, say, 1945 would focus on the economic role of military spending and on managed devaluations in fixed capital investment and consumption fund formation through urbanization and investments in the built environment. These have possibly been the dominant ways to dispose of or absorb unlimited surpluses without major crises of chaotic and unpredictable devaluation.

---

14   Ibid., *Grundrisse*, p. 128.

Long-term investments in the built environment (for both production and consumption) are able to absorb surplus capital and
surplus labour and are frequently undertaken for exactly this purpose.
Roosevelt's Works Progress Administration in 1935 is a classic case of
the conscious use of such a strategy. Idle capital and labour were put
to work by the state using deficit financing on infrastructure projects
in a desperate attempt to revive capital accumulation. The aim was to
absorb as much surplus capital and as much surplus labour as possible,
without any consideration of how productive such investments might
be. Mussolini's investments in the Mezzogiorno, Hitler's building of the
autobahn, Eisenhower's building of the Interstate Highway System in the
1950s, China's huge urbanization and infrastructure projects of 2008–9
supplemented by the Belt and Road Initiative, and, more recently, Biden's
infrastructure plans of 2021 are all moves of this sort. Some of these
investments may have turned out to be productive in the long run, but
that was not their point at the time. Even if they turned out to be productive, that impact was so far into the future as to have little relevance
for the present.

Something that was marginal in Marx's time has thus become foundational for ours. The international difficulties of 2007–8 arose, for
example, around the finance of housing and other aspects of consumption fund formation in the built environment, primarily in the United
States but also in Spain, Ireland and a number of other countries. The
general crisis was largely resolved, ironically, by a massive surge of investment into fixed capital and consumption fund formation in China, the
productivity of which is moot. About 30 per cent of China's GDP was
caught up in fixed capital and consumption fund formation (15 per cent
in housing construction alone) after 2008. Whole new cities were built
that, for a while, stood bereft of any inhabitants. More than 20,000 miles
of high-speed train network were built in a few years. No wonder the
Chinese consumed so much cement! This was mainly what stopped the
global economy plunging into a 1930s-style depression in the wake of
the financial collapse of 2007–8. Ho-fung Hung has recently argued that
the overaccumulation of capital in China was resolved 'by privileged
access to state bank loans, which were used to fuel an investment spree.
The result was rising employment, a temporary and localized economic
boom, and a windfall for the elite.'[15] But this dynamic also left behind

---

15   Ho-fung Hung, *City on the Edge: Hong Kong Under Chinese Rule* (Cambridge:
Cambridge University Press, 2022).

redundant and unprofitable construction projects: empty apartments, underused airports and unneeded coal plants and steel mills. That, in turn, resulted in falling profits, slowing growth and worsening indebtedness across the main sectors of the economy.

Unproductive or wasteful fixed capital and consumption fund formation has become, over time, a significant feature in the dynamics of accumulation. During the halcyon days of the property boom in Spain after 2000, for example, a new city – Ciudad Real – was built to the south of Madrid, replete with a new airport costing some two or three billion euros. It was built with the fantasy that a significant overflow from the congested airport in Madrid would materialize. And then came the crash of 2007–8, which hit Spain and its property sector in particular hard. The initiating company went bankrupt, and the completed airport was put up for auction. A Chinese company bid something like 50,000 euros. The bid was refused. The airport was finally bought out by a private investor for an undisclosed but presumably trivial sum, but it has never attracted commercial passenger flights. It finally found a use as storage space for planes that were put out of service during the Covid-19 pandemic.

In this case, the value of the fixed capital appeared to be lost. But the construction companies, developers and raw material suppliers produced a great deal of surplus value (profit) from their contracts to construct the airport even though the project ultimately went bankrupt. In a way, the bankruptcy did not really matter. Its economic purpose was served by creating demand for construction, raw materials, wages for workers (who then became consumers), furnishings and technical equipment for loading and unloading, and the like. The aggregate circulation of the mass of capital was less affected by the bankruptcy of the airport than would otherwise have been the case. Investments of this sort often go belly up, but, as Marx observed, the first wave of investors often go bankrupt, leaving behind use values that can be bought up at fire sale prices to then be put to profitable use later.

A large portion of the constant capital required for the running of the airport has to be paid for upfront in the form of fixed capital and the consumption fund, most of which is embedded in the land. This poses the question of how to value this in relation to its use and income stream it might generate. The only sensible way to do this is to take the third option for valuation, valuing the airport by the income it generates. The income, once it materializes, can be capitalized as a form of fictitious capital. Investors can invest in the shares of the airport company, in return for a payment which, Marx argues, means that investments of this kind circulate in return for interest which is only a part of the surplus generated. The owners of the airport do not produce anything. They simply charge a fee for its use. This is, however, a matter to which we will return.

The relation between circulating capital and fixed capital and consumption fund formation needs more explicit attention. Machinery is part of circulating capital when it is being produced and only becomes fixed capital in the hands of its users in the factory or airport. The realization of the values locked up in fixed capital and in the consumption fund depends on their valorization through consistent use over several years. Any deviation from this requirement will result in devaluation of the fixed capital and consumption fund assets and perhaps bankruptcy of their owners or operators. The continuity and direction of circulating capital has to be sufficient to realize the value locked up in the fixed capital and the consumption fund. The realization of fixed capital and consumption fund values rests on the perpetuation of certain patterns of use and the ability of users to make sufficient payments for that use. A new airport, for example, can only be valorized if enough flights arrive and enough revenues charged for airport services over the lifetime of the airport (for example, thirty years). The maintenance costs for the machinery or fixed capital investments, such as a bridge or highway, also need to be covered. And, with complex investments, such as an airport, the lifetimes of parts of the whole will vary substantially. Changing the lightbulbs will be frequent, but the air-conditioning and heating system will typically last much longer and the roof longer still. The result is a continuous flow back and forth between the circulation of fixed capital and capital circulation in general. They are codependent circulations within the totality of capital (much, to go back to a familiar analogy, as liver and lungs are codependent in the human body).

One more issue requires attention. Marx was mainly concerned with the long-term finance of physical infrastructure for both production and consumption. In our own times, social infrastructure plays just as important role as physical infrastructure. The flows of capital into the consumption fund broaden to encompass flows to all manner of social expenditures that support the reproduction of labour power in the form of education, health care, adequate shelter and physical mobility (for example, a transportation system to get workers to and from their work) (Figure 12). More detailed analysis concentrates on the manner in which knowledge, which in the manufacturing period was largely lodged in the brains of the artisans, is, in the case of machine technologies, increasingly embodied within the machine itself, leaving behind a deskilled work-force of machine minders.

When innovation becomes a business backed by the mobilization of scientific and technical know-how as a commodity for sale to the highest bidder, a whole new world opens up for capital to colonize, backed by a state increasingly obsessed with developing technologies that confer military superiority. The organization of knowledge production becomes a distinctive branch of capital. Since 1945 and the first use of nuclear weapons, it has pitted rival states against each other in a fierce competition for technological advantage. Since the 1980s, the result has been the creation of an immense repository of proprietary knowledge that can be mobilized for biophysical and biological engineering. Currently, this field is divided into two distinctive models of competition for technological superiority. China has developed a state-centric knowledge production system, which internalizes fierce forms of internally organized competition, while the US relies on lavish state support for large-scale, corporate-led innovation (such as that of Elon Musk's Tesla and SpaceX). But in both cases, it is the fixed capital of the general intellect that is at stake with the application of generic innovations of the sort promised by AI as the ultimate product that will profoundly revolutionize all forms of economic and social life. If past revolutions in technology are anything to go by, the benefits will flow to capital and the ruling classes and the costs will be visited on labour and everyone else.

In January 2025, the shares of high-tech stocks in the US fell precip-itously because a 'small Chinese artificial intelligence lab [the typical decentralized research unit favoured by the Chinese] released Deep-Seek', which revealed a capacity 'to build a large language model on a bootstraped budget' that bypassed the US ban on exporting advanced AI chips to China.[16] The Chinese model was much better, cheaper and easier to use than the American, though how long China might preserve its advantage is hard to say. This revealed something that anyone familiar with the Chinese case knows: the depth and extent of the technologically skilled labour force in China is unparalleled and that every attempt by the US to block China's further development is at best limited and at worst a stimulus to building autonomous Chinese research capability. It is also worth noting Marx's flirtation in the *Grundrisse* with the idea of the 'general intellect' and the emergence of a knowledge economy. This

16   Eleanor Olcott and Zijing Wu, 'How Small Chinese AI Start-up DeepSeek Shocked Silicon Valley', *Financial Times*, 24 January 2025.

led to a brief period in which the idea of 'cognitive capitalism' became a central topic of discussion in Marxist circles. As with many other 'adjectival' forms of capital, the idea of cognitive capitalism did not last long, even as the legal and illegal pursuit of proprietary knowledge has continued to flourish within the new fields of capital's development.

In the case of coordination between differential turnover and production times within circulating capitals, the credit system and, ultimately, the distinctive circulation of interest-bearing capital emerge as facilitators and mediators of relations between long- and medium-term fixed capital and consumption fund formation and use, on the one hand, and the dynamics of circulating capital, on the other. As often happens, however, those who helpfully perform certain mediating functions, like lawyers and bankers, can step by step emerge as organizers, managers, manipulators and eventually dictators of those they were originally supposed to serve. Marx sees the rise in the circulation of interest-bearing capital as reflecting the need to find ways to fund long-term investments in fixed capital and in the consumption fund (for example, the mortgage market for housing and the bond market for long-term additions to the built environment). Contemporary credit, Marx argued, 'has its roots in the specific mode of realization, mode of turnover, mode of reproduction of fixed capital'.[17] With capital periodically crying out for new investment opportunities consequent on the massive surpluses of both capital and labour that often become dormant at times of crisis, the financialization of flows into fixed capital and consumption fund formation, lubricated by interest-bearing capital and accompanied by financial innovation, became critical for the survival of global capital. This will be the subject of the next chapter.

---

17   Marx, *Grundrisse*, p. 732.

12

The Circulation of Interest-Bearing Capital

Until this point in the development of the theory of capital, the prime engine of growth and transformation has been the pursuit of increasing labour productivity by individual capitalists operating under the coercive laws of competition. The consequent tendency for the aggregate rate of profit to fall is countered by the law of a rising mass of profit. This engine continues to perform its role as capital becomes an abstract social force, operating over and above, and sometimes even against, the will of individual capitalists. The latter, in any case, seek to maximize their individual interest and, in so doing, often produce an aggregate result inconsistent with the capitalist class interest. This is a world where technological innovation has become an autonomous and independent business, and where the perpetual pursuit of relative surplus value, with all its manifest consequences, proceeds unabated along with a rising mass of value and of products.

But we also know that the distinctive circulation processes engaged in collating wildly different turnover and production times along with long-term fixed capital (for example, factories) and consumption fund (for example, housing) formation 'posits' (necessarily brings into existence) the circulation of interest-bearing capital as an adjunct to the general circulation process of capital. We also know (particularly from Rosa Luxemburg's exploration of Marx's reproduction schemas) that the only way the circle of capital accumulation can be converted into a spiral is by capital finding on the market, when all other possibilities are exhausted, a source of effective demand greater than that incorporated in the normal production of capital. Without this, crises of overaccumulation will become endemic. 'The ultimate reason for all real crises always remains the poverty and restricted consumption of the masses, in the face of the drive of capitalist production to develop the productive forces as if only the absolute consumption capacity of the society set a limit to them.' The answer to this problem of insufficient effective demand lies in the evolution of a credit system.[1]

The size and diversity of the money (credit) market and of its components is now huge. In the United States, the single-family residential market for mortgages is $13 trillion and the multifamily residential market is $2 trillion. In China, real estate accounted for 30 per cent of GDP in 2020, with 15 per cent due to housing production alone, all of which was accomplished with the aid of surging indebtedness in the form of an unruly and unregulated shadow banking system. This was destined to spell speculative trouble at a later date. The crises that hit large-scale urban developers like Evergrande in the summer of 2021, followed later on by Countrywide, have put the whole Chinese economy under threat.[2]

There is, plainly, something else afoot in the circulation and accumulation of capital in our own times other than that which Marx so assiduously unpacked. The pursuit of relative surplus value through increasing labour productivity had nothing whatsoever to do with George Soros's leveraging access to a huge mass of money in speculating so successfully against the British pound in 1992. Very few people have access to the mass of money capital required to yield such a dramatic return. But Soros was not producing anything. He was accumulating capital by other means. His objective was appropriation, not production. All too often, this is how the rich get richer in our times. Black Wednesday of 1992, when all this transpired, was quite different from the earlier Black Monday of 1987, when the stock market crashed for a few days. There is a downside to all this. 'The accumulation of wealth by this [rentier] class may proceed in a very different way from that of accumulation properly so called; but it proves in any case that they [the rentier class] pocket a good portion of the wealth.'[3]

Soros was later implicated, along with several other prominent and powerful financiers, in an operation to destabilize the Thai bhat in the late 1990s. But that operation was far more extensive and long drawn-out, since it turned out to be the precursor to the financial crisis that wracked East and Southeast Asia in 1997–8. Joseph Stiglitz outlines a conspiracy

1   Marx, *Economic Manuscript of 1864–1865*, pp. 480, 577.
2   Navin Vett, *The History and Untold Story of Evergrande in China and Its Liquidation* (Independently published, 2024).
3   Marx, *Economic Manuscript of 1864–1865*, p. 567.

THE CIRCULATION OF INTEREST-BEARING CAPITAL   225

theory (which he himself does not believe) to explain what happened. 'The IMF first told countries in Asia to open up their markets to hot short-term capital. The countries did it and money flooded in, but then just as suddenly it flowed out. The IMF then said interest rates should be raised and there should be a fiscal contraction, and a deep recession was induced. As asset prices plummeted, the IMF urged affected countries to sell their assets' – at bargain prices, of course. The sales were handled by the same foreign institutions who precipitated the crisis by pulling out their money. 'These banks then got large commissions from their work selling the troubled companies or splitting them up', just as they had got large foreign commissions guiding investments into the countries in the first place. 'As events unfolded, cynicism grew.' Foreign financial companies made huge 'profits from buying at fire sale prices and [later] selling at more normal prices'.

Stiglitz insists, however, that 'the IMF was not participating in a conspiracy', no matter how plausible that conspiracy theory appeared to be to those most affected by the crisis. The IMF, Stiglitz argues, was simply 'reflecting the interests and ideology of the Western financial community'.[4] In other words, the IMF was simply doing capitalist business as usual: the free-market system and the equalization of the rate of profit produced a result indistinguishable from an active conspiracy of the sort that Stiglitz outlines. Those with command over a mass of capital can wait out any turbulence in the market, while all those firms that were a payment or two away from bankruptcy can be forced (no matter what their rate of return) to give up whatever assets they control for a trivial sum when there is a liquidity squeeze. It is, as always, command over the mass that matters. As Veneroso and Wade remark:

> Financial crises have always caused transfers of ownership and power to those who keep their own assets intact and who are in a position to create credit, and the Asian crisis is no exception … there is no doubt that Western and Japanese corporations are the big winners … The combination of massive devaluations, IMF-pushed financial liberalization, and IMF-facilitated recovery may even precipitate the biggest peacetime transfer of assets from domestic to foreign owners in the past fifty years anywhere in the world.[5]

4   Joseph Stiglitz, *Globalization and Its Discontents* (New York: W. W. Norton, 2002), pp. 129–30.

5   Frank Veneroso and Robert Wade, 'The Asian Crisis: The High Debt Model Versus the Wall Street-Treasury-IMF Complex', *New Left Review* 1: 228 (March/April 1998), p. 20.

One recalls the statements attributed to once US Treasury Secretary Andrew Mellon back in the 1920s: 'during a depression, assets return to their rightful owners' (that is, him).

Consider the case of Stephen Schwarzman, co-founder and CEO of the private equity company Blackstone. By 2019, he had accumulated a personal net worth of $14.4 billion and sought entry into philanthropy heaven by donations of $350 million to MIT and £150 million to Oxford to support the teaching of the humanities. He is also an avid supporter of Donald Trump. The rise of Blackstone to being by far the largest land-lord in the world by 2018 (with more than $200 billion of asset values under management) is a classic contemporary tale. The financial crisis of 2007–8 originated in the housing mortgage market (in the consumption fund, no less) primarily in the United States, with high concentrations of distress in California and the American Southwest, along with Florida and Georgia.[6] From the mid-1990s on, high-risk low-income populations (particularly people of colour, immigrants and women as single heads of households) were enticed into homeownership by teaser mortgages and lax oversight in the granting of so-called 'sub-prime' mortgages. Financial institutions packaged these mortgages into 'collateralized debt obligations' (CDOs) sold on to unsuspecting investors all around the world (from municipal governments in Norway to investment arms of major banks such as Paribas). These investments were, it was claimed, 'as safe as houses'. The ratings agencies (fraudulently?) gave them triple-A ratings. When the housing market tanked in 2006–8, it became clear as the teaser mortgages matured that many of the CDOs were worth-less, and foreclosures surged (too bad for the municipal governments in Norway and banks in France like Paribas). The foreclosure rules were savagely enforced, in many instances illegally so.[7]

The result was a vast pool of foreclosed properties on the books of the banks (acquired, in large part, from Latinx and African Ameri-can populations, who lost up to 80 per cent of their asset wealth in the crisis). Blackstone borrowed large sums of capital to take the proper-ties off the books of the banks at fire-sale prices. It then fixed them up and put them back on the market as profitable rentals. With pension funds, insurance companies and sovereign wealth funds desperate (in the wake of the crisis) to find adequate rates of return on their capital,

---

6 Adam Tooze, *Crashed: How a Decade of Financial Crises Changed the World* (New York: Viking, 2018).

7 David Dayen, *Chain of Title: How Three Ordinary Americans Uncovered Wall Street's Great Foreclosure Fraud* (New York: New Press, 2016).

Blackstone had access to massive amounts of investment capital, which it borrowed at modest interest rates to mount large-scale real estate operations all around the world. In 2007, Blackstone had nearly $20 billion in real estate assets under management, but, by 2019, it had increased its holdings sevenfold to $140 billion. Blackstone, management bragged, was now big enough to undertake operations beyond the capacity of any competitor anywhere in the world. It plainly had not let a good crisis go to waste. It had engineered a huge transfer of property rights from one class to another:

> By December 2012, Blackstone was spending $100 million a week on houses … it had already laid out $1.5 billion to purchase ten thousand foreclosed properties. By 2014 it had spent five times that – $7.8 billion – to buy up forty-one thousand single-family homes in fourteen cities, from Seattle to Miami, with the greatest concentrations in Arizona, California, Florida and Georgia.[8]

California's crisis of lack of affordable housing deepened as Blackstone converted properties to high-end rentals after a wave of evictions of low-income populations from the troubled rental complexes it also acquired. Some of those evicted were pensioners dependent on the California State Pension Fund, which had invested so heavily in Blackstone's operations. The pensioners, in effect, secured their pensions by way of their own eviction. Blackstone is now almost certainly poised to make another killing. During the pandemic, many households could not afford to pay either their mortgage or their rent. While a moratorium on evictions was extended in the US to later in 2021, it finally gave out, clogging the courts in all the major cities with eviction claims.

Take the case of an affordable housing project run by a housing charity in a depressed area of Brooklyn. In the late 1990s, it badly needed capital for conversion and improvements. It turned to a federal programme to support affordable housing and formed a partnership with the insurance company AIG. The latter provided the funds in return for highly remunerative federal tax credits worth twice as much as the original investment over a period of fifteen years. For legal reasons, AIG and the housing charity had to set up a corporation 99 per cent controlled by AIG to channel the funding, even as the housing charity continued to

---

8   Aaron Glantz, *Homewreckers: How a Gang of Wall Street Kingpins, Hedge Fund Magnates, Crooked Banks, and Vulture Capitalists Suckered Millions out of Their Homes and Demolished the American Dream* (Boston: Mariner, 2019), pp. 162–3.

undertake daily management. It was understood that the project would revert to the control of the housing charity after fifteen years. But Brooklyn was gentrifying fast, and AIG decided to assert ownership rights (given its 99 per cent control over the investment corporation) over what by then had become much more valuable housing. In effect, the housing charity was dispensed with.

The courts so far have sided with AIG, which then decided to sell all of its interest in such projects to Blackstone for $5 billion. Blackstone promises to keep the project affordable. But its record (from San Francisco to Copenhagen and Barcelona) would suggest it is likely in the long run to keep some of it affordable by gentrifying the rest and to enhance its return on its $5 billion. AIG and Blackstone both win big. AIG not only got back in tax rebates twice its investment, but it also capitalized on the rising market worth of the complex. The housing charity and some renters desperate for affordable housing lose out and Brooklyn gentrification stays on pace.[9] This trend for big capital to colonize even affordable housing has become, in recent times, more troubling. Investors are even taking over trailer parks, which, in the United States, are by far the most important means for providing affordable housing for low-income populations, particularly in rural areas.[9]

In citing these examples, I am seeking to lay a historical materialist basis to explore the degree to which the theory of capital has to be revised, extended or radically transformed in order to grasp its qualities in its current phase. When I first investigated the role of banking, finance and the circulation of interest-bearing capital in relation to Marx's theorizing of capital's mode of production in the 1970s, I found almost nothing in English. To be sure, there were earlier studies by Lenin and Hilferding.[10] But there had been virtually nothing since, apart from some works in French by Chesnais and de Brunhoff, along with commentaries on the role of finance in fostering imperialism in the works of Harry Magdoff and *Monthly Review*. I therefore sought to correct that situation.[11] The two chapters on Marx's views on banking, interest and finance in *Limits to Capital* (1982) were largely ignored at the time because, according to my publisher, they were written by a geographer

9   Mark Vandevelde, 'Why Blackstone Made a $5bn Bet on Housing Low-Income Americans', *Financial Times*, 27 August 2021.

10   V. I. Lenin, *Imperialism, the Highest Stage of Capitalism* (New York: International Publishers, 1982 [1917]); Rudolf Hilferding, *Finance Capital. A Study of the Latest Phase of Capitalist Development* (London: Routledge & Kegan Paul, 1981 [1919]).

11   François Chesnais, *La mondialisation du capital* (Paris: PUF, 1994); S. de Brunhoff, *État et capital: Recherches sur la politique économique* (Paris: PUF, 1981).

and not by a credentialed economist.[12] These two chapters still provide, I believe, a reasonable introduction to a complex topic.

The theory of relative surplus value and all that flows from it (such as the law of the falling rate and rising mass of profit) is not at all helpful in seeking to interpret local struggles such as those over affordable housing in Brooklyn. This is not, however, the moment to debate idealist interpretations in which conceptual and policy shifts – important though these may have been – lie at the root of emergent practices of capital. I reiterate Marx's injunction in the *Grundrisse*: abstractions and ideas are

> nothing more than the theoretical expression of those material relations which are their lord and master. Relations can be expressed, of course, only in ideas, and thus philosophers have determined the reign of ideas to be the peculiarity of the new age ... This reign [then] appears within the consciousness of individuals as the reign of ideas ... [and] belief in the permanence of these ideas ... [is] consolidated, nourished and inculcated by the ruling classes by all means available.[13]

To what ideas, therefore, do the material relations and practices described in these examples give rise? The problem is not to impose a theoretical apparatus on practices but to identify the practices that give rise to the theory. To this I add a second methodological injunction: If there is indeed a compelling case for revising or even revolutionizing the concept and theory of capital so far advanced to take account of these cases, the roots of these transformations should be discernible in earlier practices and theoretical formulations.

Consider, for example, the significance of leveraging in the world of finance. If a company purchases a house for $100,000 and rents it out at 6 per cent (for an annual rent of $6,000), the rate of return on the investment skyrockets if the company borrows $90,000 at 5 per cent costing $4,500 in interest, which leaves the company earning $1,500 on its own investment of $10,000. In most countries, this is supplemented by favourable tax rules covering everything from depreciation to interest deductions. This produces a contradiction similar to that which leads individual capitalists to produce a macro-tendency for the profit rate to fall by maximizing their individual relative surplus value through increasing labour productivity. Individual capitalists seek to maximize

---

12   Harvey, *Limits to Capital*, Chapters 9 and 10.
13   Marx, *Grundrisse*, pp. 164–5.

their return (and often successfully do so) by leveraging. When Elon Musk offered $40 billion to buy Twitter, he preferred to borrow the money from banks with his Tesla shares as collateral rather than to convert the shares to cash. Most capitalist corporations therefore operate with borrowed funds. The result is more and more leveraging and spiralling indebtedness in the macro-economy. In the capitalist's world, everyone is aware that the rate of personal return is often much higher when operating on borrowed funds.

The other incentive to operate with debt is securitization. This is, in essence, the reverse of Hardin's 'Tragedy of the Commons'. If I invest $1,000 in funding a mortgage on a house, I get the rate of return (say, 6 per cent) but bear 100 per cent of the risk of default by the mortgagee. If a bank securitizes 100 mortgages in a collateralized debt obligation, then I get my 6 per cent but bear only 1 per cent of the risk of default, since the risk of 100 properties all defaulting at the same time is almost zero. The effect is to create an investment commons which maximizes individual returns while socializing and minimizing risks. But, as 2007–8 showed, the piling up of investments in high-risk housing finance eventually results in crises as the number of defaults and evictions skyrockets. 'Almost zero' is not zero.

Marx, in his chapters on money and finance, and on merchant and landed capital in what became (thanks to Engels's editing) Volume 3 of *Capital*, constructed a far more advanced basis for theorizing the inner structure of the capitalist mode of production. Most presentations on Marx's political economy fail to appreciate his admittedly incomplete findings. Marx structured his investigations around a double movement. The first is to take up particular 'moments' (such as landed capital or finance) in isolation from the totality (much as a cardiologist will examine how the heart works within the human body). In the second moment, Marx reintegrates his particular findings into the totality. In so doing, he finds concepts and ideas that function well within a sector taken in isolation. These then have to be reinterpreted (sometimes dramatically so) when looked at in the context of the totality. The cardiology that emerges out of a holistic approach to medicine is likewise rather different from that arising from narrow technical analysis. In Volume 3 of *Capital*, Marx undertakes the first of these tasks, but he never fully accomplished the second, except by way of occasional unsystematic flashes of insight.

Here, then, is some of Marx's commentary on the role of interest-bearing capital and the financial system as far as he then understood it.[14] Capital's credit system as we now know it originated as the servant of the need for monetary coordination across production systems with radically different turnover times.[15] In particular, it became more and more essential as investments in fixed capital and the consumption fund became more prominent within the circulation and accumulation of capital. In the *Grundrisse*, however, the bankers and financiers emerge as a distinctive class. Furthermore, Marx makes clear that even the simplest form of the creation and circulation of capital 'posits' the rise of a credit system and the circulation of interest-bearing capital. Here is how he explains it in an anticipatory passage in the *Grundrisse*:

> *Money*, then, in so far as it now already *in itself* exists as capital, is therefore simply a *claim on future* (new) labour. It exists, objectively, merely as *money*. Surplus value, the new growth of *objectified labour*, to the extent that it exists for itself, is *money*; but now, it is money which *in itself* is already capital; and, as such, it is a *claim on new labour*. Here, capital already no longer enters into relation with on-going labour, but with future labour. And it no longer appears dissolved into its simple elements in the production process, [or] as … the abstract form of general wealth, but as a claim on the real possibility of general wealth – labour capacity, and more precisely, *labour capacity in the process of becoming*. As a claim, its material existence as money is irrelevant, and can be replaced by any other title. Like the creditor of the state, every capitalist with his newly gained value possesses a claim on future labour, and, by means of the appropriation of ongoing labour has already at the same time appropriated future labour … (its property of existing as value separately from its substance can be seen. This already lays the basis for credit).[16]

In other words, the germ of capital's distinctive credit system was present at the birth of capital's becoming. The challenge this poses is to identify the forces that nurtured this germ and forced its growth over time. But debt as a claim on future labour explains the inner relation that depicts 'an accumulation of capital as an accumulation of debts'.[17] This takes us back to the role of credit in squaring the circle between the production and realization of surplus value in such a way as to

14   Ibid., p. 367.
15   Marx, *Economic Manuscript of 1864–1865*, p. 566.
16   Marx, *Grundrisse*, p. 367. Italics as in the original.
17   Marx, *Economic Manuscript of 1864–1865*, p. 566.

facilitate the spiral form of endless accumulation (Chapter 2). Taking up the claim on future labour presumes that the future has already been mortgaged to secure sufficient effective demand in the present. This is, of course, the essence of Keynesian economics and, to the degree that state policies have been informed by Keynesian principles, there is a specific recognition that the credit system is a foundational feature of a capitalist mode of production and one of the main levers to promote further accumulation. Furthermore, the exhaustion of the other means to fill the effective demand gap puts the burden increasingly on credit structures.

There are, of course, some residuals of former possibilities. The Catholic Church, for example, has yet to melt down the silver and gold plate it has accumulated over centuries to pay for its multiple sins (all the way from the forced and often violent re-education of indigenous peoples to sexual predation). Central Bank shots in the arm of monetary circulation, on the other hand, are becoming more rather than less significant in the short term. The working population also now plays an active role by going into debt with the help of credit cards (an innovation that came on the scene after 1980 or so and played an important role in the history of financialization and its grip as much on the poor as on the rich). The deeper we probe into the theory of capital accumulation, the more prominent does the role of the credit system become. To dismiss it as nonessential and parasitic or superimposed by outside forces is an error of monumental proportions. In the same way that corporations find themselves now forced to yield up future labour if they are to survive, so the working population finds itself increasingly enmeshed in a form of debt peonage that forecloses future options. 'Time future', as the poet T. S. Eliot put it, is 'contained in time past'.[18]

The circulation of interest-bearing capital through the credit system 'hardens' (as happened with the circulation of fixed capital) into a powerful and seemingly autonomous force regulating much of what happens in the circulation and accumulation of capital in general. Capital equips itself with a central nervous system adequate to coordinating the flows and the needs of value flow. 'In the money market', Marx observes, 'capital is posited in its totality; there it determines prices, gives work, regulates production, in a word, is the source of production.'[19] Planning for the economy increasingly shifts, as Michael Hudson insists, from the

---

18   T. S. Eliot, *Four Quartets* (San Diego: Harcourt, 1943).
19   Marx, *Grundrisse*, p. 275.

state into the offices and corridors of the financial institutions (such as Goldman Sachs), with several key links into the daily operations of the state apparatus, particularly through the Treasury Department.[20]

In Marx's time, therefore, the lineaments of today's future were clearly if partially foretold. 'In interest-bearing capital, the capital relation reaches its most externalised and fetishized form … In interest-bearing capital … this automatic fetish is elaborated into its pure form, self-valorising value, money breeding money, and in this form it no longer bears any marks of its origin', which lies, of course, in wage labour. 'The social relation is consummated in the relationship of a thing, money, to itself.'[21] The mass of centralized money power both reproduces and augments itself. This is 'capital mystification in its most glaring form'. 'For the vulgar economist, who wants to present capital as an independent source of wealth, of value creation, this form is of course a godsend, a form in which the source of profit is no longer recognizable and in which the result of the capitalist production process – separated from the process itself – obtains an autonomous existence.'[22] It is this that promotes the rise of 'a class of men' – the rentiers or an investor class – 'who by the labours of their ancestors find themselves in possession of funds sufficiently ample to afford a handsome maintenance from the interest alone'.[23]

In Marx's time merchants frequently operated on credit and loans, while the class of bankers as specialists in finance and as a distinctly financial class was relatively small, confined for the most part to a small group of very rich and powerful families such as the Rothschilds, the Pereire Brothers and the Barings, whose power rested on their own wealth, measured either in gold or land, and who had their roots in supplying finance on the collateral mainly to the state. 'Interest-bearing capital, or, as we may describe it in its antiquated form, usurer's capital, belongs, together with its twin brother, merchant's capital, to the antediluvian forms of capital which were in existence long before the capitalist mode of production and are present in the most diverse economic formations of society.'[24] But capitalism continues to develop:

---

20   Michael Hudson, *Killing the Host: How Financial Parasites and Debt Bondage Destroy the Global Economy* (Dresden: Islet, 2015), p. 294.
21   Marx, *Economic Manuscript of 1864–1865*, pp. 492–3.
22   Ibid., p. 493.
23   Ibid., p. 465.
24   Ibid., p. 693.

In the course of its evolution, industrial capital must subjugate [usu-rer's and merchant's capital] and transform them into derived or special functions of itself … Where capitalist production … has become the dominant mode of production, interest-bearing capital is dominated by industrial capital, and commercial capital becomes merely a form of industrial capital … But both of them must first be destroyed as indepen-dent forms and subordinated to industrial capital … the real way [this happens] … is the creation of a procedure specific to itself – the credit system … the credit system is its own creation.[25]

But, as credit becomes more and more indispensable in, for example, reducing the cost and time of circulation, so 'the development of the production process expands credit, while credit in turn leads to an expansion of productive and mercantile operations.'[26] But the money capital brought together within the credit system is not concerned with production per se, but only with appropriation. The money capitalist is indifferent to the ultimate source of revenue and invests in government debt, mortgages, stocks and shares, commodity futures, or whatever depending on the rate of return. 'All connection with capital's actual process of valorisation is lost, right down to the last trace, confirming the notion that capital automatically valorises itself.'[27]

The danger then lurks that lending will not be for productive pur-poses but solely for appropriation. The circulation of interest-bearing capital becomes 'the mother of every insane form.'[28] Everything 'appears in duplicate and triplicate, and is transformed into a mere phantom of the mind',[29] such that even 'an accumulation of debts can appear as an accumulation of capital.'[30] The credit system registers the height of dis-tortion in which the accumulation of claims far outruns real production. The credit system that began as a faithful servant of industrial capital thus becomes its malignant mutant master. Marx clearly saw the poten-tiality for money capital to run amok within the credit system and for the bankers to presume that they were the arbiters of capital accumulation. Nothing portrayed in the previous examples is therefore untoward or surprising.

25   Marx, *Theories of Surplus Value*, Vol. 3, pp. 468–9.
26   Marx, *Economic Manuscript of 1864–1865*, p. 574.
27   Ibid., p. 558.
28   Ibid., p. 557.
29   Ibid., p. 564.
30   Ibid., p. 566.

But we have a choice in we how view this evolutionary movement. We can interpret it as the inevitable outcome of a teleological movement, or as a contingent outcome depending on historical accidents, environmental conditions and the balance of class and other social and geopolitical forces. Contemporary ruling classes prefer the teleological interpretation – 'there is no alternative' (Thatcher) or this is the ultimate 'end of history', as Fukuyama proposes. The supposed inevitability of historical evolution confirms the bankers' consummate power. More contingent explanations pose the puzzle of identifying possible lines for collective action and social forces that might somehow change the trajectory of human history.

The most obvious point, however, where an emphasis on continuity and contingency becomes blindingly obvious concerns the role of the mass of value. George Soros had at his fingertips a mass of capital in money form, and the same is true in the case of Amazon's borrowing and Blackstone's unrivalled assemblage of investment money power. The individuals leading these enterprises all emerge as freshly minted billionaires, constituting an oligarchy with immense economic and political power. It is not hard to trace here an evolutionary thread in Marx's history of capital's becoming. If the basic law of capital is to maximize the production of surplus value and thereby produce an ever-increasing mass of capital, and if the derivative law (thanks to the emphasis on the rising productivity of labour) of falling rate and rising mass is fully operative, there is a simple way in which these modest origins might over time generate the 'monstrous masses'. But in all of the cases cited, with the exception of Amazon, no real value is produced, though plenty is appropriated. The labour of Soros, Mnuchin and Schwarzman, along with that of all those employed by them, is unproductive labour (though they will doubtless claim that they had to work very hard and take many risks). They are rentiers, not producers. They flourish on the basis of unearned income. But the latter cannot exist without someone somewhere producing earned income. The unreality of the former is bound at some point to have to confront the reality of the latter. As we shall see, however, this confrontation is often mediated and, more often than not, ameliorated by evasive state actions.

The rising mass of capital (and its seemingly magical capacity, given a fetish disguise for self-augmentation) is in the forefront of this process. But it is only the monetary mass that truly matters. While the mass of capital engaged in production can be impressive (as the Manchester case demonstrated to Marx), its growth is physically and economically

236 THE STORY OF CAPITAL

limited, even though the industrial cities of Foxconn in Shenzhen or Rana Plaza in Dhaka are astonishingly large configurations of productive activity. Merchant capital (for example, Walmart and IKEA) likewise has both economic and physical limitations in the mass it can generate and handle, in part because its very mission is to speed up and not delay circulation. There is nothing insurmountable, however, in the assemblage, concentration and centralization of money power. Money capital can be accumulated without limit. It is, therefore, to the circulation of capital in money form that we should look for clues to the current evolutionary trajectory of capital. To take a contemporary example, the number of active hedge funds in the United States in 1990 was 600 and they had under management some $38 billion. In 2020, there were more than 12,000 hedge funds with $4.3 trillion under management. This is the kind of massive increase in the mass of capital that both allows for and promotes a qualitative shift in economic dynamics. This lopsided rate of return on capital in financial form consolidates the increasing centralization of money power. Michael Roberts notes, 'In the US, the real return on equities averaged 9.2% a year between December 1981 and December 2021, far outstripping growth in average real earnings of 0.5% a year and overall GDP growth of 2.7%.'[31] (See Figure 15.)

In Volume 1 of *Capital*, Marx identifies what he calls the laws of increasing centralization of capital.[32] These laws incorporate the principle, discussed in earlier chapters, that the larger the mass of capital the faster its increase, even when the rate of profit is declining. The concentration of capital occurs as surplus value is incrementally reincorporated in the circulation of productive capital. But this incremental process is slow. It pales into insignificance compared to the centralization of capital by other means, such as competitive takeover of weaker firms, mergers and acquisitions, the formation of joint stock companies and, above all, by way of the credit system. The leveraged buyouts that currently so often accompany mergers and acquisitions permit investors to assemble a mass of borrowed capital to buy out a large enterprise while using very little if any of their own money. They then use the earnings of that large company to pay off the interest and principal in subsequent years. This, for example, was how the Glazer family acquired the UK soccer club Manchester United, and the fans have many ill-feelings at how much of the club's revenue is taken for debt service to benefit the Glazer

31   M. Roberts, 'It's Not Looking Good for 2022', Michael Roberts blog, 3 May 2022, thenextrecession.wordpress.com.
32   Marx, *Capital*, Vol. 1, pp. 777–80.

THE CIRCULATION OF INTEREST-BEARING CAPITAL 237

family rather than being applied to develop the club. Manchester United became, in effect, a milch cow for the Glazer family.

The stock market, which came into its own in Marx's time, played a major (and, in Marx's somewhat strange view, potentially positive) role in this: the increasing centralization of money power implied the prospect for the increasing socialization of capital. But it also gave rise to speculation in asset values along with takeovers of smaller companies by conglomerate groups. In our own times, the leading hedge funds and private equity companies are a major force for this increasing centralization of capital. While hedging has been a long-standing practice in the history of capitalism (for example, by farmers insuring against crop failure), the hedge funds that now dominate investment on Wall Street and in the City of London are something entirely new. Bridgewater Associates, for example, was founded in 1975 and at its peak managed $160 billion or so of funds (talk about the mass!), invested on behalf of public and private pension funds, university endowments, government entities and very wealthy individuals. It is reputed to have earned $47 billion for its investors over the years, and Ray Dalio, its CEO, is now one of the richest persons and leading financial gurus in the world on the basis of taking 20 per cent of the fund's earnings. Dalio now warns of a coming class war of poor against the rich. For Warren Buffett (another highly successful asset manager) the class war is already here: 'There's class warfare, all right, but it's my class, the rich class, that's making war, and we're winning.'[33]

However, at a certain point, Marx asserts, the capitalists themselves are forced to recognize and use the disjunction between the productive and the purely monetary aspects of their activities. When industrial capitalists find themselves in possession of capital in the money form, they face an existential choice between reinvesting in their distinctive line of production, and thereby confirming their identity as industrialists, or lending the money out to others in return for an interest payment, in which case they convert to the identity of rentier (someone living off unearned income). They can do this either directly or indirectly with the help of financial mediators. The peculiarity here is that money, the representation or expression of value, takes on a commodity form which has a use value (it can be used to produce surplus value) and an exchange value (the rate of interest). Marx divides the surplus value between that

---

33   Ben Stein, 'In Class Warfare, Guess Which Class Is Winning', *New York Times*, 26 November 2006.

part which commands a payment (profit) for the organization of productive activity and that part which pays obeisance to ownership of sheer money power in return for interest. While individual capitalists may receive the whole surplus value, they do so as divided personas. There is nothing, furthermore, that prevents an industrial capitalist operating entirely on borrowed funds in return for structured interest and principal repayments.

The question of such financial operations has been there all along. Consider what happened with Haussmann's urbanization of Paris.[34] The new breed of investment bankers backed by state power – like Isaac Pereire, who had, as Marx put it, 'the nicely mixed character of both swindler and prophet' – invented a new kind of urban political economy. This combined the creation of fixed capital of an independent kind (the railways), the building of the consumption fund (the housing, theatres and department stores along the new boulevards with their joint uses such as a fleet of omnibuses) and the circulation of interest-bearing capital through government finance as well as through the new credit institutions (such as the Crédit Immobilier), which challenged the power of the traditional bankers, such as the Rothschilds. All of this had to be put together to facilitate the rebuilding of the city.[35]

It is not as if China, to take a contemporary case, longed for or just happened to get a sophisticated financial system and credit markets.[36] After all, banks had effectively been abolished during the Cultural Revolution. China simply could not do without a certain level of financialization (as shown by development companies such as Evergrande and the massive growth in shadow banking) as it urbanized, beginning in the 1990s in its struggle to absorb the global surpluses of capital its own rapid development was helping generate. Whether or not these investments in China's built environment turn out to be productive and viable remains to be seen. But that is not their point. The immediate need, as it was in Haussmann's Paris, is to absorb surplus capital and labour in the field of circulating capital through spectacular urbanization and massive investment in long-term physical infrastructure (the metabolic relation to nature be damned!). But this could not be done without an adequate credit system bridging private capital and local state finance and the long-term circulation of interest-bearing capital. Maintaining the profitability of circulating and extractive capital by way of potentially

34   David Harvey, *Paris, Capital of Modernity* (London: Routledge, 2003).
35   Marx, *Economic Manuscript of 1864–1865*, p. 540.
36   Chaolin Gu, *China's Urbanization* (New York: Springer, 2024).

unprofitable investments and later devaluations in fixed capital and consumption fund formation, is, Marx's theory would suggest, a critical piece of capital's game at a certain point in its evolution. China is, alas, no exception. The question is whether it can avoid the malignant mutant forms that now dominate in the United States and Europe, where the credit system poses as the master but acts like the evil joker. Recent spectacular collapses in the real estate sector suggest that China in the end is doomed to repeat what happened in the US in 2007–8.

But there is yet another twist to this story. Much of the money that the financiers lend to invest in long-term fixed capital flows almost instantaneously, as we saw earlier, into the coffers of the circulating capitalists engaging in construction and development. Value and surplus value are instantaneously produced and recuperated by activity in these spheres. It is the production of value in the form of factories and houses, schools and hospitals, toll roads and public works of all kinds that we are concerned with here. At some point, the question of how the value embodied in such assets can be circulated and recuperated has to be answered. Clear property rights to the realization of these values in the built environment have to be established. Some of the value can be recuperated directly by the imposition of user charges (for example, toll roads) or the payment of rents (for example, on housing). Otherwise, the recuperation is indirect, through state taxation to support the use of assets held in common. The flow of values can be capitalized to form market rights to these financial flows. This calls for further elaborations within the financial system, in which mortgages, annuities, long-term bonds and the like become crucial. One consequence is that the circulation of interest-bearing as opposed to profit-seeking capital then prevails.

The separation out of profit from interest is, as we have seen, critical. Whereas the industrial capitalist is expected in Marx's initial formulation to gain a surplus value that combines profit with interest, the holder of the fixed capital or consumption fund asset will demand interest as their claim to a portion of the overall surplus. Marx also sees this as one of the counteracting influences to the falling rate of profit. To the degree that long-term investments of this kind have become far more prominent in capital's overall portfolio, the circulation of interest-bearing capital also 'hardens' into a distinctive circulatory system that locks on to the vast trove of monetizable assets that litter the landscape. Marx does not, however, pursue this in any detail, even as he tentatively registers its potential relevance. The idea that investments in nonproductive long-term fixed capital might help counter the falling rate of profit is mentioned only once. But the historical evidence of its growth in significance is, as we noted earlier, overwhelming.

The financial class does not appear to confront the workers directly. But here the perspective of the totality reveals something of great significance. Indebtedness becomes an alternative means to discipline whole populations to the requirements of capital. Debts are a claim on future labour. The more indebted the working population, the more bound they are to use their future labour to retire their debts. In advanced capitalism, working people and the population in general are now so thoroughly mired in mortgage debt, medical debt, student debt, auto loans, credit card and consumer debt that they find themselves in a virtual state of debt peonage. 'Debt encumbered homeowners do not go on strike' was an interesting saying in support of the mortgage finance reforms of the 1930s that held out the promise of homeownership in the United States to the working population, while in Britain the building societies that had the same policy objective were depicted as bulwarks against Bolshevism.

I was raised in a neighbourhood of working-class homeowners and support for the Labour Party was muted there at election times, compared to the enthusiastic rallies and posters in the districts where social housing predominated. It was later belatedly recognized that the Labour Party had diminished its own support base by encouraging working-class homeownership (as Margaret Thatcher clearly recognized when privatizing as much social housing as she could). But now the shadow of total indebtedness hangs over not only the present but the future prospects of the working population. The moment of monetary autonomy in the circulation of labour capacity (see Chapter 2) which, in Marx's day, dealt with rather paltry sums, has been elevated in advanced capitalist countries to be one of the most signal features of social control of the working mass. 'Wage slavery' now combines with debt peonage to ensure the political pacification of large segments of the population. The ruling ideas of the ruling classes – Thatcherite neoliberalism and its financial turn – prevail.

The world is now mired and entangled in debt. The IMF Fiscal Monitor for 2016 surveyed the state of the global credit system. It summarized the global situation as follows: 'At 225 percent of world GDP, the global debt of the nonfinancial sector – comprising the general government, households and nonfinancial firms – is currently at an all-time high.' This debt amounts to $86,000 for every man, woman and child on Planet Earth, whether they are engaged in economic activity or not.

'Two thirds, amounting to about $100 trillion, consists of liabilities of the private sector', which has become one of the major drivers of debt growth in recent times.[37] The share of government debt bottomed out in the mid-1970s at around 30 per cent of global GDP, but has since risen closer to 100 per cent.[38] A major surge occurred in response to the crisis of 2007–8. The Covid pandemic of 2020–22 released another gush of public money to ensure surplus liquidity everywhere. This rapidly rising mass of current indebtedness carries with it serious economic risks. Any attempt to retire the debt – debt deflation, it's called – could trigger a serious economic crisis.[39]

At the same time, the increasing centralization of this enormous mass of wealth and power in few hands proceeds steadily. 'The global population of billionaires rose more than fivefold and the largest fortunes rocketed past $100 billion' after 2000. The 'disruption' due to the Covid virus of 2020 reinforced this trend. 'As the virus spread, central banks injected $9tn into economies worldwide, aiming to keep the world economy afloat. Much of that stimulus has gone into financial markets, and from there into the net worth of the ultra-rich. The total wealth of billionaires worldwide rose by $5tn to $13tn in twelve months, the most dramatic surge ever registered.' The total number of billionaires worldwide increased by 'nearly 700 to 2,700. The biggest surge came in China, which added 238 billionaires – one every 36 hours – for a total of 626.'[40] This presents a serious challenge to the power, influence and authority of the Chinese Communist Party. President Xi has, in recent times, taken steps to rein in China's largest corporations and their often flamboyant owners like Jack Ma, banning them from raising capital on Wall Street and to discipline, if not harass, its billionaire class. But China is now not far behind the US, which has 724 billionaires. In the US, the billionaire class's share of national wealth doubled from 10 to 20 per cent between 2010 and 2020. By the beginning of 2021, the top 1 per cent in the US held 32 per cent of the national wealth, while the bottom 50 per cent commanded only 2 per cent of it. No serious attempt is on the horizon to do anything whatsoever about this dramatically increasing

37 International Monetary Fund, 'Fiscal Monitor: Debt: Use It Wisely', October 2016.

38 International Monetary Fund, 'Global Debt Is Returning to its Rising Trend', September 2023.

39 International Monetary Fund, 'Global Financial Stability Report: Steadying the Course: Uncertainty, Artificial Intelligence, and Financial Stability', October 2024.

40 Ruchir Sharma, 'The Billionaire Boom: How the Super-Rich Soaked Up Covid Cash', *Financial Times*, 14 May 2021.

inequality. The malignant consequences of an out-of-control expansion of the finance and credit system considered as a teleological inevitability are now plain to see.

The opening line of Marx's *Capital* reads that 'the wealth of societies in which the capitalist mode of production prevails appears as an immense collection of commodities.'[41] Perhaps that line should now read, it has recently been suggested, that 'the wealth of capitalist societies appears as an immense accumulation of debts.'

All of this places the organization of the credit system and the circulation of interest-bearing capital both privately and through the state into a central rather than peripheral role in the overall circulation of capital. Interest-bearing capital, introduced into general circulation as a servant of industrial capital, now emerges as a master force, a central nervous system, regulating the flows of capital in general. It does this in ways compatible with the spiral form of accumulation. From that position, it can also build another presence in the increasing centralization of the mass of capital in just a few hands. Most investment banks make their money out of mergers and acquisitions rather than from retail banking functions. Accelerating the centralization of the mass of capital via the credit system animates the circulation and further accumulation of capital. The greater the centralization (including that through the state sector), the larger the infrastructure projects that can be undertaken. Perhaps the largest project so far undertaken of this sort is the 56-km-long Hong Kong–Zhuhai bridge to Macau.

That $86,000 everyone on average owes is not owed to Martians but to earthly creditors. While a household, corporation or state may be a net creditor or a net debtor, the economy as a totality is seemingly founded on the tautological principle that every debt is a credit and every credit a debt. But contradictory social and economic relations are internalized within this tautology.

The modern banking system 'robs usurer's capital of its monopoly, since it concentrates all dormant money reserves together and places them on the money market ... while restricting the monopoly of the precious metals themselves by creating credit money'.[42] From this vantage point within capital's central nervous system, Marx sees some central contradictions. This 'accumulation of moneyed capital simply means that money is precipitated as loanable money' which can be used in an

---

41   Marx, *Capital*, Vol. 1, p. 125.
42   Marx, *Economic Manuscript of 1864–1865*, p. 702.

infinite number of ways in addition to that which can be used as capital. However, 'this accumulation can express elements that are very different from genuine accumulation. With genuine accumulation constantly expanding, this expanded accumulation of money capital can be in part its result, in part the result of elements that accompany it but are quite different from it (and possibly antagonistic to it)'.[43] The very fact that the accumulation of moneyed capital is augmented by elements that are independent of genuine accumulation, even if they accompany it, leads to 'a constant plethora of the moneyed capital.' We earlier encountered the concept of a plethora of capital in considering the problems of capital's ever-increasing mass and the problems of its absorption. 'This plethora develops alongside the development of the credit system. Hence there develops at the same time a need to drive the production process beyond its capitalist barriers, over-trading, over-production, and excess credit.' To which, Marx hopefully adds: 'This must always happen, however, in forms which bring about a rebound.'[44]

This is one of those cryptic comments that Marx makes from time to time which, if thought about long enough, increasingly appears as a potential flash of insight into the parlous state of capital's present condition. The only form of capital that can easily accommodate the spiral form of perpetual exponential growth is the money form (including credit moneys). There is a purely physical barrier to exponentially expanding consumption/realization of commodities (even with the shift into the production of experiences rather than things). The exponential increase of production is likewise impossible in the long run. So when the money capitalists become the dominant faction of capital, as they now clearly are in the United States and Britain – in Europe, Japan and East Asia they are powerful but not yet fully dominant – then the exponential increase in money and credit is let loose upon the land producing the plethora of money and loan capital (the surpluses of liquidity that the IMF so frequently complains about). It is this that puts such untoward pressure on industrial capital, forcing tendencies to overproduction and senseless investments in fixed capital. But ever-cheaper mass production is required to fuel the increase in mass consumption. Hence the 'antagonistic' drive to reconfigure production through deindustrialization (and devaluation) of the remnant of the Fordist system of the 1960s and the consolidation of a neoliberal regime in which money power pursuing

---

43   Ibid., p. 624.
44   Ibid., pp. 360–8.

interest dips its tentacles into almost every aspect of daily life. This occurs alongside the perpetual search to increase the productivity of labour and cheapen the costs of commodities.

What Marx calls 'genuine accumulation' surpassed its limits some-time during the last decades. We are now living in a world of 'elements', many of them fictitious, that may 'accompany' it but are 'quite different' if not 'antagonistic' to it, with no sign of a rebound in sight. The credit system may have originated as a faithful servant, but it has now become a wayward master. When Hudson warns the Chinese that this is not a model to follow, he presumably means that the 'shadow class formation' that has long threatened the Chinese path to socialism now focuses in the West on a class of financiers. Fortunately, the major banks in China are state institutions. This does not mean there are no subversive elements at work, as Wall Street firms seek to establish themselves inside the Chinese financial system. In the United States, the question is to what degree and in what ways might a re-engineering of capital's central nervous system, even from the standpoint of genuine accumulation and the common capital of the capitalist class, provide an opening for constructive and creative change as opposed to being lured into and ultimately succumb-ing to the temptations of nonproductive and parasitic practices.[45]

This is the tension that is frustrating the British model of economic development. The illusion of the Brexiteers was that Britain could surge out of its containment within the web of European constraints with a highly productive and innovative economy that would be the envy of the world (Singapore-on-the-Thames was the ideal). But London, the centre of financial parasitism, in fact anchors the British economy, and the level of support from 'the real economy' is so feeble that the whole country is in danger of dissolving into a rapid parasitic decline. Wealth contin-ues to pile up in London, of course, though some of it has leaked away to Frankfurt, Brussels and Paris. But the rest of the country is falling apart, and since Brexit the decline of the British economy relative to its European counterparts has been precipitous. When the cotton mag-nates in Marx's time gradually retired to their country estates and left their grubby industrialism behind, this signalled their ultimate demise. Rentier practices resting on fictitious forms dominate real production in the British economy today (with the City of London at its apogee). The consequences are predictable. What might be called 'the British disease'

45   Hudson, *Killing the Host*, p. 294; Michael Hudson, *The Bubble and Beyond: Fictitious Capital, Debt Deflation and Global Crisis* (Dresden: Islet, 2012).

may be contagious. It threatens the reproduction of capital everywhere. But its primary internal host in the City of London and Wall Street appears to be terminally ill.

We are thus left with a foundational contradiction. Marx's reproduction schemas as Luxemburg analyzed them posit a perpetual and chronic deficiency of effective demand that can partially be relieved by investments in the consumption fund and fixed capital (particularly of an independent kind) that partially absorb the tendency towards over-accumulation and a plethora of capital. This requires, as the Chinese have discovered, the development of a vibrant and independent credit system. The policy fix for the innumerable effective demand crises that have erupted since the mid-1970s has been some mix of austerity in state expenditures (primarily hitting social services for the lower classes while favouring the military) and the release of vast tranches of liquidity via the state and central bank credit systems, in which those like Musk and Soros who command masses of capital are given the opportunity to command even more of it at the expense of the working population. The exponential expansion of interest-bearing capital over the last three decades points to the simple fact that capital has reached its Ponzi stage, and it does not take too much imagination to figure out what that might mean.

13

The Troublesome Case of Fictitious Capital

The circulation of interest-bearing capital has its own laws of motion. It exhibits a problematic autonomy from that required solely to support its role in matching effective demand with surplus value production, standardizing different turnover times and rationalizing fixed capital circulation and consumption fund formation. The relation between circulating capital in general (Figure 1) and fixed capital and consumption fund formation (Figure 12) is mediated by credit and the circulation of interest-bearing capital. The credit system converts long-term payments into annual payments of interest and principal (for example, in a mortgage) consistent with an annual turnover time of circulating capital. An increasingly complex and sophisticated credit system and an irrepressible circulation of more and more interest-bearing capital is, however, the Pandora's box that capital perforce must open if it is to survive and grow without limit.

Some of the consequences for capital in general have already been indicated. But Marx did not complete his mission in elaborating on these topics. Until recently, these matters have all too often been treated as peripheral rather than foundational for understanding Marx's political economy. But debt, credit and the charging of interest long preceded the rise to dominance of capital's mode of production. This is one of the key forms of 'antediluvian capital' (as Marx calls them) that played such an important preparatory role in the rise of industrial capital.[1] The challenge is to define the particular roles and forms such categories continue to assume within the mature theory of capital's mode of production.

---

1   Marx, *Capital*, Vol. 1, p. 266.

Of all the categories that Marx bequeathed us, that of fictitious capital is perhaps the most problematic and troubling.[2] It arises because money-dealing capitalists do not only lend to industrial capitalists to produce surplus value. They are equally drawn to lend to (invest in) government debt, mortgages, stocks and shares, land and property rents, commodity futures, consumer (credit card) debt or whatever, depending on the rate of return on offer and the security of flow of the revenue stream that yields the interest payments. These other forms of investment are collectively categorized as fictitious forms of capital. Money capitalists are indifferent as to who they lend to and equally indifferent to the ultimate source of the revenue stream which yields the interest payments on the money they lend out. The danger then lurks that lending will not be for purposes of surplus value production but become solely oriented to the appropriation of value. We've just considered the lucrative payments extracted from an indebted working population when they use credit cards or assume student debt. In such cases, 'All connection with capital's actual process of valorisation is lost, right down to the last trace, confirming the notion that capital automatically valorises itself.'[3] Everything 'appears in duplicate and triplicate, and is transformed into a mere phantom of the mind',[4] such that even 'an accumulation of debts can appear as an accumulation of capital'.[5]

The primary contradiction in the money form is between money used as a means of circulation (to facilitate commodity exchange) and money used as a measure of value (which can be saved and preserved over time). In Marx's day the latter function took tangible form in the use of the money commodities, gold and silver.[6] The qualities of these metals (they do not oxidize and are relatively scarce, for example) uniquely equipped them to play this role. In effect, the labour input into procuring gold and silver became the standard for pricing all other commodities. The particular values of gold and silver became socially accepted as a representation of value in general. Individual and institutional wealth and power were then measured by how much gold and silver individuals or states commanded. But the money commodities are far too clumsy to function as efficient means of circulation (imagine purchasing cups of

2   Marx, *Economic Manuscript of 1864–1865*, pp. 500–836; Harvey, *Limits to Capital*, Chapter 10; Cédric Durand, *Fictitious Capital: How Finance Is Appropriating Our Future* (London: Verso, 2017); Hudson, *Killing the Host*.
3   Marx, *Economic Manuscript of 1864–1865*, p. 558.
4   Ibid., p. 564.
5   Ibid., p. 566.
6   Marx, *Grundrisse*, pp. 200–60.

coffee with grains of gold). Hence the development of coins and tokens, of paper and fiat moneys, all of which, Marx makes clear in the third chapter of *Capital*, required state monitoring and regulation if they are to work as effective means of circulation and as a measure of value.

However, when a sudden burst of commodity exchange exceeded the quantity of money in circulation, producers and merchants simply issued credit. Buying on tick and resorting to credit depended on individual capitalists. The central banks, Marx observed, could only influence the total money supply after the private discounters had ceased their activity. The resultant underlying contradiction within the money forms was bridged by the principle of convertibility: the fiat and credit moneys could be freely converted into gold and silver, wealth that could be measured and assayed. But even by Marx's time the total quantity of gold and silver already above ground could not easily be expanded to accommodate the rapid expansion of endless accumulation. Winston Churchill's return to the gold standard while he served as chancellor of the exchequer in Britain in the 1920s had disastrous consequences for the British economy. Monetary repression in the UK contributed to the slump leading into a general strike by labour in 1926. Under the Bretton Woods agreement of 1944, the US dollar was made convertible into gold at $35 an ounce, but the role of gold was restricted to interstate monetary transactions. As Marx early on noted, if the only pressing use is for liquidity in the means of circulation, fake moneys could do the job just as easily as authentic ('hard') moneys.[7] When merchants offered credit to facilitate commodity transactions, the monetary instruments in circulation could be wildly inconsistent with the amount of gold required in the event of a rising demand for convertibility. For this reason, the personal holding of gold was restricted in the United States from the 1930s on, though monetary systems in places like India still depend on gold (often in the form of personal jewellery) to this day. Finally, the gold standard and the metallic base were formally abandoned in world trade in 1971.

'There is a contradiction immanent in the function of money as the means of payment. When the payments balance each other, money functions only nominally, as money of account, as a measure of value. But when actual payments have to be made', money comes on to the scene 'as the individual incarnation of social labour' as 'the independent presence of exchange value, the universal commodity. This contradiction bursts forth in that aspect of an industrial and commercial crisis which

---

7 Ibid., p. 210.

is known as a monetary crisis.'[8] Note well here the idea that crises are multifaceted and can appear in quite different forms, though once again it is the rising mass that is implicated in crisis formation. 'Such a crisis occurs only where the ongoing chain of payments has been fully developed ... money suddenly and immediately changes over from its merely nominal shape ... into hard cash. Profane commodities can no longer replace it. The use-value of commodities becomes valueless and their value vanishes in the face of their own form of value.'[9] Just think here of what happened to the value of housing in 2007–8.

> The bourgeois, drunk with prosperity and arrogantly certain of himself [as they certainly were in 2006], has just declared that money is a purely imaginary creation. Commodities [like houses] alone are money ... But now the opposite cry resounds over the markets of the world: only money [as opposed to a house] is a commodity. As the heart pants after fresh water, so pants his soul after money, the only wealth. In a crisis, the antithesis between commodities and their value-form, money, is raised to the level of an absolute contradiction.[10]

This brilliant evocation (written in 1867) of how monetary crises unfold fits all too sadly into what much of the world went through in 2007–8, though the money commodities were no longer in play.

When convertibility into gold and silver was abandoned in international trade in favour of the US dollar becoming the monetary standard for the world after 1971, the performance of the US economy became, in effect, the gold standard for world trade. The public monetary policies of the central banks became critical and that of the US Federal Reserve with respect to debt creation doubly so. The temporary use of fake moneys (for example, some cryptocurrencies) then entered into the picture.

Money capital is the only form of capital that can be accumulated without limit. It is, therefore, to the circulation of capital in money form that we should initially look for clues to the current evolutionary trajectory of capital. An increasing mass of fictitious money capital promotes a qualitative shift in economic dynamics. 'Fictitious capital', says Cédric Durand,

---

8   Marx, *Capital*, Vol. 1, pp. 235–6.
9   Ibid., Vol. 1, p. 236.
10   Ibid., Vol. 1, p. 236.

is an incarnation of that capital which tends to free itself from the process of valorization through production. [It] is fictitious to the extent that it circulates without production ... As Marx understood, fictitious capital plays a profoundly ambivalent role. On the one hand, it is a factor favouring capitalist development, to the extent that this anticipation operation allows the acceleration of the rhythm of capital accumulation ... On the other hand, fictitious capital's anticipation of future accumulation implies a radical form of fetishism liable to mutate into unsustainable phantasmagoria. The mass of accumulated fictitious capital can, then, assume proportions incompatible with the real production potential of economies.[11]

Or, as Marx succinctly puts it, the financiers, as the primary dealers in fictitious capital, fuse the charming personas of swindlers and prophets.[12]

Fictitious capital is the accelerant applied to the form-giving fire of human labour. Since acceleration is one of the laws of motion promoted by the coercive laws of competition operating within a mature capitalist mode of production, it is not surprising to find capital embracing means to promote systematic reductions in turnover times and speed up almost everywhere (as much in consumption as in production). The rise of the stock market, Marx suggested, might well presage the abolition of the capitalist mode of production:

> It establishes monopolies in certain spheres and hence provokes state intervention. It reproduces a new financial aristocracy, a new pack of parasites in the guise of company promoters and directors (merely nominal managers); an entire system of swindling and cheating with . respect to the issue of shares and dealings in shares. It is private production unchecked by private ownership.[13]

Continuing, Marx writes, 'The credit system, centring on the quasi-national banks and the great money-lenders and usurers around them' produces 'enormous centralisation, and gives this class of parasites a fabulous power, not only to decimate the productive capitalists periodically, but to interfere. This is the most dangerous power of interference with real production, since this lot know nothing of, and have nothing to

---

11   Durand, *Fictitious Capital*, p. 50.
12   Marx, *Economic Manuscript of 1864–1865*, p. 540.
13   Ibid., p. 537.

do with, production.'[14] When the big three auto companies in Detroit changed their leadership from knowledgeable and imaginative engineers in the 1990s to grasping financiers and accountants focusing on monetary return and stock market value, they lost their competitive edge in product quality compared to German and Japanese auto companies.

The greater part of the banks' reserve funds 'consists of claims (bills of exchange and public securities) and shares (property titles, drafts on future revenues). It should not be forgotten here that the money value of this capital, as represented by these papers in the banker's tills, is completely fictitious … Added to this is the fact that this fictitious banker's capital represents to a large extent not his own capital but rather that of the public which deposits with him, whether with interest or without.'[15]

Bourgeois economics seeks to address some of these issues through the minoritarian work of Hyman Minsky, whose financial instability thesis is designed to confront the inevitability of financial crises in the absence of adequate regulation.[16] The thesis envisages the first stage of the application of the accelerant of fictitious capital through debt financing of investments generating enough income to pay off interest plus principle (in Marx's language, the fiction becomes real). But overconfident investment ('irrational exuberance', as Greenspan and Shiller referred to it, powered by the 'animal spirits' of investors and entrepreneurs) leads into a phase where simply earning interest (even at an elevated level) without repayment of principle accelerates the flow of interest-bearing capital, which at some point leads into Ponzi financing, where the return on the investment is insufficient to pay the debt service let alone retire the principle. Current debt is serviced by new investments. Everything remains fictitious until some crack occurs in the system which exposes its fictitious basis, which has not been and cannot be made real. The effect is a financial crisis which feeds back to destroy even the good investments as the effect of a credit crunch and rapidly escalating interest rates of the sort seen in the Asian crisis of 1997–8 and the housing market crisis of 2007–8. Deregulation and inability to control the shadow banking systems that sprang up all over the place (for example, in China after 2008) is now widely recognized as a critical problem, even as the role of fictitious capital as an accelerant for the system is almost impossible to stop, let alone reverse. The tendency to produce a Ponzi financial bubble

---

14   Ibid., p. 615.
15   Ibid., p. 561.
16   Hyman Minsky, *Stabilizing an Unstable Economy* (New York: McGraw Hill, 2008 [1986]).

running on fictions and fumes is increasingly manifest, leaving industrial and to some degree merchant capital to pick up the pieces.

There is an intriguing insight in a prose poem by Baudelaire made much of in Jacques Derrida's essay in *Given Time*.[17] The poet is walking in the city with his friend when they encounter a beggar. The friend reaches into his pocket and takes out a whole franc piece and donates it to the beggar. Baudelaire compliments his friend on this extraordinary act of generosity. The friend says not so fast, the coin is fake. The poet is then outraged at the deceit and remonstrates at the cruel indifference of his friend to the plight of the beggar. But the friend retorts that the beggar at that moment is overjoyed because he thinks he has in his possession a whole franc piece. Donating it brought a period of intense happiness, at least for a time, into the life of someone who otherwise lived a life of unrelieved misery. And what could be wrong in doing that? Psychic value has some role to play in understanding the circulation of fictitious capital.

This is what John Kenneth Galbraith later dubbed a 'bezzle' (a covert and hidden form of embezzlement), suggesting that it has a systematic role to play in the dynamics of capital accumulation.[18] The most obvious form is a Ponzi scheme in which interest payments to investors are based on the flow of new investments and not on any real expansion of surplus value production and its realization. Everyone is happy while the scheme lasts, but when it is uncovered everyone finds there is no there, there. Such schemes have a positive effect on accumulation, while they last. They seem virtuous until it turns out they are not. But Ponzi schemes are just one part of what constitutes fictitious capital. Fictitious capitals are titles of ownership, claims to future labour, 'paper duplicates of the real capital':

> Profits and losses, and also the concentration of these property titles, are by the nature of the case more and more the result of gambling, which now appears in place of labour as the original source of capital owner-ship, as well as taking the place of the direct use of force. This kind of imaginary money wealth makes up a considerable part not only of the money wealth of private individuals.[19]

17   Jacques Derrida, *Given Time* (Chicago: University of Chicago Press, 2017).

18   John Kenneth Galbraith, *The Great Crash 1929* (Boston: Houghton Mifflin, 1955).

19   Marx, *Economic Manuscript of 1864–1865*, pp. 566, 567.

For this reason, the latter pay great attention to the movement of asset values. But even though false, for a time investments in fictitious capitals promote real capital accumulation. 'The credit system has a dual character immanent in it: on the one hand it develops the driving force of the capitalist mode of production, enrichment by the exploitation of other people's labour, into the purest and most colossal system of swindling and gambling.'[20] What appeared as colossal in Marx's day looks, of course, trivial in ours. While the consequent growth is not a mirage, the revolutions in productive forces proceed apace and mass production and mass consumerism continue on their path of endless 'monstrous' growth.

In his book on fictitious capital, Cédric Durand concludes with a deeply troubling if fundamental conclusion:

> The insufficient profits from the molecular process of accumulation through production ... make the sovereign state responsible for resolving an ever more acute conflict over distribution ... The hegemony of finance – the most fetishized form of wealth – is only maintained through the public authorities' unconditional support. Left to itself, financial capital would collapse; and yet that would also pull down the whole of our economies in its wake ... Financial hegemony dresses up in the liberal trappings of the market [boldly proclaiming its belief in the efficient market hypothesis] yet captures the old sovereignty of the state all the better to squeeze the social body to feed its own profits.[21]

Proponents of the efficient free market hypothesis (a version of Say's Law) conveniently forget Marx's admonition that an unregulated free market always ends up in monopoly control, making the period of neoliberal deregulation a period of ever-heightening centralization of wealth, supplemented by increasing monopoly and monopsony control in almost all sectors of the economy (with the tech industries in the lead). Braudel's assertion from long ago that 'capital is the state' gets truer by the day.[22] 'Alas', Durand continues, 'we cannot see any sign of the tomorrows bearing the song of emancipation. Since the plutocrats cannot settle for stagnation, they now resort to a strategy of crushing the rest of us. Capital stole people's hopes. The lead weight of fictitious capital deprives them of what they thought they had won for good.'[23]

---

20 Ibid., p. 540.
21 Durand, *Fictitious Capital*, p. 155.
22 Fernand Braudel, *Afterthoughts on Material Civilization and Capitalism* (Baltimore: Johns Hopkins University Press, 1977), pp. 64–5.
23 Durand, *Fictitious Capital*, p. 155.

There is another feature at the very heart of the circulation of capital that underpins the seemingly inevitable rise of fictitious capital to a position of ascendency within the capitalist mode of production. It is widely held that speculation is an aberrant and unfortunate form of market exchange. It has negative connotations even when it is not characterized by underhand and even illegal behaviour. But the circulation of capital is inherently speculative. In Marx's standard account, the capitalist starts the day with a certain amount of money with the intent of using it as capital and launches it into circulation in the speculative belief that a profit (surplus value) will be realized at the end of the day. This is what capitalist entrepreneurs do. They speculate on the profitable outcome of participating in the circulation process depicted in Figure 1. They cannot do anything else. But there is much that can go wrong in this process. Risks and uncertainties abound – so much so that bourgeois theory frequently argues that profit can be justified as a reward for risk-taking. Marx is highly critical of such an assertion. But he does recognize that, until the capital traverses the whole circuit so as to be 'valorized' through realization in the market, followed by reinvestment and further valorization in production, it exists in the parlous state of 'the not yet realized or valorized', locked into the process of speculative 'becoming'.[24]

In the same way that all labour processes imagine an outcome in the mind's eye before taking shape on the ground, so a certain quantity of as yet unvalorized capital has to exist prior to its valorization. While this amount is easily identifiable within a simple circulation process (as the potential value of a stock of yet-to-be sold commodities, for example), its social form becomes more and more opaque and problematic as the 'complexification' of capital's supply chains unfolds and the phenomena of prices without values becomes more widespread. Apple's subcontractors make component parts as commodities that can only be truly valorized when the iPhone is sold to the final consumer. If the suppliers work on the basis of cash on delivery, the suppliers receive the monetary equivalent well before the final sale. If the subcontractors supplying parts do not get cash on delivery, they must take out loans of interest-bearing capital to cover their immediate production needs if they are to continue production in the face of delayed payment. Fictitious elements pervade the whole production and circulation process. Yet the point of the bezzle is to keep Baudelaire's beggar happy and feeling rich in possessing imaginary wealth in the midst of actual impoverishment.

---

24 Marx, *Economic Manuscript of 1864–1865*, pp. 584–5.

The trouble is that, once the pandora's box of unlimited speculation is opened up as economically and socially necessary to the further accumulation of capital, and as soon as fictitious capital is established as a primary accelerant and agent of time-space compression, the dynamic of capital accumulation is held hostage to forces that are limited solely by imaginary bounds and expectations. The apogee of such speculative fervour currently lies with the astonishing speculations occurring in the monetary form itself, as in the cases of cybercurrencies, blockchain technologies and NFTs (nonfungible tokens), all of which swamp investor attention even though they are ultimately imaginary claims on yet-to-be value production.

In the same way that fixated capital ultimately hardens into the circulation of fixed capital, giving rise to the circulation of interest-bearing capital, so the latter also hardens into a distinctive form of circulation. An increasing part of interest-bearing capital hardens into the circulation of fictitious capital. Since Marx's categories (like fixed and fictitious capital) are defined by use rather than physical qualities, so the rise of fictitious capital circulation depends more and more on that capital as yet unvalorized or that is unvalorizable, even as it stakes a claim to the product of future labour.

The buying and selling of such claims is facilitated by the capitalization of a host of income streams at disparate rates of interest. State debt is, as Marx points out, the pioneer in this regard, demonstrating, once again, the direct role of state finance in initiating and sustaining capital accumulation. The flow of tax revenues is capitalized into bonds (gilts, treasuries and so on) to be sold at a certain price. I buy the bond for, say, $100 and that entitles me to a fixed share of tax revenues for, say, ten years. But the bonds are tradeable such that the bond markets of the world are capitalized at the going rate of interest plus a risk premium (astronomically high in Argentina, modestly high in Italy and low in the case of US Treasuries). Stocks and shares are not far behind, and financial markets (bonds, stocks and shares) function as a powder keg central for all forms of speculative activities and possible explosions. As the mass of value in circulation increases, so more and more of this mass exists as fictitious capital, the independent creation and growth of which plays a critical role in the reproduction of capital. In Cédric Durand's words, fictitious capital 'has taken a central place in the general process of capital accumulation. Incarnated in debts, shares, and a diverse array of financial products whose weight in our economies has considerably increased, this fictitious capital represents claims over wealth that is yet to be produced. Its expansion implies a growing pre-emption of future production.'[25]

Even if financialization has no unitary structure, there does at least exist a cluster of interdependent processes constituting it as a historical and spatial incarnation of the institutional framework for capitalist mode of production. The rising power of fictitious capital is the nodal point of this shift. It is, above all, distinguished 'by the accumulation of drawing rights over values that are yet to be produced'.[26] The problem, as Marx saw it, and as Durand confirms, is that 'the institutions establishing themselves at the centre of the world's financial system use and abuse their position and the exclusive information available to them in order to make money'.[27]

If increasing time-space compression is a law of capital, then the accelerant of fictitious capital formation becomes a critical element in the speed-up that we see all around us.[28] This is, from the standpoint of capital, its positive as opposed to parasitic role. The tactics involved have a long history. When London bankers discounted bills of lading to merchants involved in the China trade in the eighteenth century, they were in effect creating a fictitious capital that could be used, often without restriction, until the 'ship came in' after many months (or sometimes not at all). The effects of such accelerants are felt everywhere within the mode of production. This has meaning on the ground.

In *Planetary Mine*, for example, Martin Arboleda reports on 'the astonishing increase' in Chile's exports of metals to China 'between 2001 and 2011, going from $460 million to $11.1 billion'. This was paralleled by a dramatic expansion in the balance of trade between China and Latin America 'going from $15 billion in 2000 to [a staggering] $200 billion in 2011'.[29] These were years, recall, when the global economy was stumbling through the aftermath of a severe financial crisis. The role of fictitious capital as an accelerant mitigates its role as a problematic claim on future labour.

While the contractual world of fictitious capital formation and circulation appears as a legal and logistical nightmare and the bankers themselves specialize in making everything so complex that only they

25   Durand, *Fictitious Capital*, p. 1.
26   Ibid., p. 4.
27   Ibid., p. 13.
28   David Harvey, *The Condition of Postmodernity: An Enquiry into the Origins of Cultural Change* (Oxford: Basil Blackwell, 1989).
29   Arboleda, *Planetary Mine*, pp. 14, 63.

can understand and legislate for it, the underlying logic of the situation is not hard to understand. Young people in the United States are told that the lifetime earnings of those with college degrees exceed those without by perhaps as much as a million dollars over a working life. It therefore makes sense to borrow to acquire a university education for those families who cannot afford the exorbitant university tuition costs. The outstanding student debt in the US now stands at \$1.77 trillion, spread across some 43 million borrowers.[30] These are people who need no further instruction in what debt as a claim on future labour might mean. Retiring this debt is a burden that governs their life chances and disciplines them to accept the coercive conditions of maintaining a steady job. The political demand to cancel this student debt is now marked.

Throughout this text, we have frequently commented on the forces that produce and the consequences that flow from the ever-rising mass of capital and surplus value in circulation. Currently, the global ecological consequences (such as climate change and habitat destruction) are particularly troublesome. But the Chile–China trade data go far beyond the growth that might be expected even under normal conditions of exponential capital accumulation.

The temptation is to attribute this to one overwhelming and unique force: China's astonishing growth. But such an explanation misses out on the radical upsurge in value circulation and appropriation since 1980, often attributed in bourgeois circles to 'financialization'. The suspicion lurks that monetary aggregates, initially understood as the material expression or representation of values, have been cut loose from their moorings in value creation and realization. This has fuelled a massive increase in fictitious capital formation and circulation. Capital accumulation in our times thus seems to be running on fumes, rather than on material incentives. From the Long-Term Capital Management and Enron bankruptcies of 1998 and 2001 to the spectacular bankruptcy of the FTX crypto-exchange in 2022 (putting \$42 billion at risk), along with successive bank failures in 2023, we see what seems to be a new phase where Ponzi schemes and vigorous asset bubbles (bezzles) have flourished. The resulting unchecked growth of fictitious capital with its mounting claims to the product of future labour is an explosive danger.

Given the strong interventions of the world's central banks via quantitative easing, the question of whether capital itself is these days nothing

---

30   Board of Governors of the Federal Reserve System, *Consumer Credit – G.19*, 2024 Q3.

more than a self-perpetuating Ponzi scheme warrants consideration. If that is so, it is only the United States, with its power of seigniorage over the dollar as a primary reserve currency that can organize it, profit from it and, most important of all, sustain it. The farcical periodic pantomime in the US Congress over raising the US debt limit signals something important. If the US should renege on its debt by the vote of some mis-guided ideologues in Congress, the lid will come off the global Ponzi scheme and much of the financial architecture built up since the 1970s will crumble with devastating economic consequences. It would take a huge collective worldwide effort to put the lid back on again. Surely it would be better to invent some alternative. There are, for example, other ways to guarantee future livelihoods than privatized pensions. The fight to save Social Security in the US from privatization (as happened in Chile in 1975 with disastrous consequences) is emblematic in this regard.

The suspicion lurks that it is only the mediations, interventions and controls of an internationally coordinated, commercially rules-based version of a state-finance nexus (see Chapter 16) that prevents the violent dissolution of further capital accumulation on a world scale. The rising tide of fictitious capital formation and circulation signals dangers beyond imagination. The failure to collectively theorize this situation is poten-tially fatal to all human ambition. While Galbraith, Minsky and Hudson have pointed the way, few have been prepared to follow it. Left to itself, capital simply produces a terrain of centralization of wealth in the form of a billionaire class who, like Baudelaire's beggar, imagine and behave as if they are supremely wealthy.

14

Accumulation by Dispossession

The story of the rise of capitalism from the feudal period in Europe onwards, or from the various precapitalist imperial and civilizational traditions elsewhere in the world, is one in which violence, conquest, robbery, piracy, dispossession, fraud, evictions, usury, slavery and thievery brooked large along with the slow dissolution of feudal, imperial and religious power structures. Whether or not such processes were legal (sanctioned by the state) or illegal was moot for much of the time, because the institutional and property arrangements that might have provided some protection against such practices either did not exist or were ineffective. Yet trading networks and merchant capitalist operations (including the trade in enslaved people) were far-flung and widespread from the fifteenth century onwards. Flickers of what looked like proto-capitalist industrialism could be seen early on in Flanders and Florence along with the increasing global role of monetization (facilitated by the rise of gold and silver as universal money commodities).

The exchange of labour power against the rising mass of revenues (led by those of church and state) meant that the preconditions were in place for the rise and deployment of money as capital engaging in profit-seeking. For these preconditions to be liberated from their social constraints and religious defences required the mass separation of labour from access to the means of production (the land in particular) and the dissolution of landed and religious powers. Hence the significance of what Marx called 'primitive' or 'original' accumulation. This process produced a wage labour force by separating large swathes of the population from access to the basic means of production. It also led to the rise of an agrarian capitalist class that allied with merchant capitalists and bankers in that phase of capitalism generally referred to as merchant capitalism. Buying commodities cheap and selling dear, along with raiding, piracy, robbery, colonial ventures and the conquest of territory became the primary sources of profit and the main means for the acquisition of wealth (usually in the form of gold). The quest for the latter was given theoretical standing in the prevailing mercantilist theories of the time. State power was increasingly judged according to how much gold was in the coffers of the state.

Original (or primitive) accumulation was, said Marx, written into the history of humanity 'in letters of blood and fire'.[1] This unspeakable violence took place over centuries and continues to this day. While Marx may have exaggerated a bit he also recognized how 'the silent compulsion of economic relations' also played its part.[2] But he did not pay enough attention to the racial, civilizational and religious dimensions of these transformations. There were processes at work that were undermining traditional forms of precapitalist economic, political and religious power. A path to 'something else' was opening up, though the monarchs, lords and priests of the time had no idea what it might be. The corrosive effects of trade on traditional class and state powers was supplemented by the impacts of usury and debt encumbrance in dissolving feudal power and land dominance. But this would have not played out in the way it did without the rise of various ways in which labour power could be corralled, managed and mobilized (sometimes through slavery and serfdom but also through indentures and guild control over apprenticeships) to produce surpluses, usually for the benefit of some ruling class. The idea of mass organization of labour into the factory system in Britain was almost certainly influenced by the earlier experience of mass management of slave labour on the West Indian sugar plantations.

What is interesting about this history is the way in which initial, seemingly developmental, steps could almost immediately become barriers to further development. While, for example, the management of slave labour may have initiated the first step, the class formation it facilitated condemned the West Indies, the American South and much of South America to what Clyde Woods later dubbed 'arrested development'.[3]

---

1   Marx, *Capital*, Vol. 1, Part 8, Chapters 26–33; see also David Harvey, *The New Imperialism* (Oxford: Oxford University Press, 2003); and David Harvey, 'The "New" Imperialism: Accumulation by Dispossession', *Socialist Register* 40, 2004.

2   Marx, *Capital*, Vol. 1, p. 899.

3   Clyde Woods, *Development Arrested: The Blues and Plantation Power in the Mississippi Delta* (London: Verso, 2017).

While the guild system of labour organization similarly took steps towards the management and social reproduction of wage labour as a commodity, it held back the rise of the free wage labour markets required for the factory system. Early industrial capitalism could not take root in the major merchant capitalist cities in Britain like London, Bristol, Norwich or Liverpool, all of which largely operated within the constraints of the corporatist guild system dominated by the power of the merchants and the bishops. The new industrial factories had to seek out greenfield sites. Small villages with names like Manchester, Birmingham and the like suddenly became industrial cities and nonconformist religions took the place of hierarchical religious powers centred on Rome. The problem of arrested development never went away. Capital is as anxious today as it was in eighteenth-century Britain to search out and favour 'greenfield' sites (for example, in the US South or in the *maquila* zones of Mexico) where labour organization and regulatory barriers are weakest. And, in many parts of the world, the power of the landowners (as in some countries of Latin America, with Chile an excellent case) has made for a perpetual battle of capital in general against arrested development through the domination of traditional local elites and landed interests. Within the orbit of the United States, Puerto Rico and the Mississippi Delta region come close to qualifying for the status of arrested development.

For purposes of theoretical clarity, Marx excluded primitive accumulation from consideration in his attempt to theorize the capitalist mode of production in its most mature form outside the confusions of a much more complex social formation. But we cannot afford that luxury. The violent dispossession of a self-sufficient peasantry and ongoing practices of proletarianization continue to play a critical role to this day in many parts of the world. If the global wage labour force has increased by more than a billion people since 1980, it has in part been through the destruction of alternative means of making a living. In China, for example, we have witnessed a state-sponsored programme of 'partial proletarianization' since 1980 in which the rural peasantry has supplied a vast migrant labour force to the booming factories in the industrial south on a temporary basis while retaining its rights of access to the land in their rural place of origin. The costs of social reproduction are borne in rural China, while the labour supply (particularly a huge cohort of young women) is applied in urban areas where migrant workers have no citizenship rights. This is the essence of the *hukou* system that still regulates much of the internal migration throughout China, even as some steps are taken towards its abolition in the face of a rising mass of a floating population of migrants in urban areas who stay on but have no citizenship rights.

Practices of original accumulation led to the formation of a wage labour force that was and still is free 'in the double sense': individuals are free to contract their labour power with whomever they wish, while being freed of all access to the means of production.[4] They have to engage in wage labour in order to live. But the continuing practices of primitive accumulation are now supplemented by a range of other practices in which capital increasingly depends on direct dispossessions, evictions and colonizations, to say nothing of cheating, theft, fraud and robbery (often backed by violence). The organized appropriation of the revenues of others (wages and other distributional incomes) now helps sustain capital accumulation. Price-gouging by merchants, fleecing by financial means, extraction of excessive land and property rents, speculation in all manner of asset values (including cybercurrencies), subsidies and redistributions through taxation arrangements, the privatization of public assets at favourable, if not fire-sale, prices, promotion of legal structures that are organized for the perpetuation of class privilege and power, are but some of the means involved. It is also significant that three of the most profitable lines of trade in our times are illicit drugs, illegal arms and human trafficking. The various 'mafia economies' and protection rackets play a prominent economic role in some parts of the capitalist social formation, impinging on the dynamics of the capitalist mode of production.

All this entails a shift to what I call 'accumulation by dispossession'. While primitive accumulation is about the violent creation of a wage labour force that has to sell its labour power in order to live, accumulation by dispossession entails the transfer from one class to another of values already created. The idea for such a category stems from Rosa Luxemburg's observation (supported by Hannah Arendt) that the relevance of Marx's theory of primitive accumulation persists into the modern era. She concluded this because, in *The Accumulation of Capital*, she could not understand where the effective demand came from that would support the continuous accumulation of capital in the spiral form. She ended up theorizing that trade with noncapitalist social formations in the throes of primitive accumulation was the only possible answer.[5] But it feels a bit odd to dub what is happening now as 'original' or

---

4   Marx, *Capital*, Vol. 1, pp. 271–4.
5   Luxemburg, *The Accumulation of Capital*.

'primitive' accumulation, particularly since the modern version, for the most part, serves a very different purpose. In classical Marxism, primitive accumulation stands for the processes whereby the working class was violently forged out of precapitalist social formations. These processes continue to play a huge role: the dissolution of peasant-based societies almost everywhere around the world since 1945 has markedly increased the global proletariat of wage labourers.

But accumulation by dispossession signifies something very different. It entails stealing, scamming or appropriating the value and surplus value already produced. It relies on the fact that money profit can be had without any surplus value production. When 7 million households lost their housing asset values in the crisis of 2007–8, they succumbed to one of the greatest asset value transfers in US history. Stephen Schwarzman became a billionaire and Blackstone one of the largest real estate operations in the world by buying up foreclosed housing at fire-sale prices. Many of the foreclosures, it later turned out, were fraudulent. Financiers, as we earlier saw, made money out of the East Asian crisis of 1997–8. Peter Singer's organization made billions by holding Argentina hostage to its distressed and defaulted indebtedness over many years. Emerging market countries are debt entrapped. They cannot afford their debt service and surrender their assets to outsiders for a song. Private equity companies take shaky public companies private, asset-strip them, renege on their obligations to employees (pension and health care rights) and finally return the now slimmed down company to the public sphere at a premium price. Profit on reorganization appears to be their business. Billionaires have murky histories of plundering the public trough while evading taxation and maximizing kickbacks. The nonpayment of wages, particularly at times of crisis, has also been a major issue in many parts of the world. United Airlines and American Airlines both underwent bankruptcy reorganizations that allowed them to discard their pension and health care obligations to past and current employees. Banks can legally foreclose on debts in times when the liquidity that the banks largely control is artificially tightened.

Significant flows of capital thus get diverted from the main circuits of capital by way of accumulation by dispossession. Capital (the value in motion) is channelled into non-value-producing activities that nevertheless yield high monetary profits. Trade in commodities that have a price but no value easily spills over into illegalities. The astonishing network of illegal side-payments associated with the construction firm Odebrecht's corruption of state officials in many Latin American countries from the

1990s onwards was economically significant.[6] It led to the suicide of an ex-president of Peru as the scandal was unravelled. In many countries, a political class gets to plunder the public treasury to stash away huge fortunes in tax havens, Swiss bank accounts or, as in the case of Senator Menendez of New Jersey, gold bars.

But there is also a good deal of legalized activity. If, for example, bankers and merchants can exploit their position in the circulation of capital to accumulate capital on their own account (as they have done on an increasing scale over the last forty years or so), the laws of motion of capital, usually specified from the standpoint of production (or industrial) capital, cannot possibly remain unaffected. If the credit system is flagrantly used to bolster the wealth and power of the investment bankers (such as Goldman Sachs or JPMorgan) or speculative property companies (like Blackstone), instead of supporting value and surplus value production, the theory of capital circulation and accumulation needs extensive revision. In the *Grundrisse*, for example, Marx suggests that conditions were arising in which the labour theory of value might no longer be operative even as the capitalists clung to it as the only meaningful metric to judge their condition.[7] Furthermore, speculative trading in income-yielding assets such as property rents, state debt, stocks and shares and the like is not necessarily a zero-sum activity. Accumulation by dispossession, profit on alienation (buying cheap and selling dear), manipulations in financial and money markets, the speculative activities of rentiers and landowners (particularly with respect to extractive activities) are all potential vehicles for not only increasing concentrations of money wealth and power in certain confined quarters but also for building new channels for further monetary accumulation in the absence of value and surplus value production. Profits increasingly accrue to operations that produce no value whatsoever. Marx was all too aware of the changing scale of mass production and the internal organization of capital that this implied. Commenting approvingly on Robert Owen, he observed:

> Almost all manufactures, to be successful, must now be carried out extensively and with a great capital; small masters with small capitals have only little chance of success ... the small masters will be increasingly displaced by those who possess great capitals ... He obtains this

6   Francisco Durand, *Odebrecht: The Corporation That Captures Governments* (Lima: Fondo Editorial de la Pontificia Universidad Católica del Perú, 2018).

7   Marx, *Grundrisse*, p. 700.

power through combination with other great capitalists, engaged in the same interest ... and thus effectively bends to his purpose those he employs. The large capitalist now swims in wealth, whose proper use he has not been taught and does not know. Through his wealth, he has gained power. His wealth and his power blind his reason; and when he oppresses altogether grievously, he believes he is bestowing favours ... His servants, as they are called, his slaves in fact, are reduced to the most hopeless degradation.[8]

This is, of course, the world of Elon Musk. It is the world in which all manner of institutional means exist to dispossess the weak for the benefit of a billionaire class of consummate wealth and power. The stock exchange, Marx notes, is a wonderful place to observe how the financial sharks gobble up the economic minnows.

Accumulation by dispossession is not to be confused with the profits garnered by merchants, consultants and honest brokers in credit and stock markets. In Volume 3 of *Capital*, Marx makes clear that value and surplus value can be created only in the act of production. The essential services of the merchant capitalists have to be paid for as the 'necessary costs' of circulation (Marx uses the term *'faux frais'*) that have to be deducted from value and surplus value production. There are some exceptions. For example, Marx holds that commodities are not completely produced until they are at market. Transport and communication costs therefore add value, while other aspects of wholesaling and retailing do not, even though they are necessary costs. Exceptions exist. For example, if improvements in the field of merchant capital delivery reduce circulation times, the fact that two or three turnovers of production of a commodity can now be procured over a year translates into considerable increase in surplus value production. Furthermore, merchant capitalists exploit the labour they employ and thereby add to the total surplus value created. Increasing efficiency in merchandising is valued and much sought after. Mass production and consumption were paralleled by the creation of the department stores, such as Le Bon Marché in Paris and Marshall Field's in Chicago in the latter half of the nineteenth century, followed by the supermarkets that proliferated everywhere in the latter half of the twentieth century.

The same logic applies to business and consulting services. An organization like McKinsey and the legal teams dealing in international

---

8   Ibid., pp. 713–14.

accountancy are in principle part of the faux frais of capital circulation. When innovation becomes a business, applications that affect the efficiency and speed of execution in organizational forms become important lines of business. The invention of all manner of apps, the proliferation of automated decision-making techniques now emerging (AI) have all manner of potential implications, but if the past is any guide they will predominantly be used to maximize rates of labour exploitation while adding to the incentive to increase the mass of value in motion many times over.

The theory of distribution has to track the appropriation of value and its increasing centralization in fewer hands even in the absence of any additional surplus value production. Capital investments in circulation, distribution and realization cannot produce value, but they do create the 'conditions of possibility' for the realization and appropriation of more and more value and surplus value in the industrial circuit.

The theoretical question that Marx poses is this: Why would industrial capitalists who undertake the primary task of organizing wage labour to produce value and surplus value tolerate sharing their spoils with merchant capitalists, finance capitalists, landed capitalists and the state? Marx does not characterize these other factions of capital or the state as inherently parasitic (as many on the contemporary left often do). All of these factions (if we can call the state a faction) have legitimate and crucial roles to play in support of capital circulation and accumulation. Each has, therefore, a rightful claim to a part of the surplus value produced by industrial capital as well as that from the extraction of surplus value from the workers they themselves employ. Marx concentrates on these claims, on what basis they are established and how a distinctive flow of value and surplus value circulates in satisfying such claims. These diverted value flows affect the laws of motion of capital in general and trigger different social relations and forms of struggle than those entailed in the circulation of industrial capital in isolation. In the case of merchant capital, for example, the basic social relation is the transaction between buyer and seller, while in the case of finance capital it is between debtors and creditors. In both cases, the class relation between capital and labour, which dominates in production and forms the class basis for surplus value production, fades into the background. This has potentially profound political consequences.

The materials that Marx was amassing on banking and finance for Volume 3 of *Capital* show that he was increasingly concerned with the question of how, why and with what effect might the bankers and financiers go beyond their rightful claims and use their position and their power over the mass of wealth under their command to appropriate as much of the value and surplus value as possible for themselves. They were, by virtue of their position and the crucial services they provided, able to legally or even illegally take from the collective pool of value and surplus value that the industrialists were creating. The same would obviously apply to merchant capitalists, and to landlords and the state. The power of these factions varied somewhat, but Marx recognized their status as autonomous and independent institutionalized factions sub-sumed within the totality of relations that constitute a capitalist mode of production. There were obvious limits to the amounts of appropria-tion that might be possible. It was also obvious that much of the value they appropriated would need, at some point, to be recycled back into production to ensure future appropriations. But the structure of indus-trial production and the organization of so-called 'commodity' or 'value chains' between different firms in the production process as a whole creates complications for analysis and theory-building. This has been particularly the case in the garment and footwear industries:

> Globalized brands exercised monopsony power over producers through their ability to select from a large pool of outside firms for almost every phase of the value chain – textiles, production, transportation, process-ing, warehousing, and so on – to capture the lion's share of the value ... Suppliers unable to reach the price demands of these transnational brands risked the loss of orders or even closure. This dependence left manufacturers in a state of perpetual instability, unable to muster the capital necessary to escape the orbit of brand power and pursue their own development, with the possibility of losing a purchasing contract an inexorable existential threat. The result was that garment workers had the lowest bargaining power of any industrial sector.[9]

From his meticulous studies of parliamentary reports and newspa-pers, Marx also understood that some sort of regulatory apparatus was needed (as happened in the case of the working day) if financial crises were to be avoided. He would not, therefore, have been at all surprised that the financial crisis of 2008 would result in something like the Dodd-Frank regulatory reforms. With respect to the Bank of England, however,

---

9   Ashok Kumar, *Monopsony Capitalism: Power and Production in the Twilight of the Sweatshop Age* (Cambridge: Cambridge University Press, 2020).

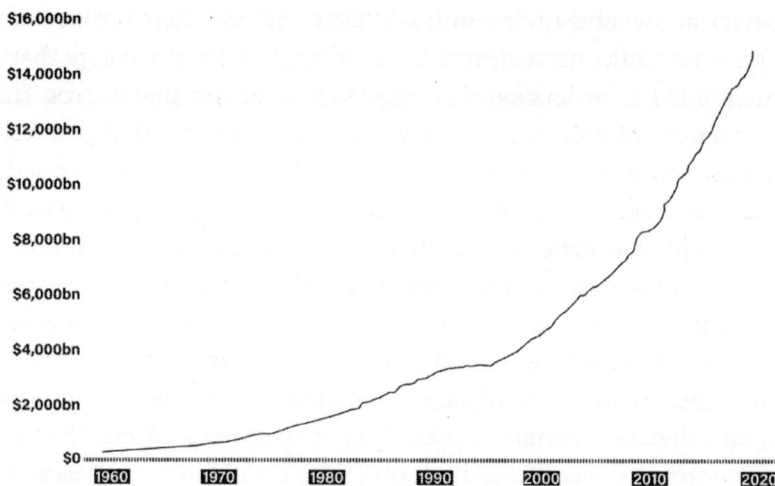

Figure 14. Total Global Money Stock (M2)

Marx also came to recognize that poor design of such institutions could deepen and lengthen crises and that 'the mistaken Bank Act of 1844' had a negative impact on continuous accumulation. The financial crises of 1848 and 1857 derived as much from the *internal* contradictions of capital as from the dynamics of class struggle. It was the failure of the working classes to respond to the crisis of 1857–8 that led Marx to plunge back into the British Museum to figure out why not.

One further point complicates not only theory and analysis but also politics. In the process of circulation and accumulation, value takes on different guises. Its three primary material forms are, as we have seen, money, commodities and production activity. Each one of these forms of appearance is a material representation of the immaterial but objective social relation we call value. But each representation has characteristics specific to itself. These characteristics have nothing to do with the value created by way of the 'form-giving fire' of labour applied in the activity of commodity production. Consider the most problematic case, that of the money form. This is, critically, the only form of capital that has the capacity to increase without limit. It is the only form of capital that can keep consistent pace with the spiral of accumulation and growth. It is perhaps significant that the growth of the world's money supply exhibits an exponential form after 1970 or so (Figure 14).

These are deep questions. But the essential point is that if the inherently contradictory money–value relation has become tenuous at best, the money forms of appropriation and accumulation can move centre stage without direct dependency on what might be happening in the immaterial but objective sphere of value relations. The only evidence we have for the continued relevance of the theory of value is that the increasingly free-wheeling monetary sphere has, since 1971, produced a large number of monetary crises with tangible effects on capital circulation and accumulation as well as sometimes catastrophic impacts on human well-being, even as the capital mass has continued to expand dramatically in spite of low growth rates. Something goes on beneath all the fetishism and the surface appearance of a dynamic financialized capitalism to suggest that disequilibria in the mass–rate relation are spelling economic and ecological trouble, even as the limitless 'bad infinity' expansion of the money supply through quantitative easing provides an easy, though temporary, remedy to every sign of crisis. The suspicion then lurks that it is quantitative easing itself that may be at the root of many contemporary economic problems. This would be true not in a direct causal sense, but because seemingly rational short-term adjustments incrementally contribute to building a far more massive problem over time, much as the easy money solution that Alan Greenspan devised in response to the stock market crash of 2001 flowed into the far deeper and damaging property market and financial crash seven years later.

It is entirely possible for merchants (like IKEA and Walmart) or financiers (like Goldman Sachs and the bondholders) to dominate industrial capital. When this happens, as Marx presciently concedes, it almost invariably results in 'a system of plunder'.[10] In the current conjuncture, the bondholders and commanders of the circulation of interest-bearing capital also exercise immense influence over the state and in some instances dominate the production and reproduction of industrial capital. 'Systems of plunder' are in evidence almost everywhere. There is no honour between the different factions of capital in their thievery. They plunder at will from each other when it suits them. Factional antagonisms also arise between industrialists, merchants, financiers and landed property, as well as between powerful family rivalries and the notoriously parasitic rentiers, to say nothing of the state. No faction hesitates to seize the opportunity to dispossess 'the other' of its asset values by any means or chicanery possible. Accumulation by dispossession is organized as a general system of competitive robbery. But who ends up controlling most of the mass, and what do they do with the wealth and power this automatically confers?

---

10 Marx, *Economic Manuscript of 1864–1865*, p. 437.

The merchant capitalist facilitates the efficient sales of commodities in the market and deserves a just reward for rendering that service to industrial capital. Merchants absorb the problem of circulation time taken in the market to procure a sale. This allows the industrial capitalists to assure the continuity of flow of value and surplus value production without regard for conditions in the market. For this reason, industrial capitalists willingly trade commodities to merchants at a discounted value. If merchants help accelerate the turnover of capital and provide credit to industrial capital on easy terms, this confers an additional claim to a portion of the value in circulation. The exercise of this claim is viewed in Marx's theory as a deduction out of the value and surplus value produced by industrial capital. But it is clear that the monopsony power of many merchant capitalists in the market can become a power over industrial capital. Pressure to lower prices on the part of the merchants can become a primary driver of appalling conditions of industrial labour throughout the value chain through which, for example, the Apple computer I am using is produced and marketed. At this point, the return to merchant capital can become parasitic rather than legitimate. The 'system of plunder' takes over.

The personas of the merchant, the banker and the landlord are such that they will all attempt to maximize their appropriations and misuse their power in furtherance of their own interest. In this the different factions become de facto parasitic rentiers rather than honourable servants of accumulation. 'The entire immense extension of the credit system', Marx laments, 'is exploited by the bankers as their private capital.'[11]

While it is useful to distinguish between the profit of merchant capital, profit of industrial capital, interest on money capital, rent on property/ landed capital and taxes to the state, these are distinctive roles rather than fixed social categories. Most corporations (along with the state) are actively involved in exploiting several of these roles simultaneously. In the automobile industry during the 1980s, for example, more money was made by deploying the auto company's financial powers in futures markets than in making cars. The nimble corporation will arrange its affairs to extract and appropriate as much value as possible in whatever form appears the most lucrative and from whatever point in the overall circulation process that can most easily be milked (and in some instances, bilked).

The theory of distribution has therefore to track the appropriation of value and its increasing centralization in fewer hands, even in the

---

11   Ibid., p. 567.

absence of any additional surplus value production. Capital investment in circulation, distribution and realization cannot produce value, but such investments do create the 'conditions of possibility' for the appropriation of value and surplus value from the industrial circuit.

Money, the representation, was in effect liberated from any direct connection to what it was supposed to represent. The floodgates of limitless money creation were opened and the question of what, exactly, the relation of money to value might be became a matter of speculation. Some even declared that the value theory is irrelevant and that only the representation – world money and the monetary policies of the world's central banks – matters. In bourgeois economics, a new monetary theory is on the rise, and among Marxists there is some interest in MELT (the monetary expression of labour time) as a new foundation for analysis.

There are abundant opportunities within the fields of distribution for the accumulation of wealth through illegitimate, unethical and, in some instances, illegal appropriations of the wealth and assets of others. Marx avoided confronting this issue by assuming, throughout the first two volumes of *Capital* in particular, that all commodities exchange at their value and that the existence of intercapitalist competition would assure a rough accord between this theoretical assumption and actual market practices. There are instances where such an assumption is plausible in today's world. The fierceness of competition among the supermarket chains in some parts of the world ensures, for example, a maximal service at minimal cost (the Aldi supermarket chain is an excellent example). The Walmart economy is super-efficient, and some now look to it as a model for a more centrally planned socialist economy.[12] It assures the efficient flow of commodities from producers located all around the world to consumers. It procures rock-bottom prices that can either diminish the value of labour power or assure material improvements in the standard of living of labour at a given wage level.

In what follows, however, I focus on illustrating how the economy of appropriation and accumulation by dispossession works across the different fields of distribution. In what ways do merchants, financiers and landed property capital organize themselves to extract far more than their justifiable rate of return, to the point where they sometimes appear to dominate rather than serve endless capital accumulation? Furthermore, how much value is appropriated by the state in the form of taxes,

---

12   Leigh Phillips and Michal Rozworski, *The People's Republic of Walmart: How the World's Biggest Corporations Are Laying the Foundation for Socialism* (London: Verso, 2019).

licenses and user charges to pay for state services that may or may not improve conditions for surplus value production and capital accumulation? The rentier state is not an impossibility, and all capitalist states take up rentier functions and practices in their drive to appropriate as much wealth and power for the state as possible. What Marx and Engels referred to as 'secondary forms of exploitation' that greet the workers on their return home in the form of greedy merchants, landlords and money lenders, to say nothing of illicit appropriations through the state apparatus cannot, in today's world, be ignored in searching out the different modalities of capital accumulation through appropriation available to the capitalist class.[13]

If capital is value in motion, the mass of value is perpetually shifting, unstable and, as we earlier saw, uncontrollable. The fluid interactions of different forms of capital intersect to shift the mass around from one part of the world to another, from one sector to another and from one group of capitalists to another. The mass moves geographically as mercantilist policies on the part of the state lead to cumulative balance of payments advantages and trade surpluses in one part of the world to the detriment of others. Similarly, different factions – producers, merchants, financiers, state enterprises – acquire hegemony for a while, only to be supplanted as the weight of the mass shifts elsewhere. In recent times and places and in certain industries the merchant capitalists have dominated over the direct producers (as seemed to be the case in the global commodity and value chains in textiles and electronics during the 1990s). But in more recent times, the reorganization of production and the rise of massive producer companies such as Foxconn in electronics have levelled the playing field. It uses its quasi-monopoly power back down its own supply chain to ruthlessly extract surpluses from suppliers. The fluidity of these relations makes it hard to track the mechanisms of surplus extraction through accumulation by dispossession (plunder) in the context of factional struggles over distributional shares between merchants, financiers, land and property owners as well as an often-avaricious state apparatus.

---

13   Marx, *Economic Manuscript of 1864–1865*, p. 711.

15

The Return of the Rentier

Resort to accumulation by dispossession paves the way for the return of the rentier. The figure of the rentier has, however, a complicated history in both economic theory and economic history. For Ricardo, the rentier was anyone who simply lived (passively) on the rate of return on their investments, whether in land, property, productive enterprises, government debt, interest on private loans or the returns on stocks and bonds. For Jane Austen, a good marriage prospect was someone who had an unearned income of £10,000 a year. For Ricardo and the Manchester industrialists, such rentiers stood in the way of the full flourishing of the capitalist mode of production. The industrial capitalists and Ricardian economists were desperate, says Michael Hudson, to free themselves from the power of a hereditary feudal landlord class and predatory usurious finance.[1] The usurer, says Marx, is 'one [who] would have the whole world perish of hunger and thirst, misery and want … so that he may have all to himself'.[2]

By the time Marx wrote, however, not only had usury largely been curbed in Britain (except for the poorest classes), but merchant capital, landed capital and money (finance) capital had all become broadly subservient to the industrial interest, both economically and theoretically (at least within the orbit of Manchester industrialism). The monopoly power of the East India Company had been broken, which opened up the Indian market to the cotton magnates. The corn laws (tariffs on wheat) were

---

1 Michael Hudson, 'The Road to Debt Deflation, Debt Peonage and Neofeudalism', Working Paper No. 709, Levy Economics Institute of Bard College, 2012; Hudson, *The Bubble and Beyond*.
2 Marx, *Capital*, Vol. 1, p. 740 n22.

repealed in 1846. Grain imports (from Chicago, Buenos Aires and Odesa) lowered the cost of bread, which meant a decline in the value of labour power and therefore rising profits for the industrialists and hard times for the British landed interest. Furthermore, the credit system was being systematically reconstructed as an aid to the increasing circulation of capital through fixed capital and consumption fund formation along with the reform of banking, the proliferation of joint stock companies and the rise of increasingly regulated stock and money markets in Britain, France and the United States. For Marx, therefore, the theoretical problem was to explain the 'necessary' or 'productive' roles of merchant capital, land rent and expanding credit and the rising market for loanable capital. This was all paralleled by the emergence of a 'class' faction of bankers and financiers, dabbling in the stock market while speculating on state debt and its conversion into capital.[3] More recently, the idea that a billionaire class is exercising much greater influence has begun to be studied.

According to Michael Hudson, the rentiers returned after the First World War to make increasing claims on the surplus, to the point where even Keynes felt moved in the 1930s to argue for 'the euthanasia of the rentier'.[4] Both Michael Hudson and Brett Christophers see the neoliberal counterrevolution that occurred from the mid-1970s on as opening the floodgates to the large-scale return of the rentiers.[5] They returned, however, in a more active role, as opposed to the passivity that so incensed Ricardo and enchanted Jane Austen. It is now the turn of the industrial capitalist to be rendered subservient either to the monopsony power of the merchants (like Walmart or IKEA), or to the monopoly power of the financiers, while the landed interest (including command over the minerals under the land) is extracting its pound of flesh (or grams of lithium) wherever it can.

Marx's conceptual formulations to understand all of this are tentative, often ambiguous and sometimes surprisingly prescient. At various points, he mentions a class of merchant capitalists. Elsewhere, he writes of a financial aristocracy, or even a seemingly independent financial class, along with, from time to time, a distinctive rentier class of billionaires. The landlord class is firmly depicted as one of the three great

---

3   Marx, *Economic Manuscript of 1864–1865*, Chapter 7.
4   John Maynard Keynes, *The General Theory of Employment, Interest and Money* (London: Macmillan, 1973), Chapter 12.
5   Brett Christophers, *Rentier Capitalism: Who Owns the Economy, and Who Pays for It?* (London: Verso, 2020); Brett Christophers, *Our Lives in Their Portfolios: Why Asset Managers Own the World* (London: Verso, 2023).

classes positioned at the heart of the capitalist mode of production. In the *Grundrisse*, he seems to suggest that a distinctly capitalist landlord class had to form prior to the rise of capital in general because this was the only way wage labour could be denied access to land as a basic and universal means of production.[6] In Marx's time, the merchants and the financiers were best conceptualized as class factions in the process of becoming fully fledged autonomous and independent class interests.

The power of finance has clearly risen significantly since Marx's time. Financiers were, for example, the principal organizers of the deindustrialization inflicted after 1980 on the core areas of capitalist class power in the United States, Western Europe and even traditional industrial districts in countries as diverse as Brazil and Argentina, Mumbai and Tokyo. Where traditional manufacturing industry did survive, it was in part because industrial corporations such as General Motors and US Steel partially morphed into financial institutions. When US Steel became USX in the 1980s and the CEO was asked what X stood for, the answer was money, not steel.

The explanation for the return of the rentier in an active role partly lies in the fact that the independent powers of the landed interests, the financiers, the merchants and the state may have been tamed but were never abolished. Like so many of Marx's categories, they exist in nascent form from the very first sign of primitive accumulation. Here is how he depicts it in *Capital*:

> The only part of the so-called national wealth that actually enters into the collective possession of a modern nation state is – the national debt. Hence ... the modern doctrine that a nation becomes the richer the more deeply it is in debt ... Public credit becomes the credo of capital. And with the rise of national debt-making, lack of faith in the national debt takes the place of the sin against the Holy Ghost, for which there is no forgiveness. The public debt becomes one of the most powerful levers of primitive accumulation. As with the stroke of an enchanter's wand, it endows unproductive money with the power of creation and thus turns it into capital ... The state's creditors actually give nothing away, for the sum lent is transformed into public bonds, easily negotiable, which go on functioning in their hands just as so much hard cash would. But furthermore, and quite apart from the class of idle rentiers thus created.[7]

6 Marx, *Grundrisse*, p. 276.
7 Marx, *Capital*, Vol. 1, p. 919.

Note here how the theory of capital's mode of production as a totality now internalizes the critical interrelations of the state and its finances (to be taken up in the next chapter), the national debt, the circulation of interest-bearing capital, merchant, financial and landed classes, all the while opening up the possibility for the formation of a growing parasitic class of rentiers.[8]

Ricardo spent an inordinate amount of time working out the distinctively legitimate form of capitalist ground rent, and Marx spent an inordinate amount of time studying Ricardo on this topic. This suggests that rent arising as ground rent derived from monopoly control over land as a primary means of production needs to be distinguished from other forms of rentierism. A key precondition for capitalist ground rent was the dissolution of the common property systems and clan inheritance structures characteristic of feudal and peasant modes of production and the creation of individualized private property in land with all its legal trappings. The enclosure of the commons from the seventeenth century onwards in Britain and much of Western Europe and the colonial imposition of private property rights in land in the Americas, Oceania and even parts of South Asia (for example, India) had broadly accomplished this task by 1870 or so. The same thing happened much later with the sudden privatization of Maoist collective agriculture in China after 1978. This led to dramatic gains in agricultural productivity in China in the short run. The result was a not-so-subtle modification of how the coercive laws of competition worked in China. Private rights to but not private ownership of land meant the retention of a certain monopoly power of individuals as to what to do with the land and how to capitalize on its fictitious value. Competition, in this case, meant monopolistic spatial competition, and that meant the attenuation of the coercive effects of competition from which the operation of the laws of motion of capital were derived:

> Landed property presupposes that certain persons enjoy the monopoly of disposing of particular portions of the globe as exclusive spheres of their private will to the exclusion of all others. Once this is possible, it is a question of developing the economic value of this monopoly, in other words valorising it on the basis of the capitalist mode of production. The legal power of these persons to use and misuse certain portions of the globe is not in itself decisive, for the use of this power depends entirely

---

8   Marx, *Economic Manuscript of 1864–1865*, Chapter 7.

upon economic preconditions, which are independent of their wills ... the legal notion of free private landed property ... arises in the ancient world only at the time of the dissolution of the organic bonds of society, and in the modern world only with the development of the capitalist mode of production ... In the section on primitive accumulation ... the direct producers are freed from the position of mere appendages of the soil ... and on the other hand the expropriation of the mass of the people from the land. To that extent the monopoly of landed property is a historical precondition for the capitalist mode of production and remains its permanent foundation ... But the form of landed property which greets the capitalist mode of production at the start does not correspond to this mode. The form that does correspond to it is only created by the mode of production itself ... feudal landed property, clan property or small peasant property is transformed into the economic form corresponding to this mode of production.[9]

It is, says Marx, one of the great achievements of capital to revolutionize agriculture and to bring to bear on that sector all the scientific knowledge of agronomy. This implied completely detaching landed property 'from relations of lordship and servitude' while completely separating the land as a condition of labour.[10] For the landowner, therefore, the land 'represents nothing but a certain money tax that his monopoly permits him to extract from the industrial capitalist.'[11] This flow of money is known as ground rent, which is 'the form in which landed property is economically realised, valorised'.[12]

In this way what began with landed monopoly of any kind as a precondition for the rise of capital becomes a result that founds the rise of a distinctive class of landed capitalists living exclusively off their appropriation of ground rents. It also sets in motion the state's regulatory role (for example, zoning, national parks, reservations, restrictions on land uses, special economic zones and so on). Beyond this, we witness monopolistic competition over land uses backed by the capacity to appropriate land rents from allocating land to specific uses. This all happens in a context of spatial differentiation in land productivity and locational advantages, with the latter very much affected by fixed capital investments not only in the land itself but also in transport and communications.[13]

9   Ibid., pp. 714–16.
10   Ibid., Chapter 7.
11   Ibid., p. 716.
12   Ibid., p. 717.
13   Ibid., pp. 885–95; Harvey, *Limits to Capital*, Chapter 11.

In the 1820s, Ricardo saw that the rising demand for food grains based on population growth and increasing wage labour was forcing grain production onto more and more marginal land in Britain. He theorized that the price of wheat was set by the production costs on the least favourable land that had to be brought into production to satisfy the rising demand. Extra profits would thus accrue to producers on the more fertile and advantageously located land. The extraction of land rent would tax away these extra profits to the benefit of the landowner (without them doing anything) and put competition between all grain producers on a more equitable basis. This was Ricardo's theory of legitimate differential rent, the first version of which focused on natural and locational advantages and the second on the differential impacts of investments in land improvements (such as land clearance and drainage) and changing relative location reflecting the new transport systems. Marx broadly accepted Ricardo's framework for handling differential rents, while adding the categories of absolute and monopoly rent, the last of which, Marx observed, dominated in urban areas.[14]

There are occasions when rental transactions appear both remunerative and appropriate and therefore not parasitic in the way Ricardo presumed. Marx has an interesting habit of portraying the rise of some new form of circulation from something that is epiphenomenal and seemingly trivial within another form of circulation. For example, the search for relative surplus value transforms 'fixated' forms of capital and hardens them into the circulation of fixed capital, which in turn sparks an important role in extending credit which hardens into the circulation of interest-bearing or loanable capital. In commenting on the latter, Marx recognizes that in the first instance, while it is money that is typically loaned out, capital can also be loaned out in material commodity form. This has hardened in our time into the renting and leasing of equipment (for example, machines or forklift trucks) rather than their purchase. This reduces the cost of constant capital while guarding against the effects of potential devaluation through accelerated obsolescence of fixed capital in production. But it also facilitates economies for consumption. It now costs $600 a month or more to garage a car in Manhattan, and when all the other expenses are added in it is far cheaper to rent a car in New York City when needed rather than own one. The car rental and equipment leasing companies are not passive rentiers in the sense that Ricardo meant them. And money capitalists are also far more likely

---

14   Marx, *Economic Manuscript of 1864–1865*, p. 752.

to actively deploy the funds they control by shaping the contextual conditions for their loans (for example, state provision of infrastructure
such as transportation, water and sewage and physical infrastructure
that favours developers). Investors may also be active participants in the
carrying trade, borrowing money at 2 per cent in Germany and investing
it at 5 per cent in Japan in the hope that the exchange rate between the
two currencies moves in their favour rather than against them. The rentierism of the private equity companies (taking a public company private,
asset-stripping it and returning it to the public domain in slimmed down
and more profitable form, for example, with new and more exploitative labour contracts) entails very active interventions (particularly
on the labour relations front). The only thing produced through such
investments is profit upon reorganization. The latter now emerges as an
important new category within the totality of capital's circulatory forms.
This is the distinctive economic niche occupied by the private equity
experts.

The term 'rentier' does not refer to a specific faction of capital but to
a raft of unproductive and parasitic practices that exist throughout the
whole capitalist system. While there are certain sectors (like landholding
and private equity operations) that are more parasitic than others, even
an organization like Blackstone may engage in productive activities from
time to time. So how, then, are we to characterize contemporary rentier
activities?

Ricardo's rationale for differential ground rent fell apart in the latter
half of the nineteenth century. The new transportation systems (railroads, steamships and the telegraph) along with the abolition of tariff
barriers made accessible far more fertile lands in Eastern Europe and
North and South America. These lands could easily out-compete in production of food grains in Britain and Western Europe. Production was
therefore moving onto more fertile, not less fertile lands, as Ricardo had
presumed. The telegraph permitted global grain prices to be coordinated
from Odesa to Chicago to Buenos Aires and Liverpool. The legitimacy of
Ricardo's (and Marx's) differential rent theory was thus challenged by a
perpetually disappearing margin. The rationale for Marx's theory of absolute rent, which presumed that agriculture was far less capital-intensive
than capital in general, likewise disappeared with the industrialization of
agriculture. This became universal after the Second World War.

But the monopoly basis for rent extraction from private property
in land remained. The consequences for the land market, land investment and extractivism were wide-ranging. While Marx concentrated

on the agricultural case, rapid urbanization was shifting the emphasis of landed elites to cultivating monopoly rents from investments in land development in rapidly expanding urban areas (for example, suburbs). Investors took to growing condominiums rather than cabbages. As late as the 1970s, the lands in Westminster and Belgravia in London along with prime land in other areas (such as North Oxford) and more suburban developments around Britain were monopolized by the aristocracy and ancient institutions such as the Church, the Crown, and the Oxford and Cambridge colleges. Properties built on the land were often traded separately from the land. Examples of this exist to this day even in the United States.

The land beneath the iconic Chrysler Building in New York, for example, is held by Cooper Union, a very old private university that specializes in training in the arts and design fields. For many years, Cooper Union was tuition-free, but financial constraints finally led to the imposition of tuition fees. In 2018, the rental payment on the land under the Chrysler Building stood at $7.75 million. It was raised to $32.5 million in 2019 and is scheduled to rise to $41 million by 2028.[15] Since there is no way the existing tenants could or would cover these rent increases, the value of the property on the land collapsed to a reported $150 million on its sale in 2019, when only ten years before an Abu Dhabi investment firm had bought into a 90 per cent share on the building for $800 million. Cooper Union legally robbed the Gulf investment firm of $650 million. This was rentier capitalism at work on the land in its most blatant form, though many might consider this to be a 'Robin Hood' operation, stealing on an asset value in a good cause. But what the case depicts is the arbitrariness of rent extractions and the huge leaps that those who control access to the land can impose on users. In most cases, this is not in a good social cause.

In New York City, land and property owners have, in recent years, raised commercial rents excessively (50 per cent rental increases are not uncommon) to drive out marginal activities, such as small specialist stores and family restaurants. Only the banks, the drug stores and the chain stores can afford to stay. The resultant rapid decline in qualities of street life and commerce, to say nothing of inadequate residential opportunities for much of the population, are a subject of daily complaints. Rapidly increasing rents (which only partially are due to a rise

---

15   Anna Kodé, 'The Fight over the Chrysler Building Escalates', *New York Times*, 23 October 2024.

in land value) lie at the root of a crisis in affordable housing, resulting in 60,000 or more homeless people in New York City. On the other hand, the erosion of retail activity through competition from online marketing has produced declining rents along local high streets and even in some up-market locations, such as Fifth Avenue in Midtown Manhattan.

An analogous example is a recent leasehold scandal in Britain. Traditionally, in Britain, households own housing on a freehold basis. But, over the last two decades, developers have taken to selling on a leasehold basis (for 999 years) so that buyers 'bought' the property but not the land, which was sold on separately and profitably to investment companies. Unsuspecting buyers did not understand that the land investment companies had the right to raise the land rent, doubling it every ten years under some contracts. The land investment companies stood to make 7.5 per cent annual rate of return, which is high by contemporary standards. The land rent to the leaseholder escalated, while the cost of commuting the land payment rose very rapidly, depressing the value of the property relative to that of the land. In this case, it was the leaseholders who were effectively being robbed by the investment companies. Pressure mounted on the developers, and some agreed to buy back the leased land and convert it to freehold. Government eventually had to step in under public pressure to regulate the whole arrangement.

These are the sorts of rentier operations on the land that have proliferated in recent times. The incredible proliferation of 'land grabs' in Africa and Latin America in particular testifies to the intense competition to acquire land and resources (particularly rare earth metals so vital to contemporary electronics). At the other end of the scale, Blackstone's fabulous fortune derives largely from rental transactions, as do the rents increasingly extracted by mining interests from the use of natural resources, mining and forestry as well as agriculture, all of which supplement the monopoly rents extensively cultivated by housing and commercial urban development. In this latter case, it is relative location that is the focus of land rent. The sharing (or not) of the increases in land value consequent on public investments in infrastructure (for example, roads) becomes a much-contested question. In Second Empire Paris, Haussmann originally managed to organize matters so that the public treasury captured the rising land values provoked by the building of the boulevards, but in the 1860s the landlord lobby successfully turned the tables so that they retained the land rights and privately benefited from public investment. The resultant crisis in municipal finance due to the loss of income from land sales led to Haussmann's downfall in 1868. In contemporary China, municipal revenues also derive from land sales to developers. In this case, it is the development companies like Evergrande that struggle rather than the municipal governments (though the finite amount of land is now causing difficulties for municipal finance).

These examples of rental appropriation so far have largely concentrated on land and, to some degree, property on the land (as in the case of long-standing physical infrastructure). This was the case that most preoccupied Marx. For a variety of reasons, land deserves to be considered separately from the other forms of rentierism, many of which have proliferated around us in more recent times. To begin with, the relation of labour to the land is of long-standing provenance and has a universal character, in which traditional beliefs of belonging have not been fully erased. Rare is it, furthermore, that any form of commodity production occurs without being located on the land and, while land and land ownership, like money and debt, have been transformed into their distinctive capitalist forms during the rise of industrial capital, there have been some clear limits in how far this transformation could go. The power of a class of landowning capitalists who have had no intention of submitting to the dictates of capital in general has to be confronted. Land, while it has been commodified and marketed in such a way as to have a price even when it bears no trace of human labour and of value, is clearly a special commodity. To begin with, it is a universal means of production which incorporates a limited form of monopoly power such that competition in the land market is a form of monopolistic competition (to be examined later). In bourgeois theory, land is viewed, along with capital and labour as part of a 'holy trinity' of key factors of production. Marx mirrors this by accepting (however tentatively) that the capitalists, the labourers and the landlords as constituting the basic class structure of a capitalist mode of production and profit, and wages and rents as basic forms of distribution that correspond to these commodities.

There are a million and one outrageous examples of rentier extractions through the monopoly pricing of commodities rather than land. Here is my favourite. Martin Shkreli, CEO of a pharmaceutical start-up, acquired the rights to Daraprim (pyrimethamine), a sixty-two-year-old drug used for protozoal infections. He promptly raised the price per tablet in 2015 from $13.50 to $750.[16] When challenged, he pointed out that few if any users actually paid cash and that he had cleared the price

---

16   Lindsay Whitehurst, 'Supreme Court Rejects Appeal from "Pharma Bro" Martin Shkreli', Associated Press, 7 October 2024.

rise with the insurance companies, for whom the financial impact was negligible, given that not many people used the drug. But this is the sort of thing that can, if multiplied, affect insurance premiums. Shkreli ultimately backed down when thoroughly condemned in the court of public opinion, though he insisted he needed the price rise to fund important pharmaceutical research 'for the benefit of humanity'. The monopoly price-gouging of pharmaceutical products remains a scandal in the United States.

While capitalists are supposed to adore the rough-and-tumble of free market competition, in practice they prefer the quiet privilege of rentierism. Given the choice between the comfortable life of living off rentier incomes and engaging with production, much of capital is sucked into the former at the expense of the latter. It is in this spirit that capitalists, when they do produce, go to extraordinary lengths to differentiate their product so as to procure monopoly rents. Every advertisement from toothpastes to sleeping pills to cars emphasizes the unique qualities of the commodity for sale, sometimes using the monopoly price as evidence of the unique qualities of the shampoo or whatever in question. Gullible consumers can all too easily be persuaded that the more expensive shampoo must obviously be the better shampoo. The cultivation of uniqueness, originality and special qualities in the realm of cultural production now commands its own market logic of monopoly rent that sometimes seems to have as much to do with money-laundering and rentier extractions as with genuine capital accumulation.[17] The monopolist at least produces something (for example, a shampoo). But, if everyone becomes a rentier and no one produces anything, a crisis will almost certainly ensue.

Consider, as well, the case of credit markets. Merchants had long been both recipients and dispensers of credit and, probably for this reason, Marx's brief history in *Capital* of precapitalist trading activities merged the two functions.[18] Long-distance trade, which often involved ventures that took a year or more, very much depended on financial support for often collectively funded and appropriately insured merchant ventures. These gave real meaning to the popular phrase 'when my ship comes in'. Skills and, above all, the development of relations of trust in proffering commercial credit, honouring bills of lading and insuring risky ventures were all on the table in the legendary coffee houses of the

---

17   Harvey, 'The Art of Rent'.
18   Marx, *Capital*, Vol. 1, Chapter 31.

major trading centres from the eighteenth century onwards. But the vast expansion of international trade that gathered pace as the nineteenth century wore on, particularly after 1850, put major demands on rationalizing the banking and credit system. This expansionary dynamic came to an end in 1914 and, as Helleiner explains in detail, to grow only tepidly until the neoliberal counterrevolution was consolidated under Reagan and Thatcher after 1980.[19] From then on, as Michael Hudson comments, the floodgates opened lopsidedly to favour a financial expansion and proliferating rentier opportunities.[20] Keeping the level of effective demand intact in the face of wage repression for the workers was largely achieved, for example, through credit card debt expansion within the working classes.

The other primary function for the bankers and financiers – the funding of governments in general and the national debt in particular – opened all manner of opportunities for the big family banking firms. The Rothschilds, for example, came to prominence during the Napoleonic Wars by lending to strapped governments on both sides of the conflict, and from that time on the big international banking conglomerates never looked back. By Europe's revolutionary moment in 1848, the bankers, it was said, could determine the fates of governments through their control over gold. The epic battle between the bankers who dealt in gold, such as the Rothschilds, and the credit-based bankers in Second Empire Paris who dealt in trust, such as the Pereire brothers coming out of the Saint-Simonian tradition, was turned into novel form in Zola's novel *L'Argent*.[21] Rothschild won the battle and the Pereires went bankrupt, even as their faith-based credit strategy won the long-term war.

After 15 August 1971, the world's monetary system lost its commodity base entirely, rendering gold and silver technically irrelevant to international trading. The resultant shifting power balance between the rentier activities of financiers and bondholders, on the one hand, and increasingly subservient state apparatuses, on the other, is the most potent sign of the return of rentier power to dominance. While control over economic power is primary, the power over politics and state functions has become more and more significant both historically and theoretically.

The carry-over and transformation of many practices from the precapitalist European world was insignificant compared to the rapid expansion of distinctively capitalist credit and finance institutions from

19   Helleiner, *States and the Reemergence of Global Finance*.
20   Hudson, *Killing the Host*.
21   Émile Zola, *L'Argent* (Paris: France Loisirs, 1991 [1891]).

the late eighteenth century on. The explicit demand for credit and interest-bearing capital emanates, as we have seen, in the first instance from the need to secure extra effective demand to maintain the spiral form of endless accumulation. But the credit system and the circulation of interest-bearing capital also derive from rapidly increasing investment in fixed capital (particularly of an independent and collective kind) plus long-term investments in the consumption fund (housing, autos, consumer durables). The surplus has then to be divided, even within the enterprise, between interest on the money advanced and profit on the commodity produced. As a result, the opening up and expansion of new lines of production becomes more likely to be fuelled by credit, set up with borrowed funds (as was the case of Amazon). Cash-based investment and even reinvestment is these days the exception rather than the rule. This is particularly the case when start-up costs are very high. As capital has matured and more and more of the mass of credit becomes necessary to assure current effective demand by pledging more and more claims to future labour as collateral, ever more massive surpluses of capital are created and put into motion.

The interest rate, Marx accepts, is determined by demand and supply conditions in the money market, though, in our times, there is a good deal of intervention by central banks. The relation between the interest rate and the profit rate is tangential for all sorts of reasons. Rarely is there any equalization. Speculative markets on the futures of interest rates, currency exchange rates, commodity prices, and in stock, shares and bonds, move according to their own mysterious logics in which the intangible of 'market sentiment' often prevails. Developers may build houses with debt finance while lending buyers the debt finance required to purchase the house. A lot of finance now flows to support consumption. This varies from housing, autos and other large consumer durable items as well as student debt. The strength of this demand relates to expectations on future wage levels, incomes and salary levels of managerial strata. Housing construction alone accounts for some 7 per cent of GDP in the United States and double that in recent years in China. It then follows that financial operations on the land and what is on the land will also play an important role in the massification of personal wealth and power. To the degree that the middle class has any financial savings, for example, they are more often than not embodied in home ownership, which conveniently provides collateral for further borrowing. The inflation of house values then underpins the rapid expansion of further borrowing. It should not therefore be surprising that homeowners in the

United States now typically spend around 40 per cent of their disposable income on servicing their housing debt.

Resort to the credit system simultaneously makes territories vulnerable to flows of speculative and fictitious capitals that can both stimulate and undermine capitalist development and even be used to impose savage devaluations on them, as in the emerging market debt crises of the mid-1980s. Territorial indebtedness within the global interstate system became more and more of a problem after 1980. Many of the poorer countries, and even some of the major countries like South Korea, Russia and Argentina, found it impossible to pay their debts and threatened default. Enter the International Monetary Fund and the World Bank. They visited structural adjustments (austerity) on the whole developing world in return for a bailout that rescued the banks and not the people. In the period from 1997 to 2003, some thirty-seven countries were forced to renegotiate their debts and undergo a structural adjustment process that cut state expenditures and attacked the already meagre living standards of working people. 'The debt trap' hooked the poorest countries to the system of circulation of interest-bearing capital in a way that sucked value over and above that which occurs through the equalization of the rate of profit. Pledging claims to future labour to cover current expenses is easy enough. But finding the future opportunity to employ that labour is a much greater challenge.

Even in the United States, it became clear, from the Clinton presidency on, that both domestic and international policy was effectively driven by Wall Street and the bondholders. 'Monied capitalists and industrial capitalists can form two particular classes only because profit is capable of separating off into two branches of revenue. The two kinds of capitalists only express this fact; but the split has to be there, the separation of profit into two particular forms of revenue, for two particular classes of capitalist to be able to grow up on it.'[22] Or again: 'the real difference between profit and interest exists as the difference between a moneyed class of capitalists and an industrial class of capitalists. But in order that two such classes may come to confront one another, their double existence presupposes a divergence within the surplus value posited by capital.'[23] This division is not a feudal residue. It is instead a consequence of the expansion and evolutionary trajectory of capital in itself. 'Both interest and profit express relations of capital', but 'interest-bearing capital

---

22   Marx, *Grundrisse*, p. 851.
23   Ibid., p. 852.

stands opposite, not labour, but rather opposite profit-bearing capital.'[24] The possibility of active struggle between industrial and banking/finance capitals to the exclusion (and possibly the detriment) of the working classes then exists.

The class relation between debtors and creditors also needs to be collectively analysed, addressed and ultimately revolutionized. While every debt is also a credit, it does not follow that debts and credits are in equilibrium any more than an appeal to Say's Law applies to commodity exchange. Accumulation by financial means is far more significant than the mere ambitions of the bankers and financiers, important though these may be. While investment in debt and in the credit markets constitutes a powerful force that demands its pound of flesh at some time in the future, it can also threaten to kill the host (as Michael Hudson puts it) and to undermine that which it purports to serve.[25]

The whole panoply of credit/debt relations becomes an ever more central feature of the drive for endless accumulation. Financial interests power monetary accumulations on in ways that are autonomous and independent of production capital while subsumed within the laws of motion of capital. But perhaps the most telling problem is the exponential growth of credit in parallel with the struggle to maintain an exponential rate of growth of the economy in general. The total money supply in the world has, along with the supply of credit, been increasing at an exponential rate. The problem is that an increasing proportion of that already increasing money supply has to earn a rate of return (either interest or profit). The amount of money functioning as capital is thus accelerating and the question of where some sort of rate of return can be had moves into the centre of what the financial system has to deal with. But what circulates in the financial system is not money but monetary claims. Much of the credit issued, as we have seen, takes the form of 'fictitious capital' and the easiest form of fictitious capital originates with the practice of leveraging.

In 2009, in the immediate aftermath of the financial crash, an article appeared in *Rolling Stone* by Matt Taibbi on Goldman Sachs, the premier US investment bank. Goldman had somehow managed to navigate the crisis profitably. Taibbi doubled down on Marx's image of the industrial capitalist as a blood-sucking vampire. 'The world's most powerful investment bank is a great vampire squid wrapped around the face of humanity, relentlessly jamming its blood funnel into anything that smells

---

24   Ibid., p. 853.
25   Hudson, *Killing the Host*.

like money.'[26] This could also be an appropriate image for what the capitalist ruling class does as it rules. The tentacles of its power are sunk deep into every corner of the social totality. Value or its representation (money) can be sucked out not only from production but from everywhere within the overall totality of capital circulation and accumulation. It can be sucked out at the point of realization, through the agency of the circulation of interest-bearing capital, through feeding at the trough of the state, through rental extractions and licenses on intellectual property rights. Extortionary credit can be extended to the working or middle classes to buy houses, cars, holidays while paying on the never-never for education, health care and a wide range of services. Finance and credit companies suck up wealth from the population as a whole, regardless of class, race, or gender. Value and its representation in monetary form can be sucked out from the financing of leveraged buyouts, through manipulation on the foreign exchange markets, through the financing of land speculation, through intermediating between buying and selling on the stock market (high-speed trading) ... the list is potentially endless. Capital and the capitalist class sink their tentacles deep into the state apparatus, sometimes legitimately fulfilling contracts to build public infrastructure, military equipment, research institutes and the like but just as often through extensive schemes of corruption. As Marx put it, capital lives, 'vampire-like ... by sucking living labour' and 'it lives the more, the more labour it sucks.'[27]

Capitalists can increase the mass of capital under their individual command without going through production. As we saw in the case of accumulation by dispossession, there are various ways – both legal and illegal – they can do this. It is, therefore, imperative to study 'accumulation by other means' in endless accumulation, even though Marx tends to relegate such features to the status of mere 'residues' of some preceding era or as secondary forms of exploitation, as in the *Communist Manifesto*. 'No sooner is the exploitation of the labourer by the manufacturer ... at an end ... than he is set upon by the other portions of the bourgeoisie, the landlord, the shopkeeper, the pawnbroker, etc.'[28] As Nancy Fraser notes, expropriation can sometimes outweigh exploitation in the appropriation of value and surplus value.[29]

---

26   Matt Taibbi, 'The Vampire Squid Strikes Again: The Mega Banks' Most Devious Scam Yet', *Rolling Stone*, 12 February 2014.

27   Marx, *Capital*, Vol. 1, p. 342.

28   Marx and Engels, *Communist Manifesto*, p. 44.

29   Fraser, *Cannibal Capitalism*.

In a prescient passage, Marx comments: 'As a nation advances in the career of wealth, a class of men springs up and increases more and more, who by the labours of their ancestors find themselves in the possession of funds sufficiently ample to afford a handsome maintenance from the interest alone.' This class 'has a tendency to increase with the increasing riches of the country … As the class of rentiers increases, so also does that of lenders of capital, for they are one and the same.'[30]

The significance of this passage – particularly the fact of their being one and the same – cannot be overemphasized. It posits the existence of a mini-circulation process rather like that of the flow of investments into fixed capital and consumption fund formation which, if they enhance the productivity of labour, produce the surpluses of capital and labour required for further investments in fixed capital and the consumption fund. In the case of the rentiers, billionaire investors create conditions for the further massification of economic and political power in billionaire hands. This is what the 12,000 private equity funds now managing $4.3 trillion are up to. But this is only the tip of an investment iceberg. The ever-increasing centralization and expansion of wealth in the hands of a rentier billionaire class in formation is now all too prominent. The power of this billionaire class has grown incrementally in recent times. Marx was well aware, as we earlier saw, that a low rate of return on a huge mass still yields a significant absolute return, while a strong rate of return (say the 9 per cent on equities since the 1980s), will yield an amount beyond belief. Billionaire power, as Trump's election in 2024 amply demonstrated, is both economic and political. Companies no longer pursue profit but focus on the shareholder values that underpin the billionaire class's wealth and power. The drive to raise asset values which the billionaire class is so heavily invested in – everything from housing (the Blackstone model) to mineral rights, stock prices and commodity futures, is ceaseless. The main objective of public policy is now increasing the wealth of the billionaire class rather than achieving more adequate standards of living for the population at large. Billionaires like Mnuchin played a prominent role in the first Trump administration, and they have been stealthily consolidating their control over the media and information flows over the past decades. Their prominence in the second Trump presidency and the appointment of Elon Musk to remake the US institutional structure is telling. Government by and for the billionaires is now the order of the day, to be enforced by an increasingly militarized state apparatus.

---

30   Marx, *Economic Manuscript of 1864–1865*, p. 465.

The potential crises of these forms of contemporary rentierism, coupled with the Ponzi structures evidenced within the credit system, altogether constitute pressing economic and political dangers that will have to be met by some sort of state response. The only possible, if implausible, way to save capital from the finance capitalists would be the evolution of a systematically deflationary, low-growth economy in which Keynes's 'euthanasia of the rentiers' is coupled with Marx's dream of 'the expropriation of the expropriators' (that is, the billionaire class). Hints of what such an economy might look like can be found in the deflationary low-growth history of the Japanese economy after the speculative crash of 1990. Whether such a possible, but implausible, economy is achieved globally would clearly involve the wise exercise of consummate power by the capitalist state, which is not renowned for either its wisdom or its theoretical acumen. Such a new strategic direction would have to rest on the takeover of state power and its mobilization to displace the bad infinity of the accumulation spiral and to construct a much happier production and consumption cycle.

16

The State-Finance Nexus

The question of the state lay at the centre of bitter controversies within Marxist circles from the 1960s onwards. These controversies had practical consequences, given the partial successes of revolutionary anticapitalist, anti-imperialist and anticolonial movements in acquiring state power in many parts of the world after 1945 (in much of Africa, for example). But since the end of the 1970s, most Marxists seem to have given up on this theoretical debate and followed Philip Abrams's advice to confine studies to what capitalist states (in all their infinite variety) actually do, rather than indulge in theoretical debates over what states inherently are or how they should be narrowly conceptualized in relation to capital.[1] The state has not, therefore, been ignored, but its role in the theory of capital has largely been left to one side.

Why Marx left the theorization of the capitalist state in limbo is some-what of a mystery. In one of the several plans of study outlined in the *Grundrisse*, for example, he proposed to study the

> state and bourgeois society. – Taxes, or the existence of the unproductive classes. – The state debt. – Population. – The state externally: colonies. External trade. Rate of Exchange. Money as international coin. – Finally the world market. Encroachment of bourgeois society over the state. Crises. Dissolution of the mode of production and form of society based on exchange value. Real positing of individual labour as social and vice versa.[2]

---

1   Philip Abrams, 'Notes on the Difficulty of Studying the State', *Journal of Historical Sociology* 1: 1 (1988): 58–89.

2   Marx, *Grundrisse*, p. 264.

He never did any of this, except by way of occasional offhand remarks. This leaves us with the task of uncovering the particular forms of the state adequate to bourgeois society as well as to capital in its never-ending process of its 'becoming'. The next step is to enquire whether the leverage of the bourgeois state can be mobilized for anticapitalist purposes and, if so, by whom?

At the outset, however, it is vital to understand why and how the capitalist state (as opposed to all other state forms) takes on the character it does. In always assuming that the market exchange system operates in its pure form, Marx is able to show that crises do not arise because of the failure of the capitalists to achieve the conditions of perfect market exchange (unlike many contemporary economists). The problem, as we have already touched on, is that individual capitalists working to maximize their own interests (the production of surplus value) produce an aggregate result inimical to capital's class interest. Marx shows instead that the more perfect the market the greater the probability of crises of accumulation. But the perfect market is rule-bound, and we must ask who makes the rules that guarantee liberty, equality and reciprocity (fraternité) in the market and how are they enforced. While moral solidarities can be produced and sustained among small groups, the experience of solidarity economies, LETS (local economic trading systems) and the collective management of the commons suggests that collective arrangements based on mutual trust can be sustained only for small groups over short periods. Such systems break down when some individuals figure out ways to game the system for their own individual advantage. The solution is the establishment of rules of law enforced by sanctions – private property laws in the market that are enforced by the state. Hence the capitalists' minimal need for a nightwatchman state. The establishment of a world market thus requires a rule of law backed by enforcement that will curb, but never eliminate, gaming the system. Corruption of both state and market is, alas, endemic.

There are some specific material features of the capitalist state that have implications for how we might theorize it. To begin with, the state is a territorial entity defined and fixed by its boundaries in absolute space and time. The state is a product of this territorialization.[3] Other primary agents of capital accumulation, such as individual labourers, consumers, firms and corporations, are not fixed in space in the same way (they can

---

3   Matthew Sparke, *In the Space of Theory: Postfoundational Geographies of the Nation-State* (Minneapolis: University of Minnesota Press, 2005).

move around and go in and out of existence), even though they obviously have a passing presence in absolute space and time. The territory over which the state has jurisdiction is for all intents and purposes fixed, but the flows of wealth and of capital, the circulation of labour capacities, the flow of investments via the circulation of interest-bearing capital and so on, all flow through the state, with obvious implications for the qualities of daily life in the territory as well as for the prospects for further accumulation within the territory. At a certain historical moment, Marx notes, loyalties to persons, families, clans were replaced by identities and loyalties to territories. At that point, the politics of governance became territorialized. The relation between state and nation is posited as is that between state and citizen (as in France) or state and subject (as in the UK). These are issues which will be taken up later.

The tension between the territorial fixity of the state and capital in motion is a matter of great theoretical as well as practical consequence.[4] Consider some very obvious features. The circulation of tax revenues has to be a major feature in any study of capital as a totality. Currently, in capitalist states, 40 per cent or more of GDP is typically taken up by state expenditures (in Denmark, which is reputed to be the happiest state in the world, it's 55 per cent). Investments in the circulation of fixed capital and the consumption fund (particularly those of a collective independent kind and even more so with investments immobilized in the land), almost invariably are organized with state support. Public–private partnerships are omnipresent in guiding investments in the built environment. States and other territorial jurisdictions (local, state and municipal) compete in all sorts of ways to entice capitalist development to locate within their respective borders. The consequences of interterritorial, interstate and interurban competition will be taken up later.

States have a wide range of powers vis-à-vis both capital and labour power. They can put up barriers (for example, tariffs) or offer incentives (for example, tax abatements or subsidies). By their investments in the qualities of labour power or in fixed capital of an independent kind, they can augment the productivity of labour and facilitate the production of extra surplus value within their territory. Furthermore, as Marx noted:

National debt, i.e. the alienation of the state – whether that state is despotic, constitutional or republican – marked the capitalist era with its stamp ... As with the stroke of an enchanter's wand, [the public debt]

---

4   Harvey, *The New Imperialism.*

endows unproductive money with the power of creation and thus turns it into capital, without forcing it to expose itself to the troubles and risks inseparable from its employment in industry or even in usury.[5]

Government debt therefore plays a key role in the formation and general circulation of interest-bearing capital. It is a privileged territory for the production and circulation of fictitious capitals. The state is alienated by and open to bourgeois capture. This has almost certainly played a major role in relation to the rising mass of fictitious capital that has flooded the globe since the 1980s. Clinton, on his inauguration as president in 1993, was advised by his secretary of the treasury, Robert Rubin, that he had no option if he wanted to be re-elected but to do what the bondholders wanted. This marked the capitulation of state power to the financial power of the bankers and investors.

Armed with substantial tax revenues, along with other instruments of public finance and public intervention (such as control over land development), state powers can be deployed across all the different moments in the circulation of capital as well as in support of other forms of circulation such as that of labour capacity, fixed capital and interest-bearing capital. State finances can be deployed to guarantee access to cheap raw materials and to low-cost but compliant labour forces. State support for technological innovation has historically been critical even beyond that arising out of military requirements. Deficiency in effective demand arising out of wage repression can be compensated for by subsidized flows into social expenditures: in the US, think of Social Security, Medicare, support for education and homebuilding as well as all manner of megaprojects, some of which may have, as we have seen, zero utility in promoting the greater productivity of labour power.

Surplus-absorbing rather than surplus-producing public expenditures are widespread. The state can be directly involved in the promotion of new modes of consumption and cultural practices. This goes back a long way. When Haussmann built the new boulevards in Second Empire Paris – 'The City of Light' – he created a framework for new cultures of consumption, including the department stores (made so much of in Zola's novel on that topic), the cafes, the street operas, the imperial spectacle and the first hints of the potential importance of the tourist trade for urban economies.[6] In all these respects, and many more, the circu-

---

5   Marx, *Capital*, Vol. 1, p. 919.
6   Émile Zola, *Au Bonheur des Dames* (London: Penguin, 2002 [1883]).

lation of state revenues becomes a crucial feature that must necessarily be integrated into the theory of capital.

This then poses the question of who controls the state and with what power. Haussmann could do his work because of the dictatorship of Louis Bonaparte in Second Empire Paris, Mussolini could drain the Pontine marshes because of the authority of his Fascist state, Robert Moses could practise his revolutionary metropolitan urbanism because of New Deal bureaucratic autocracy. Le Corbusier could build Chandigarh and Oscar Niemeyer, Brasília, because of the new-found confidence of Third World state-led developmentalism. Massive development companies like Evergrande and Country Garden could urbanize much of the Chinese space by way of the decentralized democratic centralism of the Chinese Communist Party.

It is obvious that any claim to sketch out an 'adequate' theory of capital's mode of production has to incorporate the direct impact of the circulation of tax and other state revenues and indirectly make a space for institutional and regulatory interventions and state rentierism across its cultural and political dynamics. Furthermore, state policies as to how it raises taxes and dispenses revenues can vary considerably, in part through the dynamics of class and other forms of social struggle. Taxes can be raised on income, on wealth (rarely), on property values, on consumption, on economic activity (value added taxes), on imports and exports, and in each case the distributive consequences are unequal and uneven, as reflected in the broad division between progressive and regressive tax regimes instituted by factions in the population depending on their political power. How and for what purposes the vast pool of revenues is disbursed also depends on political and policy decisions made by the factions controlling political power and dominating government's agenda.

In Marx's time, the Manchester School exercised a great deal of power over state policies in Britain. But that power was contested. As Engels argued, the state is not

a power imposed on society from without ... Rather, it is a product of society at a particular stage of development; it is the admission that this society has involved itself in insoluble self-contradiction and is cleft into irreconcilable antagonisms which it is powerless to exorcise. But in order that these antagonisms, classes with conflicting economic interests, shall not consume themselves and society in fruitless struggle, a power, apparently standing above society, has become necessary to moderate the conflict and keep it within the bounds of 'order'; and this power, arisen out of society but placing itself above it and increasingly alienating itself from it, is the state.[7]

Engels went on to summarize Marx's theory of the capitalist state as follows:

As the state arose from the need to keep class antagonisms in check, but also arose in the thick of the fight between the classes, it is normally the state of the most powerful, economically dominant class, which by its means becomes also the politically dominant class and so acquires new means of holding down and exploiting the oppressed class. The ancient state was, above all, the state of the slave-owners for holding down the slaves, just as the feudal state was the organ of the nobility for holding down the peasant serfs and bondsmen, and the modern representative state is an instrument for exploiting wage labour by capital. Exceptional periods, however, occur when the warring classes are so nearly equal in forces that the state power, as apparent mediator, acquires for the moment a certain independence in relation to both.[8]

To this we may add that different factions of capital (industrial, merchant, landed or financial) vie for power and influence within the state in pursuit of their own narrower interests. The state is the pre-eminent domain within which class forces and interests clash without cease. Finally, the struggle for hegemony on the world stage within the inter-state system gives rise to geopolitical struggles that cannot be ignored.[9] Broader global questions of war and peace are mediated through the geopolitics of capital, which will be the subject of the next chapter.

Marx in *Capital* assumes at the outset (without saying so) that the existence of some kind of 'nightwatchman' state within which market exchange occurs between juridical individuals endowed with private property rights over their own labour and over the commodities they produce, trade and consume. Marx in effect accepts the market-based framework of the classical political economists as his starting point. The traders operate in a rules-based system of legal relations and commercial law. They relate to each other under conditions of reciprocal

7   Friedrich Engels, *The Origin of the Family, Private Property and the State* (New York: International Publishers, 1993 [1884]), p. 229.
8   Engels, *Origin of the Family, Private Property and the State*, p. 231.
9   Arrighi, *Long Twentieth Century*.

independence in a market where no one individual has power over prices. But state regulation is widespread over the forms of money required as means of circulation: both the coinage and fiat moneys bear the imprimatur of particular states. Concern over the qualities of these moneys put Isaac Newton in charge of the Royal Mint to guard against coin clipping and the constant threat of debasement of the currency. Malefactors were publicly hung on Tyburn Gallows, as being burned at the stake for religious heresy gave way to a public hanging for the sin of debasing the currency.[10]

States and other administrative districts are foundational to the territorialization of capital and labour power flows. Fragmentation and geographical decentralization are advantageous for capital but not so much so for labour. The geographical divisions within the labour force are, in some cases, themselves as effective as distinctions of race, ethnicity and gender in undermining the capacity to build solidarities within the global workforce even when national and other place-based loyalties are overcome. For capital, however, nothing can be more conducive to its centralization than decentralization. It is hard to imagine a more decentralized system than that of market exchange, with trillions of transactions occurring every day but piling up at the end of each day into massive amounts of money capital concentrated in a few hands. The fragmentations of administrative regimes are similarly advantageous for capital. Decentralization is put to good use to produce the centralization of money wealth and power in the hands of an autocracy in general but a billionaire's club in our times.

The modern capitalist state originated as a fiscal-military entity shaped by violence, war, militarism, interstate competition and a social structure of management and administration that was hierarchical and class-bound in ways not inherently favourable to capital.[11] As Derrida once warned, institutions born out of the most heinous forms of violence can never erase traces of their violent origin in their future histories.[12] The history and role of slavery in the United States directly reflects that principle. The state's control over organized violence and its claim to possess a monopoly power over the means of that violence made control

---

10   George Caffentzis, *Clipped Coins, Abused Words, and Civil Government: John Locke's Philosophy of Money* (London: Pluto Press, 1989).

11   Christopher Storrs (ed.), *The Fiscal-Military State in Eighteenth-Century Europe: Essays in Honour of P.G.M. Dickson* (London: Routledge, 2009).

12   Jacques Derrida, 'Force of Law: The "Mystical Foundation of Authority"', in *Deconstruction and the Possibility of Justice* (London: Routledge, 1993).

of the state a primary target for any aspiring group or class. The disciplinary power brought to bear by the capitalist state over labour power in general and, in the United States in particular, the use of incarceration to reinforce the power of capital vis-à-vis labour follows on from the capitalist ruling class domination over the state. But, in states dominated by a caste system (such as Iran, India, Syria) or by clan-nationalist social orders (such as Japan, France, Germany and so on) the power of a dominant class may be diluted or even subsumed within some other territorial logic of governmental power. The relations between these three primary sources of power – caste, clan and class – can be indeterminate.

The social relations of late feudalism, as Braudel depicts them, combined landed wealth and power with religious obligation, kinship loyalties and cultural practices of often serf-bound peasant masses confined to an unchanging daily life. The subversive spread of market exchange allowed for the slow accumulation of merchant wealth (corporatist towns) and the growing accumulation of money commodities (gold and silver) as 'war chests' in state treasuries and in private coffers that would ultimately give rise to primitive banking practices. There were, as Arrighi points out, good reasons why this mix could evolve in the way it did in Western Europe, for it was there that traditional fragmented power structures were most easily dissolved to make way for the rise of landed and merchant forms of capital across the European space and beyond. The Hanseatic League and the Baltic trade, Bavarian banking, the Champagne market fairs and the ultimate emergence of the Italian city-states formed a long-drawn-out story. It was followed by the exploration of the Atlantic trade coupled with the weakening hold of papal power. All of this preceded the rise of manufacturing and then industrial capital in economically peripheral regions. It seems strange to imagine Britain as raw material producer during those years. But it was the locus of wool production for Flanders and Italian city-state manufacturing in the fifteenth century.

This gives Giovanni Arrighi's concept of the historical fusion of state and capital some modern purchase. 'The really important transition', Arrighi asserts, 'is not that from feudalism to capitalism but from scattered to concentrated capitalist power. And the most important aspect of this much neglected transition is the unique fusion of state and capital, which was realized nowhere more favorably for capitalism than in Europe.'[13] 'Capitalism', Braudel had earlier commented, 'only triumphs

---

13   Arrighi, *Long Twentieth Century*, p. 11.

when it becomes identified with the state, when it is the state.'[14] A some-what enigmatic entry in Marx's *Grundrisse* refers to 'concentration of bourgeois society in the form of the state. Viewed in relation to itself', and a later entry reads, 'the concentration of the whole in the state' followed by 'the international relation'.[15] State development and the increasing centralization of capital appear to go hand in hand, while the enigmatic and unexplored 'international relation' needs both prac-tical and theoretical elucidation. In other contexts, Marx would likely refer to this as a particularly close and significant metabolic relation. The problematics of the international relation will be taken up in the next chapter.

Interstate competition had and still has a fundamental role to play in directing and shaping the global flows of capital in space and time. State investments in the built environment, in social reproduction (of labour power in particular), in technological development (particularly, like gunpowder, for purposes of assuring military superiority) and in capacities for administration and production of public goods that capital can use in common: these are all presuppositions for the very existence of capital at the same time as they are produced and reproduced at the behest of a nascent bourgeois society and its capitalist state. Their qualities clearly have a direct impact on the dynamics of accumulation. Revolutions in mental practices such as double-entry bookkeeping and the rising Enlightenment views on human existence in the cosmos played their part.

Capital cannot be theorized outside the ever-changing role of the cap-italist state. The problem is, as earlier encountered in the cases of social reproduction and the metabolic relation to nature, that the territorializa-tion of administration and of the state has many functions beyond those directly relevant to the accumulation of capital. The state has one foot firmly planted within capital's mode of production and the other foot firmly planted in the particularities of capital's nascent social formation within which clan and caste interests may flourish.

The boundary between the dual functions of the modern capitalist state sprawling across the mode of production and the social formation is fluid and porous. Furthermore, the state is not a monolithic entity. It is internally differentiated, divided and 'complexified'. And here lies the difficulty of unpacking the role of the state within the theory of capital.

---

14 Fernand Braudel, *Afterthoughts on Material Civilization and Capitalism*, pp. 64–5, cited in Arrighi, *Long Twentieth Century*, p. 11.

15 Marx, *Grundrisse*, pp. 108, 227.

The possibility even exists for the state to become the primary driver of capital's mode of production. This is the question that is posed in spades by the contemporary case of China. But China is not unique. Capital's evolution in Japan, Singapore, South Korea and Taiwan (to name a few) was, and still is in some cases, tightly interwoven with the growth of an activist state with capitalist interests.

The explosion of fictitious capitals and the speculative boom that has dominated since the 1980s leads to state regulatory interventions (some of them collective through the G7, the G20 and supranational institutions such as the IMF and Bank of International Settlements) in the attempt to stave off potential crises. The alienated capitalist state is in the front line of attempting to manage and control the excesses of predation and fictitious capital formation, whose dynamics clearly indicate yet another instance of individual capitalists behaving in such a way as to undermine their own class interest. If the current wave of fictitious capital formation indeed amounts to a massive Ponzi scheme, it will take draconian state action to contain and unwind it. Consider, then, the recent history where hints of this problem become clear.

On 19 October 1987, a day known as 'Black Monday' in financial history, the Dow Jones Industrial Average dropped by 22.6 per cent in one day, its biggest drop ever. As many commentators noted, this event occurred less than a year after the 'big bang' unification of the worlds' major stock markets. The violence of the collapse in New York and London instantaneously hit the whole world of capital. The context was a debt crisis in emerging markets throughout the world that had begun with the Mexican debt crisis in 1982. The surpluses acquired by Gulf States from oil revenues in the 1970s were recycled into the global economy via the New York investment banks as development loans at easy rates to needy states. The great thing about lending to needy states, famously quipped Citibank's Walter Wriston, is that you always know where to find them if they try to renege on their payments. But when interest rates suddenly rose in 1979–80, many countries found themselves caught in a debt trap. The soaring interest rates demanded for repayment greatly exceeded the rates at which they had borrowed. The only way out was to submit to the discipline of structural adjustment programmes administered by the International Monetary Fund, backed by the US Treasury. In the United States, irresponsible speculation in the savings and loan sector was also a source of severe distress for depositors as well as for those who had invested through the S&Ls in long-term uneconomic building projects.

To this day, there is no settled explanation of the violence of the Black Monday event, though the failure of financial institutions to hedge against the risk of rapid interest rate movements was plainly the trigger. In the search to find answers, the US brought together the major players from the US Treasury and the Federal Reserve along with almost every big-name economist in the United States and elsewhere. The conference papers were a mix of the technically incomprehensible and ideologically driven. The one that stood out for me was that of Larry Summers. He focused, as did many others, on the problem of so-called 'moral hazard'. It had been clear since the New York fiscal crisis of the mid-1970s that, in the event of the financial system going belly up because of irresponsible speculative investments, state power would be deployed to rescue the banks – and would not bother about helping the people affected. The result was to encourage irresponsible, high-risk and speculative investment by the banks and other financial institutions. This plainly had something to do with the events of Black Monday and the S&L domestic crisis. Summers seemed to suggest there was a policy choice between tighter regulation of finance with at best low growth (or even stagnation) and the embrace of 'moral hazard' through further financial deregulation, which would generate far higher growth rates almost certainly punctuated by violent periodic crises. If the latter course were chosen, then preparations should be made to handle such crises and mitigate their violence. It was also clear, he said, that the US could not do this alone. The unification of global stock and financial markets in 1986 meant the inevitability of international consultation and coordination.[16]

After 1987, and particularly in the Clinton years, the moral hazard option prevailed. A detailed assessment by JPMorgan's research arm in the late 1990s suggested that most of the rather tepid growth over the previous two decades was due to moral hazard. In 1999, with Larry Summers as treasury secretary, the Glass-Steagall Act, the last regulatory barrier that had kept retail and investment banking at arm's length since the 1930s, was repealed (thus permitting unwieldy conglomerates like Citigroup to form while promoting more speculative activity on the part of the banks). This came at the end of a decade in which Wall Street effectively dictated economic and social policy to the Clinton administration. Clinton had campaigned on universal health care and social investments, but he delivered punitive neoliberal reforms in welfare and criminal justice, NAFTA and the reckless expansion of mortgage finance

---

16 Helleiner, *States and the Reemergence of Global Finance*; Tooze, *Crashed*.

304 THE STORY OF CAPITAL

to foster economic growth, culminating in the repeal of Glass-Steagall. This was pure neoliberal policy in action. Few would now deny that all of this had something to do with the catastrophic collapse of 2007–8, though there is dispute as to how much.

The immediate response to Black Monday by the monetary authorities was to flood the market with liquidity. This seemed to work (and is the strategy that has been widely deployed since), when combined with some technical reforms of the stock market (such as the introduction of circuit breakers to trading to stop the 'lemming' instinct of investors to all jump off the investment cliff at the same time). But Summers was right to suggest that the embrace of moral hazard would produce crisis tendencies. The wild west of the investment world known as the 'dot-com' bubble of the 1990s ended badly in the stock market crash of 2001, leaving a few start-ups, like Amazon, to later surge to the fore. But the coming instability was signalled by the collapse of the energy company Enron and even more significantly Long-Term Capital Management, a hedge fund run by two Nobel Laureates in economics, who speculated on Russian and Southeast Asian debt, only to be caught big-time in their collapses in 1998. Long-Term Capital was bailed out, at the behest of the New York Federal Reserve, by a consortium of fourteen banks who put up $3.6 billion to liquidate its untenable positions. Investors in Enron lost almost everything through fraudulent accounting. This was 'the bezzle' coming home to roost.

The rolling East Asian debt crisis passing from Thailand to South Korea (and lots of countries in between, except China) was causing sufficient mayhem in 1997–8 to raise the threat of contagion for the global economy. South Korea became a trigger point. It took some illicit concertation of the International Monetary Fund and the US Treasury (which is not supposed to interfere in IMF affairs) to contain the threat, again at the cost of draconian 'structural adjustments' to labour rights and government funding of social services. The East Asian debt crisis, as we earlier saw, left behind a set of seriously mauled and maimed economies and a lot of much wealthier foreign bankers and investors. The crisis spread to Russia and Argentina (2001). Yet in each case, it ended up being geographically contained. The stock exchange 'correction' in the US in 2001 was also largely confined as an internal affair. It was parlayed by Alan Greenspan, then chair of the Federal Reserve (and great fan of Ayn Rand's libertarian neoliberalism) into a passing event by lowering interest rates and bolstering liquidity. Investment flows shifted from the speculative US stock market to the speculative US housing and property market (that is, the consumption fund). And it was this that culminated in the housing foreclosure crisis and financial debacle of 2007–8. By then, the tautological 'efficient market hypothesis' (Say's Law) that had prevailed from the late 1980s on, and which held that markets were bound to clear to produce a happy equilibrium, was thoroughly discredited. Even Greenspan admitted that it had been wrong.

The crisis, when it came in 2008, caught almost everyone in or close to power by surprise. When Her Majesty the Queen asked the economists of the British Academy why they had not seen the troubles coming, they confessed that they had no idea and wrote a collective report in which they claimed that a lot of good, hard-working and dedicated economists had somehow missed something called 'systemic risk'. Missing systemic risk almost anywhere is a recipe for likely disaster. This was definitely one of those moments when the tautologies of most forms of bourgeois economics were found wanting.

The key moment came on 15 September 2008, when Lehman was forced into bankruptcy. The US Treasury (Hank Paulson from Goldman Sachs) and Federal Reserve (Chair Ben Bernanke) had tried to find a buyer but had failed and, when they tried to work out the value of Lehman's assets, did such a poor job of valuing foreclosed housing assets as to make Lehmann seem much more vulnerable than it in fact was. And by letting Lehman go under, they globalized what had, until then, largely been a New York City–based crisis. An investment arm of the French bank BNP Paribas, which had invested much of its surplus capital in dicey US mortgage securities, was the first to confess insolvency. Whether this global move was deliberate or not is hard to tell. The self-serving and self-justificatory books of Tim Geithner (then head of the New York Federal Reserve Bank) and Paulson are little help in explaining what happened. But with the failure to find a buyer for Lehman, the other obvious option was to temporarily nationalize the banks (as Sweden did when faced with an analogous problem in the early 1990s). Paulson, however, had no wish to go down in history as the first person ever to dare nationalize the US banks, even temporarily. Had he done so, every Republican in Congress would endlessly have reviled him. Obama did, however, briefly nationalize General Motors during the crisis that followed (eliciting plenty of caustic criticism from Republicans).

Bernanke and Paulson therefore went back to the tried-and-true neoliberal principle of saving the banks at the expense of the American people and foreign investors. This was done directly by flooding the banks, whether troubled or not, with liquidity in the fanciful belief that it would all trickle down to the needy masses. The Troubled Asset Relief Program (TARP) that emerged (after plenty of bickering with Congress) had begun with a joint three-page memo from Paulson and Bernanke. These two took charge, with President Bush nowhere to be seen and members of Congress taken up with trying to stuff square facts into round ideological holes. Congress ultimately converted a three-page memo into 300 pages or so of legislative text. The core principle was to give the six major banks in the country massive amounts of money and ask them to spend it and get the economy humming again. But the US banks, unlike those of China, are private institutions that do as they please, and what pleased them was to take the money, retire some of their debts and to buy back their own stocks. This increased the banks' stock market value, which in turn triggered larger bonuses for management.

The recovery from the recession therefore took place very slowly, helped by two significant features. First, President Bush convened a meeting of the G20 (as Summers had thought inevitable), which initially agreed to mount a coordinated global stimulus rescue package. This coordination fell apart a few months later as each state took its own path, rejecting US leadership. Obama was relatively isolated in the second G20 meeting. Second, and far more important, China responded to the collapse of its export market in the United States with a massive internal expansion of investments in urbanization and the built environment (fixed capital of an independent kind plus the consumption fund). This absorbed all the surplus capital and labour power that was to be found and expanded global demand for raw materials, agricultural commodities and semi-finished products. Supplying countries, like Australia and Chile, quickly recovered from the effects of the crisis. China rescued global capitalism from falling into a long-term 1930s-type depression. It plainly did not do so because of any loyalty to capital. It needed to maintain domestic employment opportunities in the face of widespread job losses if it was to preserve political stability. Its success in doing so was what saved global capital from itself. By some estimates, China created 27 million jobs in one year, leaving it with a net job loss from the crisis of only 3 million (which compared favourably to the 13 million net jobs loss in the US). China did an excellent job of making fictitious capital real, at least for a while. But the Chinese learned the hard way the truth of Engels's adage that the bourgeoisie can never overcome its crisis tendencies, it can only move them around. If this is the surface appearance of events, what theoretical insights can we generate when we dig deeper into the underlying forces at work as to the position and role of the state in relation to the inner structures and dynamics of a capitalist mode of production?

As in the cases of interest-bearing and fictitious capital, it is useful at the outset to identify the foundational internal contradictions that contain the seeds of what the capitalist state might currently be all about. Consider, for example, the contradiction that lies within the theoretical statement of absolute surplus value in Chapter 10 of *Capital*. The coercive laws of competition lead individual capitalists, firms and corporations to extend the length of the working day and to intensify production practices as far as possible. Labour consequently seeks to reduce intensity and limit the length of the working day. Both sides are right, says Marx, according to the 'law of exchange' and the dictum 'between equal rights, force decides'.[17] Hence the political struggle over the length of the working day and increasing intensification of production work. But why would a state run by capitalists and landlords consent to passing legislation on such a topic? Marx's answer is, in part, that the worker's movement was becoming more powerful, that allies among those classes not immediately affected by the question could be rallied to support the worker's demands and, finally, even capitalists could see that the depletion of creative and productive powers of labour as a result of extending the working day and increasing intensification beyond all tolerable bounds is not in capital's collective interest.

Capitalists, driven individually by the coercive laws of competition, produce an aggregate result which is not in their own class interest. This principle is observable at many points within the theory of capital (for example, the search for relative surplus value tends to produce in aggregate a falling rate of profit). This principle calls for state intervention to protect the ruling capitalist class interest against the individual activities of capitalists. State regulation of the working day was, up to a certain point, positive for both capital and labour. The definition of that point had to be worked out contingently through class struggle. When Edward Heath, faced with a fierce miners' strike, reduced the working week to three days and closed down television broadcasting at 11 pm, to cope with the shortage of electricity in the 1970s, subsequent data reflected no major drop in output and a noticeable bump in the birthrate nine months later. The return to a forty-hour week reflected the fear of capitalists that labour might become much more assertive. Such state interventions have varied motivations and impacts. Marx reminds us that the earliest state

---

17   Marx, *Capital*, Vol. 1, p. 344.

interventions on the working day focused on enforcing employment and criminalizing beggary and vagabondage with imprisonment in the stocks and public humiliation awaiting those who failed to comply. The carceral state goes back a long way. It became the bedrock of a neoliberal politics of wage repression.

While working-class demand can obviously never be sufficient to absorb all the value produced, the downward pressure exerted by competitive capital on the value of labour power (the wage rate) is concerning. Individual capitalists seek to depress wages while (Marx jokingly suggests) urging their rivals to raise theirs to invigorate market demand. The Keynesian management of effective demand through the empowerment of labour's bargaining position by supporting unionization has, at times, become significant. In the US, some firms shifted to a four-day, thirty-two-hour week during and after Covid-19.

The collective action problem for capital invites frequent state regulation and intervention to confront the contradictions between individual actions and collective requirements. Commentators as noteworthy as FDR and Keynes more than once asserted that they viewed their policy interventions as guided by a mission to save capital from the capitalists. If, as Marx argues in Volume 1 of *Capital*, capitalists (individual and corporate) acting under the compulsion of the laws of competition strive to maximize their particular interests and end up destroying the sources of all wealth – labour and the soil – then some countervailing force must be created to limit the damage that results. The same question arises with respect to the capitalists' penchant for imposing austerity on all collective forms of intervention in the social reproduction of labour power. The drive to limit the burden of taxation leads to deterioration in the level of education and the health of labour power. Given the damaging consequences of the explosive growth of fictitious capital circulation since the 1980s, it seems very likely that state intervention and regulation will become increasingly necessary to avoid the threat of catastrophic crises.

But behind this lies the thorny question of how and by whom the class interest of capital as a whole is defined, in a context where the interest of the antagonistic individual capitalists is both clear and pressing. Marx probed this question more deeply in his analysis of the struggle over the working day. The landed aristocracy was hostile to industrial capital and held on to its share of state power for most of the nineteenth century in Britain. It willingly sought ways to regulate and curb the excesses of industrialism and curried favour with the working classes. In so doing, it parlayed its privileged position vis-à-vis the monarchy into the presumption that it and it alone was in a position to define the national interest.

The definition of the class interest in general that Marx and Engels assumed, was, in the British case, conveniently masked by the embrace of a national interest dependent on the noblesse oblige of the aristocracy, combined with the popular loyalties inspired by all the institutions of the monarchy. It was this that led Engels to fantasize that the state appeared to be above class struggle and potentially able to reconcile conflicting class forces. Even after the landed aristocracy lost much of its direct power, while coincidentally using land as collateral to dominate British banking and finance, the idea of the national interest continued to conveniently mask the general class interest, thereby disguising the class foundation of the bourgeois British state. My father, who came from a professional military background, asserted that the aristocracy in Britain was born to rule and that neither the business class nor the working class could be trusted with political power, precisely because each would pursue its narrow class interest rather than look to the general interest when they gained political power. He only began to question this view after Sir Anthony Eden, who he considered a true gentleman, plunged Britain into a disastrous foreign venture with France and Israel in trying to retake the Suez Canal in 1956. The widespread mythology in Britain of the pre-eminence of the national interest guaranteed by the aristocracy and the monarchy was only challenged in the 1960s (by Monty Python) and finally put to rest by, of all people, Margaret Thatcher.

But this still poses the question of the class interest of the vast army of personnel employed within the state apparatus, in public institutions and within other collective administrative functions (such as ensuring a safe water supply). Marx had argued, in the case of services and merchant capital, that the dramatic increase in the productivity of industrial labour released an increasing amount of labour for employment in unproductive but useful functions (including the military), and there is no reason why this would not also apply to rising state employment. In the British case, as we have seen, the upper echelons of state administration, including the armed forces, were for many years taken up by an aristocracy often at odds with industrial and merchant capital. Only much later was this supplemented by the recruitment of a bureaucratic meritocracy from elite institutions (with Oxbridge in the lead in Britain and the leading research universities and the Ivy League fulfilling this need in the United States). The nonelite mass of the bureaucracy was typically recruited from the literate petite bourgeoisie.

The circulation of interest-bearing capital, however, nourishes a class of financiers and a bankocracy that has the disturbing habit of asserting its own distinctive interests rather than serving the general interest of capital. The formation of an administrative state bureaucracy and an independent civil service likewise supports the creation of a distinctive class faction (a 'political class', as Engels called it) that frequently advances its own narrow interests, again at the expense of serving the general capitalist class interest. This class faction often appears more caste- than class-like, particularly in its internal formation, and it rests on financial contributions from capitalist class interests and corporate lobbying to ensure that some often-warped version of class interest might emerge. This is the point at which Marx's recognition that 'unproductive classes' have a role to play becomes critical. The billionaire rentier element threatens to appropriate value rather than create the conditions that might support its production. Furthermore, in the United States, agribusiness, energy and pharmaceuticals are prominent sectors that rely heavily on the largesse of the state to maintain their profitability. They are in perpetual danger of systematically implanting rentierism rather that surplus value production. Hence the emphasis of capital in advocating austerity and fiscal discipline with respect to taxation and state expenditures.

The state, as a set of administrative structures and practices, has evolved over time, in part in response to the 'becoming' of capital accumulation. Perhaps the most important of its tasks is coping with the increasing massification and complexification of capital's own dynamic. The rise of enormous state bureaucracies and international political institutions has created a world radically different to that Marx encountered. The history of political economy, for example, from William Petty on, has largely been about defining the state's changing role from a needs and public goods perspective. While the claim that economics is a science like Newtonian physics is clearly spurious, the art of shaping state and other public policies in ways advantageous to capital accumulation along with the satisfaction of basic requirements for social reproduction (particularly of labour power) has produced ideological configurations that have wide-ranging effects. Ideas and ideologies can become, as Marx observed, material forces in history. Professional economics now constitutes a large field for ideological debate, culminating in dominant orthodoxies of a Brahmin caste which, for a time, can dictate certain paths of action rather than others. Political economy in its tautological guise plays its part in that superstructure of the capitalist social formation, in which we can become aware of serious problems and search for solutions ('fight them out', as Marx puts it), particularly when things go so badly wrong (as they obviously did in the 1930s, the 1970s and in 2007–8). This is supplemented by institutions of public administration (such as the Grandes Écoles in France), the elite universities (in China, India, Scandinavia, Germany, Latin America and East Asia), the national academies in Britain and Europe, the research universities in the United States, the think-tanks and law schools, the supposedly professional administrations and bureaucracies, all of which devote themselves to the clarification of their distinctive version of the national interest, along with definitions of the public good and, more often than not, a defence of capital's role. All of this occurs within a class-bound framework of the bourgeois state that remains largely hidden and subterranean. The result is a contested field throughout the social formation as to what the proper definition of the national interest and the public good should look like. Large segments of the working class are incorporated as both participants and beneficiaries contributing to the national interest. This has been a major feature of China's quasi-capitalist economic evolution since 1978.

There is, furthermore, a schism in the broad policy responses fashioned within the capitalist state. On the one hand, the 'supply-siders' have great faith in the efficiency and clarity of the market and presuppose that a perfectly functioning market will optimize outcomes in terms of both growth and distribution of the surplus value. Left to itself, they argue, the market will find an equilibrium such that crises are impossible. Deregulation is therefore the watchword. Crises are due to excessive regulation. The Keynesian 'demand-side' perspective positions itself on the other side of the underlying contradictions and seeks to pre-empt tendencies towards disequilibrium by supporting one or other side of the contradiction between capital and labour in search of some sort of acceptable equilibrium.

From the standpoint of the underlying contradictions, both sides fail. The equilibrium supposed by the supply-siders crashes and massive interventions become necessary. But the job is to rescue the market by perverting it. Meanwhile, those capitalists, who are skilled at never letting a good crisis go to waste, typically consolidate and further centralize their economic power through exploitation of crisis conditions. The demand-siders typically find themselves oscillating between the two sides of their contradiction. On the one hand, an excess of savings and of money capital (overaccumulation and what Marx referred to as a 'plethora' of capital) needs to be absorbed in a situation where market conditions are not conducive to realization. Propping up effective demand by expanding fictitious capital formation puts pressure on the consequent accumulation of debt. Given the law of endless accumulation for accumulation's sake, the accumulation of capital takes the form, as was earlier argued, of an accumulation of debts (of claims on future labour).

The US Treasury was and is intimately involved in all of capital's activities. But this is only one key department in the state apparatus. The state has to be conceptualized, therefore, as an assemblage of very different departments and circulatory systems constituting a somewhat amorphous totality with multiple links into the capitalist mode of production. The Treasury department administers fiscal policies. It deals with tax collection and distribution, with debt creation (the creation and management of the national debt) and public investments, while often assuming veto power via the state budget over other departments' proposals (when judged too costly). The Treasury, in short, lords it over the circulation of tax revenues and debt creation within the totality of capital. It is, consequently, the least sensitive department to the needs of the people and the most carefully attentive department within the state apparatus when it comes to the needs and requirements of capital. The Treasury is captive to capitalist class needs (especially when the needs of the class go against the interests of many individual capitalists). Other departments within the state may be much more attuned to meeting popular needs while having an indirect role in affecting the circulation of labour capacity and bolstering effective demand. This is why it is so important to separate out the Treasury/Finance Ministry from other aspects of the state.

Government spending is paid for by tax revenues plus the issuance of debt (a claim on future labour). The US national debt, which stood at around $10 trillion in 2008, topped $30 trillion in January 2022 (it now far exceeds annual GDP). The US Treasury Department issues and sells notes in certain denominations at a market rate of interest. This is the gold standard for the rentiers who buy it or for trading partners (such as Japan and China) who need a safe place to store their surpluses. The government then puts the borrowed money to work as loan capital which, when it comes to fruition, can become capital if it engages with the production of surplus value. When the debt has to be repaid after, say, ten years, the Treasury typically pays it off by making another debt issue. This is akin to a state-defined and -administered Ponzi scheme. In recent years, Congress has toyed with the idea of enforcing a debt ceiling, but so far has held back from refusing to increase/roll over the debt because of its disastrous consequences for the US dollar as an international reserve currency.

Other states have defaulted or do occasionally come close to defaulting on their debts. The gap in interest rates between US and German debt versus the debt of Greece, Italy and Argentina is the market measure of the relative risk of default. The circulation of tax revenues likewise expands as it circulates, and the state looks to some version of cost-benefit analysis to calculate the benefits of its tax- or debt-funded investments for capital. Marx here attributes capital formation (particularly long-term capital investments in physical infrastructure and the built environment) to state action. There are, therefore, other avenues for capital accumulation than that charted by industrial capital. The capitalist state, via the Treasury Department, provides the basis for finance capital and the debt/credit system. It also claims certain regulatory rights over the circulation of capital in general while promoting investments in the built environment (both productive and nonproductive), which, as the China case clearly shows, can be mobilized to counter the crisis tendencies of capital, at least for a while.

But the Treasury does not act alone. The central bank (in the US, the Federal Reserve) is also involved. The central bank under capital is generally construed to be the pinnacle of the private banking system, and it therefore ought to be independent and autonomous from the state apparatus. Yet when crises break out, it regularly appears as an equal partner with the Treasury Department in seeking solutions. Like the Treasury Department, the central bank tends to operate purely in the class interest of capital (though, as Marx complains, the bankers who run it frequently do so in their own personal or factional interest). Hence, there is no surprise that it was Hank Paulson from Treasury and Ben Bernanke from the Fed who authored and publicly promoted the proposals for exiting the 2007–8 crisis in a way that was adequate for the needs of capital.

From time to time, the central bank is brought inside the state apparatus but rarely with happy results. The situation in Turkey in 2022 in which President Erdoğan imposed on the Central Bank of Turkey the idea that high interest rates hurt the economy, is illustrative. The Turkish lira collapsed in international markets and inflation rates soared out of control. It is generally held (though not by Erdoğan) that the independence of national central banks should be sacrosanct. It was Labour Chancellor of the Exchequer Gordon Brown who engineered a rechartering of the Bank of England a few years ago to ensure its independence.

314 THE STORY OF CAPITAL

But from its very inception, the separation and insulation of the central bank from state power was crucial. When the British monarchy, bank-rupted by costly wars, sought loans from wealthy London merchants in the 1690s, the latter refused. Instead, it was agreed in 1694 to charter a bank controlled by the merchants but dedicated to providing loans to the state and with chartered powers of issuing fiat moneys against their holdings of money commodities, gold and silver. Members of the monarchy could become stockholders without exercising a controlling interest. What revolutionary governments from the left can do about the central bank poses a serious conundrum. In the Paris Commune of 1871, the communards protected the Bank of France, a move that earned Lenin's intense criticism, but the Soviets did not do much better. The revolutionary Morales regime in Bolivia pursued 'sound fiscal policies' and protected their central bank, which earned them praise from the International Monetary Fund but circumscribed their capacity to re-engineer their economy along socialist lines. The problem here is that the monetary system that is required for market exchange cannot easily be abolished, and the management of money is entirely within the purview of the state and leading financial institutions (that is, the finance ministry plus the central bank).

How, then, do we depict the position of the central bank vis-à-vis the finance ministry? Arrangements in the United States are illustrative. The Federal Reserve is a key institution in civil society. Its main role is to manage the real rate of interest (nominal rate minus inflation) and to ensure the stability of the monetary system. The problem is that the issue of credit is a private affair over which the Federal Reserve has no direct control. It can only intervene after the fact. Its activity is based within the capitalist social formation. But, as Marx argued, the power of the banking system can only be asserted after the private discounters cease their operations. This parallels the Treasury Depart-ment's positionality within the state apparatus, where it is charged with determining the viability of Congress's fiscal and taxation policies. The expenditures orchestrated within the other departments of the state on defence, education, health care, housing, environmental protection and the like form the bedrock of effective demand in the economy and therefore play a major role in the realization of capital through social reproduction including the reproduction of labour capacity. When, in a recession, tax revenues decline, demand can be stabilized by issuing more debt. This is a tacit acknowledgement, at a rather high level of abstraction, that the adequate management of the circulation of capital has to rest on some sort of public–private partnership between Treasury and the Fed.[18]

This structural duality, it turns out, lies at the heart of bourgeois forms of governance, as illustrated most clearly in the case of the United States. The Justice Department is within the state but relationally partners with judges and lawyers in a judicial system in the social formation that has its pinnacle in the Supreme Court. The military apparatus is within the federal state, but all the local police and militia forces and so on are embedded in the social formation. The Commerce Department is partnered by the National Association of Manufacturers and Chambers of Commerce, the Labor Department by the trade unions and so on.

Since the 1990s, it is fair to say that state political power in the United States has consolidated around the interests of the rentiers (the bondholders), the financiers and what is generally referred to as the 'tech sector'. Paulson's refusal to contemplate nationalization of the banks, even temporarily, was a clear sign of how that power has been used. But the state can take many forms, depending on contextual conditions and the mobilization of class influences. In Germany, for example, the state is not so subservient to finance as it largely is in the United States. The industrial corporations in Germany typically partner with the banks (avoiding the stock market) to shape a state-managed market system (called 'ordoliberalism') that engages in a mercantilist politics (pursuing a permanently positive balance of payments) within the interstate system. In China, matters are even more radically different. The banks, at all levels (national, regional and local), are under state control. The response of the big banks in the US to Paulson and Bernanke's proposals would be impossible in China, where the banks (starting with the four largest in the world) take orders from the Chinese Communist Party. To be sure, the shadow banking system that proliferated after the 1990s in China has proven difficult to control and, as the case of the large-scale urban development firm Evergrande illustrates, the typical crises inherent in the capitalist mode of production have been by no means abolished. The politicization of institutions (such as the Supreme Court and Federal Reserve in the United States or the Central Bank of Turkey) can have major effects on how governance is working, thus determining the direction civil society moves in. But all the evidence suggests that divergence from a rule-bound state-finance nexus produces difficulties.

---

18   Helleiner, *States and the Reemergence of Global Finance.*

Some theories of the state seek to internalize these structural duali-
ties. 'One of Gramsci's key contributions', notes Chantal Mouffe, 'is his
conception of the "integral state", which he conceived as including both
political society and civil society. This should not be understood as a
"statization" of civil society but an indication of the profoundly political character of civil society, presented as the terrain of the struggle for
hegemony.'[19] To the degree that all of these relations are suffused with
or tainted by what Althusser called 'ideological state apparatuses', then
the question of politics and political contestation moves to the forefront
of theorizing.[20] Which political faction controls which institution with
which ruling ideas is the question. It is not at all uncommon for the
state (Treasury) and civil society (the Federal Reserve) to be as much at
odds as in concordance with each other. In a crisis, however, it is critical
that both sides come together. When they do, they form what I call a
'state-finance nexus'. This was what the joint appearance of Paulson and
Bernanke signalled and their three-page policy proposal, which eventually underpinned TARP, was the tangible policy response that emerged
from their concordance.

'From the nineteenth century, if not before', says Joseph Vogl, 'the nexus
of state and finance was embodied in institutions – above all central and
national banks – that occupy an unstable, eccentric and prominent position within government ... In the second half of the twentieth century,
structures of power emerged in which power was blatantly transferred
from governments and states to the financial markets themselves.' In
the United States, the transition 'from a government-controlled financial system to a market-controlled system was forced by central banks
themselves'.[21] The effect was that financial questions became much more
central to policy-making, while financial and commercial crises became
much deeper and more frequent as the powers of the Treasury and the
Fed were consolidated and combined in the state-finance nexus as a first
line of defence in managing those crises. As Summers predicted, the
price of strong growth was financial deregulation that opened the path to
increasingly violent speculative crashes. The balance of power and influence within the state-finance nexus has consolidated in recent times in
favour of the bondholders. When in 2022 the new UK prime minster, Liz

19   Chantal Mouffe, *For a Left Populism* (London: Verso, 2019), Chapter 3.
20   Louis Althusser, 'Ideology and Ideological State Apparatuses (Notes towards an
Investigation)', in *Lenin and Philosophy and Other Essays* (New York: *Monthly Review
Press*, 2001), pp. 127–86.
21   Joseph Vogl, *The Ascendency of Finance* (Cambridge: Polity, 2017).

Truss, presented an economic programme of which the bondholders disapproved she suddenly found herself unemployed. When governments in Greece and Italy lost control of their finances, financial technocrats appointed by Brussels took over for a while.

The state-finance nexus is the organizational form that crystalizes out as the finance and credit system becomes, in effect, the central nervous system regulating capital flow and managing both the dynamics of class struggle and the other key foundational contradictions within the capitalist mode of production. The management of commodity and surplus value production, consumption capacity, land development, asset values, prices and, most important of all, control over inflation are all within its remit. The last of these is a key mandate mainly for a central bank. Clearly, the management of the creation, amortization and flows of fictitious capital is now in the trembling hands of the state-finance nexus, even as the institutional recognition of this task is in many instances only partial. The recently chartered European Central Bank has control of inflation as its sole responsibility. Elsewhere, this is usually combined with policy objectives of full employment, balance of payments positions and the like. On the other hand, the management of the debt largely falls within the remit of the finance ministry. The state-finance nexus is built to ensure what is adequate to the reproduction of capital in general, by way of the combined power of these two institutions.

Of course, particular governments in particular countries may seek to work outside the norms. But the convertibility of currencies exercises a disciplinary effect, while the world's central banks (the Federal Reserve, the European Central Bank, the Banks of England, Japan and Switzerland) coordinate their responses to market instability through the manipulation of interest rates and the circulation of interest-bearing capital. As Marx points out, in matters of this sort, the working classes have almost nothing of relevance to say and certainly no clear positions to act upon. The contradictions of capital and public finance exercise their own logic, and the responses within the state-finance nexus are barely touched on by popular class forces, even as the class effects may be striking (for example, recessions and widespread unemployment as fiscal policies shake out overaccumulated fictitious capitals). Small wonder that the Parisian communards did not know what to do about the Bank of France other than to protect it and guard the gold in its vaults. Nationalizing the central banks is a common enough sentiment on the socialist left, but every attempt to do so to date has ended in calamity. The state-finance nexus typically regulates after the fact rather than creating new paths for social change. As Marx observed in the *Grundrisse*, there is no way that monetary reforms (of the sort advocated by Proudhon) could provide paths to a socialist future, even though such a future would likely entail serious monetary and fiscal reforms, including, at some point, the demonetization and decommodification of as much of the economy as possible.

The fusion of state and capital that Arrighi sees has widespread implications. It connects the laws of motion of a capitalist mode of production with the theory of capitalism as a social formation. The inner structure of a capitalist mode of production contains, as it were, a restricted opening via the state-finance nexus into the rich complexity of economic forces at work within the social formation. Influences flow across this bridge in both directions. The theory of capital has to have one foot in capitalist state theory and another in that of the capitalist social formation. Or, put the other way round, the theory of the capitalist state internalizes the duality if not the fusion of state and capital. The three people who sat in that room and decided what to do in 2008 – Hank Paulson (Treasury), Ben Bernanke (chair of the Federal Reserve) and Tim Geitner (the Fed's Wall Street regulator) – played their roles and fulfilled their appointed tasks. In the crisis of 2007–8, collaboration between Treasury and the Federal Reserve was, as we have seen, critical in finding an exit from the crisis. This was not a unique situation. The near collapse of the South Korean economy in 1997–8 required the collaboration of the International Monetary Fund and the US Treasury. Earlier, Ronald Reagan had set in motion proposals to abolish the IMF, only to find a vital role for it in alliance with the US Treasury in dealing with the Mexican credit crisis of 1982. This crisis set the template for structural adjustment programmes subsequently sprinkled around to deal with the forty-odd countries (from Poland behind the Iron Curtain to Ecuador) that ran into debt difficulties after 1982.

Meanwhile, the struggle for control of the state-finance nexus is currently deeply engaged among the billionaire oligarchy, backed by factionalized corporate, financial and legal elites. The working population is largely sidelined as electoral cannon fodder pulled this way and that in response to the manipulative demagogy of billionaire money rather than people power. A big question is the degree to which those who ultimately seize control of the state-finance nexus can save capital from the billionaires, the financiers and the vast and growing army peddling fictitious capitals for the ruling classes against the background context of austerity politics and continuous wage repression for the masses.

17

The Geopolitics of Capital

Investigating the geopolitics of capital entails opening up the interplay of three critical forces – class, clan and caste – in shaping capital's mode of production and its socio-political formations. Each force represents a distinct but interconnected dimension of how capital operates and evolves, influencing geopolitical struggles, cultural expressions and territorial dynamics.

The class dimension originates with the collision of alienated capital and alienated labour, which drives the accumulation of surplus value and the transformation of economic and social structures. From this 'big bang' interaction arises a spiralling process that reshapes the world through the production of spaces and places, fixed capital and consumption fund formation, the circulation of interest-bearing capital and the interventions of state-finance nexuses.

The lenses of class alone cannot account for the persistence and influence of clan and caste forces. Clan forces operate autonomously yet intersect with class to shape the totality of capital's social formations. Clans, rooted in kinship, locality and tradition, have been a critical force in the evolution of nation-states and nationalism. Caste, by contrast, enforces rigid hierarchies of value and exclusion, often aligning with class and clan dynamics to perpetuate structural inequalities in the distribution of wealth and power within the interstate system.

Class relations are central to understanding capital's laws of motion. The relationship between capital and labour is not merely transactional but foundational to the processes of surplus extraction and accumulation. Marx's analysis of alienated labour reveals how capital's expansion transforms material and social geographies, creating contradictions that manifest in uneven geographical development and spiralling capital accumulation. Capital's need for endless accumulation drives the production of space. Urbanization, infrastructure development and the commodification of daily life are all mechanisms through which capital seeks to overcome its inherent crisis tendencies. For example, the rapid growth of industrial cities during the nineteenth century reflects how capital reshaped physical landscapes to maximize surplus extraction. Manchester and Birmingham became sites of intense class conflict as workers organized against exploitative conditions in order to stay alive, highlighting the centrality of class struggle in capital's expansion. Capital also relies on financial mechanisms to sustain accumulation. The expansion of the circulation of interest-bearing capital, from colonial ventures to modern financial markets, reveals how surplus value is extracted not only from labour but also through the manipulation of debt and speculation. This process intensifies inequalities, as financial capital consolidates its own class power in the hands of a few, often at the expense of workers and marginalized populations.

While class provides the backbone to capital's dynamics, the logic of clan remains a powerful force in structuring capital's social formation. Clan, as defined by Marx, includes associations based on family, kinship, locality and shared traditions. These affiliations have not disappeared in the transition to the hegemony of capital but have been transformed to serve new purposes. Nation-states are a product of territorialization rooted in clan logics. The Westphalian settlement of 1648 formalized the sovereignty of nation-states, embedding clan-based loyalties into the political and economic structures of an interstate system. Nationalism, often viewed as a modern phenomenon, draws heavily on a history of clan affiliations, whether through shared histories, cultural symbols or territorial claims. Nationalism illustrates how clan logics intersect with capital's drive for accumulation. Nation-states compete to attract capital and protect their economic interests, often resorting to nationalist rhetoric to justify policies. However, these dynamics also create contradictions. For instance, the rise of protectionism in the twenty-first century reflects a tension between global capital's need for geographical mobility and the territorial imperatives of nation-states.

The Olympic Games serve as a vivid example of how clan-based nationalism and capitalist accumulation intersect. Originally conceived as a celebration of clan-based national pride, the Olympics have evolved into spectacles of global capital. Cities invest heavily in infrastructure and marketing, often incurring significant debt to host the event. Urban developers and corporations profit from these investments, while local communities bear the long-term economic and social costs.[1] The Olympics demonstrates how clan loyalties are commodified within capitalism's broader logic.

Caste, described by Marx as the 'strictest form' of human association, introduces a hierarchical rigidity that often complements and reinforces capitalist and clan structures. While caste systems may seem antithetical to modernity, they persist in various forms, shaping how power, privilege and exclusion operate within capitalist societies. In the United States, racial hierarchies function as a caste-like system, structuring access to resources, opportunities, and political power on a seemingly rock-solid basis. The legacy of slavery, Jim Crow laws and the current forms of systemic racism underscore how caste dynamics are embedded in capitalist social formations. For instance, the racial wealth gap illustrates how economic inequalities are perpetuated across generations, aligning with caste-like exclusions. Caste-like systems intersect with class to create complex hierarchies of privilege and oppression within institutions (such as the law and academia, which is an excellent example of a modern caste system). In South Asia, caste remains a defining feature of social and economic life, dictating access to education, employment and political representation. These dynamics are further exacerbated in global labour markets, where caste-based discrimination shapes the experiences of migrant workers and diasporic communities. Patriarchy likewise operates as another dimension of caste-like exclusion. Gendered hierarchies, reinforced through cultural norms and institutional structures, limit women's access to economic and political power. These exclusions are not incidental but integral to capitalism's functioning, as they provide a reserve army of labour while perpetuating unpaid care work.

Class, clan and caste are not isolated forces but intersect in complex and often contradictory ways. This intersectionality shapes the totality of capital's social formations, influencing how power is distributed and contested. Class and clan frequently intersect to shape the geopolitical landscape. For instance, the competition between nation-states to attract capital often aligns with the interests of the capitalist class, creating synergies that drive economic and territorial expansion. However, these alignments are not without conflict. Nationalist policies, such as

---

1   Jules Boykoff, *Power Games: A Political History of the Olympics* (London: Verso, 2016).

protectionism or anti-immigration measures, can disrupt global capital flows, highlighting the tensions between class and clan logics.

While caste intersects with class and clan, it also operates autonomously, enforcing rigid hierarchies that often transcend economic structures. For example, the persistence of racial discrimination in the United States or the caste system in India reflects rigidities that resist assimilation into purely class-based or clan-based analyses. These dynamics underscore the need for a more nuanced understanding of how caste operates within the context of capital's mode of production. The Heideggerian and Aristotelian perspectives on placemaking as the 'first among all things' incorporate caste principles of rootedness, permanence and 'dwelling'. The anticapitalist answer is not to ignore placemaking but to mobilize it, as does Lefebvre, towards the construction of that 'good life' that Aristotle envisaged.

The dynamics of class, clan and caste are integral to understanding capital's evolution and its geopolitical implications. While class remains central, the persistence of clan and caste introduces additional layers of complexity. These forces shape how capital operates across different contexts, influencing everything from urban development to nationalist policies and racial hierarchies within major political and cultural institutions. This triad of caste, clan and class not only provides a framework for analysing capital's historical trajectory but also raising critical questions about its future. As capital continues to adapt and expand, the interplay of class, clan and caste will remain a defining feature within its social formations.

In exploring the evolution of capital as a totality, we need to recognize it as a dynamic system shaped by contradictions and interdependent forces. Marx's dialectical method offers a crucial lens, revealing how the different circulatory processes interact to form a contradictory whole. This totality is neither static nor deterministic but constantly evolving through the clash of opposing forces.

Capital originates as a single seed in the encounter between alienated labour and alienated money power. From this seed, capital expands, subsuming diverse aspects of social and economic life. This expansion, while innovative, is also fraught with contradictions that periodically reshape the entire system. The shock of major technological shifts, such as the factory system in Marx's time and AI in ours, is, for example, felt everywhere.

As an aid to analysis in such situations, Marx reverts to 'concrete abstractions'. Universal principles are distilled out of myriad individual moments of capital in motion. Exchange value, for example, serves as a universal designation that covers a huge number of seemingly disparate market transactions. Marx begins *Capital* with the concept of commodity because everyone, no matter their class, race, gender or ethnicity, lives by way of commodity exchange. As capital incorporates more and more concrete abstractions – such as fixed capital, interest-bearing capital and fictitious capital – the scope of its totality broadens, encompassing everything from urban development to financial markets. The mode of production is ruled by these abstractions. The totality that results is not harmonious. It is riddled with internal contradictions that both drive capital's dynamism and threaten its stability. The chaos that inevitably ensues opens the way for the formulation of alternative ways of being, from everyday life to the policy pronouncements of, say, the world's central banks.

We can illustrate this through numerous historical examples. Venice's rise to prominence in the sixteenth century was driven by a unique interplay of state-led militarization, colonial practices and individualized capital accumulation. Its economic success was rooted in clan principles. Wealthy families used state power to secure their interests and expand their own personal wealth. Venice exemplifies how state-led initiatives can facilitate capital's growth. The city's militarized colonialism allowed it to absorb surplus capital through territorial expansion, while its control over trade routes ensured a steady flow of wealth from peripheral regions to the centre in Venice. This interplay of state power and capitalist principles underscores the importance of understanding capital's totality within specific historical and geographical contexts. But Venice's dominance was not immune to the contradictions of capital. Over time, the forces that drove its expansion – such as reliance on state-led militarization – became liabilities. The city's economy could not adapt to changing global dynamics, leading to its decline. Today, Venice serves as a cautionary tale of how capital's totality is shaped by both its successes and its failures.

The state-finance nexus plays a central role in shaping and mediating capital's totality. But the state is not, as we have seen, a monolithic entity. It is a complex and fluid structure incorporating multiple functions. It straddles two realms: capital's mode of production and the social formations that arise from it. This duality positions the state as both an enabler of accumulation and a mediator of its contradictions. The state operates within two distinct logics: the first is that of capital. Prioritizing profit and the expansion of markets, this logic aligns with capital's need for endless accumulation. States support this logic by protecting private property, facilitating trade and disciplining labour. Political and economic power is rooted in the sovereignty of the nation-state. The second logic emphasizes territorial control and governance. It reflects the state's need to maintain social order, enforce laws and manage internal conflicts and contradictions within its borders. These two logics often conflict, creating tensions that define the state's role in capital's totality. For example, the state's territorial logic may clash with capital's demand for mobility, as we can see in debates over immigration, trade policies and environmental regulations. States have historically navigated these tensions through different models of state-led capitalism. From medieval Venice to contemporary China, the state has played an active role in shaping capital's trajectory. Both Bismarck's Germany and Meiji Japan illustrate how state intervention can drive economic modernization. In Germany, Bismarck's policies of industrialization and social welfare sought to balance the demands of capital with the needs of the working class, creating a model of state capitalism that influenced subsequent regimes, including that of the Nazis. Similarly, Japan's Meiji Restoration combined industrial development with strong state control, laying the foundation for its emergence as a global economic power.

China represents a modern iteration of state-led capitalism, blending authoritarian governance with market-based reforms. Through initiatives like the Belt and Road Initiative, China exports its mass of surplus capital and labour while consolidating its geopolitical influence and access to markets. This is an obvious example of what I call the 'spatial fix' for deploying capital and labour surpluses in space. This initiative also reveals the contradictions of state-led capitalism, as it creates debt dependencies and vulnerabilities for both China and its partners. Domestically, state policies direct investment into strategic sectors, such as technology and infrastructure, illustrating the state's capacity to shape capital's evolution. Since 1978, China's financial institutions have operated on state direction to fund the mass of investment to sectors of the economy considered foundational, independent of the risk as represented by variable interest rates. Despite its successes, however, state-led capitalism is not immune to contradictions. The reliance on state intervention can create inefficiencies, corruption and imbalances, as seen in China's current housing market crisis. These contradictions highlight the challenges states face in mediating capital's totality while addressing their own territorial imperatives.

The interplay between capitalist and territorial logics of power is a defining feature of modern geopolitics. Marx noted:

The concept of national wealth creeps into the work of the economist … in the form of the notion that wealth is created only to enrich the state, and that its [the state's] power is proportionate to this wealth. This was the still unconsciously hypocritical form in which wealth and the production of wealth proclaimed themselves as the purpose of modern states, and regarded these states henceforth only as means for the production of wealth.[2]

But under a regime of competing ethnic nationalisms, the production of wealth by capital is primarily put to work to serve national interests rather than those of capital alone. These two logics are not merely competing forces but ones that are deeply intertwined, influencing how states navigate global and domestic challenges. Capital's need for mobility often conflicts with the state's territorial security. For example, multinational corporations prioritize access to global markets, to labour and to resources, while states seek to regulate these flows to protect their sovereignty, along with their competitive wealth and power. This tension is evident in debates over trade agreements, tax policies and labour laws.

States necessarily emphasize territorial sovereignty and social order. This logic often manifests in nationalist policies, such as protectionism or immigration controls, which may disrupt global capital mobility and labour flows. The current turn to protectionist policies in the United States reflects a territorial response to the perceived threats posed by globalization. The dual role of the state-finance nexus becomes particularly evident during crises. In the aftermath of the 2008 financial crisis, states intervened to stabilize global markets while addressing domestic social unrest. These interventions highlight the state's power to mediate the contradictions between capitalist and territorial logics, even as they reveal the limits of that power.

Capital's geopolitical history reflects all of these conflicting forces and features. The New Deal, for example, represented a landmark case of state intervention to address certain of capital's internal contradictions, particularly those that the dominant Ricardian theorists had brushed aside in their embrace of Say's Law. During the Great Depression, the US government implemented policies to stabilize the economy, including public works projects, debt-financed investments, welfare programmes and labour protections. While these measures alleviated economic distress, they also reflected the racial and class biases of the time, as many

---

2 Marx, *Grundrisse*, p. 108.

marginalized groups were excluded from their benefits. The Marshall Plan after 1945 demonstrated how states can use capital to rebuild and stabilize geopolitical regions. By channelling funds into war-torn Europe, the United States sought to prevent the spread of communism by fostering economic recovery. This intervention illustrates the intersection of capitalist and territorial logics, as the US pursued both economic and geopolitical objectives.

The exploration of capital's totality, and the role of the state-finance nexus within it, highlights the complexities and contradictions inherent in capitalism's geopolitical evolution. The state, as both an enabler and mediator of accumulation, occupies a central position in capital's social formations. However, its dual logics of power – capitalist and territorial – create tensions that shape the trajectory of global and domestic politics.

Consider, then, some key moments in capital's geopolitical history. Capital must struggle not only against its nemesis – labour – but also wrestle with its own internal contradictions. Individual capitalists, recall, seeking to maximize their individual interest collectively produce an aggregate result inimical to capital's reproduction. Interstate competition poses exactly the same problem. If each state maximizes its own interests, then global warming and other global problems can never be addressed. Capital has to be saved from the capitalists and from wrong-headed politicians playing clan and caste politics. Roosevelt, Keynes, Kalecki and many others have clearly understood this dilemma. It then follows that the state-finance nexus must be deployed simultaneously as an economic policy and a territorial project.

This, in turn, presumes an adequate geopolitical theory to guide political action. But the history of geopolitical theorizing under capital is, to put it mildly, profoundly embarrassing, even by liberal standards. It is riddled with assertions of natural and racial superiority, invoking principles of justifiable domination and, at its best, articulating United Nations principles of a just, rules-based international order backed by the US as a ruling hegemonic power. There are those who believe, however, in the ineluctable laws of geopolitics in guaranteeing global domination. For Admiral Mahan, the execution of those laws depended on sea power.[3] But for Sir Halford Mackinder, the laws were land-based, encapsulated in the formula that whoever controlled the Eastern European states (Poland plus Hungary) controlled the heartland and whoever controlled the

---

3   A. T. Mahan, *The Influence of Sea Power Upon History, 1660–1783* (Boston: Little, Brown and Co., 1890).

heartland controlled the 'world island' (Eurasia) and whoever controlled the world island controlled the world. It is significant that the Second World War broke out with the German invasion of Poland and that the current key to the survival of the European Union rests heavily on what will happen to Hungary and Poland. Originally written in the wake of the Russian Revolution, Mackinder's *Democratic Ideals and Reality* was republished in the United States in 1942.[4]

When Hitler picked up Karl Haushofer's analogous geopolitical theories in the 1920s, for example, he concluded that Germany's future economic wealth and power and the prospects for global domination depended on open access to basic resources (oil in particular) and world markets.[5] The geopolitics of '*drang nach osten*' (the drive to the East) then followed. Expansion of capital through territorial conquest was an economic necessity, Hitler claimed, justified by rock-solid caste principles of racial and cultural superiorities and the need to bypass the barriers constructed around existing imperial and territorial structures. Theories of geopolitical superiority abounded in the inter-war years, as much in London and New York as in Berlin. After the Second World War, geopolitics became a dirty word in elite policy circles, given its tawdry history in relation to the Holocaust. But the problem is that geopolitical rivalries are not incidental to capitalism but central to its dynamism. While Hitler was certifiably mad, look at what he was enabled to do. While Trump also may be certifiably mad, watch out for what he might be enabled to do. He surely has dreams of global domination. He now proposes to rename the Gulf of Mexico the Gulf of America (with major implications for oil extraction claims). He seems ready to offer Puerto Rico's associated commonwealth status to Greenland, provided the Greenlanders cede control over the Arctic passage in the interest of US national security while giving the US exclusive rights to mineral extraction. He has already asserted that he would not defend the Baltic states (Latvia, Lithuania and Estonia) and Georgia from Russian takeover (on the Belarus model). He might possibly accede to China's takeover of Taiwan provided that TSMC, the world's largest chip maker, becomes US owned (for example, by Elon Musk, who might just be able to afford it).

There are 'respectable' forms of this kind of geopolitical thinking. When George Kennan articulated his theory of containment of the

---

4   Halford J. Mackinder, *Democratic Ideals and Reality* (London: Constable, 1919).
5   Karl Haushofer, *Geopolitik des Pazifischen Ozeans: Studien über die Wechselbeziehungen zwischen Geographie und Geschichte* (Heidelberg: Kurt Vowinckel Verlag, 1925).

communist system in general and of China in particular in the 1950s, he opened a space for the militarization of the whole East Asian archipelago from Japan to Singapore, which led the US to hold the line against the spread of communism by taking over the French colonial role in Vietnam.[6] This strategy, incidentally, entailed US support for capitalist-led development and technology transfers to bolster capital's development in East Asia as a barrier to China's communism.

These logics often operate in tandem but are also often misaligned, creating the contradictions that underpin geopolitical struggles. The expansion of global trade agreements may benefit capitalists while undermining national industries and interests, for example, leading to a protectionist backlash. How to theorize this sort of thing is the question. A historical materialist approach entails describing surface appearances, revealing what happens behind the surface appearances and fetishisms, while formulating theoretical concepts to capture the motion of the underlying forces at work. In that spirit, it is useful to go back to that moment in the First World War after most of the international socialist movement mobilized in support of clan rather than class politics.

Consider, then, what happened geopolitically in the Versailles settlement of 1919 that followed the defeat of Germany in the First World War. There were four main participants in the conference. The American 'idealist' Woodrow Wilson who, by virtue of the decisive role of US military intervention (engineered in the face of serious domestic opposition), was ostensibly in a position to dictate the terms of the settlement. He set out his 'Fourteen Points' (such as the right of peoples to self-determination) to signal his intentions. In addition, there was the liberal (in the European sense) David Lloyd George, defensive of British imperial interests and looking to further new commercial interests (particularly in the oil-rich Middle East); Vittorio Orlando from Italy, who played a minor role (though with African ambitions); and Georges Clemenceau from France, whose tough talk and social Darwinist approach made him a formidable and determined negotiator pursuing a distinctive national interest. Clemenceau apparently ran rings around Wilson (who, some assert, was not in the best of health in the wake of the Spanish Flu epidemic that ravaged the world in 1918). Clemenceau took every opportunity to weaken and humiliate Germany to France's advantage. Alsace-Lorraine, which had been ceded to Germany after the Franco-Prussian war of

---

6   George F. Kennan, *American Diplomacy, 1900–1950* (Chicago: University of Chicago Press, 1951).

1870, was returned to France. Germany lost its colonial possessions (the key one in China was given to Japan as compensation for Wilson blocking Japan's proposal for a clause in the Versailles settlement asserting the racial equality of nations). Germany faced forced demilitarization, had to accept blame for the war and contracted to pay a large sum in punitive reparations to cover the war's costs. Keynes worked out the economic implications in intricate detail and they were not positive by any measure.[7] The Germans who signed off on the agreement were subsequently pilloried in the court of German public opinion. Versailles was, for many Germans, a humiliation beyond belief. In all of this, the question of working-class interests was largely ignored, even though working-class militancy during the war itself was marked and working-class organization began to consolidate after the war ended (for example, the rise of the British Labour Party and the formation of the Chinese Communist Party).

Much of the work of the Versailles Conference was, however, taken up with drawing the boundaries and creating new sovereign states out of the remnants of the Austro-Hungarian and Ottoman Empires using the principle of the right of peoples for self-determination. National interests, both existing and incipient, predominated. This task rested heavily on the cartographic skills of the American Geographical Society, led by the geographer Isaiah Bowman, who travelled with Wilson to Versailles as an adviser as to where the boundaries might best be drawn. Within the British Treasury delegation, however, the young economist John Maynard Keynes acted as an adviser on economic affairs. Keynes fell sick before the proceedings were concluded. But he saw the way the wind was blowing. He returned to Cambridge to write a critical book, *The Economic Consequences of the Peace* (1919). It was widely read but not well appreciated at the time – and was later characterized as prescient.

The gist of Keynes's argument was that the failure to devise an economic recovery plan to cope with the economic devastation of the war and its aftermath would have serious political and economic consequences in the long run. It would condemn most of the people in Europe and beyond to misery and privation, and it was therefore a recipe for political instability. (He presumably had the example of the Russian Revolution in mind.) Struggling to align state boundaries with the rights of peoples to self-determination may have been important but could not

---

7   John Maynard Keynes, *The Economic Consequences of the Peace* (London: Macmillan, 1919).

ground a lasting peace. The separatism that would come from conflicting and competing national state interests, along with competitive regional power blocs vying for advantage, would make a European-wide economic recovery unlikely. The economic burden placed on Germany to pay reparations would hobble economic recovery not only for Germany but for Europe as a whole. One might say that Versailles was too much about geography and national interests, and too little about economics and capitalist class interests. Moreover, Clemenceau's determination to vilify, humiliate and disempower the Germans at every turn would likely backfire. It is extremely dangerous to insult and humiliate a potentially powerful defeated enemy like Germany. Humiliated populations would likely exact revenge. This turned out to be only too true when Hitler later came to power.

Capital not only needs to be saved from capitalists, Keynes tacitly inferred. It also needs to be saved from self-aggrandizing politicians and error-prone state policymakers pursuing narrowly construed national clan interests guided by mistaken economic theories, such as those of austerity. Hence Keynes's implicit view that the economy needed to be managed by skilled and wise technocrats (such as himself) rather than by politicians and idealogues like Winston Churchill. At Versailles, capital particularly needed to be defended from those, like Clemenceau, who armed themselves with social Darwinist and organicist and racist theories of the nation-state in which only the fittest could survive. Worse still, the whole atmospherics of the conference was animated by the hierarchical caste-like assumption that some nations are superior and better than others. Hence Wilson's denial of Japan's proposal for a clause in the treaty establishing the racial equality of nations.

The evidence that Keynes was right was quick to emerge. In 1921–2, a sharp deflationary recession and major unemployment hit most European countries. Hitler attempted his 'Beer Hall Putsch' in Munich in 1923. Popular discontent with Versailles and the dismal rate of post-war recovery played a central role in crystallizing support for his attempted coup. Imprisoned and then quickly released, Hitler shifted from acquiring absolute power by coup to an electoral strategy towards the same end (much as Trump did after an equally amateurish coup attempt in 2021 in the US).

Capital's performance in the inter-war years was, to put it mildly, dismal if not catastrophic, particularly in the depression years after 1929. Its condition was worsened by widespread attachment to the erroneous neoclassical economic idea that austerity was the answer to economic distress when, as was earlier noted, the smooth accumulation of capital depends, according to Marx's theorization, on the steady expansion of credit. Otherwise, it would be impossible to avoid periodic devaluations through underconsumption (or overaccumulation). The 'plethora of capital' to which Marx referred would take over. The Keynesians (and Kaleckians) struggled unsuccessfully to refute the austerity thesis in favour of deficit state financing. Perversely, it was the fascists who, in practice, gave a Keynesian tweak to the economy via militarization and Hitler's building of the autobahns (which encouraged Henry Ford to sympathize with the fascists, perhaps because his cars needed good roads to run on). It was a tragedy, wrote Keynes in the 1930s, that Ricardo had adopted Say's tautologies (that supply will always create its own demand to make general overproduction impossible). The much-maligned Malthus, Keynes argued in the 1930s, had it right, with his theories of inevitable crises of overproduction and underconsumption because of a structurally determined lack of effective demand.[8]

This was the only theorization that made sense in the Great Depression of those years. Say's Law was obviously wrong. Production plainly did not create its own demand. The Keynesian solution of deficit-financed credit expansion that lay at the heart of Roosevelt's New Deal was only fully accepted out of necessity during the Second World War. Roosevelt had succumbed to the pressures of austerity politics as urged by the Brahmin economists in 1938, thereby triggering a return to depression conditions. Deficit financing became a widely applied popular policy preference after 1945, only to be formally jettisoned in 1982 under Ronald Reagan, when austerity and supply-side economics of the Milton Friedman type returned to become a basic prop to neoliberal public policies. In that year, all the Keynesians were fired from the international and national institutions regulating finance (for example, the IMF and the US Treasury). From the early 1980s on, Keynesianism was treated as a bad joke in bourgeois economics and policy circles, while most Marxists (apart from the Paul Sweezy school) also condemned any explanation that smacked of under-consumption. Belief in Say's Law and austerity returned with a vengeance after 1982. Consequently, labour's share in GDP steadily declined, precip-itously so after 2000 (see Figure 15). So did all the problems associated with the application of that tautological law, only partly countered by the expansionist policies adopted in response to the Covid-19 virus.

---

8 John Maynard Keynes, *The General Theory of Employment, Interest, and Money* (London: Palgrave Macmillan, 1936).

— Business sector: Labour share, Q1 1948=100

— Shares of gross domestic income: Compensation of employees, paid:
Wage and salary accruals: Disimbursments: To persons, 1948=100

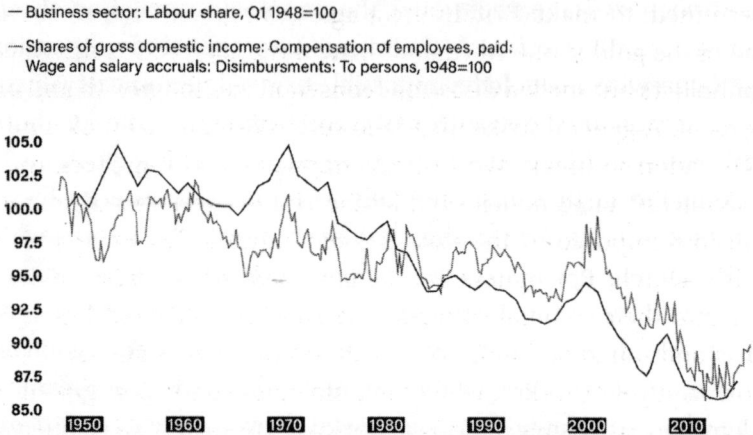

Figure 15. US Labour Share Index, 1948–2016

At first sight, it seems a strange coincidence that the two phases of global state-imposed austerity (1920–45 and 1980–present) have ended in a seemingly unstoppable turn to authoritarian and neofascistic politics in the state logic of power, leaving the capitalist logic to impose the requisite medicine of wage repression leading to rising underemployment and increasing consumer dissatisfaction. The 'austere' aspect of state-administered austerity amounts to the imposition by the state of a regime of self-discipline, of 'tough love' administered by the (increasingly reviled) state, coupled with ever diminishing expectations of the good life that Aristotle's economics had envisaged as the ultimate lot of all. Thatcherism combined the state imposition of austerity in public services for the populace with a theory of the importance of the 'entrepreneurial self'. The poverty of the mass of people was blamed on the victims for their lack of initiative and not investing sufficiently in their own human capital. Citizens with rights were supplanted by subjects begging for charity from the NGOs. The compassionate state was replaced by the humiliation of the needy as 'spongers' when they turned to the state for support. The successful self-made entrepreneurs made out fine, thus exacerbating class distinctions and social inequality. Self-love (a culture of narcissism) and popular hatred of the state was all that was left for the toiling masses. If democratic politics cannot deliver, then opportunities galore present themselves for a narcissistic leader who promises to love the people provided they love him or her back. The merger of the two logics of power produces the turn to economic fascism under conditions of austerity.

Winston Churchill, while chancellor of the exchequer in 1925, determined 'to make Britain great again' by going back to the discipline of the gold standard (the ultimate austerity), which delighted the bondholders but spelled disastrous consequences for growth and unemployment. A general strike then followed in Britain that took a military mobilization to break. World trade stagnated, held in check not only by nationalist tariff policies but by the closed markets and imperialist exclusions imposed by the main colonial powers. The French, Belgian, British, Dutch, Portuguese and Spanish colonial possessions limited trade into their colonial empires. The Japanese occupied Korea, Manchuria and much of China (obviously setting their sights on usurping British control of India), while the isolated Soviet Union lurked in the background, ostensibly offering an anticapitalist, communist alternative. It was a huge struggle to keep the capitalist mode of production freely in motion during these inter-war years, even as the relatively small class of active (as opposed to rentier) capitalists (from Krupp to Henry Ford) revelled in their immense monopoly wealth and power. While capital did very badly, the monopoly capitalists made out very well, even as the working classes (those that had jobs) struggled to stay afloat. All of this led Hitler and Mussolini to embrace 'national socialism' and the social Darwinist theory of *Lebensraum* (living space). Germany claimed the right to expand its territorial domination in order to procure and protect its imports of raw materials (particularly oil) while opening markets for its surplus products. Hitler's first step was to annex the Sudetenland from Czechoslovakia. Shortly after, he signalled his intention to absorb Poland and occupy the Romanian oil fields.

Meanwhile, the Japanese search for its own *Lebensraum* was in full flood – Japanese forces rushed into China and committed atrocities such as 'the rape of Nanking' (1937) in which the total population of that city was put to the sword, in one of the biggest crimes against humanity outside of the Holocaust. This particularly perverse version of 'the spatial fix' was coupled with an organicist theory of a state that had, like any living organism, to be materially fed if it was to survive. The result was the Second World War fought against the imposition of the fascist ('national socialist') answer to economic distress and imperialist expansionism. During this whole period, capital had to cut its cloth according to whatever opportunities for accumulation presented themselves (such as military rearmament). It was, coincidentally, the three powers that were pushing hardest to expand geographically and overcome their hitherto restricted imperial ambitions – Germany, Japan and Italy – that formed the Axis alliance that launched the Second World War. Their path to a spatial fix was blocked by imperial preferences on the part of others, so they sought to unblock it by resorting to war to assert their own imperial expansion.

In negotiating the post–Second World War economic settlement at Bretton Woods, it had seemed as if the political classes had learned their lessons from the mistakes of Versailles. Keynes headed the British delegation and doubtless reminded everyone of those earlier errors. There was little appetite in 1945 to insult and humiliate Japan, Germany and Italy, and no talk of reparations (apart from German reparations to the Jews). Germany was pacified, divided and voluntarily demilitarized. Japan likewise. The defeated powers were steadily reinserted into the circuits of capital through the US Marshall Plan to Europe (in part conceived as a defensive move to stem the communist advances) and economic assistance to Japan (supporting the authority of the emperor and other traditional caste institutions, such as the royal family). This strategy highlights how geopolitical rivalries often serve as mechanisms of capital accumulation. The Bretton Woods system, established in 1944, sought to create a rules-based international economic order to prevent the competitive chaos of the inter-war years. By instituting fixed exchange rates and creating institutions like the International Monetary Fund and World Bank, Bretton Woods provided a regulatory framework for managing global capital flows while addressing its contradictions. However, this system also entrenched the dominance of the United States, reflecting a convenient alignment of capitalist and territorial interests in the form of the Cold War.

Decolonization and dismantling of imperial preferences were imposed by the US by way of GATT (the General Agreement on Tariffs and Trade). This meant that West Germany and Japan had open access to the world market (and no need to pursue a politics of colonialism and *Lebensraum*.) To confirm this new direction, France and Germany formed a US-backed alliance that began with the Monnet Plan to create a common market for coal and steel production, leading to the eventual formation of the European Union on the basis of the Franco-German Alliance. The possibility for a repeat performance of world war by way of interstate European competition with Germany at the centre was nullified by such new territorial politics.

The US also hit on the idea that social democracy, a compassionate positioning of state supports to needy citizens, and global free trade were the best weapons to stem the advance of communism in Europe or a return to the closed-door authoritarianism of the 1930s. The US at times supported moderate social democratic parties in Europe against the advance of communism. It also conceded some degree of technology transfer to Japan (followed by 'the flying geese' of Singapore, Hong Kong, Taiwan and South Korea) as well as to Europe to foster global growth and mass consumption as a check to the promises of communism in general and China in particular. Walt Rostow had subtitled his influential book *The Stages of Economic Growth* (1960) as a 'Non-Communist Manifesto'. Its problematic road map of how to get to a society of endless mass consumption was widely followed. As the old empires were dissolved and decolonization proceeded apace, it was replaced by a far more lucrative and insidious global neocolonialism headed up by the United States as the world hegemon.

After 1945, state planning of the economy was acceptable in most places (including even the United States). Europe saw the nationalization of the commanding heights of economies (coal, steel, automobiles, transport and communications were the main sectors), and it was accepted that the state should play a vital role in assuring adequate conditions of social reproduction and capital accumulation. Such measures had been essential to the successful prosecution of the wartime economy, and it seemed natural to continue them at least for a while after the end of the war.

New international economic institutions were created, such as the United Nations, the International Monetary Fund and the World Bank, to promote capitalist forms of development everywhere and to face down the newly empowered communists within the Soviet orbit. New principles, such as those of universal human rights, aimed directly at the communist challenge, were enunciated within the framework of a new rules-based international order. By the 1980s, West Germany and Japan were the model versions of capital's mode of production operating at its best, leading many to observe that these states may have lost the war, but they had clearly won the peace. The US, however, forced Japan and West Germany to revalue their currencies upwards in the so-called Plaza Accord of 1985 to make US capital much more competitive on the international stage. Japanese and German goods became much more expensive, thus restoring the relative economic power of the US in the international order. The framework of the Bretton Woods agreement presumed competition between nation-states and their economies in a world system regulated by the supreme power of the United States and its dollar. The latter offered military protection in return for open markets.

But if the chaotic conditions of the 1930s are anything to go by, and if we are in for a repeat performance, the current dissolution of the rules-based neoliberal order of austerity for the masses and untold wealth for the ruling oligarchy will be accomplished through a slide into competitive authoritarianism and right-wing populism. This future was presciently predicted by Klaus Schwab and Claude Smadja at the 1996 Davos Symposium, when they warned the gathered global economic and financial elites of the dangers of a 'rising backlash' against neoliberal globalization and warned that a spreading mood of 'helplessness and anxiety' was promoting 'the rise of a new brand of populist politician' and that this could 'easily turn into revolt'.[9] This situation did not bode well for the perpetual world peace of which Immanuel Kant dreamed, nor the reasonably stable economic order that Keynes thought technically possible. Once more, the question will be posed, but this time more urgently than ever: Who now will save capital from the capitalists? How will the ruling classes and dominant political castes comport themselves in the face of the current surge in right-wing autocratic violence? And what kind of socialist alternative can be constructed to address both the potentialities and the contradictions posited by capital's forms in the current historical and geographical conjuncture? The old utopias are useless. A new dialectical utopianism which builds on rather than ignores the current contradictions of capital has yet to be constructed. That is the task of the next generation of anticapitalist thinkers and activists.

While our ultimate task may be to change the world, there is no escaping the preparatory task of understanding it. That is why Marx wrote the volumes of *Capital, Theories of Surplus Value* and all the associated manuscripts from the *Economic and Philosophic Manuscripts of 1844* to his final investigations into agronomy and the historical anthropology of social life. Is our mission of defining and understanding the story of capital accomplished? In this expansion of Marx's work, we have before us a remarkable legacy to understand the story of capital. We need to use it well.

What looks like a linear story that starts with the seed of money power's encounter with labour capacity as a commodity ends up, after many intermediate steps, in spiralling geopolitical conflict on the world stage. But there is, it seems, a foundational contradiction at work here between capital's evolution as a mode of production and its unfolding geopolitical expression. If, as Arrighi demonstrates, capitalist state formation and

---

9   Klaus Schwab and Claude Smadja, 'Start Taking the Backlash Against Globalization Seriously', *International Herald Tribune*, 1 February 1996.

interstate competition are preconditions for the rise of capital to domi-nance and if, as Marx asserts, territorialization, private property in land (nature as the basic means of production and the extraction of capital-ist ground rent) are also precursors to capital's rise to dominance, then capital, from its very inception, was and still is a systemic geopolitical project. Late medieval Venice was its initiating paradigm case and China is its current manifestation. The capitalist mode of production became and still is a means to the accumulation of untold money wealth and power for the dominant political caste. It is the means to an end and not an end in itself. As of 2025, the shape and form of this geopolitical project is clearly changing. Tariff barriers are being constructed by the once hegemonic United States and its closest European allies to protect themselves against a flood of cheap imports from China. Immigration, which ensures expansion of the population required to support endless accumulation, is increasingly resisted by popular forces, in turn dimin-ishing a key life force behind endless growth. This signals a major shift. When the United State was hegemonic, its advocacy of free and open trade and openness to immigrants was unparalleled. But its current embrace of protectionism and anti-immigrant politics signals that its unbridled hegemony is over, economically if not militarily. There seems to be nothing to replace it, though talk of a free trade association between China, Japan and South Korea (possibly incorporating Taiwan) suggests one possible path towards a rebalancing of global hegemonic power rela-tions. But this would mean a huge struggle against the intensity of clan and xenophobic sentiments in all three countries, as well as worldwide.

The endless reproduction of capital is politically as well as econom-ically assured, but its destructive consequences proliferate. Unbridled ethnic nationalism constitutes a grave threat to the perpetuation of capital in its current form. Meanwhile, the world seems headed towards chaotic competition and an equally chaotic reterritorialization of allegiances of a sort not seen since the post-war settlement and decolonization after 1945. The geopolitical foundation blocks for endless capital accumulation are shifting, and where this fundamental shift will lead is anyone's guess, though the odds are high that East Asia will play a collective and perhaps dominant role.

When Lefebvre set out on his mission to understand capital's mode of production and the capitalist state, he proposed to organize his studies at three different scales.[10] First, there is the scale of the individual person

10   Henri Lefebvre, *The Production of Space* (Hoboken, NJ: Wiley-Blackwell, 1992 [1974]).

338 THE STORY OF CAPITAL

in their immediate environs. This is the sphere of our everyday life and our intimate social relations, the realm in which sentient and psychically endowed human beings creatively explore their capacities and powers along with their limitations as 'species beings'. This is the scale that is most beholden to the theoretical and ideological interventions of psychoanalysis and the many forms of anarchism, anarcho-syndicalism and libertarianism that exist in different parts of the capitalist world. This is the world of which Margaret Thatcher could say there is no such thing as society, only individuals and their families.

Then there is the scale of the global economy, where the activities of individuals, firms and other economic entities are registered as a multitude of 'dot-like' interventions which, when aggregated, make up the macro-economic laws of motion of capital in a national economy within an interstate system. The inputs and the outcomes can here be subjected to statistical analysis and historical and theoretical interrogation. This is the realm of economic abstractions, where the competitive state is the primary agent of activism along with the monopoly corporations and the big investment banks. This is the structure to which Lenin appealed in constructing his theory of imperialism back in 1917. The potency of that theory was increasingly resurrected in the 1960s. The United States under Eisenhower had rebuffed the Anglo-French attempt (with Israeli support) in 1956 to take back control of the Suez Canal from Egypt. The United States had rejected the formal colonialism of the previous international order, but it increasingly resorted to neocolonial practices that often came close to imperialism. The 'best and the brightest' ruling caste summoned from Harvard by Kennedy in the early 1960s took control of US international policy with disastrous consequences. George Kennan had earlier pushed for the containment of Soviet and Chinese communism. This ultimately led the US after 1950 to the full-fledged embrace of imperialist practices, later tempered by neoliberal policies in the macro-economic realm. The aim was to preserve global capital accumulation for the benefit of the US as the global hegemon. This was recognized by the left at the time in the anti-imperialist writings of Samir Amin, Baran and Sweezy, Ernest Mandel and others. This strategy was confirmed in Pinochet's US-backed military coup in Chile against the democratically elected socialist government of Salvador Allende on 11 September 1973.

The ruling political elites of the time then resorted to supply-side neoliberal economic theory to manage these abstractions and hopefully evade or at least contain crises and enhance where possible capitalist class and ruling caste power. The geopolitical games that states play operate through diplomacy or the exercise of economic, political and, in the last resort, military force. It is almost impossible to think practically of a socialist alternative at this global scale except in terms of equally abstract measures (like a global wealth tax). It is, however, hard to organize against abstractions. And 'abstractions rule', as Marx puts it. This masks potential alternatives and plays into supporting the powers of a ruling caste of global managers and experts (consultants like McKinsey) who claim they understand how the laws of motion of capital work.

This brings us to the third, and for me the most interesting and challenging scale, which is that of urbanization, or as I prefer it, the scale of the metropolitan bioregion. This is the most elusive, vague and problematic scale in terms of its material framing, because no one can really tell where a metropolis begins or ends. Probably for this reason, it is the most undertheorized and underappreciated category. It is rarely pursued in the Marxist tradition. At no point does Marx attempt to create a distinctive theory of place, urbanization and metropolis in his exploration of capital's mode of production. Yet, 55 per cent of the world's population is now living in metropolitan areas. This compares with less than 5 per cent in Marx's time – and most of that population was attributable to London alone. Metropolitan growth has been particularly strong over the last fifty years. São Paulo, Lagos, Chicago, Shanghai, Mumbai, Cairo, Istanbul, Sydney, Delhi and so on looked very different fifty years ago compared to how they look, feel and function today. There are now more than 100 cities with more than a million people in China alone. This metropolitan scale is, in short, huge and rapidly increasing. We cannot afford to ignore it. Today, it is by far the most productive and popular scale at which the search for alternatives proceeds. Yet it is also impossible to work at this metropolitan scale without invoking processes occurring at the individual and global scales. The built environment of the metropolis, for example, is created through the global circulation of fixed capital, along with investments in the consumption fund entailing state intervention and the circulation of interest-bearing capital, all in the context of falling profit rates and a rising mass of product and of values. The abstractions of global processes form the context for building prominent infrastructure (for example, transport systems, airports, stadia) at the metropolitan scale.

The theoretical insights that come from the global and individual scales are, in fact, much more manageable and graspable when interrogated by way of the metropolitan scale. The co-presence of class, clan and caste elements is everywhere in evidence within the metropolitan body politic. At this metropolitan scale, furthermore, it is easier for relatively small groups of citizens to form solidarity groups to agitate for improved conditions of life, to foster distinctive cultural traditions or to reshape social relations and productive forces. Urban social movements – some progressive and some reactionary (NIMBY) – are all over the scene. Local governments of a progressive character abound – the Paris and Shanghai communes, the Marxist-inspired Greater London Council under Ken Livingstone and Barcelona en Comú with Ada Colau. Experiments with collective living such as Copenhagen's Freetown Christiania, the Christian Base Communities of Central America that were founded on the theology of liberation and then inspired the Zapatista movement in Chiapas, the anarchist communes that settled across the United States in the nineteenth century, the Owenite experiments in New Lanark (which Marx did write about appreciatively at length) and the solidarity communes of today. Even Milwaukee had a socialist administration for many years. The rural settlements of the MST in Brazil and the organization of assembly governance to engage the water wars of Cochabamba in Bolivia, the earlier uprisings in Soweto – these are further examples of urban-regional scale strivings to define alternatives for the metropolis and its bioregion. The whole panoply of class struggles against the power of capital as well as against all the other forms of oppression (for example, race and patriarchy) encompass a long list of place names where the battles were fought (for example, Tolpuddle and Peterloo, Harlan County and Narita).

It is at the individual localized scale that impulses from social anarchism become more prominent in affecting the search for alternatives. The anarchist contribution to the history of urban planning, for example, cannot be denied. A utopian tradition stretches back to Thomas More and encompasses Fourier, Saint Simon and many more. This tradition has affected metropolitan urban planning and creates openings for political and social interventions in which 'another world is possible'. Figures like Patrick Geddes and Lewis Mumford continue to influence thinking about the sources of metropolitan dynamism, particularly in the light of technological revolutions in the hardware of metropolitan living. Independently formulated theories of urbanization merge into strategies to build metropolitan and municipal socialism in the works of Murray Bookchin, who inspired the assembly forms of governance in the Kurdish regions of Rojava in Syria.

The thirst for metropolitan alternatives to counter placelessness and urban alienations are powerfully present, even as it is recognized that action at the metropolitan level is limited by the power of global-level abstractions. It is also clear that it is only through the consolidation of multiple and diverse urban social movements into a mass movement that it will be possible to challenge the powers of abstraction as administered by the market and profit-seeking. Alternatives that appear daunting, if not impossible, at the global level (such as erasing the competitive pursuit of profit) can more easily be embraced at the metropolitan level. By setting the metropolis in its bioregion it becomes more feasible to redesign the metropolitan spaces into configurations more suited to an adequate metabolic relation to nature. Flows of energy, water, food and wastes function reliably, and access to woodlands, pastures, mountains and leisure facilities beckons. The perspective of the metropolitan bioregion invites us to consider the metabolic relations to nature in situ.

It is much easier to grasp alternative possibilities at the metropolitan bioregional scale, and this provides a compelling incentive for embracing and privileging it. This scale is not more important than the others, but tactically it is easier at this scale to create a base from which to challenge the abstractions of global capital while addressing the idiosyncrasies of the personal in everyday life.

From the standpoint of social theory and of the totality, this means that the only kind of anarchism adequate to metropolitan perspectives is one that acknowledges the power of collective solidarities and action in the collective management of the commons. The only adequate form of Marxism, by the same token, is one that takes the production of spaces, places and environments along with the metabolic relation to nature as foundational to its quest for freedoms from multiple forms of oppression at the global level. The anarchist–Marxist distinction indeed makes little sense today. Theoretical distinctions relevant to 1872, when the global urban population was less than 10 per cent of 1.2 billion people, cannot accurately reflect conditions in 2025, when 55 per cent of 8.2 billion people live in metropolitan areas lit, incidentally, by electricity rather than oil lamps and candles. It is also the case now that some two-thirds of US GDP is produced in twenty major metropolitan regions.

But capital's laws of motion at the global scale, which Marx identified in the 1840s, are still with us. This is what makes so much of Marx's analysis so compelling for understanding our present situation. A worldwide movement of subversion of the existing order of concentrated and increasingly centralized wealth and power is required. When the Seattle disruption of the WTO meetings occurred in 1999 and gave birth to the World Social Forum and the anti-globalization movement in subsequent years, it seemed that a global movement was being born to reject the abstract laws of motion of international capitalism in favour of a far more democratic and localized organization of production and distribution. But that movement failed, in part because it was animated by moral rather than material incentives. It became a global talking shop for the NGOs, which are supposedly well-meaning bourgeois organizations trying to address the crushing needs of global poverty, environmental degradations and the death traps of inadequate health care.

The internal politics of the metropolitan region are full of dynamism. They incorporate the sentient and tactile sides of human life and understand the logic of mega projects, but they lack the capacity to scale up to revolutionary transformations at the global and abstract scale of capital flows. It is worth here taking a page out of the playbook of late medieval merchant capitalists. The German merchants set up a trading network with towns and trading stations covering all of northern Europe (with Lübeck at its centre and London on its fringe). With the moral incentives of trust and loyalty (which the Chinese to this day call *Guanxi*), coupled with the material incentive to amass gold for themselves by buying cheap and selling dear ('profit upon alienation', as Marx puts it) within a regional division of labour, the merchants, in effect, used the monopoly element always present in spatial competition to collectively protect themselves from robbery and other harms, while consolidating their status as honest traders. This Hanseatic League lasted for two centuries. I fantasize that we might build such a League of Socialist Cities that can initially work within the frameworks of market exchange to support more equitable social relations in a way that can exploit the monopoly powers of spatial competition to curb the excesses of entrepreneurial urbanization and endless capital accumulation, while step by step dismantling the institutions of power that support privileging of the profit rate.

The story of capital as here presented points to three prominent contradictions that threaten the future of endless capital accumulation. These contradictions cry out to be addressed. They are currently the subject of public debate and political action. They are therefore potential fodder for anticapitalist struggles. The first of these begins with the past forty years of wage repression, enforced through intercapitalist and interstate competition. This functions as a technical measure for the lack of well-being among the deprived and dispossessed at the bottom half of the income pyramid in the US. This population is, for the most part, demoralized, alienated, depressed and disorganized. About half of the population in the United States struggles to get by on less than $30,000 a year. This increasingly constitutes the mass of the contemporary working classes everywhere, moving ever closer to a global wage. The result is widespread malaise and alienation at the bottom of the income pyramid. It will take a mass movement of the alienated and dispossessed and some concrete results of specific struggles to awaken the hope and prospect for a better collective future. To make matters worse, AI threatens to reduce labour demand substantially, well into the future. Wage repression is more likely to increase than to decline in coming years without a vigorous campaign against it.

The second issue is the unbelievable concentration of monetized wealth and power, with all its political and economic consequences. The top 500 billionaires, Bloomberg tells us, now control $9.8 trillion. This valuation is predicated on a massive increase in the circulation of fictitious capitals, propped up by Ponzi financing and outlandish increases in asset values (for example, property in particular). The threat of massive asset deflation and financial collapse looms large, on the one hand, as does the increasing takeover of almost everything of money value by a few billionaires, on the other.

Finally, no one can doubt that an existential crisis in our metabolic relation to nature is already upon us. The threats of famine and pestilence, droughts, firestorms and floods, heat waves and ice storms, earthquakes and tsunamis, ecological collapses and pandemics have always been with us, but their intensity and frequency has ratcheted up and is now systemwide. The scale is now biblical rather than manageable. Trump's call to 'drill, baby, drill' results in 'burn, baby, burn' in Los Angeles. The rectification of our terribly unbalanced metabolic relation to nature will take massive adjustments in both production and consumption and will therefore constitute a threat to further unbridled capital accumulation.

These are today the three primary contradictions that cannot be shunted to one side, by even the most devoted follower of Ricardo. These are the contradictions that the current cohort of thinkers, activists and organizers have to confront head on. Alliances in search of alternatives are forming, and the socialist perspective has much to offer, because nothing short of total revolutions will address our metabolic relation to nature, our addiction to the enormous, centralized power of Ponzi financing and fictitious capital circulation along with the long-standing alienation and the grim cruelty of ever more savage wage repression.

Appendix: Piero and Me

During my first summer term at Cambridge in 1955, the 'Backs' – a vast stretch of grass on the far side of the River Cam – were converted into tennis courts, and I spent many an hour playing there with my fellow students. In the non-descript town of Gillingham, Kent, where I grew up, there had been a multitude of small tennis clubs, which was odd since it was neither prosperous nor culturally distinguished. Gillingham was boringly lower-middle class. My parents had met at a local tennis club sometime in the 1920s. At the end of our street, a garden had been converted into a lovingly maintained grass court and one of my earliest memories is sitting on a blanket there and watching my parents play tennis, in striking white flannel outfits. I must have been four years old, just before the war broke out.

Playing on the Backs, we were frequently watched by a sombre figure, dark and slender, usually dressed in a long black coat and a sort of peasant cap, and even in summer sporting a muffler around his throat. He had piercing eyes, and it was quite nerve-wracking having him stand behind you when you served. Many a double fault resulted from that intense gaze on my back. Worse, when winter came and I switched to playing squash, he would be there in the gallery, staring at us disconcertingly. The presence of this individual was a matter of much comment among my fellow students. Who was this mysterious figure?

In our third year, one of us solved the riddle. The man in black was an Italian economist called Piero Sraffa, who had a research fellowship at Trinity College. He had written an important article in 1926, on the strength of which Keynes had invited him to Cambridge to be a librarian at King's College.[1] As far as anyone could tell, he had written nothing of significance since then. He reputedly hated teaching, which was presumably why he still held a research fellowship. He had no position in the university's economics department, but as a fellow of Trinity, with free board and lodging and access to the college's wine cellar, he could live parsimoniously but well. The post-war cohort of students to which I belonged viewed with contempt the gentlemanly tolerance for eccentricity that allowed a supposedly leading educational institution to keep such unproductive parasites on the books. In the name of meritocracy, modernity and innovation, we were all for sweeping away those encrusted class privileges that defined the university and English society as a whole.

Some years later, I was back in Cambridge for an event. Wandering into one of the many superb bookshops that still existed at the time, I happened upon a book titled *Production of Commodities by Means of Commodities*, by one Piero Sraffa.[2] It was an exceedingly slim volume and I estimated that Sraffa's productivity must have amounted to three pages a year since 1926. The book was stuffed with mathematical equations of considerable complexity that I would never be able to understand. Later, on an impulse, I bought a copy that I still have on my shelves.

In the early 1960s, I decided to teach myself some economics. In the summer months, I often found myself driving my Mini across Europe, usually en route to Sweden, with a copy of Samuelson's introductory *Economics* in the boot. One summer I drove into East Berlin through Checkpoint Charlie, just after the Wall went up. On the way out, the guards impounded the Samuelson. (I have since fancifully imagined that the corrosive effects of its circulation through the DDR played a role in ending the Cold War.) Deprived of my Samuelson, I determined to read some Keynes and was surprised to discover *The General Theory*'s fulsome acknowledgement of Sraffa's contribution. I also learned that Sraffa was then in the process of editing *The Works and Correspondence of David Ricardo*, which was surely no mean task. Sraffa was plainly not as unproductive as I had supposed. My puzzlement deepened when I discovered that Wittgenstein's theory of language games was a result of a conversation with Sraffa on the train from Cambridge to London. Sraffa had apparently insisted that hand gestures were as much a form of linguistic

---

1   Piero Sraffa, 'The Laws of Returns under Competitive Conditions', *The Economic Journal* 36: 144 (December 1926).

2   Piero Sraffa, *Production of Commodities by Means of Commodities* (Cambridge: Cambridge University Press, 1975).

communication as the spoken or written word. As Wittgenstein put it in his preface to the *Philosophical Investigations*:

> I was helped to realize these mistakes – to a degree I myself am hardly able to estimate – by the criticism which my ideas encountered from Frank Ramsey, with whom I discussed them in innumerable conversations during the last years of his life. Even more than to this – always certain and forcible – criticism I am indebted to that which a teacher of this university, Mr. P. Sraffa, for many years unceasingly practised on my thoughts. I am indebted to this stimulus for the most consequential ideas of this book.[3]

With two intellectual giants of the mid-twentieth century expressing such appreciation for Piero, my opinion of him – and of Cambridge – had to be revised.

I then learned that a controversy had erupted in economics, counterposing the MIT economists around Samuelson and the Cambridge school, led most prominently by Joan Robinson, who was advancing interpretations based upon the complicated mathematics that Sraffa had devised. I remembered Robinson as an astonishing presence from my student years. She was a supporter of the Chinese Revolution and wore a Mao tunic and cap around town. I had attended several of her lectures, which were obsessed with Malthusian questions of demographics and the Chinese path. Word had it that Samuelson was intimidated by Robinson, and I could understand why. She was awe-inspiring, both intellectually and as a person. My views on China were profoundly influenced by her stance towards the People's Republic, in a period dominated by McCarthyism and the weird US debate over who 'lost' China (weird, in that it involved imagining a world in which China does not belong to the Chinese).

In 1969, I found myself at Johns Hopkins University, where Owen Lattimore, one of three people charged by McCarthy with responsibility for China's 'loss', had long taught. A formidable scholar of Inner Asia, Lattimore had decamped to Leeds a few years before; but controversy was still rife on campus as to whether he was a traitor. I eventually tracked him down for an interview in Cambridge, where he was happily anticipating a trip to Ulaanbaatar to receive a medal from the Mongolian

---

3   Ludwig Wittgenstein, *Philosophical Investigations* (Oxford: Blackwell Publishers, 1953), p. viii.

Academy of Sciences. Reading the transcripts of the McCarran Senate Committee hearings, at which Lattimore was ruthlessly interrogated for eight days without access to legal counsel, confirmed for me that there is no such thing as a serious academic argument that does not have a strong political dimension. Nor is there any protection from the politics of fear that periodically works its insidious way into the seemingly reclusive world of the university. It was the Professor of Geography at Johns Hopkins who sent Lattimore's name to McCarthy.

The controversy over capital theory to which Sraffa contributed so mightily was of this sort. Sraffa is hard to follow and the mathematics in the *Production of Commodities* is way beyond most people, including myself. But the controversy is vital for understanding how capital works and how economic theory is constructed. I gained some insight into this in the 1980s when I was teaching Marx at Hopkins and writing *The Limits to Capital*. I noticed that someone in the Economics Department was teaching Michio Morishima's *Marx's Economics*.[4] I hunted down Peter Newman, who went out of his way to assure me, rather fearfully I thought, that he had no interest in Marx, but that Morishima's mathematics were remarkable. I found them incomprehensible, but Morishima's conclusions were of great interest because I had already decided that Marx was not an equilibrium theorist. Morishima evaded what I call the 'everything tends to equilibrium' trap, which pervaded the history of economics. He showed that Marx's political economy produces disequilibrium, with either monotonic departures from an equilibrium growth path, or ever-increasing oscillations around it, depending on the degree of capital intensity within the economy.

I had no grasp of the mathematical path whereby Morishima generated these conclusions, but I trusted Newman's opinion of it. If Morishima was correct, then presumably state policies would have to intervene if economic stability was to be achieved. When I mentioned Sraffa to Newman he exploded in righteous wrath. It turned out that he had dedicated a few years to trying to verify Sraffa's mathematical proofs, which he had initially thought far-fetched, only to find them impeccable – because, Newman asserted, Sraffa, like Wittgenstein, was beholden to the mathematical genius of Frank Ramsey, who had died at the age of twenty-six in 1930. The study circle at Trinity that had included Sraffa,

4   Michio Morishima, *Marx's Economics: A Dual Theory of Value and Growth* (Cambridge: Cambridge University Press, 1978).

Ramsey and Wittgenstein was crucial. Newman, frustrated, published his proof of the correctness of Part One of *Production of Commodities* in a specialist Swiss journal and left it at that.[5] It turned out that I had already been deeply influenced by the intellectual circle at Trinity, for I had relied heavily on Richard Braithwaite – a fringe member – for my understanding of the history and philosophy of science in writing *Explanation in Geography*, my first book.[6]

Looking back at the Cambridge capital controversies, it is hard to separate out Sraffa's contributions from those of Robinson. Sraffa appears to have avoided controversy like the plague, but Robinson fiercely embraced it. Robinson was not mathematically inclined and preferred, she said, to use her brain and intelligence instead. That meant it was easier for me to follow her arguments. She was not hostile to Marx, but she did complain about his use of Hegel: 'What business has Hegel putting his nose in between me and Ricardo?'[7] Foundational to her reading of Sraffa was an emphasis on the rate of exploitation of labour power as the motor for capital accumulation. But she also emphasized the role of the world market and wrote an introduction to an edition of Rosa Luxemburg's *Accumulation of Capital,* which she called 'one of the masterpieces of socialist literature'. By the 1980s this was one of my gospel texts. But here I should pause to acknowledge my own immediate interest in the questions that Sraffa posed.

After publishing *Social Justice and the City,* I resolved to try to integrate Marx's political economy into my studies of urbanization and uneven geographical development at a variety of scales, from the neighbourhood to the globe.[8] This entailed grappling with Marx's theorizations of ground rent, merchant capital, state investments, banking credit and finance, all the while confronting the problematics of differential turnover times and the production of time and space, in consumption as well as production. The questions of fixed capital circulation and consumption fund formation – for example, housing and the built environment, which formed the second part of Sraffa's book – loomed large in my thinking. I also needed to work more carefully over the circulation and

5   Peter Newman, 'Production of Commodities by Means of Commodities', *Swiss Journal of Economics and Statistics* 98: 1 (March 1962).

6   David Harvey, *Explanation in Geography* (London: Edward Arnold, 1969).

7   Joan Robinson, 'Open letter from a Keynesian to a Marxist', *Collected Economic Papers* 4 (Oxford 1973): p. 115.

8   David Harvey, *Social Justice and the City* (Baltimore: Johns Hopkins University Press, 1973).

reproduction of labour capacity. These issues were explored theoretically in *The Limits to Capital*, and historically and geographically in *Paris, Capital of Modernity*.[9] If I was to understand the role of capital in the rebuilding of Paris during the Second Empire, or in contemporary New York, then I had to understand what capital was and the different forms it might take in the built environment. If I was to take Marx's path, then I needed to know how Marx's definition of capital differed from that of the bourgeois economists.

Robinson pointed out that the neoclassical 'production function' – where Q, the output, is a function of labour and capital – lacks a satisfactory understanding of the units in which capital can be measured. When capital is in money form there is no problem; but capital also consists of a heterogeneous stock of use values such as machinery, plant and equipment, whose value cannot be established without invoking their impact on the value of Q. In other words, it rests on a tautology. But as Robinson noted, before the economist gets round to querying this, 'he has become a professor, and so sloppy habits of thought are handed from one generation to the next'.[10] The net effect is that neoclassical economic modelling is circular. And Sraffa proved it so.

This is a pretty devastating finding. But the response by bourgeois economists over the years has been to ignore the problem, or to treat it as a 'tempest in a teapot'. As Marx observed, whenever a crisis occurs, bourgeois economists simply complain that it can only be because the economy is failing to perform according to their textbooks. In fact, a few Marxist economists, led by Ian Steedman's *Marx After Sraffa*, were the only ones to take Sraffa seriously as having undermined one of their key concepts, the labour theory of value.[11] My view was that Steedman is correct if Marx's theory of value is identical to that of Ricardo, the object of Sraffa's critique. This is Steedman's position. But Marx does something different when he insists that the 'socially necessary labour time' that constitutes value presumes sufficient effective demand. If the commodity cannot be sold, then there is no value (it is not socially necessary), no matter how much labour is used up in its production. In Marx's scheme, consumerism can on occasion lead production. From this perspective, the great divide between the utility-maximizing consumerism

---

9   David Harvey, *The Limits to Capital* (London: Verso, 1982); *Paris, Capital of Modernity* (New York: Routledge, 2006).

10   Joan Robinson, 'The Production Function and the Theory of Capital', *The Review of Economic Studies* 21: 2 (1953): p. 81.

11   Ian Steedman, *Marx After Sraffa* (London: New Left Books, 1977).

APPENDIX: PIERO AND ME   351

of the neoclassical paradigm and the class-based profit-maximizing pro-
ductivism of the Robinson paradigm look more like different sides of a
single coin. In my work, I have found this relation enlightening rather
than troublesome. After all, urbanization is very much about individual
and collective cultures of consumerism to which production incentives
attach. To attribute everything to the evolution of the productive forces,
as G. A. Cohen did for example in *Karl Marx's Theory of History*, is a step
too far.[12]

Sraffa and Robinson both died in 1983. Since then, there has been a small
though persistent trickle of articles testifying to the significance of the
issues they posed, but no mainstream discussion of their implications
for neoclassical theory. It was possible to take a quiet but smug satisfaction in the thought that the economists who so often assumed they were
the Brahmin caste within the social sciences had a knowledge structure
founded on tautology; but there things seemed to stand. However, in
2003 a helpful article on the Cambridge capital controversy by Avi Cohen
and Geoff Harcourt revived my interest in the subject.[13] The essential
point they make is that Sraffa correctly exposed a fatal flaw in Ricardian
economics. There can be no measure of the value of capital (understood
as a free-standing factor of production) that does not depend upon the
value of what it produces. All economic reasoning in this tradition is
tainted by the fact that it is inherently tautological. This is particularly
true with respect to the circulation of fixed capital, the Achilles heel of
theoretical economics. The value of a machine cannot be determined
independently of the value that the machine helps to produce. The question is whether this flaw carries over to marginalist neoclassical theory.
Samuelson eventually accepted that Sraffa was formally correct about
Ricardo but claimed to find a way to wriggle out of Sraffa's conclusions.
It all came down to how best to interpret Sraffa's mathematical findings
and confront the tautologies.

Cohen and Harcourt put it this way: 'Has there been continuity in the
evolution of economic theory from Adam Smith to the present, or dis-
continuity, with the marginal revolution setting neoclassical economics
on a different path from earlier classical political economy and Marx?'
The neoclassicals envisioned 'the lifetime utility-maximizing decisions

---

12   G. A. Cohen, *Karl Marx's Theory of History: A Defence* (Oxford: Clarendon
Press, 1978).
13   A. J. Cohen and G. C. Harcourt, 'Whatever Happened to the Cambridge Capital
Controversy?', *Journal of Economic Perspectives* 17: 1 (winter 2003).

of individuals as the driving force of economic activity, with the allocation of given, scarce resources as the fundamental economic problem'.
In contrast, the Cambridgians argued 'for a return to a classical political
economy vision' in which 'profit-making decisions of capitalist firms are
the driving force'. Rates of profit depend upon 'differing power and social
relations in production and the realization of profits is brought about by
effective demand associated with saving and expenditure behaviours of
the different classes and the "animal spirits" of capitalists.'[14]

Evoking 'the spectre of Marx', Robinson had argued that the 'meaning
of capital lay in the property owned by the capitalist class, which confers
on capitalists the legal right and economic authority to take a share of the
surplus created in the production process'. Of course, mainstream economists in the capitalist world would not subscribe en masse to Robinson's
class-bound, surplus-value producing and profit-maximizing vision. The
textbook that Robinson wrote with John Eatwell incorporating this alternative vision, *Introduction to Modern Economics*, had very few takers,
leaving lifetime individual utility-maximizing behaviours as the only
game in town.[15] Indices of consumer confidence have become the bell-
wether of the present and future health of the economy, and the stock
market wobbles accordingly. Once more, politics trumps mathematics.

Sraffa tantalizingly leaves the matter open. Having established 'the
central propositions' in the 1920s and elaborated them in the 1930s and
'40s, he offered only a 'prelude' to a critique of political economy in the
1950s. It is, he says in the preface to *Production of Commodities*, 'a peculiar feature of the set of propositions now published that, although they
do not enter into any discussion of the marginal theory of value and distribution, they have nevertheless been designed to serve as the basis for
a critique of that theory'.[16] Though Sraffa's foundation appears to be solid,
the critique itself has yet to appear. I have my doubts that it ever will. It
would take the genius of someone like Sraffa, the mathematical brilliance
of a Ramsey and the dedicated persistence of a Newman, assembled in
an institutional setting of the sort that Cambridge provided in the inter-
war years. The capture of the Cambridge Economics Department by the
neoclassicals in the 1970s more or less ruled it out.

∾

---

14   Ibid., pp. 207–8.
15   Joan Robinson and John Eatwell, *An Introduction to Modern Economics* (London:
McGraw Hill, 1973).
16   Preface to Sraffa, *Production of Commodities*, p. vii.

In *The Structure of Scientific Revolutions*, Thomas Kuhn persuasively argued that science does not evolve in an incremental, linear way. It had gone through periods when theory and practice were sufficiently aligned to pose and answer key questions of the time. But at some point, anomalies that could not be explained or accurately predicted became more salient. These eventually provoked a revolution in theoretical framings, methods and conceptual understandings, forming a new paradigm. Einstein's physics superseded that of Newton, only to be superseded by Niels Bohr's quantum theory. In each case a new normal science came into being. It is tempting to see the relations between neoclassical and Sraffian economics as evidence of an arrested and incomplete paradigm shift in economic theory. But in the same way that Newtonian mechanics is perfectly adequate to the task of building bridges and knocking them down again – rendering relativity and quantum theory irrelevant to that purpose – so the neoclassical paradigm and its vast trove of data and empirical information may be adequate for a wide range of economic tasks.

But Sraffa had not set out to create an alternative economic theory. He had simply undermined the theoretical basis of the old, both Ricardian and neoclassical. Where, then, are the anomalies that make a revolution in economic theory necessary? In the late sixties, with urban uprisings from Chicago and Paris to Bangkok and Mexico City, the case for a revolutionary transformation of urban economics was for me unassailable. The neoclassical urban economists had nothing meaningful to say about these events in general, or their urban dimensions in particular. I was faced with a theoretical world constituted by thing-like factors of production such as land, labour and capital, whereas I wanted to know what was happening to the labourers, capitalists, financiers, merchants, landlords, state officials, the political class and state and legal officials; to say nothing of exploring the implications of sharp differences within populations based on race, religion, ethnicity, culture and gender. This was the paradigm shift – from objectified things to social relations – that I was searching for in an article that became the transitional piece from liberal to revolutionary perspectives in *Social Justice and the City*.[17] It was not too hard to describe how the 1960s uprisings unfolded. But it was more difficult to explain why they occurred. It was this seemingly intractable 'why' that drove me to interrogate Marx for answers, seeing that neoclassical economics plainly had none.

---

17   David Harvey, 'Revolutionary and Counter-Revolutionary Theory in Geography and the Problem of Ghetto Formation', *Antipode* 4: 2 (July 1972).

354 THE STORY OF CAPITAL

So, what would Marx have had to say about all of this? Here, I must register two complaints. First, there is an immense literature on Marx in relation to Hegel, and rightly so, but very little on Marx in relation to Ricardo. In the *Grundrisse*, Marx engages deeply with Ricardo throughout whereas Hegel is merely mentioned. Similarly, the second volume of *Theories of Surplus Value* focuses on Ricardo and the Ricardian School of the time, many of whom expressed socialist sympathies on the simple grounds that if value is given by labour input, as Ricardo claimed, then the labourers should surely receive a lion's share of the value they produce. Hence the redistributive socialism of J. S. Mill, and its contemporary version in the work of Thomas Piketty. Second, as Walter Rodney complained, 'there is one common uniting strand to all bourgeois thought: they make common cause in questioning the relevance, the logic, and so on, of Marxist thought.' 'In the English tradition', he continues, 'it is fashionable to disavow any knowledge of Marxism'; 'one knows it is absurd without reading it and one doesn't read it because one knows it is absurd, and therefore one glories in one's ignorance.'[18]

Exhibit A is Keynes's claim to have never read Marx. But then, Keynes was bourgeois to the core and dedicated his life to saving capital from the capitalists, which was and remains no easy task. For Keynes, though, this was a technical problem.

Keynes did object, however, to the Ricardians' embrace of Say's Law, which states that supply creates its own demand – a tautological claim if ever there was one. Marx dismissed Say's Law as 'childish babble'. Keynes held that its broad acceptance by the Ricardians hobbled economic theory for a century or more. In the 1930s, Keynes sought to revive the reputations of Malthus and Sismondi, who had long ago rejected Say's Law since it implied there could be no general over-accumulation of capital or over-production of commodities. Such propositions made no sense in the Depression years, when Keynes was stressing the importance of state-managed effective demand. In the 1980s, after a generation of Keynesian hegemony, his followers were hounded out of policy-making chambers in London, New York, Washington and Basel, and the economics departments of the major research universities. They were replaced by neoclassical 'supply-siders' armed with a new version of Say's Law and its counterpart, the efficient-market hypothesis. Thereafter it became difficult to think seriously about Keynes, let alone take up the

---

18 Walter Rodney, 'Marxism and African Liberation', in *Decolonial Marxism: Essays from the Pan-African Revolution* (London: Verso, 2022), p. 35.

implications of Sraffa's arguments. But here we must deal with the consequences of 'putting Hegel's nose' between us and Sraffa's Ricardo.

Since Sraffa's work is a critique of Ricardo, the link to Marx is indirect. In the introductory chapter of the *Grundrisse*, however, Marx takes up a critique of the basic categories of classical political economy – production, consumption, distribution, realization, exchange. All of these 'moments' in the circulation of capital are loosely linked in bourgeois economics to form a 'weak syllogism' within an 'organic totality'.[19] 'Capital in general' could only come into being if enforced wage labour pre-existed the rise of capital. This presumably occurred through the buying and selling of labour services supplied by wage workers to the church, the state, the military, rich merchants, the feudal lords and so on. Adam Smith, says Marx, reduces these necessary preconditions to 'a few very simple characteristics, which are hammered into flat tautologies'. Could it be that Marx is intuiting here the tautological qualities of neoclassical theory? At several points in *Capital*, Marx hints at the danger of lapsing into tautological reasoning. But the main thrust of his argument lies elsewhere.

In the *Grundrisse*, however, Marx spelled out a mission:

> The exact development of the concept of capital is necessary, since it is the fundamental concept of modern economics, just as capital itself . . . is the foundation of bourgeois society. The sharp formulation of the presuppositions of the [capital] relation must bring out all the contradictions of bourgeois production, as well as the boundary where it drives beyond itself.[20]

Notice here the importance of contradiction. 'We are the last to deny', Marx writes, 'that capital contains contradictions. Our purpose, rather, is to develop them fully. But Ricardo does not develop them. But rather shifts them off . . .'. Malthus, on the other hand, 'senses the contradictions, but falls flat when he himself tries to develop them'. Contradiction is not a term to be found in the neoclassical or Ricardian playbook. But it is foundational for Marx's conception of capital.

Marx defines capital as 'value in motion', as a circulation process rather than a thing. It is, he writes, a 'moving contradiction'.[21] It first

---

19   Karl Marx, *Grundrisse*, trans. Martin Nicolaus (London and New York: Penguin, 1973), p. 86.

20   Ibid., pp. 331, 351, 353.

21   Ibid., pp. 705–6.

takes on the money form. Not all money is capital but capital takes on the guise of money capital when the money is used to buy labour power and means of production as commodities in order to put them to work in a labour process organized under the authority (as Robinson had noted) of the capitalist to produce new commodities whose value is expressed in money form after being sold in the market. This converts the value back into the money form, whence it can go back into circulation as money capital once more. In this circulation process, capital takes on different material forms: labour power and means of production, a labour process, new commodities for sale. The different material qualities of each moment matter. A steel works worth ten million dollars is very different from having ten million in cash. The ease of geographical mobility differs markedly from one moment to another.

The incentive that drives this circulatory system is profit, or as Marx prefers to call it in the *Grundrisse*, 'the production and realization of surplus value'.[22] Capital's circulation process is not cyclical. It is constituted as a spiral of perpetual expansion and accumulation of capital. How to absorb this ever-expanding accumulation – a 'bad infinity' as Hegel would put it – was the problem with which both Luxemburg and Robinson grappled. In Luxemburg's case, the answer was colonial imperialism. This was the best explanation she could find. Robinson's support for Keynesian policies of debt-financed state interventions probably arose for the same reasons. For purposes of analysis, it is reasonable to hold certain aspects of a contradiction constant. In Volume One of *Capital*, for example, Marx assumes throughout that all commodities exchange at their value (therefore no overproduction or overaccumulation). The question of where the extra effective demand comes from to pay for the expanding production of surplus value is left to be dealt with in Volume Two of *Capital* and the *Grundrisse*.

Given Marx's emphasis on contradictions it is useful to give a sense of how they operate. In Marx's scheme of things, the internal contradictions (as opposed to external contradictions such as a viral epidemic) invariably take the same form. Individual capitalists driven by the coercive laws of competition engage in practices that maximize their individual rate of return while producing aggregate results that collectively threaten the reproduction of the capitalist class and its power. The question then arises as to who will rescue capital from the capitalists. In our times the answer is the state. Hence debates over the role of the state and which

---

22   Ibid., pp. 348–458.

kind of economic theory will be most effective. In the interstate system, the individuation of capitalist states depends on the primary contradictions each confronts – say, oil extractivism versus tourism – and the particular strategies they develop to manage these trade-offs. This formulation applies to local governments as well as nation states, making urban entrepreneurialism and inter-urban competition prominent features in the political economy of the present.

But the contradictions need to be systemically situated if they are to be properly understood. The key concept here is that of capital as a mode of production within which wages, profits, exchange, consumption, realization, rents, finance, merchant profits, interest and state functions, including interstate relations, dynamically intersect with each other to constitute the totality of contemporary capital at a particular place and time. Marx speaks of the different elements – production, distribution and consumption – as 'moments' in order to capture the transitoriness and contingency of everything within the totality of capital's mode of production. Thus, the moment of 'production' refers to the whole panoply of commodity production processes under the direction and class power of capital, while the moment of 'consumption' refers to how all that is produced in the way of commodities for sale in the market is used up in different ways in all manner of different places and times.

Capital's totality is conceptualized holistically as an organic system in perpetual evolution. This system, says Marx, 'has its presuppositions, and its development to its totality consists precisely in subordinating all elements of society to itself, or of creating out of it the organs which it still lacks. This is historically how it becomes a totality. The process of its becoming this totality forms a moment of its process, of its development.'[23] While the idea of totality undoubtedly derives from Hegel, Marx reworks and revolutionizes it. For him, the totality of capital is an ever-changing network of historically specific social practices and relations built, evolving and ultimately dissolving, only to be rebuilt again through human action. This network is constantly in the process of growth and transformation – perpetually 'becoming' as Marx puts it – even as it exhibits certain proclivities towards solidity and permanence. Marx's concept of capital's totality is, therefore, open, evolving and self-replicating, but in no sense self-contained, given its internal contradictions and its penchant for disharmony and breakdown. Capital exists as a complex ecosystem of value flows in continuous internal tension,

---

23 Ibid., p. 278.

thus forcing permanently revolutionary transformations, such as AI, and continuous historical evolution.

How the coercive laws of competition work is epitomized in Marx's chapter on the working day. The incentive for capitalist producers to extend the working day and increase its intensity tends to deplete the quantity and quality of labour power, culminating in 'death from overwork' – a live category in today's East Asia. The remedy is state intervention ostensibly on behalf of the workers but also to the benefit of capital through the improvement in labour health and quality. Inter-capitalist competition likewise produces continuous increases in labour productivity through technological and organizational innovations which reduce labour inputs and thus reduce the surplus value resulting in an aggregate fall in the rate of profit. Wage repression also reduces consumption capacity, making the question raised by Luxemburg and Robinson of where the compensatory effective demand might come from a vital issue. In all these cases, the capitalist state becomes critical to regulating the deepening contradictions of capital. Contradictions cannot be eradicated; they can only be managed. But the coercive laws of competition apply no less to interstate dynamics, say when it comes to acquiring military hardware, space technologies and new technologies in general. Interstate competition shapes aggregate paths of technological and organizational change in capitalist social formations.

And then there are the contradictions that surround fixed-capital and consumption-fund formation (the consumption fund being all those long-lived items used to support final consumption like cars, houses and kitchen equipment), essential to thinking about the built environ-ment. In his *Stages of Economic Growth*, Walt Rostow identified a critical period of investment in fixed-capital infrastructures as vital in creat-ing the necessary preconditions for 'take off' into sustained economic growth.[24] Marx had long recognized that such investments were essential but noted that it took the mobilization of surpluses of capital and labour at the expense of present consumption to fund such investments. But when capital matures, such investments in increasing labour productiv-ity produce even more surpluses of both capital and labour to fund even more such investments. This expansive cycle is potentially crisis prone. Marx notes:

---

24   W. W. Rostow, *The Stages of Economic Growth: A Non-Communist Manifesto* (Cambridge: Cambridge University Press, 1960).

There are moments in the developed movement of capital which delay this movement other than by crises; such as, e.g. the constant devaluation of part of the existing capital; the transformation of a great part of capital into fixed capital which does not serve as agency of direct production; unproductive waste of a great portion of capital.[25]

Capital has a choice as it matures of overaccumulation in real estate, as in China after 2020, or using urbanization as a dumping ground for surplus capital and labour, as in the US, by building bridges to nowhere. The other form of deliberately wasteful capital flow is into military expenditures, which are equivalent, Marx tells us, to dumping value in the ocean. It is sobering to try to imagine capital's dynamic in the US since 1945 without ever-expanding military expenditure and chronically wasteful suburbanization. If capital is value in motion, then fixed capital slows that motion down, while the same competitive forces that produce a falling rate of profit produce an acceleration in the motion of circulating capital. One part of capital speeds up while the other part slows.

There occurred an important coda to my Sraffa-driven understanding of all of this in the mid-1990s. My students at Johns Hopkins told me of a new appointment in political science whom they found interesting and suggested I teach a course with him. I readily agreed and so met Mark Blyth. My only stipulation was that we not engage in the usual graduate school seminar practice of pretending to read fifty major authors over a semester. We should each select one book and build the course around reading them carefully together. I had previously done this with Giovanni Arrighi. Reading my *Limits to Capital* along with his *Long Twentieth Century* proved really illuminating. I chose Gramsci's *Prison Notebooks*. My jaw dropped when Mark chose Keynes's *General Theory*. He hastened to reassure me that he would deal quickly with the technical stuff and concentrate on the psychology and expectations aspects in the latter part of the book. I was still not excited but reluctantly went along. The course got more and more interesting and ended up being, for me at least, a splendid experience. I distinctly remember waking up one morning and realizing I was teaching a class about Keynes, who thanked his good friend Sraffa for his help in writing *The General Theory*, and Gramsci, whose *Prison Notebooks* might well not have been written let alone preserved had it not been for Sraffa's support and help.

---

25   Marx, *Grundrisse*, p. 750.

This brings me to the coup de grâce, as it were, in the history of my encounters with Sraffa, albeit at a distance in space and time. I had long been aware that Sraffa supported Gramsci during his prison years in a variety of ways, such as opening an account in Gramsci's name with a Milan bookstore. But I had never looked into the significance of this in any depth. In 1991, a compact but extremely informative biography of Sraffa by Jean-Pierre Potier was translated from French into English.[26]

The book covers the salient phases of Sraffa's intellectual and political career, documenting his relations with Keynes and the Cambridge economists of the 1930s and 40s, and even more importantly his work with Gramsci, who was a close friend from his student days. Although never a member of the Italian Communist Party, Sraffa was a key figure among the left intellectuals in Italy struggling to combat fascism. In 1924, for example, there was an open debate between Gramsci and Sraffa in which the latter contended that the revolutionary path to communism was effectively blocked by fascism and that priority had to be given to supporting the bourgeois anti-fascist movement, in order to clear the decks for a better organized working-class movement to pursue its goals. Gramsci disagreed, while recognizing that Sraffa held to revolutionary perspectives in the long run.

This debate is taken up in Andy Merrifield's *Roses for Gramsci*.[27] Here is another strange connection born out of historical accident. Andy was a student of mine and we have remained close friends for decades. Having relocated to Rome he decided to write a memoir reflecting on Gramsci's legacy in the current conjuncture. Andy had already written several studies on left thinkers – Guy Debord, Henri Lefebvre, John Berger – concentrating on their lives and animating preoccupations. His method is to immerse himself in the material circumstances of his subject's life and writings. He uncovered much more detail about Sraffa's role during Gramsci's incarceration, when he offered as much support as he could, at his own expense. The primary contact with Gramsci, however, was his sister-in-law Tatiana Schucht. She painstakingly copied out letters from Gramsci to send on to Sraffa. It was primarily she who rescued Gramsci's notebooks after his death and, possibly with Sraffa's help, secured their transfer to Moscow. What role Sraffa played in influencing Gramsci's thinking we shall probably never know, even from the many letters and documents cited in Potier's book and others that are yet to be published.

---

26   Jean-Pierre Potier and Piero Sraffa, *Unorthodox Economist (1898–1983): A Biographical Essay* (London: Routledge, 1991).

27   Andy Merrifield, *Roses for Gramsci* (New York: Monthly Review Press, 2025).

But if Sraffa could influence Wittgenstein, Keynes and Robinson in such fundamental ways, then surely Gramsci would not have remained unmoved. Gramsci, with his interest in the Southern Question, Americanism and Fordism, the organic intellectuals and a host of other topics, is one of my favourite Marxist thinkers, and for this I have, I suspect, Sraffa partly to thank.

What future might we predict for 'that epoch-making book', as Maurice Dobb liked to call it, *Production of Commodities by Means of Commodities?* That remains an open question. I think it safe to assert, however, that it is more meaningful to work through and with Marx's contradictions than wallow in Smith's 'flat tautologies'. So, here am I, in my ninetieth year, looking back on my career as a geographer interested in explaining, with a little help from Marx, how urbanization and uneven development work, finding myself obliged to some extraordinary scholars, such as Sraffa and Robinson; and to people, events and political currents that open doors to new ways of thinking, hopefully more adequate to confront the central contradictions of our times. It is, however, one thing to open doors but quite another to pass through en masse, to explore what might exist on the other side. The American empire that has sheltered capital for so long is starting to crack. This is a moment of opportunity as well as of peril. A little bit of optimism of the intellect is called for, if only to jump-start the optimism of the will.

Index